To Share, Not Surrender

I0866318

To Share, Not Surrender

Indigenous and Settler Visions of Treaty Making in the Colonies of Vancouver Island and British Columbia

Edited by Peter Cook, Neil Vallance, John Sutton Lutz, Graham Brazier, and Hamar Foster

UBC Press 1971–2021

© UBC Press 2021

All rights reserved. No part of this publication may be reproduced, stored in a retrieval system, or transmitted, in any form or by any means, without prior written permission of the publisher, or, in Canada, in the case of photocopying or other reprographic copying, a licence from Access Copyright, www.accesscopyright.ca.

Printed in Canada on FSC-certified ancient-forest-free paper (100% post-consumer recycled) that is processed chlorine- and acid-free.

Library and Archives Canada Cataloguing in Publication

Title: To share, not surrender : Indigenous and settler visions of treaty making in the colonies of Vancouver Island and British Columbia / edited by Peter Cook, Neil Vallance, John Lutz, Graham Brazier, and Hamar Foster.
Names: Cook, Peter (Associate professor of history), editor. | Vallance, Neil, editor. | Lutz, John S. (John Sutton), 1959– editor. | Brazier, Graham (History scholar), editor. | Foster, Hamar, 1948– editor.
Description: Includes bibliographical references and index.
Identifiers: Canadiana (print) 2021021290X | Canadiana (ebook) 20210217065 | ISBN 9780774863827 (hardcover) | ISBN 9780774863834 (paperback) ISBN 9780774863841 (PDF) | ISBN 9780774863858 (EPUB)
Subjects: LCSH: Indigenous peoples—Legal status, laws, etc.—British Columbia—History. | LCSH: Indigenous peoples—Land tenure—British Columbia—History. | LCSH: Indigenous peoples—British Columbia—Government relations—History. | LCSH: British Columbia—Ethnic relations—History. | LCSH: British Columbia—Race relations—History. | CSH: Indigenous title—British Columbia—History.
Classification: LCC KIB1810 .T6 2021 | LCC KF8210.T76 T6 2021 kfmod | DDC 342.71108/72—dc23

Canadä

UBC Press gratefully acknowledges the financial support for our publishing program of the Government of Canada (through the Canada Book Fund), the Canada Council for the Arts, and the British Columbia Arts Council.

Printed and bound in Canada
Set in New Baskerville and Galliard by Apex CoVantage, LLC
Copy editor: Lesley Erickson
Proofreader: Judith Earnshaw
Indexer: Lillian Ashworth
Cover designer: Alexa Love
Cover image: *View of Victoria, Vancouver Island* by Hermann Otto Tiedemann. Courtesy UBC Library, Rare Books and Special Collections

UBC Press
The University of British Columbia
2029 West Mall
Vancouver, BC V6T 1Z2
www.ubcpress.ca

Contents

Treaty Timeline

Hamar Foster and Neil Vallance

For thousands of years before first contact in the eighteenth century, the Salish peoples of southern Vancouver Island, the Nu-chah-nulth on the west coast of the Island and the Kwakwa̲ka̲'wakw on its northeastern coast, hunted, fished, conducted their seasonal rounds, and lived in winter villages. They made treaties among themselves concerning the allocation and use of the land and its resources, they resisted raiding parties from northern nations such as the Haida, and they occasionally engaged in conflicts with one another and with more distant nations.

1774 Juan Perez (Spain) encounters Haida off Haida Gwaii but does not go ashore.

1778 Captain James Cook (United Kingdom) and his crew are the first Europeans known to have come to what is now British Columbia, at Nootka on Vancouver Island. News of the value of the sea otter pelts they obtained and sold in China sparks the maritime fur trade on the Island's west coast. Spanish, British, and American ships all take part.

1790 Spain, in the Nootka Convention, acknowledges Britain's right to trade in the area. Manuel Quimper and Gonzalo López de Haro (Spain) sail up the Strait of Juan de Fuca, stopping at Sooke and Royal Roads.

1791 Francisco de Eliza and José Maria Narvaez (Spain) sail up Haro and Georgia Straits to Saturna Island, Howe Sound, and Texada Island, stopping in the harbour at Nanaimo on their way south.

1792 Captain George Vancouver (United Kingdom) and Juan Francisco de Bodega y Quadra (Spain) negotiate at Nootka, which is abandoned in 1795.

1806 The first land-based fur trade posts are established at Stuart Lake and Fraser Lake, signalling the beginning of the end of the maritime fur trade. By 1830, the number of ships trading on the coast had shrunk from a high of twenty-three (in 1801) to only two.

1818 Britain and the United States agree to defer the question of the boundary between British North America and the United States west of the Rockies.

1821 The North West Company and the Hudson's Bay Company (HBC) amalgamate.

1836 The HBC steamer *Beaver* arrives on the coast to transport furs, leading eventually to the closing of some of the HBC's coastal trading posts.

1837 Prompted by the dangers of crossing the Columbia River Bar to get to Fort Vancouver, and by increasing American immigration into Oregon, the HBC sends Captain William McNeill and the *Beaver* to look for a suitable place to locate a new HBC headquarters. He finds one at the tip of southern Vancouver Island.

1842 James Douglas, on the *Cadboro,* examines possible sites for a new headquarters on southern Vancouver Island, including the one found by McNeill at Camosack (or Camosun), and recommends it.

1843 The HBC builds a fort at Camosack (Victoria). Local First Nations trade salmon and other food for blankets and trade goods.

1846 The Treaty of Washington (or Oregon Treaty) between Britain and the United States extends the international boundary westward along the forty-ninth parallel to the Pacific Ocean, dipping south to include all of Vancouver Island in British territory.

1849 Britain grants title to Vancouver Island to the HBC for ten years, on the condition that the company promote colonization. The HBC moves its western headquarters to Fort Victoria. HBC chief factor James Douglas takes charge of the fort, and company executives in London instruct him to extinguish any Indigenous interest in land around Fort Victoria.

1850 Before receiving instructions from the HBC in London, Douglas meets with representatives of the Songhees, Esquimalt, Beecher Bay, and Sooke First Nations and enters the names of the representatives on nine sheets of blank paper. No minutes are kept. He then writes to London requesting that a "proper form" be sent "by return of post." Several months later, the template is received by Douglas, the blanks are filled in, and the completed text is inserted onto the sheets of paper. Each completed text contains a surrender of First Nations land in return for compensation paid mainly in blankets, reserving only their "village sites" and "enclosed fields." The documents also confirm their right to hunt over "the unoccupied land" and guarantee their fisheries "as formerly."

1850 Richard Blanshard is appointed governor of Vancouver Island, but authority over land remains with Douglas and the HBC.

1851 Blanshard resigns as governor, and Douglas replaces him, making similar agreements with two First Nations at Fort Rupert, near present-day Port Hardy.

1852 Douglas makes two more agreements with the First Nations resident on the Saanich Peninsula.

1854 Douglas makes a fourteenth and apparently final agreement with First Nations representatives at Fort Nanaimo.

1855 Britain confirms that the grant of Vancouver Island will expire in 1859.

1858 Douglas resigns from the HBC when he is made governor of the new Colony of British Columbia. He is now governor of both colonies. Apart from federal Treaty 8 in 1899, which Ottawa made with First Nations whose land rights extended into northeastern British Columbia (the BC government took no part), no treaties with First Nations are made in British Columbia until the Nisga'a Treaty in 2000.

1862 The *British Colonist* reports that a treaty similar to the first fourteen has been made at Cowichan, but no official record of it exists. It is not usually included in the list of "Douglas Treaties."

1863–64 Douglas retires as governor of the Colonies of Vancouver Island and British Columbia.

1864–1964 Awareness of the fourteen treaties in the settler community is vanishingly small.

1866 The Colony of Vancouver Island becomes part of the Colony of British Columbia.

1871 British Columbia joins Confederation. Under the Terms of Union, Canada assumes responsibility for "Indians and Lands reserved for the Indians."

1875 A booklet titled *Papers Connected to the Indian Land Question* is printed, reproducing (for the first time, and after much prevarication) the written versions of the fourteen Vancouver Island (Douglas) treaties.

1913 Snuneymuxw Elder Dick Whoakum testifies before the McKenna-McBride Commission. He provides his recollection of the 1854 Nanaimo treaty terms, claiming there was no surrender of land.

1934 Saanich Chief David Lattass tells his story of the formation of the Songhees and Saanich Treaties in a newspaper article, claiming they agreed to share, not cede, their land.

1964 The *R v White and Bob* case is decided by the BC Court of Appeal. As a defence to a charge of hunting out of season, the defendants, members of the Snuneymuxw First Nation, rely on the hunting guarantee in the 1854 Nanaimo treaty. The Crown argues that the agreements are merely private agreements with the HBC. The Court of Appeal (affirmed by the Supreme Court of Canada) disagrees: they are treaties under the Indian Act, so the hunting guarantee takes priority over provincial game laws.

1973 *Calder v Attorney General of BC* is decided in the Supreme Court of Canada, holding that Aboriginal title is a legal right but splitting three to three on whether the land rights of the Nisg̱a'a were implicitly extinguished by colonial legislation.

1982 Section 35 of the Constitution Act, 1982, recognizes and affirms Aboriginal and treaty rights.

1984 The *R v Bartleman* case is decided by the BC Court of Appeal. Another hunting case, it affirms that the Saanich treaty right to hunt on unoccupied land includes lands anywhere in their traditional hunting territory.

1986 In *Hunt v Halcan,* the BC Supreme Court issues an injunction to halt logging on Deer Island until trial or other disposition of the matter. One of the grounds upon which the injunction is issued is that there is a "fair question" to be tried between the asserted Aboriginal and Douglas treaty rights, on the one hand, and the Land Title Act, on the other.

1989 The *Saanichton Bay Marina* case is decided by the BC Court of Appeal. The Tsawout people use their 1852 treaty to stop development of a marina that would adversely affect their treaty right to enjoy "their fisheries as formerly." This marks the first time that a Douglas Treaty is used as a sword to fight development rather than as a shield against charges of illegal hunting or fishing.

1990 In *Regina v Joseph,* the BC Supreme Court holds that a fishing closure – although a valid conservation measure that applies equally to sport, commercial, and "Indian" food fishing – violates Douglas Treaty rights protected by section 35 of the Constitution Act, 1982, because it treated "Indian" fishing rights as having no priority over other rights.

1992 In *R v Ellsworth,* the judge who decided *Joseph* states that "when the Indian people by the Douglas Treaty were given a right 'to carry on [their] fisheries as formerly,' this included fishing, conservation, and the use of the fish by the Indian people for whatever purpose the fish were used [for] by the signatories to the treaty."

1992 Canada, British Columbia, and the BC First Nations Summit sign an agreement to create the BC Treaty Commission, and the Treaty Commission Act is passed the following year.

2006 In *R v Morris,* the Supreme Court of Canada holds (four to three) that the provisions of the BC Wildlife Act that prohibit hunting at night with a light do not apply because of the Douglas Treaty guarantee of the right to hunt "as formerly."

2017 Esquimalt and Saanich Elders produce the first versions of their treaties written in local Coast Salish languages.

Acknowledgments, *Haichka*

THIS BOOK IS ONE OF the enduring outcomes of a remarkable gathering at the Songhees Wellness Centre in February 2017, and there are so many people to thank for making that event and, therefore, this book possible.

Most important, we would like to thank our friends at the Songhees Nation who so enthusiastically embraced the idea of a public discussion of the Vancouver Island (or Douglas) Treaties and Indigenous land rights. Chief Ron Sam leaped at the idea and offered his support throughout this project. Chief Sam asked his councillor John Rice Jr. and his staff members Cheryl Bryce and Mark Salter to represent the Songhees Nation on our organizing committee. Mark took on the role of local arrangements coordinator and masterfully handled the myriad challenge of seating, feeding, and touring three hundred people. Thanks, too, to Charlotte Charlie and the Songhees Youth Leadership Council for volunteering at the event.

It is also a pleasure to thank Songhees Elder Dr. Elmer George and W̱SÁNEĆ Elder John Elliot, Sr., for translating the treaties into their own languages for the first time and presenting them to the BC Archives. John Elliot also served as our keynote speaker. We want to thank the Songhees Dancers for welcoming us and Elder Sellemah, Joan Morris for leading us in a water tour of Songhees Territory.

It is imperative to thank Sarah Taekema for graciously handling the logistics on the University of Victoria side and for recruiting and leading a group of student volunteers. Sean MacPherson did a masterful job of filming each of the presenters and making the video summaries available online as another lasting outcome. We also want to thank Dr. Nick Claxton who joined our organizing committee.

There would be no book without the presentations of community members and academics at the gathering. We thank all the presenters! Summaries of their presentations are available in videos on our website.

At the event, we called four witnesses to respond to what transpired over that weekend with their reflections, and we wish to thank all of them: Robert Clifford, Stephen Hume, Maxine Matilpi, and Douglas White III. We offer special thanks to all those who offered up their words as chapters in this volume.

For their help in turning these presentations into a book, we wish to thank the three anonymous reviewers for their thoughtful suggestions, cartographer Ken Josephson, indexer Lillian Ashworth, and, at UBC Press, Darcy Cullen, Meagan Dyer, and the other dedicated people who had a hand in shepherding this collection into print. Publications like this need financial support to be accessible, and we have benefitted from the generosity of the Social Sciences and Humanities Research Council, the Songhees First Nation, the University of Victoria Faculties of Law and Humanities and the Department of History, as well as Frey and Company, JFK Law, Arbutus Law Group, and Woodward and Company. This book also received support from the University of Victoria Book and Creative Work Subvention fund.

Hay'sxw'qa si'em nakwilia! We thank you all!

To Share, Not Surrender

Introduction

IT ALL BEGAN SIMPLY ENOUGH. Four of us, who had done historical research on the colonial history of Vancouver Island on the west coast of Canada, met in fall 2015 to discuss the possibility of a one-day symposium on the policies of James Douglas concerning First Nations and land. In recent years, volumes of research had been completed by scholars in the form of confidential reports prepared for different land-title court challenges. One of these researchers expressed the concern that if this research was not made public, First Nations and governments would continually have to hire "experts" to do the same research over again every time a land-title case went to court. The symposium was planned as a first step in making this grey literature publicly available; it would be followed by a peer-reviewed publication of the presentations.[1] However, an unexpected chain of events changed the plans and the book.

The Conference

At the first meeting, we decided to invite both the Songhees First Nation and the University of Victoria to cohost the event. Songhees Chief Robert Sam immediately agreed and suggested that the event take place at their beautiful new Wellness Centre on Reserve 1-A. Serendipitously, the proposed conference dates coincided with the annual meeting of the Working Age Members of the Temex'w Treaty Association, composed of five Vancouver Island Treaty First Nations, the Songhees, T'Sou-ke, Beecher Bay, Malahat, and Nanoose First Nations. They decided to register en masse for the conference, instantly providing 140 registrants. To make this a truly collaborative effort, five new members were added to the organizing committee. The committee set out to encourage participation by the general public, who responded by filling the remaining 160 spots, yielding a total of 300 attendees, greatly exceeding all previous estimates. The topic and locale of the conference clearly appealed to the Victoria "settler" population, who were eager to be part of an event devoted to a better understanding of settler–First Nations history in the region and, consequently, participate in the truth and reconciliation process.

The expanded committee quickly came up with new ideas for the conference, including a tour for attendees of Songhees Territory, adoption of First Nations meeting protocols, and the recruitment of two Elders to produce versions of the treaties in their own languages. First Nations communities were encouraged to submit presentations on their views of Indigenous land, colonization, and James Douglas. The conference lost its originating impetus – white academics sharing their versions of history – to become a dialogic engagement of different views of history. In the process, it gained a much wider scope and appeal for both First Nations and settler audiences and produced a different kind of knowledge.

The "First Nations, Land, and James Douglas: Indigenous and Treaty Rights in the Colonies of Vancouver Island and British Columbia, 1849–1864" conference, which took place on February 24–26, 2017, was an historic, unprecedented event for Victoria. Three hundred people, half-settler, half-Indigenous, gathered for a weekend to learn from and share with one another the history of this region. The conference was opened by Robert Sam, Chief of the Songhees; Jamie Cassels, president of the University of Victoria; and the Songhees dancers. The keynote speech was given by W̱SÁNEĆ Elder STOLȻEŁ John Elliott, Sr. The formal presentations were rich, but much of the success of the event came from lively discussions among conference-goers, which happened at meal-times, coffee breaks, and open-mic sessions after each presentation. Between sessions, attendees were encouraged to move to different tables and start conversations.

The first event of the conference was a land-sea tour of Songhees Territory, featuring a visit to Tl'ches (Chatham and Discovery Islands), where Songhees Elder Sethlema (Joan Morris) told stories of her early childhood on the islands, which had been a sanctuary for her people during the devastating smallpox epidemic of 1862. The land tour included excursions to archaeological sites in Beacon Hill Park and culturally modified trees at the base of Mount Douglas, known to the W̱SÁNEĆ people as PKOLS. As part of the opening ceremonies, four "witnesses" were appointed and charged with the responsibility of summing up the conference as part of the closing ceremony on Sunday afternoon. The evening concluded with a keynote address by STOLȻEŁ John Elliott, Sr., titled "Sacred Teachings." Fittingly, he addressed the audience alternately in SENĆOŦEN and English, explaining the close spiritual and linguistic connections between

W̱SÁNEĆ origin or Creator stories and the SENĆOŦEN names for natural features such as mountains, islands, and trees.

The second day of the conference began with a formal presentation of the translations of the Vancouver Island (Douglas) Treaties into SENĆOŦEN and Lekwungen to the Royal BC Museum by STOLȻEŁ, John Elliot and Dr. Elmer George (Esquimalt). This dramatic moment – a moment when, for the first time, the Vancouver Island Treaties were available in local languages – was followed by performances in dance, song, and words of the Kwakiutl view of the treaties by the Chiefs and Elders of Fort Rupert, whose ancestors also made a treaty with James Douglas.

Throughout the day, the question periods provided the audience with an opportunity to probe the presenters, and it soon became clear that there was a diversity of views within the settler population. No surprise, then, that equally diverse views were expressed by Indigenous members of the audience, including a moment when an audience member of the Kwakiutl Indian band told the audience that the presenters from her community did not represent all members of the band and that deep divisions existed within the Kwakiutl community at Fort Rupert. Tension was also created by a brash young member of the audience who expressed his opinion that the scholarly presentations were boring and irrelevant, a view with which other audience members disagreed.

Sunday was a relaxed day. Attendees comfortably table-hopped between sessions, met new people, and initiated new conversations. It was also time for the four witnesses – one settler representative and three First Nations spokespeople – to have their say. Their takes on the conference were of course different, but all were positive. Three of the witnesses prepared summaries of their reflections, which are included in this volume.

By the end of the conference, it was clear that the publications, while still meeting academic standards, would also have to honour the conference participants' widely expressed desire to extend their learning experience beyond the three-day meeting. This book is therefore only one of three legacies of the conference. The second is a permanent website maintained by the University of Victoria. It includes video summaries of the presentations plus an array of resources about the conference topics.[2] The third will be a multimedia blending of text and video, oral and written summaries, and our combined learning on UBC Press's innovative web platform RavenSpace.[3] The success of this conference and an earlier one on pre-Confederation treaties hosted by the Snuneymuxw First Nation and Vancouver Island University in 2012 are persuasive arguments for having more such events and moving them off the usual campus setting and onto First Nations locales. In sum, the conference and this book are bellwethers of change.

The Context

Treaties, whether through their presence or absence, are central to any discussion of Indigenous land and British colonialism. In the case of British Columbia, the "treaties" are the fourteen agreements concluded between various Indigenous groups on Vancouver Island and James Douglas, land agent for the Hudson's Bay Company from 1849 to 1858 and governor of the Colony of Vancouver Island from 1851 to 1864 and the Colony of British Columbia from 1858 to 1864. No treaties were concluded on the mainland Colony of British Columbia.

The Vancouver Island Treaties have endured long periods of governmental and scholarly neglect. The written texts preserved in Victoria were edited and published in 1875 as the first seven pages of a long compendium of documents titled *Papers Connected to the Indian Land Question.* They were presented as conveyances, not as treaties.[4] Subsequently, they virtually disappeared from public view.[5] When the Canadian government published the texts of all the "Indian" treaties and land surrenders on file in Ottawa in 1891, the Vancouver Island Treaties were not included. (Nor did they appear in a third volume published in 1912.)[6] Aside from the occasional consideration in unpublished academic work, the treaty making of 1850–54 languished in relative obscurity for more than a century until two men charged with violating British Columbia's Game Act defended themselves successfully by invoking the hunting provisions of the 1854 Nanaimo treaty in a court of law. Upheld by the Supreme Court of Canada in 1965, the ruling in *R v Bob and White* affirmed the status of the negotiations of 1850–54 as treaties.[7]

Subsequent scholarship – historical, legal, and otherwise – has wrestled with fundamental questions regarding the meaning and significance of the treaties, and the essays in this volume bear witness to the ongoing efforts of scholars to do so. One recurring problem is context. It is clear, for example, that the Vancouver Island Treaties do not fit neatly into the long trajectory of alliance formation and treaty making between Indigenous peoples and colonizing powers that began in the late sixteenth century on the Atlantic coast of the continent and that culminated in the so-called Numbered Treaties in the Plains and Subarctic regions of what is now Canada in the late nineteenth and early twentieth centuries. These "historical treaties" – so labelled to distinguish them from the results of modern land claims and other agreements that have emerged since the 1970s – had their roots in local solemnized agreements worked out between Indigenous communities and the European fishers, whalers, and fur traders who frequented the coast seasonally in the late sixteenth century. In the seventeenth century, a persistent European presence at strategic points, such as Quebec, led to the formation of enduring alliances between Indigenous nations and colonizing agents. The intercultural diplomacy of the era focused on relationships (routinely expressed through the metaphor of kinship) and was shaped strongly by Indigenous political rhetoric, rituals, and protocols. European preferences – such as formal written records bearing the signatures of principals – crept in only gradually. Trade relations, territorial access, mutual defence, military cooperation, and even religious exchange were all negotiated in this way; the surrender of land, however, was not the principal object of treaty making for nearly two centuries. (The gradual dispossession of Indigenous peoples commenced nonetheless, but by other means.[8])

Only in the last half of the eighteenth century did British officials – as a matter of imperial policy in the context of military struggle with, first, France and then the American breakaway republic – begin to regularize to some degree the practice of formal negotiations regarding land with the aim of maintaining alliances with Indigenous powers who had repeatedly objected to, and opposed forcefully, the methods and outcomes of white settler encroachment. By 1850, British territorial treaty making in Upper Canada (now Ontario) had evolved into a bureaucratized process, and although the practices of face-to-face negotiations still bore testimony to the long history of nation-to-nation "peace and friendship" treaty making, the written texts had evolved to foreground the colonial state's preoccupation with land surrender. They emphasized "cessions" of extensive tracts of land (well in advance of actual settlement or exploitation), the assignation of reserves, the recognition of hunting and fishing rights, and the payment of annuities to members of "bands" whose leaders were signatories to a given treaty – all characteristics that would feature in treaty making for years to come. Two major Upper Canada treaties of 1850, negotiated with Anishinaabe nations around Lakes Huron and Superior, were emblematic of the gradual evolution of the form and practice of treaty making over more than two centuries on the eastern half of the continent.[9] The written texts of Douglas's treaties of the very same year are, however, markedly different; they are, as Neil Vallance underlines in his essay in this volume, *hors catégorie.* A central purpose running through the wide-ranging essays presented here is to illuminate, in all their complexity, the various contexts of the Vancouver Island Treaties and, thus, to help modern readers understand them on their own terms.

The chapters in this book contribute to a larger international discussion of the "great land rush," to use John Weaver's phrase, and the displacement of Indigenous populations from traditional territories from the Arctic to Australia. In some cases, as in parts of Vancouver Island, treaties were the instrument by which that dispossession occurred and were legitimized in the laws and discourse of the colonizers. In other places, such as the Mainland, treaties were rejected in favour of other strategies. Violence, forced removal, and even genocide were the strategies of choice in some colonial spaces. But in British Columbia, the colonizers' technology of dispossession was what Mary Louise Pratt has called the "anti-conquest" and John Sutton Lutz calls "peaceable subordination": in other words, British law, or rather a flawed conception of British law.[10]

The essays that follow look at the idea of treaties from both Indigenous and British colonial viewpoints and offer a rethinking of what makes "treaties" the formative, primal texts for colonial states. "Britain's empire," says John Weaver, "accorded indigenous peoples legal interests in land. British recognition of entitlements originated from secular ideas of humanism ... that venerated the rule of law."[11] As we learn, James Douglas in representing the Empire was inconsistent in his "veneration" of Indigenous title to land, but when he did, he encountered a sophisticated Indigenous legal network of property rights.

In her edited collection on treaties, Saliha Belmessous says we assume at our peril that Indigenous peoples did not understand the idea of land ownership or land laws. Belmessous argues that Indigenous societies each had a long-established set of Indigenous land laws and that colonialism is the on-the-ground interaction of European and Indigenous land laws. There is, she says, a surprising amount of overlap in the two; both recognize, for example, conquest and treat it as a legitimate means of acquiring ownership.[12]

At different times, First Nations, Canadian courts, and governments have relied on the literal words in particular treaties to define ownership, clarify rights and responsibilities, and award compensation – but to what extent are treaties stable and credible texts? To what extent do the words capture the agreements? Do they capture a meeting of minds and a shared understanding of a colonial future? Or are they better read as colonial impositions, fantasies, and wish lists disingenuously imposed on Indigenous peoples? The stability and reliability of treaty texts are central questions across the colonial world, but they have even more import in British Columbia because, as these essays show, the "texts of the treaties" were sent and arrived from London six months after the "actual oral treaties" were finalized between Douglas and the first nine Indigenous groups he treated with. The *x*'s next to the printed names of the Indigenous participants and the signatures of the European witnesses were attached to pages with a blank where the text was later added.

To understand what the oral and written treaties meant to the participants at the time requires a dive into the "situational" – the particular thinking of the 1840s and 1850s and the specific personalities involved in their creation. It also requires knowing the "global" context. European understandings of "treaties" as instruments of international law and of Indigenous people as legal entities who could be parties to agreements concerning land need to be placed alongside Indigenous conceptions of land ownership, their laws and customary practices of sharing, and their understanding of Europeans as legal beings in their world.

The situational was also embedded in settler ideas of race. The essays here directly and indirectly explore European ideas of the humanity of Indigenous peoples. Indigenous rights of land ownership are at the centre of the debate settlers were having among themselves between a stadial theory of race (in which Indigenous groups could potentially achieve the European ideal) and a biological theory (in which qualities such as intelligence and empathy were innate, immutable, and lacking in Indigenous populations). Stadial thinkers such as Douglas saw treaties as a way to protect and anticipate the day when Indigenous people would achieve a higher state of being and struggled against other settlers who rejected their improvability and, therefore, the need for land and treaties.[13]

While we can never lose sight of the focus – the dispossession of Indigenous land – the pivot on which this turned in this place and time was James Douglas. He makes a fascinating study because he was, for six years, the governor of two adjacent colonies at the same time. In one colony he initiated treaty making and in the other he ignored it.

The Essays

The overarching goal of the book is to shed light on the origins of the continuing struggle of First Nations and settlers to identify and implement an equitable sharing of the land we cohabit. The essays demonstrate that the problem arose from a fundamental absence of will on the part of the Hudson's Bay Company, James Douglas, and settlers to comprehend and accommodate First Nations traditional relationships with land. The role of James Douglas is crucial because the Hudson's Bay Company, the British Colonial Office, and newly arrived settlers all looked to him to ensure that First Nations did not stand in the way of land development; First Nations, in turn, looked to him to ensure that the growing settler population would not destroy their all-important relationships with the land.[14]

The volume is divided into four sections. Part 1 delves into the wider colonial, settler, and Indigenous context of the period. Part 2 focuses on First Nations perspectives on treaty formation, while Part 3 drills down to the contentious issue of why the treaty process was short-lived. Part 4 carries the story onto the mainland Colony of British Columbia, where, from 1858 until Douglas's retirement in 1864, the creation of Indian reserves replaced treaties as the site of contestation over the control of land. A treaty timeline (see pages vii–xi) and two maps (Figures I.1 and I.2) are provided to help situate historical events and locations.

FIGURE I.1 Hudson's Bay Company forts and First Nations–language groups in the Pacific Northwest in the mid-nineteenth century. | Map by Ken Josephson.

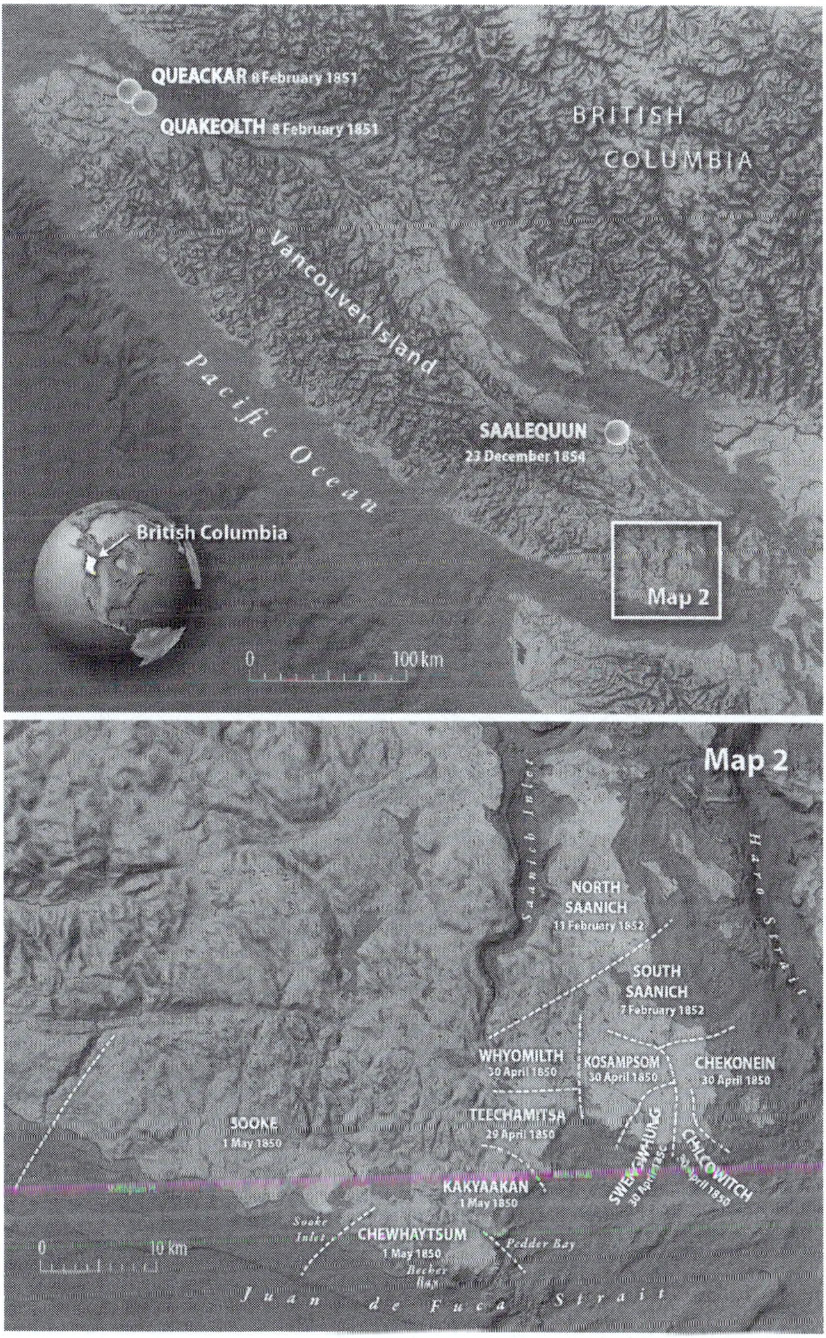

FIGURE I.2 Approximate location of the land described in each of the written versions of the Vancouver Island Treaties, 1850–54. | Map by Ken Josephson.

The three chapters in Part 1, by Adele Perry, Laura Spitz, and Hamar Foster, explore First Nations and colonial understandings of Indigenous land rights. Perry and Spitz provide the broader geographical context in which ideas about Indigenous lands developed in the decades leading up to the agreements between Douglas and First Nations on Vancouver Island. They are followed by Foster's account of British imperial views as to Aboriginal title to land.

Perry delves into the early geographic and family influences that shaped Douglas's attitudes towards Indigenous lands. Of the various colonial locations through which Douglas passed and remained tied to, Perry focuses on two: the Caribbean (especially Guyana) and the historical Northwest (especially Red River). Douglas's complicated connections to Indigenous peoples were imbedded in the historical context within which they occurred and were made meaningful by the imperial world he travelled through and remained linked to in multiple ways. Douglas also retained strong family ties, and Perry addresses the complexities of connecting his relationship with his Creole mother and Cree wife to his policies towards First Nations and land in the Colonies of Vancouver Island and British Columbia.

Spitz takes a more theoretical approach in her discussion of colonialism, law, and the social construction of humanity on Vancouver Island between 1849 and 1864. Although James Douglas is sometimes valorized for having recognized Aboriginal title in unceded land, the underlying assumption that Indigenous people were in fact "human" does not reveal a robust and nuanced view of humanity, nor was it especially progressive except in contrast to the discriminatory views of others. Rather, it was fundamentally liberal in the sense that it recognized that Indigenous people could be (legal) persons capable of holding and exercising rights in property. Moreover, it was consistent with early nineteenth-century European norms. But this conception would likely not have resonated with, nor made sense in the context of, Coast Salish legal traditions and Coast Salish understandings of themselves and their material, spiritual, and natural environment(s). Being human was not so much a status to which legal rights attached as a largely relational way of being in the Coast Salish world, and even then, it was potentially transitional or temporary and invariably subordinate to more powerful nonhuman forces.

By way of contrast, Foster tackles the imperial law of Aboriginal title as it existed at the time of the Vancouver Island Treaties, asking what exactly was the relevant, non-Indigenous law of Aboriginal title in the

1850s, when the Vancouver Island, or Douglas, Treaties were drawn up. The question sounds simple, but the answer is complex. Using the Supreme Court of Canada's 1973 decision in the *Calder* case as an important clue to interpreting the history of Aboriginal title law in British Columbia, Foster explains the role that the doctrine of sovereign immunity played in this history and how it permitted popular but erroneous understandings of Indigenous rights to flourish. Still, a law of Aboriginal title was generated by common-law courts in the nineteenth century, albeit indirectly. Traces of it may be found in imperial legislation; in criminal cases from the Indian Territories (of which Vancouver Island was a part until 1849); in legal opinions by government lawyers as well as lawyers acting for First Nations; and in superior court decisions in other jurisdictions. To paraphrase Sir Henry Maine's *Early Law and Custom,* the law of Aboriginal title was secreted in the interstices of cases involving land disputes between settlers. Its contours have only been developed fully in the last forty years or so, but its basic elements are much, much older.

Part 2 opens with Neil Vallance's chapter, which argues for a fundamental distinction between what he calls the "Douglas Forms" – the short, written quitclaims that up until now have been regarded as authoritative – and the "Vancouver Island Treaties." The latter are what was orally agreed to at the meetings between 1850 and 1854, and Vallance argues, they were, in general, agreements to share the land. The devil, of course, is in the details, some of which may be forever irretrievable. But breaking with scholarly tradition to date, Vallance begins with what are, to the best of our knowledge, all the documented records of First Nations understanding of these proceedings. He then proceeds to make comparisons with the almost equally scanty colonial record.

The SENĆOŦEN and Lekwungen versions of the treaties are introduced by Vallance, who explores the issue of communication at the Vancouver Island treaty meetings and the bilingual nature of the treaties. Emchayiik, Robert Dennis, Sr., and Kevin Neary's chapter provides a much-needed outline of a contemporary First Nations laws concerning land and treaties. The chapter demonstrates how these laws informed relations with early settlers, as illustrated by the story of William Banfield's residence on the west coast of Vancouver Island in the mid-nineteenth century. In particular, Neary examines an 1859 agreement entered into by Banfield with the Huu-ay-aht, which purported to be an outright transfer to him of a small island in Barkley Sound; under Huu-ay-aht law, however, the agreement was merely a temporary assignment of rights to use and occupy the land.

In Part 3, Graham Brazier and John Sutton Lutz look at the roles of the various colonial actors in the treaty-making process on Vancouver Island. In Brazier's view, although Douglas had sympathy with the Indigenous peoples of the new colony and was concerned for their well-being, his fur trade background hindered his ability to embrace the notion of Aboriginal title – which meant that he only "went through the motions" of treaty making. Brazier focuses on the years between the founding of Fort Victoria in 1843 and the establishment of the Colony of Vancouver Island six years later, arguing that the lack of consideration devoted to Indigenous land issues in this period suggests that the treaties were the result of a land policy that was an "afterthought." He concludes that there was no strong driving force behind the treaty-making process Douglas undertook in April–May 1850, and when it proved to be "troublesome," Douglas decided that, on the whole, treaties were not worth the effort unless they were intended to deal with specific issues.

John Sutton Lutz takes a different view. In his essay, he harkens back to a suggestion made by the first scholar to examine what was then called "Indian" policy in British Columbia, George Edgar Shankel. In 1945, Shankel noted that the Vancouver Island House of Assembly had "objected to the voting of money to extinguish [Indian] land title when they had no control of funds from the sale of land." However, the "House viewed with approval the extinguishment of title from the proceeds of land sales but refused money from general revenue."[15] Lutz goes well beyond Shankel in making a strong case that Douglas was not alone in wanting treaties – so, too, did newspapers, settlers, First Nations, the Colonial Office, the Vancouver Island Legislative Assembly, and his successor as governor, Arthur Kennedy. Why, then, did treaty making appear to end in 1854? Because, Lutz argues, the colony's archaic constitution pitted the governor and assembly against each other on important fiscal matters and because, after 1859, the HBC and the imperial government were unable to agree on the compensation owed to the company on returning the colony's title to Britain. So, even though all the relevant actors wanted treaties of some kind, it was not a lack of funds but a financial impasse that paralyzed and, in the end, terminated the treaty process.

Part 4 shifts the focus from the Vancouver Island Treaties to Indigenous title and reserve creation in the Colony of British Columbia after 1858. Sarah Pike proposes a new approach to understanding Douglas's reserve policy on the Mainland. Her chapter examines what may be called the BC unsurveyed land system, a set of rules Douglas devised to meet settlers' insistent demands for land while preserving – or, at least, intending to preserve – Indigenous interests in land and balancing the colony's needs with the Colonial Office's directions. The BC unsurveyed land system's focal point was the right of pre-emption, a practice adopted from the United States that allowed British subjects to acquire unsurveyed land without paying for it prior to occupying it. Yet through the BC unsurveyed land system, Douglas also sought to preserve for Indigenous people the lands they had occupied before settlers came by precluding an "Indian reserve or settlement" from lands available for pre-emption.

The essay by Keith Thor Carlson invites a different perspective on James Douglas and his "Indian" land policies. Carlson uses a major gathering hosted by Douglas just before he retired in 1864 as a way to introduce his thoughtful analysis of what an earlier scholar has called the Douglas "system,"[16] one that was both committed to the emerging liberal and Christian order but that also saw an important place in that order for the colony's Indigenous population. With all its faults, he concludes, the system was nonetheless "something that Indigenous people then regarded as workable and that in hindsight was greatly preferable to what replaced it following Douglas's retirement." In essence, Carlson argues that Douglas's vision of a settler colonialism was not predicated on assumptions of Indigenous peoples' racial inferiority; this vision caused significant anxiety in the settler community, which increasingly regarded Douglas as too sympathetic to the needs and interests of Indigenous inhabitants. Douglas had, after all, seen at close hand what had happened in Oregon, and Carlson argues that Douglas – enjoying extraordinary executive and legislative power and confident that he had the Colonial Office's backing – believed he could foster a colonial society in which (unlike Washington, Oregon, and California) not only warfare but also marginalization and displacement could be avoided. For him, the threat to this project was the prejudice and greed of settlers more than the liberal economic order he believed in and was appointed to establish. Indeed, as a man whose mother was a "free coloured woman" and whose wife's mother was Cree, the threat posed by this prejudice, especially to his children, was both personal and palpable.

Taken together, three major themes recur throughout this volume. One is the desire of European explorers, traders, and colonists to lay claim to the land, to obtain exclusive possession. This obsession is forcefully described by Thomas King in his book, *The Inconvenient Indian:*

> The issue that came ashore with the French and the English and the Spanish, the issue that was the raison d'etre for each of the colonies, the issue that has made its way from coast to coast to coast and is with us today, the issue that has never changed, never varied, never faltered in its resolve is the issue of land.[17]

A second thread is the spirit of *cel'an̲'en,* defined in the Lekwungen language as "Our culture, the way of our people."[18] In the SENĆOŦEN language, the word is written as "C'ELA'N̲EN," but the meaning is the same. In 1987 Saanich Elder Gabriel Bartleman described the relationship between C'ELA'N̲EN and land: "We have what they call a C'ELA'N̲EN, and the word C'ELA'N̲EN does not allow any other foreign agreements. There's no way we can sell a C'ELA'N̲EN or trade it off, it is a way of life."[19] First Nations had no intention of handing over their way of life, or their land, to the newcomers.

The worldviews of Indigenous peoples and newcomers were clearly at odds with respect to land, and yet they all faced the enormous challenge of coexisting on the same land. The final thread follows the career of James Douglas as he tried to fulfill his responsibility to dispossess First Nations of all land potentially required for colonization while protecting them from the worst excesses of land-hungry settlers. Every contribution to this book demonstrates his pervasive influence on efforts to resolve the conflict from 1849 to 1864, through treaty making along the inner coast of Vancouver Island and then through reserve formation on the Mainland. He did not succeed then, and the tension remains unresolved now. The current project is an attempt to understand why, to untangle the threads, and to move the urgent task of reconciliation in Canada forward.

Notes

1 The problem of grey literature and reinventing the wheel was identified some time ago, at the outset of the BC treaty process: see Hamar Foster and Alan Grove, "Looking behind the Masks: A Land Claims Discussion Paper for Researchers, Lawyers and Their Employers," *UBC Law Review* 27 (1993): 213–55, esp. 235–37.

2 "Vancouver Island Treaties," n.d., https://hcmc.uvic.ca/songheesconference.

3 RavenSpace, http://ravenspacepublishing.org/.

4 British Columbia, *Papers Connected to the Indian Land Question* (Victoria: R. Wolfenden, 1875), 5–11.
5 The exception was heated but short-lived debates in the *Victoria Daily Colonist.* See Neil Vallance, "Sharing the Land: The Formation of the Vancouver Island (or 'Douglas') Treaties of 1850–54 in Historical, Legal, and Comparative Context" (PhD diss., University of Victoria, 2015), 244–50, 250–53.
6 Canada, *Indian Treaties and Surrenders from 1680 to 1890,* 2 vols. (Ottawa: Brown Chamberlin, 1891), and *Indian Treaties and Surrenders from No. 281 to No. 483* (Ottawa: C.H. Parmelee, 1912).
7 Vallance, "Sharing the Land," 274–79.
8 Allan Greer, *Property and Dispossession: Natives, Empires and Land in Early Modern North America,* Studies in North American Indian History (Cambridge: Cambridge University Press, 2018).
9 The best historical overview of early Canadian treaty making is J.R. Miller, *Compact, Contract, Covenant: Aboriginal Treaty-Making in Canada* (Toronto: University of Toronto Press, 2009).
10 Mary Louise Pratt, *Imperial Eyes: Travel Writing and Transculturation* (London: Routledge, 1992), 7; and John Sutton Lutz, *Makúk: A New History of Aboriginal-White Relations* (Vancouver: UBC Press, 2008), 24–25.
11 John Weaver, *The Great Land Rush and the Making of the Modern World, 1650–1900* (Montreal/Kingston: McGill-Queen's University Press, 2003), 134.
12 Saliha Belmessous, *Native Claims: Indigenous Law against Empire, 1500–1920* (Oxford: Oxford University Press, 2012), 4–5.
13 Scholars today debate whether we should understand this settler conflict from a humanist point of view, which rejects the idea of race in favour of a continuity of humanism, or from a posthumanist perspective, which rejects thinking of humans as essentially different from animals and separated from nature. See, for example, Alan Lester, "Humanism, Race and Colonial Frontier," *Transactions of the Institute of British Geographers* 37, 1 (2012): 132–48.
14 The ongoing attempts by Douglas to juggle these priorities is discussed in Neil Vallance's chapter in Part 2 of this volume. The scholarly consensus is that, for all his faults, Douglas was much better than what came after him. As Marianne Ignace and Ronald E. Ignace state, his "'pro-Indian' attitude in the negotiation of treaties and subsequent intent to establish 'Douglas Reserves' has been hailed as well intended, [but] the downfall of British Columbia Aboriginal peoples was Douglas's neglect to codify his intents in the form of laws that protected Aboriginal title": see *Secwépemc People, Land, and Laws* (Montreal/Kingston: McGill-Queen's University Press, 2017), 438. A recent and outspoken critic of this consensus is Tom Swanky, who asserts that Douglas "seems a murderer, a thief, an outlaw, a usurper, a liar, a profane violator of sacred customs, prone to abuse of authority and a keen practitioner of amoral virtues"; see *The True Story of Canada's "War" of Extermination on the Pacific* (Burnaby, BC: Dragon Heart Enterprises, 2012), 24. Swanky regards historians who have anything good to say about Douglas's Indian policy as "apologists and collaborators in genocide" and suggests they are "criminally negligent" (11, 219).
15 George Edgar Shankel, "The Development of Indian Policy in British Columbia" (PhD diss., University of Washington, 1945), 45.
16 Paul Tennant, *Aboriginal Peoples and Politics: The Indian Land Question in British Columbia, 1849–1989* (Vancouver: UBC Press, 1990).

17 Thomas King, *The Inconvenient Indian: A Curious Account of Native People in North America* (Toronto: Doubleday Canada, 2012), 217.

18 Songhees Nation, *Songhees: Gaiʔ ataʔeyʔ šqal'o'wen/Songhees: To Work with Good Mind, Good Feelings* (Victoria: Songhees Nation, 2013), 8.

19 *Saanichton Marina Ltd v Louis Claxton et al., and Louis Claxton et al v Saanichton Marina Ltd and Her Majesty the Queen in right of the Province of Columbia,* Actions nos. 85/2872 and 85/2873, trial transcript for September 2, 1987, at 29–30.

Photo Essay

Songhees dancers welcome the conference participants. | Photograph by Spencer Pickles.

Members of the conference organizing committee observe the opening of the conference with Songhees Chief Ron Sam. *Left to right:* Songhees Chief Ron Sam, Graham Brazier, Hamar Foster, Neil Vallance, and Peter Cook. | Photograph by UVic Photo Services.

Graham Brazier of the conference organizing committee offers tokens of gratitude to conference witness Robert Clifford, YELḰÁTTE (W̱SÁNEĆ and Osgoode Hall Law School) at the beginning of the conference. | Photograph by UVic Photo Services.

Graham Brazier *(right)* offers tokens of gratitude to conference witness Douglas White III, Kwul'a'sul'tun (Snuneymuxw). | Photograph by UVic Photo Services.

Left to right: W̱SÁNEĆ Elder STOLȻEȽ John Elliott, Sr., Songhees Chief Ron Sam, and John Sutton Lutz (conference organizing committee) welcome attendees to the opening of the conference on Saturday morning, February 24, 2017. | Photograph by UVic Photo Services.

Songhees drummers lead the procession of Songhees and W̱SÁNEĆ Elders with the SENĆOŦEN and Lekwungen versions of the treaties into the conference hall. | Photograph by UVic Photo Services.

Songhees Elder Dr. Elmer George enters the conference hall with the Lekwungen version of his community's treaty with James Douglas. On his right is Chief Ron Sam (Songhees) and on his left is Songhees Councillor Garry Albany. *Behind, left to right:* John Rice (Songhees), STOLȻEȽ John Elliott, Sr., and Nick Claxton, XEMŦOLTW̱. | Photograph by UVic Photo Services.

Songhees Elder Dr. Elmer George addresses the conference attendees. | Photograph by UVic Photo Services.

Left to right: Dr. Elmer George (Songhees), Songhees Councillor Garry Albany, STOLȻEŁ John Elliott, Sr. (W̱SÁNEĆ) presenting the SENĆOŦEN version to Lucy Bell and Angela Williams of the Royal BC Museum. | Photograph by UVic Photo Services.

Members of the Kwakiutl Nation sing and drum before their presentation. | Photograph by Spencer Pickles.

Tony Hunt, Hereditary Chief of the Kwakiutl, addresses the conference attendees. | Photograph by Spencer Pickles.

Conference attendees in the gymnasium of the Songhees Wellness Centre. | Photograph by UVic Photo Services.

Conference participant Diane Sam (Songhees) compares a facsimile of the Vancouver Island Treaties with new SENĆOŦEN and Lekwungen versions. | Photograph by UVic Photo Services.

Neil Vallance (conference organizing committee) and a young member of the Songhees Nation participate in an icebreaker dance on Day 2 of the conference. | Photograph by Spencer Pickles.

Maxine Hayman Matilpi (Lakwa), witness of the conference. | Photograph by UVic Photo Services.

Stephen Hume, witness of the conference. | Photograph by John Sutton Lutz.

Part 1

First Nations and Colonial Understandings of Indigenous Land Rights

1

Indigenous Lands, Imperial Travels, and James Douglas

Adele Perry

It is for good reason that James Douglas (1803–77) is most associated with the particular space of British Columbia and the consequential decades of the middle of the nineteenth century.[1] In these years, Douglas sat at the helm of a fractious and violent settler state, and the ways that this state both did and did not recognize Indigenous peoples and Indigenous lands have had enduring consequences for Indigenous peoples, British Columbia, and Canada, which British Columbia became a province of in 1871. But Douglas's story – and, I would argue, his particular imprint on the questions that lay at the heart of this volume – was also shaped and given meaning by other geographies and temporalities. In this essay, I put Douglas and his complex interactions with Indigenous peoples and lands in a wide-angle lens and examine them over the *longue durée,* over the course of the long nineteenth century and in relation to Douglas's own experiences and connections beyond British Columbia. I do so by focusing on three documents: a 1798 map of Guyana, the Selkirk Treaty of 1817, and a photograph of Amelia Connolly Douglas and her household in 1885.

I use this map, this treaty, and this photograph to anchor a discussion that ranges throughout British North America, the United Kingdom, and the Caribbean from the end of the eighteenth century until the 1920s. This research reflects my ongoing work on the extended families and peers of Douglas and his wife, Amelia Connolly Douglas (1812–90), much of which was published in 2015's *Colonial Relations.*[2] This work is rooted in three historiographical manoeuvres. First is the long-standing but still vital contention that women, family, and intimacy are worthy, possible, and provocative subjects of historical inquiry. Our analysis shifts and is enriched when we acknowledge and explore women's multiple pasts, examine men and women as gendered subjects, and put the presumed schism between private and public into question. In this I have been lucky to benefit from the research of Sylvia Van Kirk, Charlotte Girard, and

John Adams into Douglas's and Connolly Douglas's families and peers.[3] Second is the rejection of the presumption that history is best framed within the nation-state or within the related category of the region. This means that historians can and should follow stories, connections, and lives across national and regional spaces. The third manoeuvre is to try to put into practice what might be broadly called decolonizing historical practice, one informed by Indigenous historians and postcolonial scholarship and committed to unpacking rather than reifying colonialism, its ontologies, its violence, and its remarkable staying power. This includes attending to questions of voice and being mindful of the limits of myself as a white settler historian who works primarily with colonial archives.

What are the implications of these three frames for our discussion of Douglas, Indigenous peoples, and treaty rights? To read Douglas through a feminist, transnational, and critical colonial lens does not displace analyses that centre Douglas within the thick histories of Lekwammen and Kwakwa̱ka̱'wakw peoples and lands. But it can put those histories within wider contexts. Of the various colonial locations through which Douglas passed and remained tied to, I focus on two: the Caribbean, especially Guyana, and the Northwest, especially the Red River settlement. These wide histories are best understood when we firmly locate them within their specific temporal context and when we reject the idea that Douglas was somehow outside of his time – whether behind it or ahead of it, as has more often been the case in discussions of Douglas and his legacies, including his influence on Indigenous lands. Douglas's complicated connections to Indigenous peoples were imbedded in the historical context within which they occurred and were made meaningful by the imperial world he travelled through and remained multiply tied to. Douglas's imperial and racial thinking was not tidy, coherent, or consistent, but it can be traced through different moments and different archives.

Thomas Walker's map of Guyana was drawn about four years before James Douglas was born in 1803. The map is enormous, over four feet in both width and length. It reflects a part of the colonial world in political flux. The parts of South America along the Caribbean coast territorialized as Guyana were repeatedly shuffled between colonial empires in the complicated years at the end of the eighteenth century. In 1803, the colonies of Demerara, Berbice, and Esquibbo would be remade as British. The orientation of the map reflects this uncertainty. As Graham Burnett notes, Walker's map inverts the usual north-south relationship and puts

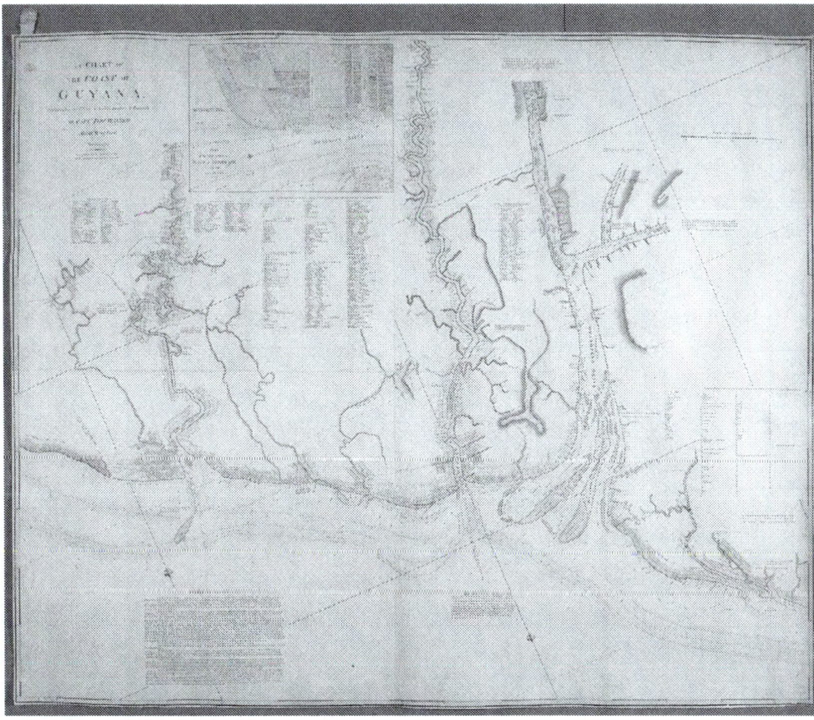

FIGURE 1.1 Captain Thomas Walker, *A Chart of the Coast of Guyana, Comprehending the Colonies of Berbice, Demerary and Essequebo,* October 1, 1798. | British Library, 124/40/11, Guyana 1798, Ktop CXXIV/40 (London: C.G. Playter, 1799).

the south on the top of the sheet, conveying "the impression of a view from a high point above the coast down the interior."[4] It pays attention to the boundary between Guyana and neighbouring Spanish claims.

Walker's map is also remarkably detailed, almost granular. It documents a particular spacialization of Guyana, located on the eastern coast of South America and sharing a history of intensive plantation slavery with the islands to its immediate east. Walker's map shows us long lots organized around private, if often absentee, ownership of plantations that were, in turn, dependent on slavery. It makes clear that this is about ownership of land as well as people. Walker's map identifies the "Names of Proprietors & Estates" in different regions, including "From Malcouny to Mahaica." Number 19 on the map is a plantation owned by "Ramsay, Felfair and Douglas." These names could refer to a number of people – the surname "Douglas" was and is common in both Guyana and Scotland. This Douglas could also be the family of John Douglas, James's father.

In the early years of the nineteenth century, the Douglas family was regularly associated with different branches of the Atlantic economy that connected Scotland and the Caribbean. Family members kept shops and traded goods and owned plantations in Demerara and Berbice. John Douglas was in and around Georgetown in the early nineteenth century but seems to have returned to Scotland, perhaps with his two sons, James and Alexander, in the 1810s, leaving daughter Cecilia. John Douglas would marry a Scottish woman and have another, somewhat parallel, family. In 1834, he applied for compensation for property under the legislation that finalized the abolition of slavery in the British Empire. His application identifies him as absentee owner of colonial property and enslaved people, the kind that Guyana had long been organized around, and as a Glasgow merchant tied to the J.T. and A. Douglas Company. Douglas was awarded over £12,407 compensation for 236 slaves at Good Hope. Nicholas Draper's remarkable research allows us to see that the Douglas family is as good an example as any of the economic and political work performed by slavery and slave compensation in nineteenth-century Britain.[5] John Douglas died in London in 1840 and is identified in his death certificate as a "West India Merchant" living in Edinburgh. The money of slave compensation likely contributed to his estate being valued at more than £70,000.[6]

The inset in Walker's map marks out a different kind of Caribbean space – the city. Here, it carries the Batavian name of Stradbroek, which would be renamed Georgetown in 1812. Martha Ann Telfer and Rebecca Ritchie – the women who Girard suggests were James Douglas's mother and grandmother – were most associated with this place. Telfer was one on a long list of "free coloured" people who paid their 1808 taxes for owning slaves, in her case, twenty-four of them. In 1817, the British Colonial Office enumerated enslaved populations and found that Telfer owned twenty-eight slaves, well above the average urban household in Guyana.[7] By the time Telfer applied under the Slave Compensation Act, she had only one slave to her name.[8] Telfer had social as well as material resources. She could write or at least sign her name to legal documents. When she died in 1839, the goods she left suggest her status as a well-to-do and distinctly Caribbean woman: a press, a large mahogany bedstead with bedding and curtains, a "colony-wood" bedstead, and a large mahogany sideboard.[9] Girard suggests that Telfer's mother was Rebecca Ritchie, a "free coloured woman" who acted in the local courts on matters of property and who bought and sold land and buildings in Cummingsberg, one of the districts specified on Walker's map.[10] Ritchie owned slaves in both Demerara and Barbados[11] and would be awarded just under £2,000 for thirty-three slaves and almost £200 for four slaves of Amelia Jacobs, a minor under her guardianship.[12] This was presumably the source of some of the approximately £500 that Ritchie left to James Douglas's daughters in her 1855 will.[13]

This is a strikingly detailed map that still imagines the expansive interior as more or less empty and devoid of people and places, with the brief exception of one building labelled an "Indian House." The map replicates a strategic colonial erasure of Indigenous peoples, an erasure that legitimated the dispossession of Indigenous peoples and territories throughout the Americas and the Antipodes. But Guyana was Indigenous space, established on the Traditional Territories of Arawakan, Cariban, and Warrauan peoples.[14] In Walker's map, these spaces are imagined as revealingly blank, broken only by an occasional river or topographical feature. Here was a different version of the erasure of Indigenous peoples, one that would recur, with different emphasis, in northern North America. Behind Walker's vague pink spaces were histories of Indigenous peoples and colonial states.

Historian Mary Noel Menezes analyzes how the British colonial state continued parts of Dutch and French practice and wrestled with where Indigenous people and labour fit within a system of chattel slavery. British colonial administrators had a range of opinions on practices of annual gifting, but Indigenous people found ways to ensure that this practice, which could be a form of treaty making, continued. In November 1812, one official reported that a "large body of Indians had arrived in the neighborhood of the Colony to demand presents." He met the Crown's obligations but tried to sever them from a reckoning of treaty, and rights, explaining that the gifts should be "a boon and not a right, as a reward for their past good conduct rather than as the purchase of their future friendship."[15] As the threat of slave resistance diminished, the alliance of Indigenous peoples mattered and was valued less, and by the 1860s what was now British Guiana was absorbed in a gold rush.[16] "The British policy towards Indians in Guiana meant many things to many men," explains Menezes. In the pink parts of Walker's map, the question of whether the British state ought to recognize Indigenous title, how it should maintain its alliance with Indigenous peoples, and how much it mattered were very much alive in the years of James Douglas's childhood.

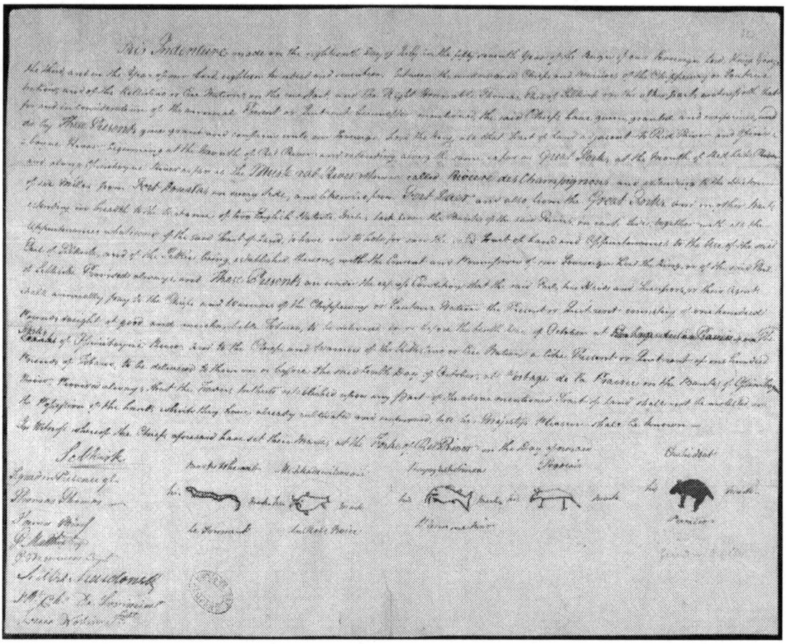

FIGURE 1.2 Deed conveying land adjoining the Red and Assiniboine Rivers from Saulteax and Cree Chiefs to Lord Selkirk [the Selkirk Treaty], July 18, 1817. | Hudson's Bay Company Archives, E.8/1, folio 10.

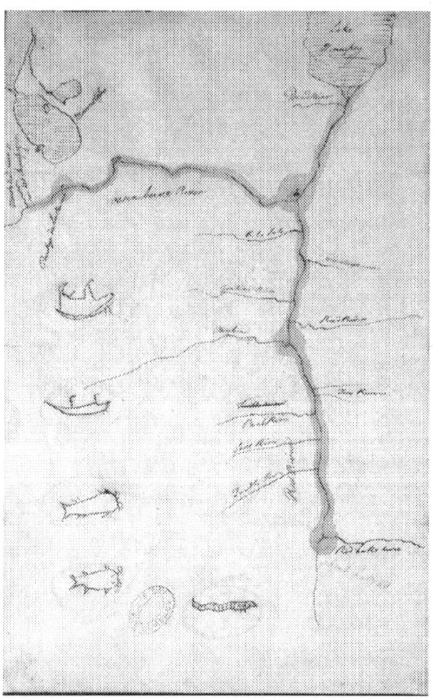

FIGURE 1.3 Map accompanying the Selkirk Treaty. | Hudson's Bay Company Archives, E.8/1, folio 11.

In 1817, Annishinaabeg and Inninuwak or Swampy Cree leaders put their dodems and Lord Selkirk signed his name to a map of the Red and Assiniboine Rivers drawn on parchment and accompanied by a paragraph of alphabetic text. The map documented places and peoples along the rivers. The accompanying agreement allowed for the settlement of Scottish settlers in exchange for, as Adam Gaudry explains, "a substantial amount of tobacco as an 'annual present,' or as the Annishinaabeg saw it, rent."[17] Two years after the Selkirk Treaty was concluded, James Douglas entered its fur trade world, and he would remain associated, in one way or another, with the fur trade for the rest of his life. In 1819, in Montreal, a teenaged Douglas entered the service of the North West Company as a clerk.[18] He then travelled Indigenous territory north and west of settler British North America during years of protracted violent conflict resulting from the merger of the North West Company and the Hudson's Bay Company (HBC) and the development of a rich, enduring Métis culture. In 1825, Douglas moved to the Caledonia District but reaffirmed his ties to the Northwest and its particular Cree-Métis culture with a marriage by Indigenous custom to Amelia Connolly. Connolly was born in 1812, probably at Fort Assiniboine, the daughter of a Canadian fur trader and a Cree mother.[19] In 1830, Douglas moved to Fort Vancouver, the HBC's major west coast post. Amelia Connolly travelled after her husband, making the long journey with her father and the brigade dressed in elite Métis style – embroidered leggings and moccasins "stiff with the most costly beads."[20]

Since 1670, the Royal Charter had formally given the private interests of the Hudson's Bay Company the exclusive right "to trade" in the expansive territory draining into Hudson Bay. It was not unusual for Britain to grant a private company a peculiar sort of colonial authority in the seventeenth century, but it was unusual for this arrangement to persist into the nineteenth.[21] In the Northwest territory that Douglas worked in, HBC claims to rule were, as Gaudry explains, grandiose and fantastical.[22] Historian Michael Witgen lays this argument out in terms that historians of Canada might pay closer attention to. Until the middle of the nineteenth century, Indigenous peoples controlled the vast majority of the North American continent, and claims otherwise were more or less "a political fabrication." It was into the Annishinaabeg, Cree, Assiniboine, Dakota, and Métis parts of this complex and vibrant Indigenous world that Douglas would enter, becoming one of those traders "who lived in the Native New World."[23]

The fur trade was not much interested in land per se but in the resources, labour, knowledge, and kin relations of the Indigenous world. Trade was the mechanism that transferred them to Europeans, and treaty making was a central and well-developed means by which Indigenous peoples of the continent's interior managed relations with other nations. Legal scholar Aimee Craft explains that Annishinaabeg law utilizes treaty as a means of establishing relationships of mutual care, assistance, and, ultimately, *mino-bimaadiziwin,* or good life.[24] Despite the sweeping claims of the Charter, the HBC found it "prudent" to negotiate what scholars Frank Tough and Jim Miller describe as "Aboriginal consent to build posts and conduct trade in their territories."[25] Gifting, the ceremony of the pipe, and making newcomers kin, especially through mechanisms of marriage, all built on Cree, Annishinaabeg, and Dakota practices of treaty making.

Treaty allowed for trade, and in the case of the 1817 Selkirk Treaty negotiated between Annishinaabeg and Cree leaders and the HBC's Lord Selkirk, it allowed for non-Indigenous settlement on limited and specific terms at the confluence of the Red and Assiniboine Rivers. As a document, the Selkirk Treaty is substantially nonalphabetic, marking its meanings through a map and, more particularly, through Anishinaabe dodems, each linked to a signatory Chief and placed in clear relationship to the territories they were most associated with. As Heidi Bohaker explains, Anishinaabe dodems represented "a tradition of inscription" that predated European arrival, that functioned as a rough equivalent to the seals that indicated the consent of colonial states, and that spoke of deep environmental knowledge and relations of kinship and obligation, both to humans and to other-than-humans.[26]

The Selkirk Treaty reminds us of a wider tradition of treaty making in the fur trade and the Northwest; the connections that linked Indigenous peoples in eighteenth- and nineteenth-century North America, including on either side of the Great Lakes; and the range of possible meanings that could be and were attached to treaty. Its central use of Annishinaabeg dodems situates the Selkirk Treaty alongside the better-known documents of the eastern Great Lakes, including the 1701 Great Peace of Montreal.[27] The textual component of the treaty refers to it as an "indenture," and Selkirk reported that he was proposing "not a sale but a gift" or quitrent that might be renewed annually.[28] And as Gaudry explains, the idea that the Selkirk Treaty legitimated British governance and sovereignty was "bitterly contested" by Annishinaabeg leaders for years."[29] Here, as elsewhere, Indigenous peoples have argued that the oral and in some cases written agreements of treaties were agreements not to cede land but to conditionally share parts of the land and live in relationship.[30] These more nuanced and Indigenous interpretations of treaties are worth keeping in mind when recourse is made to brittle distinctions between "ceded" and "unceded" lands. Political scientist Gina Starblanket has analyzed the Numbered Treaties, including Treaty 1 (1871), which superseded the Selkirk Treaty. She reminds us that "simplistic narratives of land cession and surrender through treaty making have always been contested by Indigenous peoples, who understand treaties as having involved the negotiation of far more complex political arrangements."[31]

In 1885, on the day she posed with her children, grandchildren, and great-grandchildren on the porch of her Victoria home, Amelia Connolly Douglas was a widow in her seventies, and her husband had passed away some seven years earlier. Douglas and Connolly Douglas had thirteen children and raised five daughters and a son to adulthood. The 1885 photograph depicts a large extended family, rooted in their James Bay home, and signals, in multiple ways, the family's affluence, prestige, and respectability. As a document, this photograph speaks to the ways that family and place were woven through Douglas's history.

FIGURE 1.4 Amelia, Lady Douglas (seated centre) surrounded by family to the third and fourth generation, ca. 1885. | Royal BC Museum and Archives, Image A-00840.

In 1843, Douglas had established a new fort on Vancouver Island, first dubbing it "Camousack," which one contemporary explained signified "beads of necklaces" in Cree. This was the working language of much of the fur trade, whether it was in Cree territory or not and one that Douglas "was fairly familiar" with.[32] A little later, a generic imperial renaming made it Victoria. Douglas was named chief factor, and he, his wife, and a family of four daughters – a son and another daughter would be born in Victoria – took up residence within the walls of the fort. Like HBC posts elsewhere, Fort Victoria was a kind of palisaded village, a militarized commercial space that spoke to the blunt material aspirations and colonial authority of the private fur trade company. Fort Victoria had residential buildings for various categories of employees, warehouses, a blacksmith's shop, a bakery, and, at the centre, a belfry, which was rung for rising, meals, work, and for Christian service on Sunday. The fort walls distinguished who and what belonged to the HBC, what did not, and what was at its margins. Outside the fort were the cabins of HBC servants and their Indigenous families, many of them Coast and Straits Salish, unlike the mainly Métis women married to HBC officers.[33]

Fort Victoria was a built testament to both the powers of the British Empire and its desire to remake the lived experience of the diverse spaces it awkwardly and often violently claimed. The fort's gates, watchmen, and bastions spoke to empire, and so, over time, did the land. The cultivation of gardens served as particularly potent symbols of empire, as tangible reminders of its capacity to rearrange and repurpose space. James Robert Anderson was sent from Fort Alexandria to Fort Victoria to attend school and, like many fur trade children sent to a major post for schooling, was placed in the care of the chief factor and his family, in this case James Douglas and Amelia Connolly Douglas. Anderson recalled the fort's garden as being "redolent with the perfume of mignonette, stock and wallflower and gay with echoltsia, mallow, hollyhock, marigold, candytuft, sweet William and others of the old-fashioned flowers." He also remembered the peas, turnips, carrots, cabbage, potatoes, and onions and, especially, the apple trees. They were grown from seeds sent from Fort Vancouver, which had, in turn, been grown from seeds brought from England. Anderson recalled being given an apple by "kind, motherly Mrs. Douglas." The apple was "a great favour," and Anderson soon learned to appreciate its strange taste. He also experienced Connolly Douglas as a fine hostess. Anderson recalled a memorable picnic and wrote of the "lurid happiness of that delightful day"; he recalled another given by

Douglas and his wife in honour of the arrival of a new British ship as being characterized by "lavish hospitality in the dispensation of wines and spirits for which the Company was so justly celebrated."[34]

Vancouver Island was established as a colony in 1849. Usually described as a Crown colony, its particular structure of governance owed quite a bit to the Caribbean, including to Guiana's complicated constitutional history.[35] In May 1851, Douglas was appointed governor and vice-admiral, adding these titles to the one of chief factor. News of Douglas's appointment did not reach him until late October of 1851.[36] Douglas's appointment and the way it was carried out again signalled how metropolitan reckonings of empire were disciplined to its local iterations. Much like the Dutch nationals entrusted with British rule in the Guyana of Douglas's childhood, Douglas's greatest qualification for governor was that he was *there* when *there* was literally and metaphorically beyond the metropole's reach.

The scope of Britain's colonial project and Douglas's authority within it expanded and was redefined in 1858. Knowledge of gold on the Mainland adjacent Vancouver Island brought new attention and a substantial non-Indigenous population who arrived via American territory to the south, were largely male, and often followed the complicated itineraries that characterized nineteenth-century Pacific gold rushes. Douglas did not wait to receive official permission to proclaim British jurisdiction over the gold fields. "The torrent of immigration is setting in with impetuous force, and to keep pace with the extraordinary circumstances of the times; and to maintain the authority of the Laws, I have been compelled to assume an unusual amount of responsibility," Douglas explained to London, seeking approval for actions he had already taken.[37] London did not approve of all of Douglas's actions, but he was made governor nonetheless. "The ceremonies of swearing in the Governor & reading the various proclamations went off most admirably & his Excellency was very well received," reported the admiral of the Royal Navy's ship *Ganges*.[38] Some ten years earlier, Douglas had been appointed governor of Vancouver Island for some six months before he was made aware of it. Now Douglas began to assert British authority long before the Colonial Office declared him governor of the new Colony of British Columbia and gave him temporary emergency powers to legislate by proclamation alone. In May 1859, Britain terminated the HBC's grant, made Vancouver Island a Crown colony under its direct control, and streamlined the two colonies' baroque constitutional apparatus. Douglas began to receive a salary as governor and was required to sever his formal connection with the HBC.[39]

It is within this context that the issues we generally associate with James Douglas, land, and First Nations emerged. Particularly key are the fourteen land "purchases" or "conveyances" that Douglas negotiated with Vancouver Island First Nations between 1850 and 1854, first as chief factor and then as chief factor and governor. What came to be known as the "Vancouver Island Treaties" have long attracted the interest of Indigenous peoples, scholars, and activists. Analyses of them have paid due attention to the wider context of land and treaty making, including the role of advice from the Colonial Office, the precedent of New Zealand, and comparisons to treaty making in the wider Pacific Northwest region, including Oregon.[40] Here, I want to push further in these directions and suggest some of the wide-angle and long-haul trajectories within which Douglas's practice pertaining to Indigenous land might be read. In connecting Douglas's response to Indigenous peoples and lands to the Northwest and the Caribbean, I do not mean to make easy causal links but instead to situate these histories within the longer histories they were lived and understood within.

These connections were made by contemporaries when Douglas was either praised or critiqued. In 1854, an American newspaper was one of the many voices that criticized Douglas for appointing his Guyanese brother-in-law chief justice of Vancouver Island. They did so through the language of race, respectability, and civilization, explaining that Douglas was a "servant to a company of fur traders – this man over whom the sun of civilization has not dawned these thirty years, and who, does not, perchance know a windmill from a spinning-jinney, and who is bound by the ties of sympathy and affection more closely to the savage than the White man."[41] Douglas's supporters saw his fur trade background and ties as effective rather than problematic but noted them all the same. Douglas's adroit use of Indigenous and fur trade practices of governance was routinely noted. Naval officer Richard Mayne recalled Douglas defusing a conflict with well-worn and distinctly Indigenous rituals of generosity and gifting. Douglas instructed his men not to arm the bastion of the fort against Indigenous men but to instead "give them a little bread and treacle." Another would recall biscuits and molasses, but the point is that Douglas made use of Indigenous practices of generosity and gift giving, delivered through the particularly imperial medium of Caribbean sugar.[42]

These connections were lived and renewed through ties of friendship and kinship. Most of all, he remained profoundly tied to his own family, something historian Margaret Ormsby only hints at when she describes him as a "devoted family man."[43] Observers in Victoria connected Connolly Douglas to the geographies and cultures of the fur trade, choosing language that separated her from proximate Indigenous communities and connecting her to Red River – for instance, as a "lady from Red River Settlement" or a "red river Indian."[44] Private correspondence and memory register Connolly Douglas's maintenance of ties and knowledge of Métis culture. Friends spoke of her joy at hearing "the old language" (a mixture of French, "Indian," and English, or Michif), her fondness for bison tongue and camas, and her "desire to see the Indian country before she died."[45] Unsympathetic and baldly racist observers criticized Amelia Connolly Douglas and tied their critiques of Douglas to his Indigenous family, as when a British naval officer wrote that "Mrs. Douglas is a good creature, but utterly ignorant: she has no language, but jabbers french or english or Indian, as she is half Indian, half English, and a French Canadian by birth." He explained that the colony deserved a different governor, one with "enlightened feelings and ideas, and a lady for his wife."[46]

Douglas maintained active connections with fur trade families in Victoria and throughout the continent. Douglas, Connolly Douglas, and their daughter Cecilia each corresponded with Amelia's sister Marguerite, a nun with the Soeur Grises in St. Boniface.[47] When Jane Douglas's husband, Alexander Grant Dallas, was named governor of Red River, Jane became governor's wife and, within the connected social world of Red River, a Métis granddaughter and niece. Letters home provided updates on old friends, promises to look after her grandmamma and, after she died, to care for her grave.[48] That Douglas's critics focused on the "family compact" and his connections to the HBC and Métis kin is axiomatic but perhaps worth sitting with as we consider the histories of James Douglas, Indigenous peoples, and land. In 1862, Jane Douglas Dallas was the governor's wife in Red River; the newspapers there reported that her father had retired and been named to the Order of the Bath, relayed mundane family news, and noted that "Mr. Douglas is father of Mrs. Dallas."[49] When a party of Lakota Sioux refugees fleeing an increasingly aggressive and militarized American settler state to the south arrived at the Dallas home in Red River, Douglas Dallas spoke of them in genteel racist language and noted the military threat the Lakota posed to the essentially Métis settlement. She also showed them "Papa's likeness."[50] When we note that James Douglas's photograph was present in Red River when the Lakota Sioux arrived, we further open up the interpretative possibilities of seeing connections between histories of Vancouver Island and British Columbia and other colonial locations, including the Caribbean and Northwest.

That Douglas had an Indigenous wife and family should not be presumed to indicate anything in particular about his politics around Indigenous people and colonization in general. But Douglas reckoned race and Indigenous identities in ways that reflected long-lived histories as well as global languages. In 1853, Douglas wrote about "half-Whites" he had pressed into service.[51] A few years later, Douglas conducted a census of Vancouver Island, and he seems to have counted many of the Indigenous people directly tied to the HBC as white; otherwise, his enumeration of 774 "whites" would have made little sense.[52] Here, Douglas used a kind of fur trade racial logic that registered Indigenous people who lived within the walls of the fort differently than those who lived outside of it. As in Red River and the Northwest, this was a variegated and shifting social landscape, and Douglas and his peers drew regular distinctions and, at times, hierarchies between different kinds of Indigenous people.[53] Historian Elizabeth Vibert has shown how the idea that interior and Plains Indigenous peoples were distinct from and superior to the coastal Indigenous peoples was a staple of nineteenth-century writing within the circles in which Douglas moved.[54] Intimate relationships – including long-standing ones of the sort shared by Douglas and Connolly Douglas – were practised throughout the colonial world, often alongside and in support of some of the most calcified and brutal practices of inequality, including transatlantic slavery and frontier violence. As historian Damon Salesa has argued, racial crossings were not themselves "intrinsically troublesome to colonialism."[55]

Douglas consistently traded in languages and practices of race that denied Indigenous peoples' full and robust humanity but still extended to them certain rights. Douglas's land policy accorded Indigenous peoples the signal right of liberal citizenship – the right to own land and, more particular in the context of settler colonialism, the capacity to pre-empt it.[56] Writing to the metropole in 1859, Douglas made clear that he considered Indigenous people rational and economically autonomous subjects within the conventions of liberal thinking. Douglas explained how he would implement his newly expanded jurisdiction over the Mainland, arguing that Indigenous people "should in all respects be treated as rational beings, capable of acting and thinking for themselves."[57] In 1861, Douglas reported to London on a meeting he had had with "Native Indian Tribes" at Cayoosh, explaining that he "strove to make them conscious that they were recognized members of the Commonwealth, and that by good conduct they would acquire a certain status, and become respectable members of society."[58]

Douglas's private and public correspondence contains a range of sometimes conflicting ideas about Indigenous peoples and where they fit in an imperial world and in Vancouver Island and British Columbia in particular. Douglas's words are steeped in mid-nineteenth-century racial knowledge, including knowledge that located Indigenous peoples as fundamentally distinct and lesser. In the 1840s, he explained that he would like to be "obliged to leave the Columbia and to withdraw to Vancouvers Island, to rusticate, among the savages there."[59] A decade later, Governor Douglas described northern Indigenous peoples as "Savages" and "Barbarians" who might only be transformed with tutelage, wage work, and great difficulty.[60] In his retirement, Douglas wrote of First Nations as peoples in a perpetual "primal state of ignorance & natural improvidence."[61] We are thus mistaken if we see Douglas as somehow outside of the pervasive racial and colonial logics of his day. As chief factor, as governor, and in his retirement, Douglas drew on the global language of empire to write about Indigenous peoples in deeply racialized and demeaning ways, and he seemingly saw no contradiction between these views and his love for his wife, his commitment to his family, or his long history in the fur trade. The family that posed on the porch of the Douglas home in 1885 speaks to the persistence of these ties after Douglas's passing in 1877.

There were four years between 1850 and 1854 when James Douglas, first as chief factor and then as chief factor and colonial governor, negotiated fourteen treaties with Vancouver Island First Nations. Within the context of the settler government of British Columbia that followed, these agreements are amenable to interpretations that register them as anomies, as somehow outside of their own history. I would also like us to consider different geographic and temporal contexts and how they might have informed and shaped the Vancouver Island we are principally concerned with here. Kenton Storey probes the connections and disconnections between Vancouver Island and New Zealand at mid-nineteenth century.[62] In this essay, I have focused on some of the imperial registers through which Douglas moved and remained connected to, as brought into focus by three documents: the 1798 map of Guyana, the 1817 Selkirk Treaty, and a photograph of Amelia Connolly

Douglas and her descendants in 1885. These documents remind us that Douglas was also a Guyanese son, an HBC chief factor, and a kinsman to family with Métis histories, connections, and sometimes identities. Each of these histories shaped the treaties that were brokered in the 1850s and the meanings that were made of them.

Acknowledgments

This research was undertaken, in part, thanks to funding from the Canada Research Chairs program. I am also grateful to Cambridge University Press for letting me reproduce material that was published, albeit in a very different form. Laura Ishiguro did important research that I draw on here. I also appreciate the feedback of the editors and readers of this volume.

Notes

1 Note the titles of these books: Julie Ferguson, *James Douglas: Father of British Columbia* (Toronto: Dundurn Press, 2009); Walter Sage, *Sir James Douglas and British Columbia* (Toronto: University of Toronto Press, 1930); and Dorothy Blakey Smith, *James Douglas: Father of British Columbia* (Toronto: University of Toronto Press, 1971). Derek Petick was a dissenting voice in his *James Douglas: Servant of Two Empires* (Vancouver: Mitchell Press, 1969).

2 Adele Perry, *Colonial Relations: The Douglas-Connolly Family and the Nineteenth-Century Imperial World* (Cambridge: Cambridge University Press, 2015).

3 Charlotte S.M. Girard, "Sir James Douglas' Mother and Grandmother," *BC Studies* 44 (Winter 1979–90): 25–31, "Some Further Notes on the Douglas Family," *BC Studies* 72 (Winter 1986–87): 3–27, "Sir James Douglas' School Days," *BC Studies* 35 (Autumn 1977): 56–63; and "The Guiana World of Sir James Douglas' Childhood," unpublished MS; John Adams, *Old Square Toes and His Lady: The Life of James and Amelia Douglas* (Victoria: Horsdal and Shubert, 2001); and Sylvia Van Kirk, "Tracing the Fortunes of Five Founding Families of Victoria," *BC Studies* 115–16 (Autumn–Winter 1997–98): 148–79.

4 D. Graham Burnett, *Masters of All They Surveyed: Exploration, Geography, and a British El Dorado* (Chicago: University of Chicago Press, 2000), 70n13.

5 Slavery compensation record, British Guiana, 550, John Douglas, ID 8520. I thank Nicholas Draper for his willingness to share his valuable database on British slaveholding and compensation with me. Also see "Legacies of British Slave-Ownership," University College London, http://www.ucl.ac.uk/lbs/; and Nicholas Draper, *The Price of Emancipation: Slave Ownership, Compensation, and British Society at the End of Slavery* (Cambridge: Cambridge University Press, 2010). The Douglas family is discussed on page 241.

6 Will of John Douglas, April 16, 1841, National Archives of Scotland, Edinburgh, SC70/1/60. Death certificate of John Douglas, July 8, 1840, copy in W. Kaye Lamb, "Ancestry of Sir James Douglas," BC Archives (BCA), B/90/D74.

7 *Essequebo and Demerera Gazette* (*EDG*), September 25, 1810; Colonial Office, "Slave Registers, 1817–1832," Demerara, entry for Martha Ann Telfer, 1817, National Archives (UK) (NA), 874, T71/399; and Thompson, *Unprofitable Servants,* 15.

8 "Compensation: Registers of Claims," NA, T71/866, Claim 1366, Martha Ann Telfer.

9 *Royal Gazette of British Guiana,* February 11, 1840, NA, "Royal Gazette of British Guiana," CO 115/2. Thanks to Laura Ishiguro for this.

10 *Royal Demerara and Berbice Gazette,* October 29, 1825, CO 115/2; *EDG,* May 16, 1812, and July 18, 1812; and Baker, *Guide to Demerara,* 337. Pagination added.

11 Rebecca Ritchie to John Murray, July 12, 1820, in "Petitions," 1820–21, WRNA, A01/5; *EDG,* May 16, 1812; Slave Registers, Demerara, entry for Rebecca "Rithie," 1817, NA, T71/392, 800–1; Slave Registers, Barbados, St. Michael's Parish, 1817, T71/520, 485 and 1823, T71/529, 505, www.ancestry.ca.

12 "Compensation: Register of Claims," NA, T71/886, Claim 1364, December 14, 1835; NA, T71/886, Claim 1365, December 14, 1835.

13 James Douglas to James Stuart, October 7, 1868, and James Douglas to Jane Dallas, June 11, 1869, both in "Private Letter Book of Sir James Douglas, Correspondence Outward, March 22, 1867–Oct. 11, 1870," BCA, Add MSS B/40/2, transcript.

14 W. Edwards and K. Gibson, "An Ethnohistory of Amerindians in Guyana," *Ethnohistory* 26, 2 (1979): 161–76. For an analysis of settler colonialism in Guyana, see Shona N. Jackson, *Creole Indigeneity: Between Myth and Nation in the Caribbean* (Minneapolis: University of Minnesota Press, 2012).

15 Earl of Bathhurst to A. General Carmichael, November 25, 1812, Colonial Office, British Guiana, NA, CO 111/10.

16 Mary Noel Menezes, *British Policy towards the Amerindians in British Guiana, 1803–1873* (Oxford: Clarendon Press, 1977), 296.

17 Adam Gaudry, "The Selkirk Treaty, 1817," Guest Curator Series, Canada Who Do You Think We Are?, *Library and Archives Canada Blog,* July 20, 2017, https://thediscoverblog.com/tag/treaties/.

18 North West Company Indenture, James Douglas, July 6, 1819, 2344, Fort William Historical Park. See also details for the contracts for "James Douglass" and "Alexander Douglass" in the voyageurs database, Centre du patrimoine, http://voyageurs.shsb.mb.ca/.

19 James Douglas, "Notes," "Private Account," BCA, Add MSS B/90/1.

20 N. de Bertrand Lugrin, *The Pioneer Women of Vancouver Island, 1843–1866* (Victoria: Women's Canadian Club, 1928), 14.

21 See Edward Cavanagh, "A Company with Sovereignty and Subjects of Its Own: The Case of the Hudson's Bay Company, 1670–1783," *Canadian Journal of Law and Society* 26, 1 (2011): 25–50; and Philip Girard, "Imperial Legacies and Chartered Enterprises in Northern British America," in *Legal Histories of the British Empire: Laws, Engagements, and Legacies,* ed. Shaunnagh Dorset and John McLaren (London: Routledge, 2014), 127–40.

22 Adam Gaudry, "Fantasies of Sovereignty: Deconstructing British and Canadian Claims to Ownership of the Historic North-West," *Native American and Indigenous Studies* 31, 1 (2016): 50–52.

23 Michael Witgen, "The Native New World and Western North America," *Western Historical Quarterly* 43, 3 (2012): 292 and 297. Also see Witgen's *Infinity of Nations: How the Native New World Shaped Early North America* (Philadelphia: University of Pennsylvania Press, 2012). On a related point, see Hamar Foster, "Law and Necessity in Western Rupert's Land and Beyond, 1670–1870," in *Laws and Societies in the Canadian Prairie West,*

1670–1940, ed. Louis A. Knafla and Jonathan Swainger (Vancouver: UBC Press, 2005), 57–91.

24 Aimee Craft, "Living Treaties, Breathing Research," *Canadian Journal of Women and the Law* 26, 1 (2014): 1–22. Also see Aimee Craft, *Breathing Life into the Stone Fort Treaty: An Anishinabe Understanding of Treaty One* (Saskatoon: Purich, 2013).

25 Frank Tough and Jim Miller, *Bounty and Benevolence: A History of Saskatchewan Treaties* (Montreal/Kingston: McGill-Queen's University Press, 2000), chap. 1. Also see Harold Cardinal and Walter Hildebrandt, *Treaty Elders of Saskatchewan: Our Dream Is That Our Peoples Will One Day Be Clearly Recognized as Nations* (Calgary: University of Calgary Press, 200).

26 Heidi Bohaker, "Reading Anishnaabe Identities: Meaning and Metaphor in Nindoodem Pictographs," *Ethnohistory* 57, 1 (2010): 11–33, and "*Nindoodemag:* The Significance of Algonquian Kinship Networks in the Eastern Great Lakes Region, 1600–1701," *William and Mary Quarterly* 18, 1 (2006): 23–52.

27 See Gilles Havard, *The Great Peace of Montreal of 1701: French-Naïve Diplomacy in the Seventeenth-Century,* trans. Howard Scott and Phyllis Aronoff (Montreal/Kingston: McGill-Queen's University Press, 2001).

28 Lord Selkirk to W.B. Coltman, July 17, 1817, reproduced in "Lord Selkirk's Treaty with the Indians, July 18, 1817," *Manitoba Pageant* 21, 2 (1976): http://www.mhs.mb.ca/docs/pageant/21/lordselkirktreaty.shtml.

29 Gaudry, "Fantasies of Sovereignty," 53.

30 See Craft, *Breathing Life into the Stone Fort Treaty;* and Treaty 7 Tribal Council, Walter Hilderbrandt, Sarah Carter, and Dorothy First Rider, *The True Spirit and Intent of Treaty 7* (Montreal/Kingston: McGill-Queen's University Press, 1996).

31 Gina Starblanket, "The Numbered Treaties and the Politics of Incoherency," *Canadian Journal of Political Science* (2019): 2.

32 James Douglas to John McLoughlin, July 12, 1842, copy enclosed in Great Britain, Colonial Office, Vancouver Island, National Archives (UK) (NA), Records of the Colonial Office (CO), 305/1, in *The Colonial Despatches of Victoria Island and British Columbia, 1846–1871,* ed. James Hendrickson and the Colonial Despatches Project, https://bc-genesis.uvic.ca (hereafter *Colonial Despatches*); and James Robert Anderson, "Notes and Comments on Early Days and Events in British Columbia, Washington and Oregon, Including an Account of Sundry Happenings in San Francisco; Being the Memoirs of James Robert Anderson, Written by Himself," BCA, MS 1912, box 9, transcript, 149.

33 See Anderson, "Notes and Comments," 153–54; and James Dean to Mr. Monleith, May 12, 1878, in James Dean, "Settlement of Vancouver Island," BL, Bancroft MS, P-C 9, microfilm 1, 1–2.

34 Anderson, "Notes and Comments," 152–53, 181.

35 For more on Vancouver Island and governance, see Stephen Royle, *Company, Crown, and Colony: The Hudson's Bay Company and Territorial Endeavour in Western Canada* (London: Macmillan, 2011). On Guiana, see L.M. Penson, "The Making of a Crown Colony: British Guiana, 1803–33," *Transactions of the Royal Historical Society,* 4th series, 9 (1926): 107–34.

36 Margaret A. Ormsby, "Douglas, Sir James," *Dictionary of Canadian Biography,* vol. 10, Université Laval/University of Toronto, 2003–, http://www.biographi.ca/fr/bio/douglas_james_10F.html.

37 Hendrickson, "Introduction," xxxiv; James Douglas to Lord Stanley, July 26, 1858, CO 305/9, *Colonial Despatches.* More generally, see Daniel Marshall, "Mapping the New El Dorado: The Fraser River Gold Rush and the Appropriation of Native Space," in *New*

Histories for Old: Changing Perspectives on Canada's Native Pasts, ed. Ted Binnema and Susan Neylan (Vancouver: UBC Press, 2007).

38 Admiral Baynes to Sir Julian Stafford Corbett, December 4, 1858, National Maritime Museum (Greenwich, UK), Sir Julian Stafford Corbett Papers, CBT/29/S.

39 Hendrickson, "Introduction," xxxii; and Ormsby, "Douglas."

40 See R. Cole Harris, *Making Native Space: Colonialism, Resistance, and Reserves in British Columbia* (Vancouver: UBC Press, 2002), chap. 2; Kent McNeil, "Negotiated Sovereignty: Indian Treaties and the Acquisition of American and Canadian Territorial Rights in the Pacific Northwest," and Hamar Foster and Alan Grove, "'Trespassers on the Soil': *United States v. Tom* and a New Perspective on the Short History of Treaty Making in Nineteenth-Century British Columbia," both in *The Power of Promises: Rethinking Indian Treaties in the Pacific Northwest,* ed. Alexandra Harmon and John Borrows (Seattle: University of Washington Press, 2009). More generally, see Wilson Duff, "The Fort Victoria Treaties," *BC Studies* 3 (Fall 1969): 3–57; Hamar Foster, "Letting Go the Bone: The Idea of Indian Title in British Columbia, 1849–1927," in *Essays in the History of Canadian Law: British Columbia and the Yukon,* ed. Hamar Foster and John McLaren (Toronto: University of Toronto Press for Osgoode Society for Canadian Legal History, 1995), 28–86; and Raymond Frogner, "'Innocent Legal Fictions': Archival Convention and the North Saanich Treaty of 1852," *Archivaria* 70 (Fall 2010): 45–94.

41 "The Vancouver Island Resolutions, Relative to Judge Cameron, &c," *Pioneer and Democrat* (Olympia, Washington Territory), August 5, 1854.

42 Mayne, *Four Years in British Columbia and Vancouver Island,* 54; and Good, "British Columbia," 11.

43 Orsmby, "Douglas."

44 Robie L. Reid, ed., C.C. Gardiner, "To the Fraser River Mines in 1858," *British Columbia Historical Quarterly* 1, 1 (1937): 253; and John Emmerson, *Voyages, Travels, and Adventures by John Emmerson of Wolsingham* (Durham, NC: William Ainsley, 1865), 34–35.

45 Christina McDonald McKenzie Williams, "The Daughter of Angus McDonald," *Washington Historical Quarterly* 13 (1922): 116; and F.W. Howay, William S. Lewis, and Jacob A. Meyers, "Angus McDonald: A Few Items of the West," *Washington Historical Quarterly* 8, 3 (1917): 225.

46 Edmund Hope Verney to Harry Verney, July 20, 1862, in Allan Pritchard, ed., *Vancouver Island Letters of Edmund Hope Verney, 1862–1865* (Vancouver: UBC Press, 1996), 75.

47 Marguerite Connolly to Cecilia Douglas Helmcken, May 8, 1858, BCA, Helmcken Papers, vol. 14, file 2; James Douglas to Jane Douglas Dallas, March 2, 1863, BCA, James Douglas, "Letters," reel 246A.

48 Jane Dallas to Cecilia Helmcken, July 19, 1862; and Jane Dallas to Amelia Connolly Douglas, August 9, 1861, and December 19, 1862, BCA, Helmcken Papers, vol. 14, file 9, transcript.

49 "Sir James Douglas," *Nor'Wester* (Red River Colony), October 14, 1863; and "Accident to Sir James Douglas," *Nor'Wester,* July 2, 1864.

50 Jane Dallas to Cecilia Helmcken, January 1, 1862, and Jane Dallas to Amelia Connolly Douglas, December 30, 1862, BCA, Helmcken Papers, vol. 14, file 9, transcript.

51 James Douglas to John Packington, January 21, 1853, CO 305/4, *Colonial Despatches.*

52 "Indian Population, Vancouver's Island, 1855," in James Douglas to Henry Labouchère, October 20, 1856, CO 305/7, *Colonial Despatches.* Also see "The Census of Vancouver Island, 1855," *British Columbia Historical Quarterly* 4, 1 (1940): 51.

53 See Norma J. Hall, *A Casualty of Colonialism: Red River Metis Farming, 1810–1870,* ebook, 2015, accessed April 24, 2017, https://casualtyofcolonialism.wordpress.com/.

54 See Elizabeth Vibert, *Traders' Tales: Narratives of Cultural Encounter in the Columbia Plateau* (Norman: University of Oklahoma Press, 1997), especially chap. 7; and Elizabeth Vibert, "The Contours of Everyday Life: Food and Identity in the Plateau Fur Trade," in *Gathering Places: Aboriginal and Fur-Trade Histories,* ed. Carolyn Podruchny and Laura Peers (Vancouver: UBC Press, 2010).

55 Damon Ieremia Salesa, *Racial Crossings: Race, Intermarriage, and the Victorian British Empire* (Oxford: Oxford University Press, 2011), 2.

56 See Paul Tennant, *Aboriginal Peoples and Politics: The Indian Land Question in British Columbia, 1849–1989* (Vancouver: UBC Press, 1990), chap. 3; and Robert E. Cail, *Land, Man, and the Law; The Disposal of Crown Lands in British Columbia, 1871–1913* (Vancouver: UBC Press, 1974), 177–78.

57 James Douglas to Edward Bulwer-Lytton, March 14, 1859, 4800, CO 60/4, *Colonial Despatches.*

58 James Douglas to Duke of Newcastle, January 2, 1861, CO 60/8, 11678, 196, *Colonial Despatches.*

59 James Douglas to James Hargrave, March 24, 1847, Hargrave Papers.

60 James Douglas to Edward Bulwer-Lytton, May 25, 1859, Colonial Office, Original Correspondence – Secretary of State, Vancouver Island, "Despatches 1859 Jan–July," PAC, CO 305/10, reel B-238.

61 James Douglas to Lt. Col. Powell, October 14, 1874, in BCA, Sir James Douglas, Correspondence Outward, 1874, F/52/D74, transcript.

62 Kenton Storey, *Settler Anxiety at the Outposts of Empire: Colonial Relations, Humanitarian Discourses, and the Imperial Press* (Vancouver: UBC Press, 2016).

2

Colonialism, Law, and the Social Construction of Humanity on Vancouver Island, 1849–64

Laura Spitz

THERE ARE FEW CONTESTED CATEGORIES as significant and consequential as subjects and objects in a liberal legal order. Subjects have rights and duties; objects are property. Subjects own objects. For the most part, contemporary common-law legal systems have little difficulty in deciding the legal character of a being or thing. If I take your table without your permission, I have stolen your property. If I take your son, I have kidnapped a person. In neither case would the court typically spend any time inquiring into the question of whether the table was an object or the child a subject. These characterizations operate as underlying assumptions. But there was a time when children were formally objects – or property – in the common-law tradition, and what might seem obvious or natural to us oftentimes represents an evolution in the law's attitude. In other words, characterizations we now take for granted are in fact informed by legal histories, both recent and ancient, that necessarily shaped – and naturalized – contemporary understandings. In many cases, those histories map onto the most significant Canadian and American civil rights struggles of the last two centuries.

Today, most questions in this context are settled. Still, the concept of subject (or person) remains contested in political and legal debates about nonhuman animals,[1] natural resources,[2] fetuses,[3] prisoners,[4] artificial intelligence,[5] and corporations,[6] cases where its complexity – and perhaps inadequacy – continues to occupy the courts' time and attention. Several features of legal subjecthood contribute to this complexity. First, it is not an all-or-nothing proposition. For example, African American slaves were the property (objects) of slaveholders but also persons (subjects) capable of being criminally prosecuted. Second, not all humans enjoy full subjecthood,[7] and not all subjects are human. In other words, the terms are not coextensive. Third, the rights of legal subjects may be so limited as to suggest they are subjects in form only, lacking virtually all substantive markers of subjectivity. Or, legal subjects may have some rights commonly associated with the status, but not others.[8] Finally, the concept of subjecthood is complicated by its interaction with related but distinct legal concepts, including citizenship, suffrage, and capacity.

Although human and legal subjects are not synonymous concepts in common-law legal systems, a "human being"[9] is still the most salient instance of a "legal subject."[10] As a consequence, the extent to which the law views someone (or something) as more or less human is relevant to the question of their (or its) status as a subject. But the inquiry into the question of whether someone or something is a subject is not as simple as asking whether it is human or human-like. Rather, judges, litigants, advocates, and legislators engage in practices of humanization and dehumanization for the purpose of constituting subjects and objects as such.[11] In other words, law is both reflective and constitutive of the connection between human being and legal subject.

Several academic disciplines explore the practice of personification or anthropomorphism of nonhumans, including animals, land, trees,[12] spirits, machines, and corporations. At the same time, scholars explore the processes and implications of dehumanization, especially as normative justifications for treating beings as something less than human. Surprisingly, these phenomena – humanization and dehumanization – are rarely considered together.[13] In the context of law, this gap may be because humanization is often an explicit juridical move, and dehumanization is often implied, unacknowledged, or even unconscious.[14] But each process implicates and informs the other. To understand what it means to be human in a legal sense, it is necessary to understand who is in and who is out, why, and for what purposes.

This essay contributes to these larger conversations by exploring the legal practices of de/humanization in the Colony of Vancouver Island in the mid-nineteenth century and seeks to make several points. First, this period marked the beginning of colonial legal "sorting" or "ordering" in the region, and practices of humanization and dehumanization were used in the construction of a consequential set of categories all bearing on legal subjecthood, including "alien," "Indian," "corporation," "white," and "citizen."[15] They were consequential because common-law categories, once constructed, endure. Many of the most visible categorical contests surfaced through or in connection to contests about land, of course.[16] Determining both the subjects and borders of categories was bound up in contests over who was entitled to land and for what purpose. But it was not only about land. There was another story there, too: a much more basic story about who counted as fully human in the nascent colony. The question of who counted as fully human had broader implications for naturalizing legal and cultural practices of violence, oppression, and exclusion.

Second, notwithstanding colonial or settler practices of dehumanizing Indigenous peoples in the process of colonization, the colony's governor, James Douglas, believed that Indigenous peoples were in fact human[17] and, therefore, proper subjects of law. This was evident in his Indigenous land policies and practices, including treaty making.[18] Nevertheless, while Douglas is sometimes valorized for having recognized Aboriginal title in unceded land,[19] the underlying assumption that Indigenous people were in fact human, or at least potentially human, does not reveal a robust and nuanced view of humanity in emergent settler law, nor was it especially progressive except in contrast to the even more discriminatory views of others. Rather, Douglas's view was fundamentally liberal in the sense that it recognized that Indigenous people could be legal subjects, capable of entering into contracts and exercising rights in property. On that view, "human" was a status and "humanity" was essentially the "totality of human beings."[20] This paradigm was not significantly different from those that came after; the chief difference was one of lines, not frames. Douglas would have drawn the line so as to include Indigenous peoples in the category of human and, therefore, subject; in the years that followed his retirement, administrators set about drawing the line to exclude them.

Third, Douglas's conception of what it meant to be human would likely not have resonated with or made sense in the context of Coast Salish[21] legal traditions and Coast Salish understandings of themselves and their material, spiritual, and natural environments.[22] Being human was not so much a status – legal subject – to which rights attached as it was a largely relational way of being in the world, and even then it remained potentially transitional or temporary and invariably subordinate to more powerful nonhuman forces.[23] According to that view, humanity was not so much the totality of human beings but something one *expressed* towards others, both human and nonhuman.[24]

Finally, the disconnect between early colonial approaches to the question of whether Indigenous people were human (as exemplified by the views and policies of Douglas), on the one hand, and Coast Salish understandings of the meaning and significance of being human, on the other, was more than conceptual. It had material consequences still in evidence today. In its calls to action, Canada's Truth and Reconciliation

Commission highlighted the importance of naming and interrogating concepts and doctrines used to justify European sovereignty over Indigenous lands and peoples.[25] Subjecthood is such a concept. Surfacing the ways in which practices of de/humanization structured critical misunderstandings and influenced the construction of Indigenous peoples as less than or unhuman – and consequently, objects of law – is necessary if the work of reconciliation[26] is to be taken seriously.

In this essay, I begin by outlining my theoretical framework and key definitions. To provide context, I then introduce the history of the territory now known as Vancouver Island; the man who became the second governor of that colony, James Douglas; and the prevailing scientific norms. I then examine how legal subjects (and citizens) were constructed and managed in the nascent colony through legal and political practices of humanization and dehumanization. I also explore what these practices might tell us about Douglas's views on the meaning and relevance of being human, and how those understandings helped shape relevant legal categories. After exploring these questions, I shift the focus to how Indigenous peoples in the colony might have viewed the same questions, arguing that Coast Salish views and practices indicate a conception of humanness and humanity quite distinct from Douglas's. These differences were not reflected in the emerging colonial legal system; rather, the Coast Salish were forcibly incorporated into a system reflecting settler priorities and values. I conclude that it did not much matter to the question of cultural erasure whether Douglas regarded Indigenous peoples as (potential) legal subjects. Regardless of whether Coast Salish people were recognized as full subjects in the emerging legal order, the system did not leave space for Indigenous knowledge, culture, values, belief systems, and law.

Theoretical Framework and Definitions

Although others may embrace different understandings of legal and social constructivism, in this essay *constructivism* is defined in general terms as the approach where "X, or X as it is at present, is not determined by the nature of things; it is not inevitable."[27] Instead, the meaning of *X* is socially constructed and mediated through practices, relationships, interactions, and language over time and across space.[28] It is fundamentally an iterative process.

In everyday life and depending on the context, human beings and social institutions participate in constructivist practices as a matter of course.

For example, many personify nonhumans for cultural, emotional, material, literary, and spiritual reasons. Among the Coast Salish nations, it is not uncommon to talk about rocks and trees having human characteristics as part of a spiritual belief system. This personification practice is in some sense literal; Keith Thor Carlson explains that in the Stó:lō tradition, for example, transformers reward people by turning them into valuable resources, such as cedar, sturgeon, and beaver.[29] At the same time, spirits and nonhuman animals are able to take human shape.[30]

In law, beings and things can be humanized through a variety of legal practices and institutions. In New Zealand, for example, the Te Urewera National Park and the Whanganui River have both been recognized as persons under the law as part of recent treaty settlements,[31] with the result that they are entitled to a range of human rights. In the United States, courts have protected the religious freedom of for-profit corporations based on their status as persons, so that a corporation does not have to provide certain benefits to employees or services to the public if doing so would contravene the corporation's "honestly held religious beliefs."[32] In these cases, the law humanizes nonhumans to extend human-like rights to them. It does this, at least in part, by giving them attributes commonly associated with humanness, such as volition, intention, independence, vitality, spirituality, cooperation, morality, competence, and social connectedness.[33]

Conversely, humans can be made unhuman through law by emphasizing "nonhuman"[34] or "not-yet-human" qualities commonly associated with things, objects or children, such as detachment, atavism, lack of feeling, lack of will, lack of control, disregard for others, and amorality. This is often done to justify harsh – or inhumane – treatment, such as state-sanctioned torture, solitary confinement, Indian residential schools,[35] and the failure to extend due process rights to inmates and migrants in detention in the United States. Courts also emphasize the ways in which nonhuman animals lack human qualities when making decisions adverse to their interests.[36] Once a group of beings has been rendered unhuman or less than human, a stereotypical label commonly associated with them – such as "savages" in the case of Indigenous peoples – may be used as a label to dehumanize others.

At the same time that law defines and delimits legal subjects and objects through practices of humanization and dehumanization, it also authorizes certain subjects to speak about – including to deny – humanness.[37] Constructivism foregrounds the fact that law not only works to develop and then police categories relevant to the question of who gets to be fully human and for what purpose, it also naturalizes or constitutes certain actors as legitimate participants in discussions and decisions about those contests. An obvious example is judges, but there are others: lawyers, legislators, arbitrators, professors, and so on. Constructivism is also useful to highlight the coconstitutive ways that "[c]oncepts, practices, and people interact with each other"[38] to produce and naturalize hierarchies.[39] These features make constructivism especially useful for the focus of this essay: a nascent colony and emerging colonial legal order, superimposed over existing Indigenous political, social, legal, and economic systems,[40] where definitional contests often worked to mask the violence of underlying contests.

As with constructivism, there is variation in the ways humanization and dehumanization are used. For example, some scholars use *humanization* to mean "the process of representing *nonhuman agents* as humanlike."[41] In this essay, the term *humanization* refers to any practice by which any subject (including human beings) or object (including things) is rendered human, more human, or human-like. Similarly, *dehumanization* is sometimes deployed in an overly narrow sense, often limited to the practice of "representing *human agents* as nonhuman objects or animals."[42] For example, Second World War propaganda depicted enemy combatants as "vermin of various kinds, and in the United States, Black people have often been derogated by associating them with apes."[43] In this essay, *dehumanization* also includes processes constituting nonhumans and is defined as any process by which a subject or object is made inhuman, unhuman, or less human. Cases in which the nonhuman characteristics of beings are emphasized or reinstantiated in order to draw distinctions between them and humans can be instructive. In denying nonhumans[44] what might be described as human-like rights, their lack of humanness is often drawn in the strongest terms.

Historical Context

The Colony of Vancouver Island, 1849–64

The mid-nineteenth century was a unique period in Vancouver Island's history.[45] Socially, politically, and economically, it represented a marked departure from what had occurred during the hundreds of years before James Douglas's arrival in 1849.[46] It also differed from the years that followed his retirement as governor in 1864.[47] At least two factors contributed to the distinctiveness of this period. The first was the focused colonization project of the Hudson's Bay Company on behalf of the British Empire between 1849 and 1859,[48] which followed the signing of the Oregon Treaty in 1845 and the establishment of the border between the United States and Britain in the Pacific Northwest.[49] The second was the fact that these particular colonization efforts were led by Douglas,[50] who viewed – and for the most part treated – Indigenous peoples as human or potentially human,[51] in contrast to other settlers and the provincial and national governments that followed.[52]

There is evidence that Indigenous peoples occupied what became the Colonies of Vancouver Island and British Columbia as early as five thousand years ago.[53] When Europeans first arrived, virtually "every part of British Columbia was 'within the owned and recognized territory of one or other of the Indian tribes,' and boundaries were delineated by physical landmarks."[54] It is worth emphasizing that prior to European contact, First Nations in the region had established systems of international relations and trade, intranational governance, knowledge transmission, resource allocation,[55] justice systems, and dispute resolution.[56] But from the point of view of most European settlers and American expansionists, the original inhabitants of Vancouver Island did not live within a cognizable legal order. In fact, nineteenth-century western regions of North America are still described in popular culture as the "Wild West," a term synonymous with lawlessness.[57] This was informed, at least in part, by the dominant view in eighteenth- and nineteenth-century Europe that the original inhabitants of North America were "savages." To the extent that Indigenous justice systems were recognized as such, they were widely thought to be primitive when compared to the British legal system. The development and imposition of British-like "law and order" was thus essential to the colonial project.[58]

Between the first arrival of British and Spanish ships in the late eighteenth century and the establishment of Fort Victoria by the Hudson's Bay Company in 1843, interactions between Europeans and the Coast Salish on Vancouver Island were mostly stable[59] – although sometimes violent – and relatively infrequent outside the context of trading. In 1843, however, the Hudson's Bay Company established a fort at Victoria as a permanent base from which to trade with local First Nations,[60] thus placing the traders and other settlers in daily proximity with the Songhees. In 1849, Britain granted the company an exclusive ten-year licence to trade with First

Nations in the region and to establish the colony on its behalf; at that point, colonization began in earnest.[61] As the company's chief factor, Douglas led those efforts.

The decision to establish a colony "carried with it the assumption that British settlers were entitled to a voice in their own government,"[62] and while it took some years to establish (mostly because there were too few British subjects to establish any democratic institutions), the colonial government of Vancouver Island was eventually made up of a governor and a bicameral legislature that included a council with both executive and legislative functions and an "assembly elected by Freeholders and others according to the electoral Law of [the] colony."[63] Richard Blanshard was selected to be the first governor of the colony, notwithstanding the strong recommendation of the Hudson's Bay Company to appoint Douglas.[64] From Blanshard's arrival in 1850, however, he found himself in an almost impossible position because the settlers were mostly employees of the Hudson's Bay Company.[65] As a consequence, Douglas exercised effective authority over the European population in the colony; Blanshard resigned within a year, and Douglas replaced him as governor in 1851.[66]

One of the conditions of the Hudson's Bay Company licence was that the company effectively take title to the Colony of Vancouver Island "subject to Aboriginal title."[67] Very soon after his arrival, Douglas set out an agreement-making[68] process aimed at extinguishing Aboriginal title. Many scholars have described the ways in which this process was deeply flawed.[69] Very briefly: between April 29 and May 1, 1850, Douglas met with representatives of the Lekwungen (including the Songhees and Esquimalt), Beecher Bay, and Sooke First Nations and entered their names on sheets of blank paper. No records of their conversations were kept. He then wrote to London requesting that a "proper form" be sent "by return post." Several months later, he received a template, filled in the blanks, and inserted the completed text onto the sheets of paper with the Indigenous names. Subsequent treaties were similarly made with the First Nations at Fort Rupert (1851), the Saanich Peninsula (1852), and Fort Nanaimo (1954). Together, the fourteen agreements are commonly described as the Douglas Treaties. For reasons having mostly to do with "an appointed governor and council at perpetual loggerheads with an elected assembly,"[70] the British government's decision not to provide Douglas with additional funds for treaty making,[71] and Douglas's own evolving land policies,[72] there were no more treaties made by Douglas after 1854.[73]

While Douglas remained the governor of Vancouver Island until 1864,[74] in 1858 he was also made the first governor of the Colony of British Columbia, and he resigned from the Hudson's Bay Company. In 1859, the British government terminated the Hudson's Bay Company charter and took direct control of the Colony of Vancouver Island, forcing the new Assembly to think about how to raise its own revenue.[75] At the same time, the gold rushes – first in Haida Gwaii (the Queen Charlotte Islands) and then later in the Fraser River Valley – brought thousands of Americans across the border into the British colonies, transforming Victoria and increasing demands for public works and government services. This presented a fresh set of challenges to the region, not least because the miners were simultaneously difficult to govern and potential citizens in a colony seeking to increase its population.[76] Douglas retired as governor of British Columbia in 1864. In 1866, the Colony of Vancouver Island became part of the Colony of British Columbia,[77] and in 1871 British Columbia joined Confederation.

James Douglas, 1803–77

James Douglas was born in 1803 in British Demerara (now Guyana). Most historians agree that his parents were a Scottish plantation owner, with a second family in Scotland, and a free woman of colour.[78] There is very little known about Douglas's early life, which was likely spent among his wealthy Creole relatives,[79] but we do know that Douglas and his brother were educated in Scotland at Lanark Grammar School, where they "received the kind of middling education which gave so many Scots cultural capital to parlay into the daily administration of empire."[80] In 1819, he moved to North America to become a fur trader, first with the North West Company then with the Hudson's Bay Company.

Between 1826 and 1841, when he was charged with establishing the fort at Victoria, Douglas worked primarily from Fort Vancouver on the Columbia River (or New Caledonia), first as an accountant and then as chief trader. In 1828, he married a Métis woman, Amelia Connolly. Connolly's Irish father, William Connolly, was a fur trader and Douglas's supervisor. Her Cree mother, Miyo Nipay, had married her father according "'to the usages and customs of the Cree nation to which she belonged,' which emphasized mutual consent, the approval of her family, and local repute."[81] Like her parents, Amelia Connolly first married James Douglas according to local rather than British customs – *à la façon du pays* – but in 1837 they were married again in the Anglican Church. Together, they had five children. As described previously, Douglas assumed the role of governor of the Colony of Vancouver Island from 1851 until 1864, and of the Colony of British Columbia from 1858 until 1864.[82] From 1864 until they died in 1877 and 1890, respectively, Douglas and Connolly lived primarily in their James Bay home on Vancouver Island, although immediately after his retirement, Douglas travelled alone to the United States, the Caribbean, England, Scotland, and Paris.[83]

Douglas, Connolly, and their families were multiracial in ways that were largely invisible to the metropole – Britain – by virtue of their location and class.[84] That does not mean they were not racialized and coded in a variety of interlocking ways,[85] only that their lived experiences with race were geographically and historically specific. Douglas, for example,

> lived nineteenth-century Blackness in different circumstances and on different terms. In Victoria, as in Oregon Territory, Black/White hierarchies were not the sole or main racial cleavage. The amount of social latitude accorded to the mixed-descent elite had certainly shrunk over the course of the nineteenth-century, but it had not, as the history of the Douglas-Connolly family surely indicates, disappeared altogether. Self-invention and re-invention were made possible by a far-flung empire tied together with limited communication networks. It was in this context that a man born into the complicated location of free people of color and married into an elite Métis family, or at least an especially careful and diligent one who was repeatedly in the right place at the right time, could serve as the highest representative of the British Empire in a northern North American colony.[86]

In essence, Douglas and Connolly were the racial and racialized embodiments of the complexity of nineteenth-century empire.

Scientific Developments in the Metropole

While colonies inevitably took shape in conversation with local geographies and histories, historical developments in Europe inevitably influenced colonial norms. For example, both eighteenth- and nineteenth-century European scientists agreed, with very few exceptions, that Indigenous peoples and communities were "savage," "primitive," or "child-like," and settlers brought these views to the colonies with them. Indeed, it motivated their early efforts to "civilize" local First Nations.

Significantly, however, eighteenth- and nineteenth-century views were informed by a very different "science." The eighteenth and early nineteenth centuries were deeply marked by the Age of Enlightenment and the view that the "savage state was ... the childhood of humanity."[87] Still racist, it was a fundamentally liberal position. So-called primitive societies were thought to be at an earlier stage of development[88] and, therefore, the proper focus of "civilizing" projects: "[L]iberal humanitarians assumed that all people were essentially similar. As participants in a shared and universal humanity and with proper guidance, Native peoples would share and appreciate a universal, civilized culture."[89] In this sense, early European settlers saw images of non-European peoples as "elaborations of European categories."[90] To that extent, there was nothing intrinsic in individual people that explained why their societies were at different stages of so-called development; rather, it was mostly a function of converging social and environmental circumstances.[91]

What made the latter half of the nineteenth century distinctive was the emerging view that differences between western Europeans and others – including Indigenous peoples – were biologically, not socially, produced.[92] This view was buttressed by a variety of social and physical sciences, including biology, psychology, "physiognomy," and anthropology. Claims rested, at least in part, on an "established" link between anatomical features and intelligence. A biological explanation "of race differences had a wide appeal, first in the context of slavery and later in that of colonialism."[93] By 1863, biological racism had joined with social evolutionary theory and early anthropology to produce some of that century's most extreme and essentialist racial views.[94] Sir John Lubbock's 1863 treatise, *The Origin of Civilization and the Primitive Condition of Man,* for example, was tremendously influential.[95] Other writers, including James Sully (psychology), James Hunt (anthropology), and Charles Letourneau (psychology), relied on Lubbock for the view that Indigenous people – not societies, but the people themselves – were not only child-like but inherently animal-like. Gustav Jahoda observes that Hunt was perhaps the worst of these writers, "essentially a publicist who trawled through publications of others, seeking ammunition for his stance."[96] Notably, he is the man who founded the Anthropological Society of London in 1863.[97]

We know that Douglas did not share the views of biological racists, even though they had taken hold in parts of the British Colonial Office – and increasingly among settlers – by the 1850s. There is little known about why his ideas and approach to Indigenous peoples continued to embody the ideals of Enlightenment in this shifting ideological landscape,[98] but it would not be a stretch to suppose that it "come[s] back to the [question] of biography, of history and *of their intersections.*"[99] At least three factors stand out. Douglas would have been exposed to liberal humanitarian and other Enlightenment concepts at school in Scotland; he was a fur trader from the years when traders and First Nations mostly enjoyed a mutually beneficial relationship; and many family members – including his mother and his wife[100] – were multiracial. "[H]is life had been spent at the interface of the European and the non-European,"[101] first as a child in Demerara and then as an adult in North America, living and working near Indigenous peoples and their communities. Thus, his lived experiences would likely have suggested that all people were, in the words of Cole Harris, "essentially similar."[102] However much Douglas's land policies evolved over the time he was governor, these views were evident throughout. He fell squarely among those who believed in the possibility, value, and inevitability of assimilation, a framework that depended on the "enlightened" view that, while First Nations were primitive, this was a function of social rather than biological features.[103]

Douglas and a New Legal Ordering

It was against this historical backdrop that the Colony of Vancouver Island sought to establish itself. It did this, in part, through the creation and imposition of a legal order over and without regard to existing Indigenous legal systems,[104] not least because it did not recognize Indigenous legal systems as such.[105] The emerging colonial legal system was not an entirely "new" legal order so much as the British system adapted to meet local circumstances,[106] but given the colony's small British population and distance from the metropole, Douglas had tremendous autonomy in developing and implementing laws and policies.[107] Especially in the early years, he "governed almost absolutely."[108] His power was relevant in another respect: it constituted and naturalized him as a legitimate participant in discussions and decisions about categorical contests, especially vis-à-vis the Colonial Office in Britain.[109] Unsurprisingly, the development and evolution of a new legal order was not an even or smooth process,[110] and although it has been described as peaceful self-invention,[111] in contrast to the American experience,[112] from the perspective of local First Nations, it was confusing, oppressive, and violent.[113]

As with any new liberal legal order, the subjects and objects of law required definition and elaboration. There were at least two features of this particular colonization effort that pushed first for clarification of legal categories vitally connected to (1) commerce and (2) British citizenship. First, the colonization's original *raison d'être* had been economic trade, and the Crown's agent was a corporation. Even after the British government terminated the Hudson's Bay Company's exclusive licence to trade with Indigenous peoples on Vancouver Island, gold rushes and other economic opportunities fuelled the desire to grow and regulate the colony.[114] This was a modern capitalist project, and in the minds of Douglas and other government officials, it required Western legal structures and systems for effective operation,[115] putting the emerging legal system under intense pressure to essentially "keep up."

Second, the future of the colony as a British colony was by no means a sure thing. It is worth noting that when the Hudson's Bay Company first established its fort at Victoria, permanent settlement on the West Coast had not been envisaged by the British.[116] Consequently, when Douglas became governor, there were few white settlers on the Island – and even fewer on the Mainland – especially as compared to the Indigenous population.[117] To Douglas and the British, this uncertainty presented at least three threats to the colony's continued existence. First, while the Treaty of Oregon settled the border between the British colonies and American territories, Americans continued to make noises about expansion and annexation.[118] In addition, Russian traders remained a competitive threat,[119] as well as a security threat while Britain and Russia were involved in the Crimean War of 1854–56.[120] Finally, when compared to the relatively small numbers of white settlers, the large numbers of Indigenous people were perceived as a threat to both the economy and security of the British colony.[121] While Douglas pursued policies aimed at assimilation, he understood the situation to be volatile, as many settlers and other colonial administrators did not share his optimism about the potential or benefits of assimilation.

In response to these threats, Douglas focused on policies aimed at the peaceful settlement of Indigenous peoples on reserves[122] and shoring up the strength and numbers of settlers that could be counted on to support the British.[123] Examples included pathways to citizenship for Americans who crossed the border to mine for gold; negotiating the Douglas Treaties; advocating for reserves in locations and of sizes requested by First

Nations;[124] and looking for new immigrants who could be counted on to support the British, especially against American expansionism. As one example, he cultivated a relationship with African Americans seeking to leave California to escape racism in the mid-nineteenth century.[125] These families were especially eager to leave in the wake of the US Supreme Court's *Dred Scott* decision, which held that Black people remained the property of their former owners and could not be US citizens, regardless of whether they were currently free or enslaved.[126] Douglas, on the other hand, offered them a path to citizenship in the new colony. In addition to seeking immigrants, Douglas implemented a licensing system aimed at controlling the miners.[127] He seems to have genuinely believed in the potential of a "proper system of laws" to bring about "peace and order."[128]

Because capitalism and nationalism featured so prominently in the minds and motives of Douglas and the British Colonial Office, two legal categories – "Indian"[129] and "citizen"[130] – were especially important. More specifically, the ways in which these categories were constructed and managed through practices of humanization and dehumanization of (a) Indigenous peoples and (b) miners was and remains consequential, entitling some human beings to rights and freedoms not available to others. These include rights to land and full participation in the economy as legal subjects, among others. Importantly, Renisa Mawani and others have argued that the evolution and imposition of these categories produced racial knowledge, racial ordering, and racial governance that continue to have relevance today.[131]

To understand what practices of humanization and dehumanization might tell us about how Douglas viewed the meaning and relevance of humanness, Douglas's journals, correspondence, and papers are instructive. I do not claim to have conducted a comprehensive empirical review for the purposes of this essay; rather, I offer touchpoints and examples that suggest the particular view of humanness and humanity that informed Douglas's policies as governor. More specifically, I examine how Douglas and others talked about and treated Indigenous peoples and gold miners in the mid-nineteenth century.

Indigenous Peoples ("Indians")

The meaning of *Indian* changed several times between the decades following contact and the enactment of the Indian Act in 1876.[132] This tells us that its meaning could not be assumed to be self-evident nor coextensive with *Indigenous* but was (and continues to be) socially constructed. The law – including legal practices of humanization and dehumanization – played a significant role in the evolution of the term's meaning, and the 1996 report of the Royal Commission on Aboriginal Peoples observed that "[r]ecognition as 'Indian' in Canadian law often had nothing to do with whether a person was actually of Indian ancestry."[133] For Douglas, however, the meaning of the term was likely both self-evidently simple and transitional. We can infer with confidence that he meant "Indigenous people" in the broadest sense; he did not put "Indian" outside the category "human"; and to the extent that "Indian" was a legal category, he likely saw it as temporary in the sense that, after assimilation, "Indians" would become "British subjects." In this view, humanization would have been the process by which Indians became British subjects (the ideal human).

The ways in which Indigenous peoples were humanized and dehumanized depended, in part, on the motives of the speaker or actor. Douglas was motivated by at least two objectives: assisting Indigenous peoples on the road to full participation in the colony and convincing peers and others of the soundness of his views and methods. Consequently, his acts of humanization were part substantive and part performative, reflecting both a fairness and a pragmatism.

Humanizing practices took several forms, including speech, actions, and writing, in which human-like features or attributes were emphasized or ascribed. As described above, these included traits such as volition, intention, independence, vitality, spirituality, cooperation, morality, competence, and social connectedness. Turning first to Douglas's writing and speech, he often invoked the characteristic of friendliness in reference to Indigenous people, implying several of the attributes just listed. In Douglas's report of a canoe expedition along the east coast of Vancouver Island in 1852, for example, he describes "the Cowichins" as "a warlike people, mustering about 500 fighting-men, among a population of about 2100 souls. They were extremely friendly and hospitable to our party, and gave us much information about the interior."[134] In recounting another encounter in the same report, he observes that Indigenous communities were "eager to trade."[135] Of note are Douglas's choice of words to describe the people he met (*people, men, souls*) and their attributes (*friendly, hospitable, eager to trade*). Speaking in the Assembly of Vancouver Island in 1863, Douglas stated, "I have great satisfaction in stating that the native Indian tribes continue to evince a friendly disposition."[136] He made a similar statement to the Council of Vancouver Island that same year.[137]

Douglas's correspondence on the question of assimilation and reserves is also illustrative. Douglas believed in the possibility of assimilating Indigenous people into colonial society, assuming that they were, in his words, "rational beings, capable of acting and thinking for themselves."[138] In a letter to the secretary of state for the colonies in 1859, Douglas wrote:

> SIR, – I have the honour to acknowledge the receipt of your ... instructions directing me to inform you if I think it would be feasible to settle [the Vancouver Island] tribes permanently in villages; suggesting in reference to that measure, that with such settlement civilization would at once begin; that law and religion would become naturally introduced among them, and contribute to their security against the aggressions of immigrants; that through indirect taxation, on the additional articles they would purchase, they would contribute to the Colonial Revenue, and with their own consent, some light and simple form of taxation might be imposed, the proceeds of which would be expended strictly and solely on their own wants and improvements.
>
> 2. I have much pleasure in adding, with unhesitating confidence, that I conceive the proposed plan to be at once feasible.[139]

Douglas drew a distinction between his conception of reserves, described above, which he imagined would produce the social conditions necessary for Indigenous peoples to not only survive, but thrive, and Spanish attempts to "civilize" First Peoples in what became California. In the latter case, he believed that Spanish methods dehumanized Indigenous peoples to the detriment of both Indigenous peoples and society more broadly: "[T]hey were kept in a state of pupilage, and not allowed to acquire property of their own, nor taught to think or act for themselves, the feeling and pride of independence were effectually destroyed."[140] Douglas appeared to believe that if the state treats human beings as less than human, it destroys their human capacities. Later in that same letter, he states: "To avoid the rock on which were wrecked the hopes of the Spanish missions, I think it would be advisable studiously to cultivate the pride of independence, so ennobling in its effects, and which the savage largely possesses from nature and early training."[141] In this passage, we see that Douglas ascribes the attribute of independence to Indigenous peoples "from nature," connoting both self-sufficiency and volition.[142]

Douglas's attitude towards Indigenous peoples can also be inferred from his land policies. First, Douglas envisioned a colony in which Indigenous peoples would ultimately have land rights equal to those of white settlers.[143]

Second, he executed agreements with Coast Salish nations on the island on a nation-to-nation (or government-to-government) basis. On the Mainland, he allocated large reserves, and Indigenous people were free to purchase, pre-empt, or lease land on the same terms as anyone else.[144] In asking for funds to continue to purchase Indigenous lands from First Nations, he wrote to the Duke of Newcastle, the colonial secretary: "As the native Indian population of Vancouver Island have distinct ideas of property in land, and mutually recognize their several exclusive possessory rights in certain districts, they would not fail to regard the occupation of such portions of the Colony by white settlers, unless with the full consent of the proprietary tribes, as national wrongs."[145] In all these instances, we see a strong emphasis on First Nations' capacity to act as nations, which in and of itself signals the capacity of members for self-direction. In addition, we continue to see humanizing language – *ideas, recognition, rights, consent, national wrongs* – in reference to Indigenous peoples.

At the same time, Douglas plainly believed that Indigenous peoples had some way to go to exercise their full humanness – British subjecthood – and in that regard it might be more accurate to say he regularly expressed a commitment to their *potential* humanness. His civilizing rhetoric of the colonial enterprise encapsulated the coexistence of "humanizing" and "dehumanizing" discourses. On the one hand, laws and other social practices designed to civilize/humanize Indigenous peoples required an assertion of the innate humanness of Indigenous peoples. On the other hand, his civilizing rhetoric was also founded on the idea that their current ways of knowing and being were subhuman, and as not-yet-civilized, Indigenous peoples could not be counted in the colonial population nor extended the franchise. But still, this is where Douglas departs from others, particularly biological racists: to the extent that Indigenous peoples displayed characteristics associated with "savagery," he believed this reflected their ignorance, not inherent inferiority. Douglas would have called it a developmental stage akin to something like childhood. In a letter to the British Colonial Office, for example, Douglas wrote in 1859: "I have much pleasure in adding, with unhesitating confidence, that I conceive the proposed plan [for reserves on the Island] to be at once feasible, and also the only plan which promises to result in the moral elevation of the native Indian races, in rescuing them from degradation, and protecting them from oppression and rapid decay."[146] Consequently, he was quick to urge the benefits of education and religion for "civilization" and assimilation.[147]

Contrast this, for example, with how (some) administrators, settlers, and miners viewed and treated "Indians." Their dehumanization took many forms and was expressed variously as paternalism, fear, violence,[148] racism, and law[149] in the government,[150] press,[151] and other areas of public and social life. "Indians" were equated with dogs and other nonhuman animals; constituted in local newspapers as drunken, immoral, savage, and degenerate;[152] described as inherently inferior and untrustworthy; and otherwise treated as something to be feared and contained away from the colony. While these practices, especially in later years, are beyond the scope of this essay, they are important to acknowledge because they help contextualize Douglas's (mostly) different ideas, policies, and actions.[153]

Miners ("Citizens")

Although the Queen Charlottes Gold Rush brought Americans through Victoria, it was the Fraser Valley Gold Rush that transformed the colony forever. Thousands – perhaps as many as twenty-eight thousand – American miners from California came through the colony on their way to the Mainland. These miners – not unlike Indigenous peoples – represented a paradox of sorts for colonists. They were simultaneously perceived to be a threat to the colony[154] and potential citizens. Consequently, miners were *dehumanized* to emphasize their threat and *humanized* – both rhetorically and legally – to emphasize their potential. Perhaps unsurprisingly, then, Douglas's approach to the miners was similar to his approach to Indigenous peoples; he was focused on creating the conditions for their pathway to British subjecthood and peace in the colonies.

First, in an effort to control the Fraser River miners and bring out the so-called better aspects of their nature, Douglas issued proclamations declaring that all gold belonged to the Crown and could be mined only under licences issued at Victoria.[155] He did this even though he had no jurisdiction on the Mainland at the time. In Douglas's view, an established system of laws would not only control – humanize – the miners and foster a sense of belonging and allegiance but would also offer miners a stake in the burgeoning colony. This meant the establishment of rules aimed at entitling them to hold land, on declaring their intention to become British subjects and taking the oath of allegiance. Not long after, Britain established the separate Colony of British Columbia and made Douglas governor. A series of conversations with Britain and local government led to the enactment of the Aliens Act, 1859, which provided that aliens resident in either colony – British Columbia or Vancouver Island – for a period of three years, with the intent to settle there, would be entitled to naturalization. More, every alien would "have the same capacity to take, hold, enjoy, recover, convey and transmit title to lands and real estate of every description."[156] These steps – naturalization and land holding – paved the way to enfranchisement.[157] But this is not to suggest that the Act was immediately effective. Douglas's attempts to impose British-like law and order in mining towns were aspirational, with more or less success depending on the competence, loyalty, and skill of men and institutions charged with keeping the peace.[158] This is not surprising given the few numbers of police officers and government officials compared to the numbers of gold miners, the newness and vulnerability of legal institutions, the ambivalence of settlers to miners, and the history of violent labour practices in the region (especially among fur traders and coal miners).

Looking at the ways in which Douglas, the Legislative Council, the British Colonial Office, and settlers spoke about the American gold miners, we may observe a number of things about practices of humanization and dehumanization in that context. First, miners were often described in ways that emphasized nonhuman characteristics such as detachment, lack of feeling, lack of control, disregard for others, and amorality,[159] with most attention paid to their inhumane treatment of others, especially, but not only, Indigenous peoples. Second, Indigenous populations were sometimes invoked to emphasize just how "bad" the miners were, to wit: miners were "worse" than Indigenous peoples. For example, the Colony of Vancouver Island's first magistrate said of Indigenous people at Fort Rupert: "[T]hese Indians were peaceable and better conducted than the inhabitants of mining or frontier towns."[160] In other words, practices of humanization and dehumanization of different groups were bound up with one another.

Of course, it might be argued that this was a different case of dehumanization, more a *description* of miners' particular behaviours than a *practice* of dehumanization per se. Some miners in fact evinced behaviour rationally viewed as inhumane, and in that sense characteristics might have been emphasized to justify harsh treatment. At the same time, however, these descriptions readily coalesced into stereotype, with the effect of dehumanizing all miners.[161]

Notably, Douglas was convinced these characteristics were socially, not biologically, determined. As a consequence, he continued to focus on the potential for humanization. Evidence for this observation may be found in Douglas's correspondence with British officials and statements to the Council of Vancouver Island as well as his work on legislation aimed at offering miners and other aliens a pathway to citizenship.

More or Less Human

That Douglas regarded First Peoples and miners[162] as fundamentally human distinguishes him from other colonists and settlers, but that is not the end of the inquiry. What can his words and actions tell us about how he regarded the category itself? And what can that tell us about his conception of humanity? First, Douglas was clearly a liberal humanitarian to the extent that he saw all people as essentially similar,[163] with the potential to fully express their humanness in the right social conditions. Second, to a large degree, *human* was the functional equivalent of "law-abiding British subject," and colonization represented a concerted effort to humanize everyone within the borders of the Empire. Douglas's words and actions reveal an almost single-minded commitment to that project. Third, evidence suggests that Douglas approached humanity as a status; he was fundamentally hopeful that it could be universally achieved, but he believed it to be conditional. Finally, within the terms of this worldview, Douglas would have set much store in the subject-object divide, especially in the common law. He differed from other colonists in his view that Indigenous peoples should be constituted as subjects and not objects, but not in his acceptance that legal subjects and objects were fundamentally different. Douglas would have drawn the line between them so as to include Indigenous peoples in the category "human" and therefore "subject"; others disagreed, and in the years that followed his retirement, administrators set about drawing the line to exclude "Indians." Similarly, he believed the miners could be made into British subjects with the right incentives and under a system of clear law and order. But Douglas's underlying assumption that Indigenous peoples (and gold miners) were in fact human, or at least potentially human, does not suggest he held a robust and nuanced view of humanity, nor does it suggest that he was progressive in his treatment of Indigenous peoples, except in contrast to the even more discriminatory views of others.

What can this conception of "human" tell us about how Douglas would have defined *humanity?* The dictionary provides two possibilities, the first founded in the expression of humanness, and the second in the "totality of human beings" or humankind.[164] Douglas's conception of humanness suggests the latter. For Douglas, humanity was "all human beings collectively."[165] Again, it would be a mistake to overstate such a conclusion, but from the evidence we have, his language, attitude, and actions suggest an emphasis on what might be called a "membership" model of humanity. Of course, he was deeply embedded in the colonial project of civilizing/humanizing large numbers of not-yet-British subjects towards the goal of making them human, so this worldview would not be surprising. But it would not have resonated with the Coast Salish on Vancouver Island in the mid-nineteenth century.

On Being Human and the Coast Salish

Here, I explore Coast Salish practices and stories for evidence of how Indigenous peoples in this part of the world might have understood the relevance and meaning of being human in the mid-nineteenth century. Specifically, I focus on the Songhees,[166] but I draw from a broader range of Halkomelem-speaking (Halq'eméylem) and Straits-speaking (Lkungeneng or Lekwungen) Coast Salish examples,[167] as there were significant shared cultural practices and common understandings among them. This was especially true when it came to spiritual and social practices relevant to this inquiry.[168] But it is critically important to acknowledge the limitations posed by the tremendous diversity among Coast Salish First Nations and the fact that most of what we "know" about precontact practices is based primarily on records created by non-Indigenous people after contact.[169] Still, these examples suggest Douglas's conception of humanity was sufficiently different from Indigenous peoples on the Island that communication across those differences, especially in different languages and *without acknowledging the existence and validity of those differences,* would have been very difficult, if not impossible. Miscommunication across cultures was dangerous and consequential where the stakes included legal subjecthood in the emerging colonial order, especially given the enduring nature of categories once established in a common-law system.

There were several aspects to Coast Salish belief systems and cultural practices that are instructive here. First, "there was no firm divide between the natural and the spirit world."[170] This had both internal (within the self) and external (between the self and others) dimensions. Additionally, there were (and are) two categories of Coast Salish narratives: the *sqwelqwel,* often translated as "true news," and the *sxwoxwiyam,* often interpreted as "legends" or "myth-age stories." Keith Thor Carlson suggests that these two types of narratives do not refer to well-bounded sets of mythical as opposed to historical incidents since the spirit world described in the sxwoxwiyam often impinges on historical events,[171] thus emphasizing the absence of a stable divide between the natural and spiritual worlds.

Second, human was a not a singular concept. Human beings were thought to be made up of several distinct but integrated[172] components, including the body, the soul, the breath/vitality/life,[173] the shadow/reflection, and the spirit power,[174] and each component carried its own unique features. For example, the soul could be seen by some, continued after death, and could be lost; the shadow self could be lost or stolen; and the life force could be disassociated from the body but might also be returned.[175] In addition, the life or spirit force lived not only in humans but also in ancestors, the rocks, the trees, the grass, and so on; it "connects us all."[176] Importantly, not everyone acquired a spirit power (as distinct from the life or spirit force in everyone), but if they did, they became a "different kind of human being," drawing nearer to the nonhuman world. According to anthropologist Bruce Miller: "The private relationship with the spirit power [became] dangerous if spoken of, and if the spirit [was] offended, and upset in the relationship [it could] cause the death of the human partner. A healthy person, then, knows who they are (their self) and maintains a proper spirit relationship."[177] The absence of a firm divide between the natural world and the spirit world also had implications beyond the self. Not only could human beings acquire a spirit power that transformed them into a "different kind of human being," but they regularly interacted with external, more powerful, nonhuman forces. Humans were not the only meaningful agents.[178]

Third, humans could themselves be transformed into nonhuman beings and objects – including fish, trees, and rocks[179] – and move between the spirit and natural worlds. As just one example, Grant Keddie, the Royal BC Museum's curator of archaeology, recounts the story of the "Origin of the Willow Fish," as told by Songhees Elder David Latess.[180] In the story, a young woman from a village threatened with famine married a mysterious young stranger who made the villagers a "net sgwala" and "showed them how to use it and taught them the expressions that should accompany its handling. Then they were able to catch plenty of fish again." The village prospered once again, and the young man expressed a desire to take his bride home with him. They embarked in a canoe "toward a very deep place in the sea not far from shore" – where they vanished. Days later, the girl reappeared on the water to show herself to her people and vanished again. She never returned because she had "married the fish-spirit sgwala."[181]

Fourth, like humans, superhuman and other nonhuman beings and objects – including rocks and trees – moved in and out of the natural world, interacting with human beings and making up a part of the community (and vice versa).[182] To illustrate this point, think of environmental conservation. Concern for the environment was not some abstract concern for something external to the self; it was self-preservation. Humans would not be concerned with saving the planet because we live on it but because it is us.[183] Importantly, "Coast Salish cultural ideas of the self emphasized humans' subordination to, and dependence on, more powerful nonhuman forces"[184] and, according to Carlson, "interpersonal relationships operate[d] within a range of possibilities rather than according to a series of fixed rules."[185]

Finally, First Nations on the Island understood territory to be held collectively, so individual community members – human and nonhuman – *occupied* rather than *owned* land.[186] The scope of First Nations territories were not marked by areas of "distinct delineated space but, rather, as ... ever-decreasing interest[s] in lands the farther one moved from the core of a tribe's territory."[187] Concepts such as stewardship – contra ownership, for example – make sense in a framework where land itself is alive, a part of a community of human and nonhuman beings and things and spirits.

As critical as cultural differences are, it is important to acknowledge similarities. Like the British, Coast Salish cultural practices and belief systems revealed a class system, including slaves. Slaves were akin to property and generally not considered fully human or "people of life."[188] Carlson tells us that "[w]hile the subject of slavery is delicate due to the stigma still attached to people of slave ancestry, Coast Salish historical narratives contain many references to slavery and the tension between slaves and free people."[189] There was also a lower or inferior class of people made up of the children of slave mothers and noble fathers known as "history-less"[190] and a noble or elite class.[191] The elite class defined community goals and values.[192] Nonetheless, class, like power, had spiritual and material dimensions specific to the Coast Salish; so, while class was evident in both settler and Coast Salish communities, its enactment was inflected by those dimensions.

Taken together, Coast Salish views and practices indicate a conception of humanness and humanity quite different from Douglas's. For the

Songhees, humans were one kind of being in a larger community of beings, and not even the most important. More, the self could take other forms. What would differentiate them in their human form, then, is how they *expressed* that beingness. In addition, as a category, "human" was *not a singular* concept; the embodied self encompassed many dimensions, both natural and spiritual, and legal concepts such as the common-law "person" were insufficient and maybe inappropriate for describing "who" someone was.[193] Certainly, the common-law human-nonhuman binary as a measure of relevance would not have resonated with Coast Salish people at contact. When Douglas engaged in practices of humanization and dehumanization, it was clearly bidirectional in the sense of moving towards or away from an ideal. But outside the human-nonhuman binary, practices of humanizing and dehumanizing took on a multidirectionality that was simultaneously more robust than, and inconsistent with, liberal settler values.

Significantly, the embodied self was *transitional,* not just in the sense that humans are born and die but in the sense that living beings could be transformed into nonhuman beings and things.[194] Moreover, beings could move back and forth between human and nonhuman world(s); in other words, transformation need not be permanent.[195] This aspect of humanness would not fit nicely into the common-law "status" box and would have been largely incoherent to the settlers. It could not be easily equated with legal subjecthood, for example. Nor was it a status in the sense that, with proper civilizing or training, it could be "achieved." True, the Songhees had social classes, and class is evocative of status, but in the context of "transitionality," it could not have held the same liberal connotations as it did in the British common law.

Finally, community was constructed as an expansive and capacious concept, inclusive of not only living human beings but also ancestors, spirits, and other nonhuman and superhuman beings and things.[196] Thus, the Songhees and other Coast Salish on Vancouver Island were not likely to have viewed humanity as "human beings, collectively" or as a community to which someone belonged or in which someone might be a member. Humans were not the relevant, nor even most important, component in delineating community. Coast Salish conceptions of human and community would have rendered that idea incoherent.

As described above, Douglas was the principal face of colonialism on Vancouver Island in the mid-nineteenth century. Consequently, his assumptions, views, and policies were everywhere embedded in the emerging legal – and consequently, political, social, and economic – system(s). Given differences in language, culture, and law, it seems impossible that Douglas's deep commitment to building a liberal order premised on the subject-object binary would have been cognizable to the Coast Salish as such. This was not a system that would have translated easily into Coast Salish languages or cultures. John Sutton Lutz has observed that "comparing Indigenous and explorer accounts of the same meetings brings the collision of fundamentally different systems of thought into sharp relief."[197] My argument is that one of these fundamental differences was how each would have understood the meaning of *human* and, in consequence, *humanity*. For Douglas, "human" was very nearly coextensive with "legal subject"; "humanity," the "totality of subjects." For the Coast Salish on the Island, "human" was a far more complex category, and "humanity," the full expression of that complexity.

It is worth acknowledging that for ordinary people, this question – what is a human being? – is esoteric. One is either human or not. Rarely would the answer be: it depends. But, in fact, it does. Were it otherwise, we would not expect to see so much evidence of humanizing and dehumanizing practices in contests implicating human and other rights today. In the mid-nineteenth century on the Colony of Vancouver Island, practices of humanization and dehumanization were evident in the construction of a consequential set of legal categories – including but not only "Indian" – and then inclusion within those categories. Over time, their boundaries became less permeable, with real material and symbolic consequences. Stakes were high. Depending on if and how one fit into one or more categories, one might be entitled to participate in public life, vote, hold land, and so on. More, law played an outsized role in the formation of identity through the construction of these categories, in part because the legal order was forefront in Douglas's mind as he set about establishing the colony.

What made Douglas unique among colonial administrators and settlers in the latter half of the nineteenth century was his commitment to the idea that Indigenous peoples and American miners were (at least potentially) human, capable of being made into productive citizens. After Douglas retired, however, the borders around "citizen" were drawn so as to effectively exclude Indigenous peoples. Miners fared better. But Douglas's views did not differentiate him in ways that would ultimately make a difference. Douglas worked hard to impose a liberal system of governance; he would have included Indigenous peoples in the polity and recognized Aboriginal title in the colonies, but there was nothing about the system itself that required such a conclusion. So while he tried to humanize Indigenous peoples in the eyes of colonial administrators, settlers, and miners, towards the goal of inclusion, others dehumanized them towards the goal of exclusion. Both sets of practices were possible within the emerging system. Equally, if not more importantly, regardless of whether Indigenous peoples were full subjects, the system itself precluded the possibility of incorporating Indigenous legal traditions or culture into colonial practices. The emerging legal order depended on the erasure of Indigenous ways, culture, values, belief systems, and law. In some ways, this was a greater violence, and sustained dialogue about its legacy is essential for creating pathways to reconciliation.[198]

Acknowledgments

This project was motived in part by my commitment to reconciliation in Canada and, in particular, the values expressed by the Truth and Reconciliation Commission of Canada's calls to action, particularly nos. 28 and 45. I am extraordinarily grateful to the members of the Songhees, Tsartlip, Pauquachin, Tseycum, Tsawout, and Esquimalt First Nations who listened to my ideas and asked challenging questions at an early presentation of this research, and to the Songhees First Nation members and staff who subsequently met with me and generously shared ideas and stories. I am also grateful to John Borrows, Gillian Calder, Grant Keddie, Pooja Parmar, the editors of this volume, and the anonymous reviewers at the UBC Press for carefully reading and commenting on earlier drafts; Michael Contino, Oakley Ramprashad, and Jena Ritchey, for superb editorial and research assistance; and my writing group – Eunjung Kim, Mike Gill, and Yvonne Zylan – for support throughout.

Notes

1 *See Reece v City of Edmonton,* 2011 ABCA 238, 85 MPLR (4th) 36, [2011] AWLD 3436, [2011] AWLD 3422, 46 Alta LR (5th) 1, [2011] 11 WWR 1, 335 DLR (4th) 600, 9 CPC (7th) 21. In the American context, see *Nonhuman Rights Project, Inc ex rel Tommy v Lavery,* 31 NY 3d 1054, 100 NE 3d 846 (NY Sup Ct 2017); and *Liriano v Sardina,* No Mem 19–53 (Me 2019).

2 There is growing interest in extending rights to nature to meet the challenges of environmental crises in Canada, Australia, New Zealand, India, Ecuador, Bolivia,

Colombia, and the United States. In 2014, Katherine Sinclair walked around Lake Winnipeg in an effort to draw attention to the ways in which the lake needed to heal. Her ultimate goal, she said, was to have the lake declared a person: see Connie Walker, "Lake Winnipeg Should Be 'Recognized as a Person,' Says Advocate," *CBC News*, July 12, 2014, https://www.cbc.ca/news/indigenous/lake-winnipeg-should-be-recognized-as-a-person-says-advocate-1.2703350. See also *The Colorado River Ecosystem a/n/f Deep Green Resistance, the Southwest Coalition, et al v State of Colorado*, 1:17-cv-02316-RPM (D Colo 2017); *Juliana v United States*, 339 F Supp 3d 1062 (D Or 2018); Constitution of the Republic of Ecuador, 208, s 71; Law No 071, Rights of Mother Earth (Bolivia, 2010); Framework Law No 300, Mother Earth and Integral Development for Living Well (Bolivia, 2012); and *Salim v State of Uttarakh* (March 20, 2017) PIL No 126 of 2014 HC of Uttarakhand at Nainital (India). While some of these movements were initiated by Indigenous peoples and informed by Indigenous values (New Zealand, for example), others were not (the United States, for example). The latter cases are troubling for that reason. See Laura Spitz, "Red River, White Law," *Tribal Law Journal Blog*, June 19, 2019, https://triballawjournalblog.wordpress.com/2019/06/19/red-river-white-law/. For the argument that legal personhood for nature is counterintuitive from an Indigenous perspective, see Virginia Marshall, "Overturning Aqua Nullius: An Aboriginal Perspective on Personhood," in Gabriel Eckstein, Ariella D'Andrea, Virginia Marshall, Erin O'Donnell, Julia Talbot-Jones, Deborah Curren, and Katie O'Bryan, "Forum: Conferring Legal Personality on the Worlds' Rivers: A Brief Intellectual Assessment," *Water International* 44, 6–7 (2019): https://doi.org/10.1080/02508060.2019.1631558.

3 But see Jen Gerson, "The Uproar over Unplanned," *Maclean's*, July 10, 2019: "Most Canadians support abortion rights ... Support is so high and so entrenched that it would be absurd for any party to shake the status quo."

4 In the American context, see Michelle Alexander, *The New Jim Crow: Mass Incarceration in the Age of Colorblindness* (New York: New Press, 2012).

5 In the American context, see Toni M. Massaro and Helen L. Norton, "Siri-ously? Free Speech Rights and Artificial Intelligence," *Northwestern Law Review* 110, 2 (2016): 1179–83; and Toni M. Massaro, Helen L. Norton, and Margot E. Kaminski, "SIRI-OUSLY 2.0: What Artificial Intelligence Reveals about the First Amendment," *Minnesota Law Review* 101, 6 (2017): 2497–99, 2510–12.

6 In the American context, see *Citizens United v Federal Election Com'n*, 558 US 310 (2010); and *Burwell v Hobby Lobby Stores, Inc*, 573 US 682 (2014).

7 For an historical example, see *Edwards v Canada (Attorney General)*, [1930] AC 124, 1929 UKPC 86.

8 This tracks with an argument made by Jens Ohlin in the context of persons: "[P]ersonhood is a cluster concept, an umbrella that shelters diverse and conflicting intuitions." See "Is the Concept of the Person Necessary for Human Rights?," *Columbia Law Review* 105, 1 (2005): 212.

9 Scholars have convincingly made the case that in several contexts – prisons, for example – humans are subjects in name only, stripped of many of the rights associated with subjectivity and treated like property. See, for example, Alexander, *The New Jim Crow;* and James Forman Jr., *Locking Up Our Own: Crime and Punishment in Black America* (New York: Farrar, Straus and Giroux, 2017).

10 Ngaire Naffine, "Legal Personality and the Natural World: On the Persistence of the Human Measure of Value," *Journal of Human Rights and the Environment* 3, Special Issue (2012): 78, discussing John Finnis and Ronald Dworkin.

11 Christopher Stone makes the case that there is nothing natural about legal personhood or the connection between humans and persons. Instead, subjecthood or personhood

is a cluster concept and, most importantly, a legal abstraction. In his view, this is its potential for nonhuman subjects. There is room there for more than human beings. See Christopher Stone, *Should Trees Have Standing? Law, Morality, and the Environment,* 3rd ed. (New York: Oxford University Press, 2010), and "Should Trees Have Standing?," *Southern California Law Review* 45, 2 (1972): 450–501.

12 For a fascinating elaboration on plants as "active and communicative organisms," see Monica Gagliano, John Ryan, and Patricia I. Vieira, *The Language of Plants: Science, Philosophy, Literature* (Minneapolis: University of Minnesota Press, 2017). See also, Stone, *Should Trees Have Standing?*

13 A notable recent exception is the growing body of social-psychology literature on these processes. See, for example, the collection of essays in Paul G. Bain, ed., *Humanness and Dehumanization* (New York: Psychology Press, 2013); and Adam Waytz, Nicholas Epley, and John T. Cacioppo, "Social Cognition Unbound: Insights into Anthropomorphism and Dehumanization," *Current Directions in Psychological Science* 19, 1 (2010): 58–62.

14 See, generally, the Truth and Reconciliation Commission of Canada, *Honouring the Truth, Reconciling for the Future: Summary of the Final Report of the Truth and Reconciliation Commission of Canada,* 2015, http://nctr.ca/assets/reports/Final%20Reports/Executive_Summary_English_Web.pdf. See also Nathan Goetting, "The Marshall Trilogy and the Constitutional Dehumanization of American Indians," *Guild Practitioner* 65, 4 (2008): 207–26.

15 For an incredibly rich description of the encounters that produced racial knowledge, racial ordering, and racial governance in late nineteenth- and early twentieth-century British Columbia, see Renisa Mawani, *Colonial Proximities: Crossracial Encounters and Juridical Truths in British Columbia, 1871–1921,* Law and Society Series (Vancouver: UBC Press, 2009).

16 Hamar Foster has observed that in Europe at the time of contact, law was generally concerned with resource allocation and dispute resolution: "British Columbia: Legal Institutions in the Far West, from Contact to 1871," *Manitoba Law Journal* 23 (1995): 300. See also British Columbia, *Papers Connected to the Indian Land Question, 1850–1875* (Victoria: R. Wolfenden, 1875).

17 At times, he expressed inconsistent views. See, for example, his address to the Vancouver Island Assembly and Council, August 12, 1856, in which he describes the "Northern Indians" as being "accustomed to follow the impulses of their own evil natures": James E. Hendrickson, ed., *Journals of the Colonial Legislatures of the Colonies of Vancouver Island and British Columbia, 1851–1871,* vol. 2 (Victoria: Provincial Archives of British Columbia, 1980). See also Cole Harris, "The Native Land Policies of Governor James Douglas," *BC Studies* 174 (Summer 2012): 101–22. But the preponderance of evidence clearly establishes that he regarded Indigenous people as human beings, with the potential for full participation in colonial public life.

18 In fact, several First Nations in the region had negotiated prior agreements concerning land. See Neil Vallance, "Sharing the Land: The Formation of the Vancouver Island (or 'Douglas') Treaties of 1850–1854 in Historical, Legal and Comparative Context" (PhD diss., University of Victoria, 2015), 57–58.

19 In February 2017, for example, I was honoured to attend a conference on Songhees Territory, cohosted by the University of Victoria and the Songhees Nation, "First Nations, Land, and James Douglas: Indigenous and Treaty Rights in the Colonies of Vancouver Island and British Columbia, 1849–1864." The unifying thread that ran through much of the conference was the idea that James Douglas and the Douglas

Treaties were distinct and even admirable in their recognition of Aboriginal title in the land or territory we now know as Vancouver Island.

20 *Merriam-Webster Dictionary,* 11th ed. (2016), s.v. "humanity."

21 In this essay, I am primarily focused on the Coast Salish in what became British Columbia, but I recognize that this reinstantiates or reinforces the significance of the political border between Canada and the United States in ways that do not map onto "prior Aboriginal reality, before contact with whites and before treaties and borders": see Bruce Granville Miller, "Introduction," in *Be of Good Mind: Essays on the Coast Salish,* ed. Bruce Granville Miller (Vancouver: UBC Press, 2007), 6. See also Daniel L. Boxberger, "The Not So Common" in Miller, *Be of Good Mind,* 55: "One of the most dominant features of Coast Salish territory is the international boundary that bisects it."

22 Linguistic and cultural diversity among First Nations renders generalizations tricky, of course, and most of what we "know" about precontact practices is based on ethnographic records created by non-Indigenous people after contact. See Bruce Granville Miller, "Rereading the Ethnographic Record: The Problem of Justice in the Coast Salish World," in *Coming to Shore: Northwest Coast Ethnology, Traditions, and Visions,* ed. Marie Mauzé, Michael Eugene Harkin, and Sergei Kan (Lincoln: University of Nebraska Press, 2004), 306, and *The Problem of Justice: Tradition and Law in the Coast Salish World,* Fourth World Rising (Lincoln: University of Nebraska Press, 2001), 14–15. Still, evidence suggests there were significant shared cultural practices and common understandings among the Coast Salish, especially when it came to spiritual and social practices relevant to this inquiry. For example, "Indigenous peoples on the northwest coast and their ethnographers tell us that when Europeans arrived, the Native people lived in a world where there was no firm divide between the natural and the spirit world": John Sutton Lutz, "First Contact as a Spiritual Performance: Encounters on the North American West Coast," in *Myth and Memory: Stories of Indigenous-European Contact,* ed. John Sutton Lutz (Vancouver: UBC Press, 2007), 35.

23 Miller, "Rereading," 313.

24 This is not to say that the Coast Salish and other Indigenous communities were without internal class or other divisions. In *S'iltexwáwtxw* structures, for example, the "worthy people" "occupied the warmest and safest portions of the house – most often the middle section farther removed from doorways and drafts ... The lower status *s'téxem* ('worthless people') and *skw'iyéth* (slaves) slept nearer the draft doorways along the smokier back end of the house, serving as the early warning and defense system against intruders": Keith Thor Carlson, Albert Jules McHalsie, and Stólō Heritage Trust, *A Stó:lō–Coast Salish Historical Atlas* (Vancouver/Seattle/Chilliwack: Douglas and McIntyre/University of Washington Press/ Stólō Heritage Trust, 2001), 43. See also Foster, "British Columbia," 300: "The Tsimshian, Haida and other [coastal] nations ... were organized along strictly hierarchical lines. Although a certain amount of controversy continues in the literature about how rigid the categories were, most researchers agree that much depended upon whether one was a noble, a commoner, or a slave."

25 "Recommendation 45," *Truth and Reconciliation Commission of Canada: Calls to Action,* 2015, http://trc.ca/assets/pdf/Calls_to_Action_English2.pdf.

26 See, generally, the Truth and Reconciliation Commission of Canada, *Honouring the Truth.*

27 Ian Hacking, *The Social Construction of What?* (Cambridge, MA: Harvard University Press, 1999), 6, cited in Stacie Goddard, "Hiding in Plain Sight? The Not-So-Secret Constructivism of Relationalism: Proceedings of Seizing the Constructivist Ground?

Practice and Relational Theories" (paper presented at the Proceedings of International Studies Quarterly Online Symposium, 2017), on file with author.

28 For an application of constructivism as a theoretical method in the context of contemporary Indigenous institutions, see Justin B. Richland, "'What Are You Going to Do with the Village's Knowledge?' Talking Tradition, Talking Law in Hopi Tribal Court," *Law and Society Review* 39, 2 (2005): 235–72. See also, Elizabeth Mertz, "Legal Language: Pragmatics, Poetics, and Social Power," *Annual Review of Anthropology* 23 (1994): 447: "There is an exciting convergence among a number of disciplines on the role of legal language as socially creative and constitutive in the struggle over power in and through law. Anthropological linguists have developed a framework that permits detailed consideration of the contextual structuring of language to be linked with analysis of wider social change and reproduction. Legal anthropologists and critical legal theorists have outlined the ways in which law serves as a site for struggle and imposition of hegemony. Legal theorists focusing sensitively on language from critical race theory, feminist, and deconstructionist perspectives add a dynamic, daring, and vivid understanding of the impact of legal language in those struggles." Cited above in Richland, "What Are You Going to Do," 236.

29 Carlson et al., *Historical Atlas,* 6.

30 *S̱x̱wõx̱wiyám,* for example, are the Stó:lō oral histories describing the distant past when animals and people could speak to one another and assume one another's forms. For example, mountain goats on Lhilheqey (Mount Cheam) could take off their coats to become human. Ibid.

31 Isaac Davison, "Whanganui River Given Legal Status of a Person under Unique Treaty of Waitangi Settlement," *New Zealand Herald,* March 15, 2017. In September 2017, a suit was filed in Federal District Court in Colorado naming the Colorado River ecosystem as plaintiff, claiming *inter alia* that the Colorado River is a person with rights under the law. See Julie Turkewitz, "Corporations Have Rights: Why Shouldn't Rivers?," *New York Times,* September 26, 2017.

32 *Burwell v Hobby Lobby Stores, Inc,* 134 S Ct 2751 (2014), finding that persons capable of exercising free religion within the meaning of the Religious Freedom Restoration Act of 1993 – and thereby entitled to such protections as the Act affords – include for-profit corporations. For a more recent example, see *Masterpiece Cake Shop, Ltd v Colorado Civil Rights Commission,* 138 S Ct 1719 (2018), finding that a bakery did not have to make a wedding cake for a same-sex couple because of sincere religious objections.

33 *Reece v City of Edmonton,* at paras 39, 85, 85, 104, 123 for Chief Justice Fraser in dissent (elephants are among the most social of all animals). See also Charles Siebert, "An Elephant Crackup?," *New York Times,* October 8, 2006, asking whether elephants should have legal rights to protect them from psychological trauma. Cited in Jessica Wilen Berg, "Of Elephants and Embryos: A Proposed Framework for Legal Personhood," *Hastings Law Journal* 59, 2 (2007): 369–406.

34 Conceptually, "nonhuman" is a judgment in and of itself. In other words, attaching the label in conjunction with any of the above-mentioned characteristics is to say those characteristics are undesirable.

35 See, for example, Leslie Thielen-Wilson, "Troubling the Path to Decolonization: Indian Residential School Case Law, Genocide, and Settler Legitimacy," *Canadian Journal of Law and Society* 29, 2 (2014): 181: "In [Indian residential school] case law, this violence consists of the dehumanization of the Indigenous collective as property."

36 *Reece v City of Edmonton; Tilikum, Katina, Corky, Kasatka, and Ulises v Sea World,* 842 F Supp 2d 1259 (2012), finding that the Thirteenth Amendment to the Constitution of

the United States, prohibiting slavery and involuntary servitude, does not protect five wild-captured orcas held by Sea World.

37 I am aware, as I have noted elsewhere, that the choice of legal discourse – over political or economic discourses, for example – is not without consequences: "[L]aw as a specific set of institutions engages in a variety of rendering and disciplining processes that tend to sacrifice social, economic, and political complexity in favor of the production of discrete, singular, and disconnected 'questions.' Specifically, legal practice and procedure constrain the form and substance of argument, drastically limit what counts as relevant evidence bearing upon contested inquiries, and naturalize legal judgments in such a way as to produce the appearance of a deeper and broader analysis and resolution of a given conflict." See Laura Spitz, "The Evolving Architecture of North American Integration," *University of Colorado Law Review* 80, 3 (2009): 735–92. See also, Yvonne Zylan, *States of Passion: Law, Identity, and the Social Construction of Desire* (New York: Oxford University Press, 2011).

38 Hacking, *Social Construction of What?*, 29.

39 See Jeffrey R. Dudas, "Review: Law at the American Frontier," *Law and Social Inquiry* 29, 4 (2004): 859–90.

40 As John Borrows has observed, the sources of Canadian law concerning First Nations are "grounded in complex spiritual, political and social customs and conventions, namely those of European nations." In other words, it would be a mistake to position First Nations legal systems as "spiritual" and the emerging (European) colonial law as somehow "objective" or "apolitical": "With or Without You: First Nations Law (in Canada)," *McGill Law Journal* 41, 3 (1996): 632.

41 Waytz, Epley, and Cacioppo, "Social Cognition Unbound," 60, emphasis added.

42 Ibid.

43 Nathan A. Heflick and Jaime L. Goldenberg, "Dehumanization: A Threat and Solution to Terror Management," in *Humanness and Dehumanization*, ed. Paul G. Bain, Jeroen Vaes, and Jacques-Philippe Leyens (New York: Routledge, 2014), 111. Victoria Lee and Lasana Harris emphasize that "traditionally dehumanized individuals are perceived as low in both trait competence and warmth, resulting in feelings of disgust or contempt" for them. See Victoria K. Lee and Lasana T. Harris, "Dehumanized Perception: Psychological and Neural Mechanisms Underlying Everyday Dehumanization," in *Humanness and Dehumanization*, ed. Paul G. Bain, Jeroen Vaes, and Jacques-Philippe Leyens (New York: Routledge, 2014), 68.

44 See, for example, cases brought on behalf of nonhuman animals for their improved treatment, especially in zoos or on farms: *Reece v City of Edmonton.*

45 On the history of this period generally, see Vallance, "Sharing the Land," 19.

46 Historian Adele Perry writes, "In the latter half of the nineteenth century, the northwestern North American territories ... witnessed social and political change on a seismic scale": *Colonial Relations: The Douglas-Connolly Family and the Nineteenth-Century Imperial World, Critical Perspectives on Empire* (Cambridge: Cambridge University Press, 2015), 176.

47 British Columbia, *Papers Connected to the Indian Land Question*, provides a useful example of how the colonial posture towards "Indians" and "tribes" shifted after Douglas left office. See, for example, "The Memorandum as to the Songish Indian Reserve at Victoria," 65–68.

48 In this sense, the Hudson's Bay Company exhibited and enacted many of the features commonly associated with statehood, and the line between Britain and the company was not always clear.

49 The Oregon Treaty settled the border between the United States and what became Canada.

50 Cole Harris testified in the *Tk'Kemlups Indian Band v Canada and BC* trial that "Douglas had the making of Native land policy on Vancouver Island, and particularly in the mainland colony of British Columbia, much to himself. The Colonial Office trusted him": Harris, "Land Policies," 104.

51 In his essay in this volume, Keith Thor Carlson notes that Douglas did not view Indigenous culture as equal to settler or British culture, but he did see Indigenous peoples as "capable of being equal."

52 J.R. Miller, *Skyscrapers Hide the Heavens: A History of Indian-White Relations in Canada,* 3rd ed. (Toronto: University of Toronto Press, 2000), 178–86.

53 For example, there is evidence of an established settlement in the Fraser River Valley from that time period.

54 Foster, "British Columbia," 300, citing Wilson Duff, "The Indian History of British Columbia," in *Anthropology in British Columbia: Memoir* (Victoria: British Columbia Provincial Museum, 1964), 8.

55 See Miller, *The Problem of Justice,* 2–3.

56 For an interesting account of Indigenous dispute-resolution practices in the precontact era, see Foster, "British Columbia," 300–3.

57 *Merriam-Webster Dictionary Online* (https://www.merriam-webster.com), s.v. "Wild West," accessed September 27, 2019. See, for example, an article published by *Duhaime's LawMAG* on September 26, 2012, titled "Wild, Wild West Law" (http://www.duhaime.org/LawMag/LawArticle-1459/Wild-Wild-West-Law.aspx), in which the author simultaneously ignores the prior and continuing existence of Indigenous justice systems while minimizing the violence of colonization to say that "the wild and crazy shenanigans of the early establishment of law and justice in what is now the modern city of Victoria, British Columbia, represent a looking glass into the rough world of justice over 100 years ago throughout the North American *Wild Wild West*" (italics in original). Moreover, "to use the example … of Vancouver Island, the *nicest* description would be 'wild, wild west'" (italics in original).

58 Despite the very visible imposition of British law in the colony, First Nations legal principles continued to operate within and across Indigenous communities. They also remained relevant in interactions between Indigenous peoples and settlers, shaping and informing Indigenous points of view. Their continuing existence has been acknowledged by the Supreme Court of Canada: see Borrows, "With or Without You," 633. Professor Borrows persuasively argues that contemporary courts should be wary of replicating or reinstantiating the supposed superiority of European law. In his view – which I share – "the intersection of these various legal genealogies is sometimes portrayed as a conflict, in which one source of law is incompatible with, or should gain preeminence over, the others. In such instances, the Aboriginal source of law is generally not applied because of its perceived incompatibility with, or supposed inferiority, within the legal hierarchy. It is unnecessary, however, for courts to approach the interpretation of Aboriginal laws in such a manner. The Supreme Court of Canada has defined Aboriginal rights in such a way that these various sources can often be harmonized and need not obstruct each other" (ibid., 633–34).

59 Miller, *Skyscrapers,* 175–76; and Foster, "British Columbia," 303–7.

60 It is worth remembering that forts "were simultaneously corporate and military spaces." See Adele Perry, "'Is Your Garden in England, Sir?': James Douglas's Archive and the Politics of Home," *History Workshop Journal* 70, 1 (2010): 73.

61 This included land and an exclusive licence to trade with local First Nations, provided the company paid for civil and military establishments; and 90 percent of the profits from land sales and royalties were used for the public. James E. Hendrickson, ed., *Journals of the Colonial Legislatures of the Colonies of Vancouver Island and British Columbia, 1851–1871,* 4 vols. (Victoria: Provincial Archives of British Columbia, 1980), vol. 1. Ostensibly, Britain was worried about the threat of American expansionism and believed the Hudson's Bay Company was best situated to manage this threat.

62 Hendrickson, *Journals,* 1:xxvi.

63 Ibid. Ultimately, Hendrickson observes that it was "ludicrously complex for such a miniature community" (ibid., 1:xxxiv). See also Perry, *Colonial Relations,* 177. On the emergence and organization of the new judicial system, see David M.L. Farr, "The Organization of the Judicial System in the Colonies of Vancouver Island and British Columbia, 1849–1871," *University of British Columbia Law Review* 3, 1 (1967): 1–35.

64 Douglas was apparently taken by surprise at Blanshard's appointment. See Perry, *Colonial Relations,* 178.

65 In addition, "he had accepted the governorship without salary on the understanding he would receive a grant of one thousand acres of land, only to learn from Douglas upon his arrival that the land was attached to the office and not for his private use": Hendrickson, *Journals,* 1:xxviii.

66 Ibid., 1:xxix. Interestingly, news of Douglas's May 1851 appointment did not reach him until October of that year. According to Perry, "His appointment and the way it was carried out again signaled how metropolitan reckonings of empire were disciplined to local iterations of it. Much like the Dutch nationals entrusted with British rule in the Guyana of his childhood, Douglas's greatest qualification for governor was that he was there when there was literally and metaphorically beyond the metropole's reach": *Colonial Relations,* 180.

67 Foster, "British Columbia," 308. The recognition of Aboriginal title was not uniform across the colonies. See Harris, "Land Policies," 105. Nevertheless, Douglas probably agreed with the view that Indigenous peoples had prior claim to the land (ibid., 106). See also Grant R. Keddie, *Songhees Pictorial: A History of the Songhees People as Seen by Outsiders, 1790–1912* (Victoria: Royal BC Museum, 2003), 48.

68 Cole Harris notes that while they are described as treaties today, Douglas himself called them agreements. See Harris, "Land Policies," 105.

69 Ibid., 106. See also Keddie, *Songhees Pictorial,* 48–49.

70 Foster, "British Columbia," 307. See also Paul Tennant, *Aboriginal People and Politics: The Indian Land Question in British Columbia, 1849–1989* (Vancouver: UBC Press, 1990), 17–20.

71 See Secretary of State for the Colonies to Douglas (Dispatch no. 73), October 19, 1861, British Columbia, *Papers Connected to the Indian Land Question,* 180, which reads in part:

> SIR, – I have had under my consideration your despatch No. 24, of the 25th of March last, transmitting an Address from the House of Assembly of Vancouver Island, in which they pray for the assistance of Her Majesty's Government in extinguishing the Indian title to the public lands in the Colony, and set forth the evils that may result from a neglect of this precaution.
>
> I am fully sensible to the great importance of purchasing without loss of time the native title to the soil of Vancouver Island; but the acquisition of the title is a purely colonial interest, and the Legislature must not entertain any expectation that the British taxpayer will be burdened to supply the funds or British credit pledged for the purpose.

72 Harris, "Land Policies," 107–9.

73 The *British Colonist* reported that a similar treaty had been made at Cowichan in 1862, but no official records exist to substantiate the report: see Neil Vallance and Hamar Foster, "Douglas Conference Program," 4.

74 Some historians put 1863 as the date of his retirement as governor of Vancouver Island; others use 1864. I will use 1864 because the Executive Council's meeting minutes put it at March 14, 1864 (Hendrickson, *Journals,* 1:117), but whether it is 1863 or 1864 does not much matter for the purposes of this essay.

75 Hendrickson, *Journals,* 1:xxxii.

76 The colonial secretary, Sir Edward Bulwer-Lytton, wrote to Douglas, "All claims and interests must be subordinated to that policy which is to be found in the peopling and opening up of the new country, with the intention of consolidating it as an integral and important part of the British Empires": Lytton, Sir Edward George Earle Bulwer to Douglas, Sir James 1 July 1858, CO 410:1, 128. The Colonial Despatches of Vancouver Island and British Columbia 1846–1871, Edition 2.1, ed. James Hendrickson and the Colonial Despatches project. Victoria, BC: University of Victoria. https://bcgenesis.uvic.ca/V587202A.html.

77 Interestingly, Douglas was unhappy with the process, "writing that he had 'no patience either with those who planned or those who are carrying out the new system of Government,' blasting the policies that left Vancouver Island 'prostate and bleeding at every pore.'" See Adele Perry, "Beyond Biography, Beyond Canada," *Canadian Historical Review* 98, 2 (2017): 321–37.

78 Charlotte S.M. Girard, "Sir James Douglas' Mother and Grandmother," *BC Studies* 44 (Winter 1979–80): 25–31. See also Perry, *Colonial Relations,* 20–47.

79 Perry, "Is Your Garden in England," 69 (relying on Girard, "Sir James Douglas's Mother," 79). Adele Perry suggests this is not surprising: "The babies born in nineteenth-century colonial societies were a complicated problem for empire, one that was in part managed by practices of non-recognition ... The colonial state in early nineteenth-century Demerara recorded ordinary people in the greatest detail when they bought property, sold property, or themselves became property through practices of slavery. I know most about Douglas's probable mother and grandmother when colonial governments regulated, taxed, or compensated them for their slaveholdings": *Colonial Relations,* 4.

80 Perry, "Is Your Garden in England," 71, relying on Girard, "Sir James Douglas' Mother," 79.

81 Perry, *Colonial Relations,* 33. Perry notes in an earlier article that William Connolly went on to marry "his wealthy and much younger second cousin, and the status of his two marriages and sets of children was a locus of debate around the politics of race and marriage in nineteenth-century Canada": Perry, "Is Your Garden in England," 72–73.

82 Interestingly, Douglas was also appointed lieutenant-governor of a new colony in 1853 – the Queen Charlotte Islands (Haida Gwaii) – and remained so until he became governor of the Colony of British Columbia in 1858 (which included the Mainland and coastal islands). The appointment was in direct response to British concerns that Americans might try to annex the islands during the Queen Charlottes Gold Rush. Donald E. Waite, "Our History: The Early Days of BC's Gold Rush," *Times Colonist,* December 12, 2015.

83 Perry, "Is Your Garden in England," 78.

84 See Perry, *Colonial Relations,* 124–25.

85 Ibid., 121–32, 157; see also Mawani, *Colonial Proximities.*

86 Perry, *Colonial Relations,* 205.

87 Gustav Jahoda, "An Anthropological History of Dehumanization," in *Humanness and Dehumanization,* ed. Paul G. Bain, Jeroen Vaes, and Jacques-Philippe Leyens (New York: Routledge, 2014), 18.

88 Take the example of Lord Kames, who argued that "as, with respect to individuals, there is a progress from infancy to maturity, so too there is a similar progress *in every nation* from its savage state to its maturity in arts and sciences": Henry Home, Lord Kames, and Eighteenth Century Collections Online, *Sketches of the History of Man: Considerably Improved in a Third Edition,* 2 vols. (Dublin: 1779), 468–69, cited in Jahoda, "An Anthropological History," 18. For a contemporary example demonstrating that "the relationship between the settlers and those whom they have dispossessed, and continue to dispossess ... [continues to be] a relationship that is spatially and racially organized, as one between modern subjects and those who must be assisted in modernity," see Sherene H. Razack, "Memorializing Colonial Power: The Death of Frank Paul," *Law and Social Inquiry* 37, 4 (2012): 908–32.

89 Harris, "Land Policies," 104.

90 John S. Lutz, "Introduction: Myth Understandings – First Contact Over and Over Again," in Lutz, *Myth and Memory,* 4, citing Natalie Zemon Davis.

91 Jahoda, "An Anthropological History," 18.

92 Ibid., 19.

93 Ibid., 18.

94 Sir John Lubbock, for example, published a treatise in 1863 on the primitive condition of man, in which he wrote that "savages have the character of children with the passions and strength of men": *The Origin of Civilization and the Primitive Condition of Man: Mental and Social Condition of Savages* (London: Longmans, Green, 1882), 21, cited in Jahoda, "An Anthropological History."

95 Lubbock, *The Origin of Civilization,* 21.

96 Jahoda, "An Anthropological History," 21.

97 Ibid.

98 J.R. Miller suggests that it was a combination of the fact that Douglas had a Métis wife and was a fur trader rather than a settler. See Miller, *Skyscrapers,* 181–82.

99 C. Wright Mills, *The Sociological Imagination* (New York: Oxford University Press, 1959), 143, emphasis added.

100 On the claim that having a Métis wife influenced his views, see Miller, *Skyscrapers,* 181. But also see Miller, *Skyscrapers,* 164: "[O]bservers noted that fur traders began to turn more and more towards the mixed-blood daughters of ... earlier marriages between Indian women and European traders," perhaps reflecting a preference for lighter-skinned women.

101 Harris, "Land Policies," 104.

102 Ibid., 103.

103 Ibid.

104 By 1860, the Council of Vancouver Island made it clear that British colonial law would be applied to Indigenous peoples: Hendrickson, *Journals,* 1:148.

105 See, for example, Dudas, "Law at the American Frontier," 862: "The implanting of modern, Western legal orders throughout the non-Western world was a central means by which European colonizers exerted control over Native peoples and their resources. At the same time ... law worked as a conceptual resource with which both the colonizers and the colonized made sense of, and negotiated, the new realities ushered in by colonial processes. Law thus ordered the colonial project directly and indirectly, dislocating Native life both with formal rules and institutions and with unfamiliar logic, symbols, and vocabularies."

106 On the evolution and organization of the judicial system and its relationship to the legislative assemblies in the new colony, see Farr, "The Organization of the Judicial System."

107 See, for example, "Despatch from the Right Hon. Sir E.B. Lytton, Bart., to Governor Douglas (July 31, 1858)," in British Columbia, *Papers Connected to the Indian Land Question,* 12: "At this distance, and with the imperfect means of knowledge which I possess, I am reluctant to offer, as yet, any suggestion as to the prevention of affrays between the Indians and the immigrants. This question is of so local a character that it must be solved by your knowledge and experience, and I commit it to you, in the full persuasion that you will pay every regard to the interests of the Natives which an enlightened humanity can suggest," emphasis added.

108 Farr, "The Organization of the Judicial System," 3.

109 See notes 38 to 41 above and accompanying text. This is not to say everyone agreed with him – we know when it came to the question of Indigenous subjecthood that many did not – but to say that his position authorized him to legitimately speak. Conversely, by the same logic, Indigenous voices were rendered irrelevant.

110 For a succinct and thoughtful elaboration on the ways in which external and internal colonization(s) simultaneously operated to facilitate (a) the transplanting of Europeans to what became Canada and (b) the disappearance of Indigenous peoples as "free peoples with rights to their territories and governments" through political, economic, cultural, physical, and social displacement, see Mary Eberts, "Still Colonizing after All These Years," *University of New Brunswick Law Journal* 64 (2013): 128, citing James Tully, "The Struggles of Indigenous Peoples for and of Freedom," in *Political Theory and the Rights of Indigenous Peoples,* ed. Duncan Ivison, Paul Patton, and Will Sanders (New York: Cambridge University Press, 2000), 39.

111 See, for example, the University of Ottawa's 2015 "Destination 2020" letter from President Allan Rock, outlining the university's five-year strategic plan, in which he states: "Canada is a unique country, born not of war or revolution but in a conscious act of self-invention." On file with author.

112 For one historian's exceedingly positive account of how and why the western Canadian experience was unlike the American one, see Barry M. Gough, "Keeping British Columbia British: The Law-and-Order Question on a Gold Mining Frontier," *Huntington Library Quarterly* 38, 3 (1975): 269–80.

113 See Renisa Mawani, "Legal Geographies of Aboriginal Segregation in British Columbia: The Making and Unmaking of the Songhees Reserve, 1850–1911," in *Isolation: Places and Practices of Exclusion,* ed. Carolyn Strange and Alison Bashford (New York: Routledge, 2003). Even the Douglas years, which were arguably less violent than the years that followed, "deployed an elaborate theatre of power that in its milder representations was expressed in dress, present giving, speech making, and ceremonial cannonades; and in its more severe in-public beatings and executions conceived as spectacles intended to instill fear ... If trouble brewed in a coastal village, Douglas might send a warship, anchor it just offshore, and have its crew ostentatiously prepare the guns": Harris, "Land Policies," 103. Indeed, this latter tactic was deployed against the Songhees. See James Douglas to F. Victoria Grey, April 15, 1852, CO 305/3, 103–8. See also Perry, "Beyond Biography," 335, emphasizing the violence of Confederation. See also James W. Daschuk, *Clearing the Plains: Disease, Politics of Starvation, and the Loss of Aboriginal Life* (Regina: University of Regina Press, 2013), also cited in Perry, "Beyond Biography," 335.

114 R. Cole Harris, *Making Native Space: Colonialism, Resistance, and Reserves in British Columbia* (Vancouver: UBC Press, 2002).

115 Modern capitalism is not in and of itself a sufficient explanation. The legal systems in the British colonies that ultimately became Canada were sufficiently different from their American analogues that capitalism/commerce does not tell the whole story. Rather, it was capitalism in the context of British imperial culture and the imperatives of the metropole.

116 Mawani, "Legal Geographies," 165.

117 John Garner, *The Franchise and Politics in British North America, 1755–1867,* vol. 13 (Toronto: University of Toronto Press, 1969), 162; Robin Fisher, *Contact and Conflict: Indian-European Relations in British Columbia, 1774–1890* (Vancouver: UBC Press, 1977), 201; and Adele Perry, *On the Edge of Empire: Gender, Race, and the Making of British Columbia, 1849–1871* (Toronto: University of Toronto Press, 2001), 13.

118 See Gough, "Keeping British Columbia British," 113. As described previously, Douglas was especially concerned during the Queen Charlottes Gold Rush, and he wrote to authorities in London that "'American Adventurers' were bound for the island from San Francisco, that their purpose was to dig for gold, and that if they were successful they would colonize the islands 'and establish an independent Government, until by force or by fraud they became annexed to the United States'": ibid., 271–72, quoting a letter from James Douglas to the Earl of Grey, January 29, 1852, copy, Hudson's Bay Company Archives, A 8/6, folio 6.

119 Miller, *Skyscrapers,* 176–78.

120 Concerns about the threat of Russian violence were expressed by the Council of Vancouver Island at various points. See, for example, the minutes from the July 12, 1854, meeting of the council: Hendrickson, *Journals,* 1:14.

121 Of particular concern to Douglas and other settlers was the violence between First Nations in the region. See, for example, Douglas's address to the Vancouver Island Council and Assembly on August 12, 1856: "Gentlemen, The Colony has been again visited this year by a large number of Northern Indians, and their presence has excited in our minds a not unreasonable degree of alarm": Hendrickson, *Journals,* 2:6. For a detailed description of these battles, see Keddie, *Songhees Pictorial,* 34–47. Also of concern were "drunken Indians" that purportedly endangered the peace of the colony: Hendrickson, *Journals,* 1:14–15. A full examination of the social construction of the "drunken Indian" and its attendant consequences is beyond the scope of this essay, but it clearly contributed to the dehumanization of Indigenous people by casting them as immoral and out of control. The evolution of legislation making it illegal to sell alcohol to Indigenous people is documented in the journals and minutes of the Council of Vancouver Island, including both the Executive and Legislative Council, 1851–66: Hendrickson, *Journals,* vol. I.

122 Justification for the dispossession of Indigenous peoples was provided by assumptions about the benefits of "civilizing savages" and of turning wasteful land uses into productive ones: Harris, "Land Policies," 101.

123 At one point, the Council of Vancouver Island considered arming local Indigenous peoples to help protect the colony; however, "it was considered dangerous to arm and drill the natives, who might then become more formidable to the Colony than a foreign enemy": Hendrickson, *Journals,* 1:13.

124 Miller, *Skyscrapers,* 180. See also Douglas's letter of October 14, 1874, to I.W. Powell, Superintendent of Indians (ten years after Douglas retired as governor of British Columbia): "The principle followed in all cases was to leave the extent and selection of the land entirely optional with the Indians who were immediately interested in the Reserve": Harris, *Making Native Space,* 43–44. And see also Douglas's letter of March 14, 1849, to Lytton: "[R]eserves should in all cases include their cultivated fields and village sites, for which from habit and association they invariably conceive a strong attachment": British Columbia, *Papers Connected to the Indian Land Question,* 17.

125 According to novelist and historian Crawford Kilian ("Sir James Douglas and the Black Pioneers," Library and Archives Canada, http://www.collectionscanada.gc.ca/):

> San Francisco's Black community was actively discussing the idea of emigrating to some more welcoming country, and Douglas moved quickly to promote his own colony as a destination. In April 1858, he sent Captain Nagle of the steamer Commodore to San Francisco, inviting Blacks to settle in Victoria.
>
> The community responded at once, delegating 35 Blacks as a "pioneer committee" to inspect the colony. They sailed on the Commodore back to Victoria, arriving on April 25. Three delegates met with Douglas that same day and found him "very cheerful and agreeable."
>
> Douglas glossed over the embarrassing problem of expensive land (prices were set in London). He emphasized that all landowners would have the right to vote and sit on juries. After seven years, he promised, they could become British subjects with all rights and privileges. Until then, they would enjoy the full protection of the law.

According to Kilian, approximately four hundred families eventually immigrated to Vancouver Island, immediately building a community and contributing as labourers and business owners in the new economy of the colony: "In the crucial early years of British Columbia's existence as a colony, the Black settlers provided Douglas with a 'most orderly and useful and loyal section of the community,' as the widow of polar explorer Sir John Franklin observed when she met some of them in 1861. They were to provide a solid centre of political gravity in the colony, and they helped to define the terms on which it entered Confederation in 1872 [sic]" (ibid.). Interestingly, these families represented the first large wave of African Americans to settle in what would become Canada. While they had been assured there would be no legal discrimination against them, they in fact encountered many instances and kinds of racism in the new colony.

126 *Dred Scott v Sandford,* 60 US 393 (1857).

127 Gough, "Keeping British Columbia British," 273.

128 James Douglas, 1857, cited in Keddie, *Songhees Pictorial,* 44.

129 There are many excellent articles and books exploring the ways in which Indigenous identity and indigeneity have been socially constructed and imposed in Canada and the United States. See, for example, Rebecca Tsosie, "American Indians and the Politics of Recognition: Soifer on Law, Pluralism, and Group Identity," *Law and Social Inquiry* 22, 2 (1997): 363: "Tribal identity ... is both socially and politically constructed. The term *tribe* can be understood to refer to an ethnologically defined group and also a legally recognized political entity, although the two uses of the word do not always coincide. The law has been a powerful influence on American Indian political identity, from defining the groups with which the United States would enter into treaties and which were eligible to reside on trust 'reservations,' to contemporary concepts of 'Indigenous rights' that tend to 'encourage the formation of coalition groups that cross tribal lines,' thereby fostering 'a sense of political identity beyond the individual's tribe.'" See also Colin Samson and Carlos Gigoux, *Indigenous Peoples and Colonialism: Global Perspectives* (Cambridge, MA: Polity Press, 2017), 1–37.

130 I am using *citizen* in its broadest sense to include something like "British subject," even though the meaning of both terms was in flux during this period.

131 Mawani, *Colonial Proximities,* and "Legal Geographies." On the creation and enforcement of racism through law, see Constance Backhouse, *Colour-Coded: A Legal History of Racism in Canada, 1900–1950* (Toronto: University of Toronto Press, 1999).

132 A brief but succinct description of this history may be found online in William B. Henderson, "Indian Act," *Canadian Encyclopedia,* 2006 (updated October 23, 2018), http://www.thecanadianencyclopedia.ca/en/article/indian-act/.

133 Quoted in Henderson, "Indian Act."

134 James Douglas, *Report of a Canoe Expedition along the East Coast of Vancouver Island* (London: Royal Geographical Society, 1854), 246. In that same report, he describes another First Nation as friendly as well. In fact, it is a word that shows up in the governor's references to First Peoples throughout his career. See, for example, James Douglas, "Opening of the Third General Assembly of Vancouver Island, September 3, 1863," in James E. Hendrickson, ed., *Journals of the Colonial Legislatures of the Colonies of Vancouver Island and British Columbia, 1851–1871,* 4 vols. (Victoria: Provincial Archives of British Columbia, 1980), 3:7.

135 Hendrickson, *Journals,* 1:246, 249.

136 Ibid., 3:7.

137 Ibid., 1:239.

138 Douglas to Lytton, March 14, 1859, British Columbia, *Papers Connected to the Indian Land Question,* 16–17. According to Cole Harris, Douglas's "views on Native people turned on the following assumptions: Native peoples were as able as any others; their assimilation into non-Native society was possible, beneficial, and their only possible future in a settler colony; and during an inevitable period of transition they required the means to support themselves": "Land Policies," 103.

139 British Columbia, *Papers Connected to the Indian Land Question,* 16.

140 Ibid., 17.

141 Ibid. Paul Tennant suggests that "[b]y 'self-government' Douglas plainly meant that of the individual, not of communities": *Aboriginal Peoples,* 244.

142 Douglas's use of the word *savage* here would not have precisely the same meaning as it might today, but it undoubtedly reflected his view that Indigenous peoples were largely "uncivilized" and provides a good example of how "humanizing" and "dehumanizing" discourses related to Indigenous peoples coexisted in the colonial cultural lexicon.

143 Tennant, *Aboriginal Peoples,* 37; and Harris, *Making Native Space,* 35–36.

144 Harris, "Land Policies," 107, 116, quoting Douglas. These rights were taken away from Indigenous peoples after Douglas retired. See Foster, "British Columbia," 310; and Harris, *Making Native Space,* 43–44.

145 Douglas to Newcastle, March 25, 1861, British Columbia, *Papers Connected to the Indian Land Question,* 19.

146 "Despatch No. 114 from Douglas to Lytton, March 14, 1859," in British Columbia, *Papers Connected to the Indian Land Question,* 16. It would be ironic if it were not so tragic, but of course it was colonization itself that produced systems of "oppression and rapid decay."

147 See, for example, "Despatch No. 62 from the Right Hon. Sir Bartholomew E.B. Lytton to Governor Douglas, December 30, 1858," in British Columbia, *Papers Connected to the Indian Land Question,* 15: "The success that has attended your transactions with these tribes induces me to inquire if you think it might be feasible to settle them permanently in villages; *with such settlement civilization at once begins.* Law and Religion would become naturally introduced amongst the red men, and contribute to their own security against the aggressions of immigrants," emphasis added. See also Douglas's response, "Despatch No. 114, March 14, 1859": "I conceive the proposed plan to be at once feasible, and also the only plan which promises to result in the

moral elevation of the native Indian races, in rescuing them from degradation, and protecting them from oppression and rapid decay," ibid., 12, emphasis added. See also "Despatch No. 49 from the Secretary of State for the Colonies to Governor Douglas, April 11, 1859": "Especially I would enjoin upon you, and all in authority in both colonies, the importance of establishing schools of an industrial as well as an educational character for the Indians, whereby they *may acquire the arts of civilized life* which will enable them to support themselves, and not degenerate into the mere recipients of eleemosynary relief," ibid., 18, emphasis added. Finally, see "Despatch No. 61 from the Right Hon. Sir E.B. Lytton, Bart., to Governor Douglas, May 20, 1859": "locating the Indians in native villages, with a view to their protection and civilization," ibid., 18.

148 The violence of the miners, in particular, was feared. See, for example, Aborigines Protection Society to E.B. Lytton, August 10, 1858: "The reckless inhumanity of the gold diggers of [California] toward the unfortunate Indians, is thus described in a recent number of the *New York Times:* 'It is the custom of miners generally to shoot an Indian as he would a dog; and it is considered a very good joke to shoot at one at long shot, to see him jump as the fatal bullet pierces his heart. And when, in the spirit of retaliation, some poor hunted relative watches his opportunity, and attacks a straggling white man, the papers at once teem with long accounts of Indian outrages ... There never existed so bad a set of men on the face of this fair earth as a certain class of the highly respectable sovereigns of the states who find their way to the frontiers'": British Columbia, *Papers Connected to the Indian Land Question.*

149 Only in British Columbia and Nova Scotia, for example, were "Indians" specifically disenfranchised. See Garner, *The Franchise,* 218.

150 Garner cites the example of Governor Seymour's response to the so-called Chilcotin Uprising of 1864: "Governor Seymour informed the secretary of state for the colonies that he might 'find [him]self compelled to follow in the footsteps of the Governor of Colorado ... and invite every white man to shoot each Indian he may meet. Such a proclamation would not be badly received here ... ' Cardwell replied that he did not understand what Seymour meant, and that he was to do no such thing": ibid., 306.

151 Mawani, "Legal Geographies," 169: "The local press played a pivotal role in fuelling discourses of racial degeneracy ... Through stories ... local newspapers (re)constituted and reinforced derogatory images of the Songhees reserve and its inhabitants. The reserve came to signify a perilous zone, a place of racial disorder where 'savage' Indians practised their 'uncivilized' customs, a space where whites could never be safe."

152 Mawani, "Legal Geographies."

153 While many of Douglas's own colleagues disagreed with him, there were still some who supported his approach. See, for example, "Despatch from Then Colonial Secretary, E.B. Lytton, to Douglas, July 31, 1858": "I have to enjoin upon you to consider the best and most humane means of dealing with the Native Indians. The feelings of this country would be strongly opposed to the adoption of any arbitrary or oppressive measures towards them ... *[Y]ou will pay every regard to the interests of the Natives which an enlightened humanity can suggest,*" emphasis added, British Columbia, *Papers Connected to the Indian Land Question,* 12. See also Aborigines Protection Society to E.B. Lytton, forwarded to Douglas by Lytton in "Despatch no. 12," September 2, 1858 (ibid., 13, emphasis added):

> The Indians, being *a strikingly acute and intelligent race of men,* are keenly sensitive to their own rights as the aborigines of the country, and are equally alive to the value of the gold discoveries ...

> As therefore, the Indians possess an intelligent knowledge of their own rights, and appear to be determined to maintain them by all the means in their powers … [T]he English Government should be prepared *to deal with their claims in a broad spirit of justice and liberality.*

154 On the perspective of California miners who did not respect English law and had no plans to obey it, see Gough, "Keeping British Columbia British," 269.

155 Foster, "British Columbia," 322.

156 Sections 1 and 8, Aliens Act, 1859, in British Columbia, *Papers Connected to the Indian Land Question.*

157 In the words of the Council of Vancouver Island: "Such a measure might pave the way for the adoption of the widest form of the subject which was expressed in the principle that all persons should be allowed to deal in land & to hold & transfer landed property with the same liberty & facility as in any other article of merchandise": Hendrickson, *Journals,* 1:23.

158 Foster provides a thoughtful account and analysis in "British Columbia," 326–28.

159 See "Theoretical Framework and Definitions," this chapter.

160 Dorothy Blakey-Smith, ed., *The Reminiscences of Doctor John Sebastian Helmcken,* vol. 1 (Vancouver: UBC Press/Provincial Archives of British Columbia, 1975), 326.

161 Evidence of practices of dehumanization also gives us important information about the observer, suggesting their ideal human: the person against whom all others are being measured.

162 I do not mean to suggest these groups were alike in other ways. Indigenous peoples were victims of colonial violence and oppression. Miners, on the other hand, were encroaching on traditional Indigenous Territories to exploit natural resources for their own gain. I only mean to draw attention to the fact that both groups were regularly dehumanized by settlers and colonial officers; at the same time, Douglas – perhaps uniquely – believed in their potential humanness.

163 Harris, "Land Policies," 104.

164 *Merriam-Webster.com,* s.v. "humanity," accessed September 27, 2019.

165 *Dictionary.com,* s.v. "humanity," accessed September 27, 2019.

166 Keddie reminds us that "[w]hen we say the Songhees are a Coast Salish people, we mean that they are one of many coastal groups whose language shares a common origin." But he also reminds us that "[t]his is equivalent to saying English is part of the Indo-European language family that includes most languages in Europe and others with a common origin stretching across Turkey and India": Keddie, *Songhees Pictorial,* 13.

167 Wayne Suttles would describe the Halkomelem-Straits region as the "Central Coast Salish," of which the Songhees Nation is one. I am guided by his reasoning and focus therefore on this region. See Wayne P. Suttles, *Coast Salish Essays* (Vancouver: Talonbooks, 1987).

168 See Brian Thom, "Entanglements in Coast Salish Ancestral Territories," in *Entangled Territories: Negotiating Indigenous Lands in Australia and Canada,* ed. Françoise Dussart and Sylvie Poirier (Toronto: University of Toronto Press, 2017), 159–82.

169 Miller, "Rereading," 306. Prior forms of justice practice, for example, are often attenuated and overlaid by new practices and concepts. See also ibid., 312.

170 Lutz, "First Contact," 35.

171 Keith Thor Carlson, "Reflections on Indigenous History and Memory: Reconstructing and Reconsidering Contact," in Lutz, *Myth and Memory,* 46–68. See also Patrick Moore, "Humour and Power in Kaska Contact Narratives," in Lutz, *Myth and Memory,* 70.

172 Although everyone has all four components, "they are not well integrated in the young, the feeble, the ill, and others who are consequently vulnerable to spiritual dangers": Miller, "Rereading," 313.

173 Albert (Sonny) Naxaxalhts'I McHalsie, "We Have to Take Care of Everything That Belongs to Us," in Miller, *Be of Good Mind,* 104.
174 Miller, "Rereading," 313.
175 Ibid.
176 McHalsie, "We Have to Take Care," 104.
177 Miller, "Rereading," 314. While not everyone had access to spiritual power, Miller notes that "[v]irtually all appropriate adults had access to spiritual power of some sort," and "[t]hose without spiritual helpers were thought to be insignificant and weak."
178 Sylvie Poirier, "The Dynamic Reproduction of Hunter-Gatherers' Ontologies and Values," in *A Companion to the Anthropology of Religion,* ed. Janice Boddy and Michael Lambek (New York: John Wiley and Sons, 2013), 50–68.
179 McHalsie, "We Have to Take Care," 104.
180 Grant R. Keddie, *Supplement to the 2003 Book – Songhees Pictorial: A History of the Songhees People as Seen by Outsiders, 1790–1912,* Royal BC Museum, 83–84, http://staff.royalbcmuseum.bc.ca/wp-content/uploads/2013/08/Songhees_supplement-Grant-Keddie.pdf.
181 Ibid., 84.
182 McHalsie, "We Have to Take Care," 104.
183 Ibid., 106. See also John Elliott, nephew-in-law of Songhees Chief David Latass, who said: "When Douglas said we should fish and hunt as formerly, that's what it means. You have a sacred responsibility to do this, to look after our land. We even refer to the islands as our relatives." Cited in Sarah Petrescu, "Lost in Translation: The Douglas Treaties," *Times Colonist,* February 19, 2017, https://www.timescolonist.com/islander/lost-in-translation-the-douglas-treaties-1.10099656.
184 Miller, "Rereading," 313.
185 Keith Thor Carlson, "Toward an Indigenous Historiography: Events, Migrations, and the Formation of 'Post-Contact' Coast Salish Collective Identities," in Miller, *Be of Good Mind,* 147.
186 McHalsie, "We Have to Take Care," 98.
187 Carlson, "Indigenous Historiography," 150, citing Suttles, *Coast Salish Essays.*
188 In the Halq'eméylem language, the word for slaves is *sky'iyéth:* ibid., 150.
189 Ibid., 159.
190 Interestingly, Carlson tells us that the word for lower-class people was *s'texem,* which translates into "worthless people" because they have "lost or forgotten their history." In other words, s'texem were "history-less." See Carlson, "Reflections on Indigenous History," 49.
191 Conversely, the Halq'eméylem word for upper-class people – *smela:lh* – translates into "worthy people": ibid., 48–50.
192 Miller, "Rereading," 314.
193 I say this even though personhood is also a cluster or umbrella concept: Ohlin, "Is the Concept of the Person Necessary?," 229–30. But in the case of legal personhood, the components look very different from those contained by *human,* as that word or concept might have been used by the Songhees.
194 *Things,* like *objects,* does not feel like a satisfactory term or concept in this context, but I use it rather clumsily to signify things Europeans would have regarded as not living, such as rocks.
195 Again, it is not easy to describe these concepts in English, but when I say "move back and forth between" I want to be careful not to suggest that the worlds were entirely separate but instead to call attention to the fact there was no firm divide between them. In that sense, it was one "world" with several dimensions or registers.

196 "We even refer to the islands as our relatives": Latass, in Petrescu, "Lost in Translation," https://www.timescolonist.com/islander/lost-in-translation-the-douglas-treaties-1.10099656. See also Brian Thom, "Entanglements in Coast Salish Ancestral Territories," in Dussart and Poirier, *Entangled Territories,* 159, describing the spirit snake.

197 Lutz, "Introduction," 2.

198 See the "Principles of Reconciliation" that guided the work of Canada's Truth and Reconciliation Commission, especially Principles 3 and 10: "3. Reconciliation is a process of healing of relationships that requires public truth sharing, apology, and commemoration that acknowledge … past harms," and "10. Reconciliation requires sustained public education and dialogue … about the history and legacy of … Treaties, and Aboriginal rights": Truth and Reconciliation Commission of Canada, *What We Have Learned: Principles of Truth and Reconciliation,* 2015, 3–4, http://nctr.ca/assets/reports/Final%20Reports/Principles_English_Web.pdf.

3

The Imperial Law of Aboriginal Title at the Time of the Douglas Treaties

Hamar Foster

"The law is a hard, queer thing. I do not understand it."

– Poundmaker, a Cree Chief, addressing the court at his trial for treason, August 17, 1885

In 1846, Great Britain and the United States decided that the forty-ninth parallel would be the boundary between British and American territory west of the Rockies and that this boundary would dip south of forty-nine degrees in order to include Vancouver Island within British North America.[1] The British established a colony on the Island in 1849 and a second colony on the Mainland – British Columbia – in 1858. The latter absorbed the former in 1866 and this new, larger entity joined the Canadian federation in 1871. In 1997, the Supreme Court of Canada decided that 1846 was the effective date of British sovereignty and was therefore the critical year for establishing Aboriginal title in British Columbia.[2]

In 1910, however, the *Victoria Daily Colonist* had already stated its position on this issue. The Crown had acquired sovereignty over British Columbia by settlement, the editors declared, and "the acquisition of that sovereignty extinguished *ipso facto* every right or claim that may have been held or enjoyed by present occupation or immemorial possession by any other sovereign people, or tribe. This is no new principle. It is as old as history itself."[3]

Almost all of this statement is untrue.[4] It was, nonetheless, a common misunderstanding among non-Indigenous British Columbians at the time, and the editors' decision to express it so forcefully may have been in response to an interview the newspaper had published only a week earlier. The interviewer had asked some members of the Nisga'a Land Committee why they thought their case for Aboriginal, or as it was then called "Indian," title was solid. The men's initial response was to quote scripture

(Deuteronomy 27:17: "Cursed is he that removeth his neighbour's landmark") and to assure the reporter that their title would be recognized because "God hates injustice." The reporter was not impressed, commenting that, if this was the only argument they had, they were in trouble. He asked if they had anything more. Yes, they replied, the Royal Proclamation of 1763, which they quoted and correctly claimed as having "the effect and operation" of an imperial statute. They continued in this vein, citing other statutes, the Vancouver Island (or Douglas) Treaties and more. The reporter was clearly gobsmacked: "I'm a white man and yet I had no idea of what you are telling me – how do you know?"[5] So they told him: they had a good lawyer.

I suspect that the editors' contrary view still slumbers on in the brainpans of some people, occasionally kicking into explanatory gear when the noise generated by a headline or sound bite wakes it up. It is therefore important to understand the reasons people thought this and why some may continue to do so.

There are obvious reasons, of course, ones associated with racism (or at least prejudice and ethnocentrism), competition for land, inadequate education, and so on. But there is another reason, one that may be less dramatic than racial prejudice and land hunger but that is nonetheless important. It is the fact that, if governments refused to acknowledge that Indigenous peoples had a legal interest in their traditional lands, there was really only one way to oblige them to do so: by going to court. However, this course of action faced a formidable legal obstacle. That obstacle was the doctrine of sovereign, or Crown, immunity from suit, which required anyone wishing to sue the Crown to first seek the Crown's permission to do so. This immunity is therefore critically relevant to any attempt to answer the question, What was the imperial law of Aboriginal title at the time of the Douglas Treaties? and to appreciate why all of us – like Chief Poundmaker – may find legal understanding somewhat elusive.

In what follows I propose, first, to start at what is in a sense the end of the story: the decision of the Supreme Court of Canada in the *Calder* case in 1973 (which also marked the beginning of another story, one that is still unfolding).[6] This involves examining the doctrine of sovereign immunity and what lawyers refer to as the *ratio decidendi* of *Calder*.[7] Then I will attempt to answer the question above by looking at documents and records, published and archival, in which the matter of Indian title is addressed, from the fur trade era to the early twentieth century. These include everything from imperial statutes and fur trade cases to legal opinions and litigation over settler land rights. This winding road through such a variety of sources will help to explain why reaching a conclusion is not as straightforward a task as it should be. And why the flawed understanding of title and sovereignty displayed by the *Daily Colonist* in 1910 has had such a long life.

Calder v British Columbia

The significance of the *Calder* case, which the Supreme Court decided in 1973, is well known. Six of the seven justices were of the view that Aboriginal title was – and, by inference, always had been – part of the law of Canada. Three of those six said that the title of the Nisga'a plaintiffs – the descendants of the men who had so perplexed the staff of the *Daily Colonist* sixty-three years earlier – had never been extinguished. This prompted Prime Minister Pierre Trudeau to concede that "perhaps" the Nisga'a had more "legal rights" than he had thought.[8] Indeed, by the 1960s, the view expressed in 1910 by the *Daily Colonist* had become so ingrained that the Court of Appeal in *Calder* had pretty much adopted it when that court heard the case in 1969; virtually every First Nation other than the Nisga'a expressed reservations about an appeal to the Supreme Court of Canada.[9] So a certain amount of surprise was justified when the Supreme Court's decision, along with developments in the courts respecting the Cree of James Bay, prompted the federal government to reverse course and initiate, for the first time, a comprehensive land claims policy for the country. The case is what is referred to colloquially as a "game changer."

However, what is less well known outside specialist legal circles is that the views described above were not the ratio decidendi of the *Calder* decision; that is, they were *obiter dicta*, or nonbinding comments, and did not constitute the binding proposition of law for which the case stood. The ratio of the case is to be found in the reasons of the seventh justice, with whom three of the others agreed. And he ruled that he could not address the merits of the case because the plaintiffs were not properly before the court: that is, they did not have the permission of the provincial government to sue. This was so even though the Nisga'a were not seeking a concrete remedy such as compensatory damages or an injunction but simply wanted a declaration that their title had never been extinguished.[10] So the ratio of the case, agreed to by four justices out of seven, is simply that, without the provincial government explicitly permitting the action, the merits could not be heard.

Sovereign Immunity

This reasoning reflects a basic reality of the common-law tradition for most of its existence: the doctrine of sovereign immunity. Subjects (whether Indigenous or non-Indigenous) were free to sue one another but could not sue the Crown without a *fiat* from the attorney general, that is, without the Crown's permission; the attorney general would issue a fiat authorizing the suit only if he concluded that it had merit.[11] In the twentieth century, jurisdiction after jurisdiction repealed the doctrine. In Canada, British Columbia was the last to do so, in 1974 – too late for the Nisg̲a'a.[12] Because the province had a long history of opposing any and all attempts to have the courts decide the "BC Indian Land Question," the Nisg̲a'a had not sought a fiat, and the four-to-three decision in *Calder* was the result.[13]

For more than a decade after 1973, the BC government took the position that, because the ratio of the Supreme Court decision said nothing about Aboriginal title, the law in British Columbia was what the provincial Court of Appeal in *Calder* had held it to be. And that court had stated that Aboriginal rights or title did not exist at common law but had to be supported by a legislative pronouncement, a prerogative act (such as a treaty), or some "course of dealing that has been proved from which that can be inferred."[14] As there was neither legislation nor a treaty, and no such course of dealing had been proved at trial, the Nisg̲a'a had lost.

However, in 1986 the Court of Appeal put paid to this argument and disowned its earlier decision. Noting that for some years the provincial government had taken the position that the decision in *Calder* had been unaffected by that of the Supreme Court of Canada, the court said this was a "fallacy."

> The judgment of this court in *Calder* has not, since the pronouncement of the judgment of the Supreme Court of Canada in the same case, been binding on anyone ... The view that [it] remains binding is apparently based on a misapplication of the rule that, where a court composed of an even number of judges divides equally on the question whether the appeal should be allowed, the judgment of the final court is one dismissing the appeal. So the result is that the judgment of the lower court is upheld. It does not follow that, where the judges in the highest court divide equally in their reasons for judgment, those reasons are to be treated as if they did not exist. Even less can the equal division on certain issues justify ignoring the agreement

> of a majority in rejecting a conclusion of the lower court. Six judges of the Supreme Court having joined in rejecting the view that aboriginal title can exist only if conferred by a treaty, statute or agreement, there can be no justification for continuing to treat that view as binding.[15]

Why have I gone on about this? For three reasons. First of all, to note that as late as 1973 the doctrine of sovereign immunity from suit was alive and well in British Columbia. Second, to emphasize that the Supreme Court of Canada in that year was clearly (six to one) of the view that Aboriginal title is a doctrine that is part of Canadian law (notwithstanding that the court also held that it had no authority to adjudicate the dispute between the Nisga'a and the province in the absence of a fiat). And, third, to make the point that, because no one could sue the Crown without permission in British Columbia until 1974, and because, relatively early on, the province set its face against having the courts address Aboriginal title, the task of ascertaining what the law was in British Columbia in 1846 is not a straightforward one. *Calder* was in fact the first time the courts considered the issue of whether there was unextinguished Aboriginal title in British Columbia – well over a century after 1846.[16] Still, decisions of BC courts are not the only place to look for law.

The Law in 1846

The first thing to acknowledge in addressing this issue is that obviously more than one legal system is relevant. Wherever an imperial power penetrated and set itself up in Indigenous territory the same issue arose: whose system of law governed – European, Indigenous, or international – and to what extent?[17] The answer may have seemed obvious to many imperial officials, but the choice was often obscured by terminology based on implicit assumptions. Thus, the conflict between the British and a confederation of tribes that erupted in 1763–64 after the defeat of the French in North America is often referred to in the literature as "Pontiac's Rebellion" – which is accurate only if one assumes that this was an insurrection against a lawful British regime rather than resistance to an invader. Similarly, colonial authorities originally referred to the conflict that developed in the Chilcotin region of British Columbia in 1864 as the "Chilcotin War." But when these same authorities came to deal with the captured Tŝilhqot'in warriors, they had to re-characterize the conflict as an uprising against the legitimate government of the colony in order to justify hanging the warriors as criminals and murderers rather than treating them as prisoners of war.[18] The point for present purposes is this: although more than one legal system is relevant to this inquiry, I am confining myself to the statute law and the common law of the empire claiming sovereignty, that is, the British Empire.[19]

Of course, questions to be answered must first be asked. If the questions are difficult legal ones, this usually means submitting them to a court competent to answer them – if there is such a court. And even if there is, not only were Indigenous peoples in nineteenth-century British Columbia generally without the resources to litigate – not to mention pursue a case all the way to the Judicial Committee of the Privy Council in England – but the doctrine of sovereign immunity from suit stood in the way.

Still, until colonies were established, the Indian Territories were well described by their name, which is at least as old as the Royal Proclamation of 1763: apart from a relatively small number of fur traders, they were, after all, the *Indian* Territories.[20] There were no courts or legislatures and, except for Oregon after the mid-1830s, no settlers.[21] There was, however, a form of long-distance justice in this vast region, the records of which are generally to be found in archives and special collections rather than conventional law reports. And some of these are judicial decisions, mainly criminal ones, with respect to the Indian Territories said to be under British jurisdiction – although their number is few and they do not deal, at least not directly, with land title.

Imperial law in British North America depended on geography, and the political, and therefore legal, geography of British North America when the Treaty of Washington (the "Oregon Treaty") was signed in 1846 was as follows. In the east there was (1) Canada, which included the old Upper Canada and Lower Canada, both of which were much smaller than Ontario and Quebec are today; and (2) the colonies on the Atlantic coast.[22] In most of these colonies, English law applied by virtue of a legal fiction: in settled colonies, British settlers were said to have brought their law with them, which was usually acknowledged after the fact by the enactment of a local statute that set a precise reception date.[23] The colonists in such settler colonies were also entitled to a representative assembly, unless the imperial Parliament provided otherwise (which it did in the case of British Columbia in 1858). An exception was Quebec, where, after a difficult hiatus, French civil law coexisted with English criminal law.[24]

West of Canada, which is to say west of the former Upper Canada's vague western boundary, there were two legally distinct but geographically somewhat fluid regions where the applicability of English law was less clear. The easternmost was Rupert's Land, granted by the Crown to the Hudson's Bay Company (HBC) in 1670. Defined in its Charter of Grant as comprising all the land whose rivers drained into Hudson Bay, Rupert's Land was a proprietary, as opposed to a Crown, colony that supposedly extended west of Canada as far as the Rockies in the south. It also included most of what are now northern Ontario, northern Quebec, and Labrador. Because the charter required the company's laws to be reasonable and not contrary to the laws of England, and required the company to judge cases according to the laws of England, it can for present purposes be assumed that English law, as modified by HBC law, applied to the traders and settlers in Rupert's Land. But the details are controversial.[25]

Beyond Rupert's Land, "westward to the western shores of America" and "northward to the Frozen Ocean" were the "Indian Territories," which included Vancouver Island and what would become British Columbia.[26] Significant portions of this region were at various times claimed by Spain, Britain, Russia, and the United States. These competing claims were resolved in stages, and eventually all land west of the Great Lakes and north of the forty-ninth parallel – plus that portion of Vancouver Island south of it – was acknowledged by the other European claimants to be British. But until colonies were established, the lands west of Rupert's Land remained the Indian Territories.

One legal difference between Rupert's Land and the Indian Territories was that the HBC, by virtue of its charter, had legislative and judicial authority in the former that it did not enjoy in the latter. Even when the company acquired the exclusive right to trade with the "Indians" of the Indian Territories in 1821, this difference remained. Another difference, not apparent at first, was that the imperial statutes discussed below may not have applied to Rupert's Land in the way they applied in the Indian Territories.

A final complicating factor is that in 1818, when Great Britain and the United States settled on the forty-ninth parallel as the international boundary, they could not agree on where the boundary was on the Pacific Coast. They therefore decided that they would jointly occupy Oregon until this question could be settled. After 1818, Oregon, which stretched from Spanish California in the south to Russian Alaska in the north, was therefore really a third region. It was within the Indian Territories, but until the boundary of the forty-ninth parallel was extended to the coast in 1846, both Great Britain and the United States claimed sovereignty.

Until 1849, Vancouver Island was therefore part of the Indian Territories of British North America. As such, it became subject to two imperial statutes, the Canada Jurisdiction Act of 1803 and the Regulation of the Fur Trade Act of 1821.[27] The first of these statutes was a response to fur trade violence and the perception that crimes committed in the Indian Territories were "not cognizable by any Jurisdiction whatever." The Act therefore made provision for trying such cases in the courts of Upper and Lower Canada and for the appointment of justices of the peace for the Indian Territories. It was not a success. The HBC and the North West Company disagreed as to whether the company's ineffective judicial authority over serious crimes in Rupert's Land had been superseded by the Act, and this generated numerous legal opinions and courtroom arguments. What was even more disruptive, both fur companies used the Act and the justices of the peace whose appointment it authorized as weapons in their trade war.

The imperial Parliament tried again in 1821 with the Regulation of the Fur Trade Act, which, among other things, authorized the Crown to appoint trial judges with authority to hear civil and criminal causes in both Rupert's Land and the Indian Territories. None were ever appointed. The new Act also obliged the HBC to produce malefactors for trial and to send important civil cases (of which there were none) and capital cases to Upper Canada.[28] This statute was more successful than the Canada Jurisdiction Act but not, in my view, because of its highly theoretical judicial provisions. The reason for its success is that the North West Company and the HBC merged in 1821 under the name of the latter, and the Act authorized the Crown to grant an exclusive licence to trade with "the Indians" in all parts of North America except Rupert's Land (where the HBC already had such rights). When the Crown granted an exclusive, twenty-one-year licence to this new company, which was really an expanded HBC, the resulting monopoly ensured an era of relative peace. In 1838, the licence was renewed for a further twenty-one-year term, to end in 1859.

These developments also sharpened the legal distinction between Rupert's Land and the Indian Territories because, as I state above, the HBC had title and legislative and judicial authority in the former, but in the Indian Territories it was simply a licensee with certain law enforcement obligations.[29] Nonetheless, the company's unchallenged authority now extended, in one form or another, all the way to the Pacific in the west and the Arctic in the north.[30]

Because of these legal considerations, the letters patent granting the conditional fee in Vancouver Island to the HBC in 1849 were accompanied by an imperial statute that repealed the long-distance justice of the 1803 Act and the judicial portions of the 1821 Act in the colony. It also authorized the imperial Crown (and, once an assembly was summoned, the colonial legislature) to make laws and provide for a judiciary.[31] The grant itself was in free and common socage, and it, too, reflected the pre-existing state of the law, in that it reserved a right in the Crown to repurchase the fee from the HBC when its licence to trade with the Indians expired.[32] The grant also reserved a right in the Crown to revoke if, within five years, the HBC did not satisfactorily meet the condition of the grant, which was to colonize the Island.[33]

The grant was, in other words, a temporary measure, and everyone knew this. Many of the senior officers of the company in New Caledonia and the Columbia Department thought that combining settlement with the fur trade would never work; the Colonial Office knew that a quasi-proprietary colony was an anachronistic throwback to the seventeenth century that would last only so long as the colonists were "too few and feeble to shake it off"; and the metropolitan press was, if anything, even more skeptical.[34] As *The Times* put it, the HBC was a company of "fur traders and monopolists, and in neither capacity can they give hearty encouragement to the pursuits of civilized or colonial life." Such people "want beavers and sables to multiply, hunting grounds to be preserved, and hunters and trappers to thrive. Their function is to perpetuate what it should be the aim of a colony to destroy."[35] In fact, by then the HBC was diversifying into fisheries, cranberries, and agriculture, and the fur trade on Vancouver Island had never amounted to much; indeed, if anything hindered the colonization of the Island, it was the Wakefieldian approach to land sales opposed by Governor James Douglas but foisted on him by the Colonial Office.[36] Nonetheless, this was its image, and it took its toll: until gold was discovered on the Mainland in 1858, the settler population of Vancouver Island was negligible.

The HBC had fended off challenges to its charter almost since its inception, and as enthusiasm for free trade peaked in the nineteenth century, opposition to the company's monopoly intensified. The Province of Canada's designs on Rupert's Land and complaints about HBC rule in both Red River and Vancouver Island fuelled this opposition and led to a parliamentary inquiry. When the select committee that conducted the inquiry recommended in 1857 that the company's connection with the

Island be terminated "as soon as it can conveniently be done," the end was foretold.[37] On the expiration of the HBC's licence to trade in 1859, the Crown exercised its right to repurchase the Island.[38]

Title to the Soil of the Indian Territories

During the fur trade era, conflict between the various trading concerns before 1821 and a few isolated homicides between 1821 and 1849 had generated cases for the courts of Upper and Lower Canada to hear. In addition to the merits, all involved questions of jurisdiction and constitute a primary, if limited, source of legal argument about the relationship between British law and sovereignty, on the one hand, and Indigenous law and sovereignty, on the other. As such, they shed some light on the legal status of the dispute-resolution mechanisms and land tenures of Indigenous peoples after Britain asserted its sovereignty over the Indian Territories but before the establishment of actual colonies. I have canvassed these cases in some detail elsewhere and give only the briefest summary here.[39]

What is striking in these records is the vigour with which distinguished counsel argued, especially before the boundary treaty between Britain and the United States in 1818, that the Indian Territories were "Indian" in the fullest sense; that is, that the imperial Parliament could not legislate with respect to them because they were not part of His Majesty's Dominions. Although unsuccessful, these arguments were taken seriously, and, at one point, even the Colonial Office expressed the opinion that the Indian Territories were, in law, Indian, not British.[40]

On the question of title to the soil, the consensus was in favour of some sort of Indian title, as it was referred to at the time. The Earl of Selkirk, for example, made treaty in 1817 with the Cree and Saulteaux for rights to the land that he had already purchased from the HBC.[41] Other evidence of title comes from a number of cases that arose out of the destruction of Selkirk's Red River Settlement and the "massacre" at Seven Oaks in 1816. Although these confirmed the sovereignty of the Crown, after one of them, Chief Justice William Dummer Powell reported to the lieutenant-governor of Upper Canada that "the soil was in the aborigines and inhabited only by the Indians and their lawless followers."[42] This was the accepted opinion at the time, although those who had actual contact with the Indigenous inhabitants knew better than to describe them as lawless.

The principle that "the soil was in the aborigines" is consistent with the well-known civil case of *Connolly v Woolrich,* involving the estate of Governor Douglas's father-in-law. Citing in support a leading US Supreme Court decision, Justice Samuel Cornwallis Monk concluded in 1867 that

> the territorial rights, political organization such as it was ... [and] the laws and usages of the Indian tribes, were [not] abrogated ... when [France and Great Britain] began to trade with them ... In my opinion it is beyond controversy that ... so far from being abolished, they were left in full force, and were not even modified in the slightest degree in regard to the civil rights of the natives.[43]

As a consequence, William Connolly's "country" marriage to his first, Cree wife was ruled valid under Cree law and given priority over his subsequent marriage. Lady Amelia Douglas and her siblings therefore received shares in the estate.

Clearly some sort of Indigenous legal interest, or Indian title, had survived Britain's assertion of sovereignty over the Indian Territories in 1818 and the enactment of imperial legislation in 1803 and 1821 respecting those territories. When the Treaty of Washington with the United States brought the part of the Indian Territories that is now British Columbia (according to European law) within exclusive British jurisdiction in 1846, this change in status had no more effect on Indian title than it did east of the Rockies in 1818. Further, I can find nothing in the imperial legislation or letters patent establishing the Colony of Vancouver Island in 1849 to suggest that such title did not survive colonization.[44] Indeed, the Colonial Office's almost total lack of knowledge concerning the Indigenous peoples of the Island led it to omit any reference to Indian title in the grant – apart from a fond hope that colonization by British settlers would promote "the protection and welfare of the native Indians." But a confidential memorandum raised the issue squarely. In "parting with the land of the island [to the HBC]," it stated, "Her Majesty parts only with her own right therein, and ... whatever measures she was bound to take in order to extinguish the Indian title are equally obligatory on the Company."[45] This memorandum captures both the legal reality of Indian title as a burden on the underlying fee of the Crown and the uncertainty that characterized how the imperial and colonial authorities approached the issue.

For his part, James Douglas was under no illusions concerning the views of the Indigenous inhabitants.[46] In a well-known dispatch he made this clear:

> As the native Indian population of Vancouver Island have distinct ideas of property in land, and mutually recognize their several exclusive possessory rights in certain districts, they would not fail to regard the occupation of such portions of the Colony by white settlers, unless with the full consent of the proprietary tribes, as national wrongs; and the sense of injury might produce a feeling of irritation against the settlers, and perhaps disaffection to the Government that would endanger the peace of the country.[47]

So: imperial legislation and a few cases from the Indian Territories during the fur trade era suggest a consensus that the law recognized some sort of legal interest that Indigenous peoples had in their traditional territories. Is there anything else?

An Interstitial Law of Aboriginal Title

The view that responsibility for the fair treatment of Indigenous peoples lay with the Crown, not the courts, was not only consistent with the Crown's role in imperial expansion but with the doctrine of sovereign immunity described above. But this did not prevent the issue of whether Indigenous peoples had a legal interest in their traditional lands from arising in a number of court cases in the nineteenth century. Nor did it prevent eminent jurists from pronouncing on the issue. Given the limitations imposed by sovereign immunity, how did this happen?

The short answer is that in the United States and in British colonies such as Canada and New Zealand disputes over land titles in the settler community arose in which questions involving the nature of Indigenous land title required an answer. The context of such cases was often a dispute between a settler who had purchased a parcel of land directly from the Indigenous proprietors and a settler who had purchased the same land from the colonial government. The disputants were private citizens, so the doctrine of Crown immunity from suit was not relevant. Even so, these cases were usually test cases facilitated by the colonial government or, less frequently, cases referred by government directly to the courts (the equivalent of a fiat in a case brought by a private citizen).

One of the earliest examples is *Johnson v M'Intosh* in the US Supreme Court in 1823.[48] In that case, the plaintiffs had inherited land purchased before the American Revolution from one of the Amerindian tribes, which apparently had subsequently sold the same land to the new United States government – although these facts may well have been distorted simply to make a test case possible. In any event, the defendant obtained title to the land from that government, and the issue was which party had the better title. The answer the court gave was the one that would become standard: once a European power's claim to sovereignty over a particular territory was recognized, that power had the exclusive right to extinguish the legal interest of the Indigenous proprietors. Therefore, a good title could not be obtained by a colonist directly from such proprietors, and the defendant's title prevailed.

An example from New Zealand is similar, and was decided a year after the Treaty of Washington in 1846 and two years before the establishment of the Colony of Vancouver Island in 1849. In *R (ex rel McIntosh) v Symonds,* the New Zealand Supreme Court had to decide a test case engineered by the colonial government.[49] The background is of interest.

In an effort to encourage land sales at a time when the colonial government did not have adequate resources to buy enough Māori land for resale, the governor had issued pre-emption certificates to purchasers that purported, in such cases, to waive the rule that Māori could sell land only to the government. Concerned about the validity of such waivers, holders of these certificates were "holding out for Crown grants" to land covered by the certificates.[50] The result was "a bitter wrangle within the ... settler community" that the new governor decided had to be authoritatively settled.[51] That the solution was a government test case is clear when one considers who the parties were. On the one side was C. Hunter McIntosh, the holder of a pre-emption certificate who had been secretary to the Land Commission when the previous governor had authorized the certificates. (Indeed, it had been McIntosh's duty to have them copied and registered.) On the other side was John Jermyn Symonds, the native secretary and protector of aborigines, to whom a Crown grant to a portion of the land covered by McIntosh's certificate had been issued in order to create the dispute for court.

In concluding that only the government could give good title to land previously owned by a tribe, the American court in *Johnson v M'Intosh* declared that the Indians had "a *legal* as well as a just claim" to the soil even after Britain had declared itself sovereign over the territory.[52] In like fashion, the New Zealand court asserted that the practice of extinguishing Native title by Crown purchase was "now part of the *law* of the land."[53] In another case, the US Supreme Court ruled that grants of colonies conveyed only "the title which, according to the common law of European sovereigns, they might rightfully convey, and no more [i.e.,] ... the exclusive right of purchasing such lands as the natives are willing to sell."[54] And in yet another, the Indian right of occupancy was said to be "as sacred as the fee simple of the whites."[55] Of course, these pronouncements did not generally affect the tribes involved, who were almost never party to such cases.[56] They had parted with their land years before, and the dispute was simply as to which settler or group of settlers now had good title to it.

Nonetheless, in the course of these proceedings, the judges were invariably obliged to say something about Indigenous title. And when they did, they described it in legal terms. Even if their pronouncements are regarded as *Calder*-like obiter dicta, they categorized the interest that Indigenous peoples had in their lands as a legal one, requiring consensual extinguishment. In this they reflected the wording of the Royal Proclamation of 1763 and often explicitly invoked that document in aid.[57] However, as important as the proclamation is, it did not constitute a waiver of the rule that subjects cannot sue the Crown without permission. It can, therefore, with some justification be said that – paraphrasing Sir Henry Maine – so great was the doctrine of sovereign immunity that the law of Indigenous rights and title has at first the look of being gradually secreted in the interstices of cases about *settler* title to land.[58]

There were no such cases in British Columbia. But there was an interesting development in 1875. After Confederation in 1871, it became clear not only that British Columbia had not extinguished Indian title by treaty but also that the provincial government was unwilling to allot land for Indian reserves that Ottawa considered sufficient. By 1874, the two governments were deadlocked over these issues. In a report dated January 19, 1875, the minister of justice for the Dominion, Telesphore Fournier, expressed concern that an "Indian war" could break out in British Columbia over land policy. He therefore felt it necessary to call the Dominion government's attention "to the legal position of the public lands of the province." In particular, he concluded that British Columbia's Crown Lands Act, 1874 – which ignored the issue of Indian lands and title altogether – was seriously flawed. In doing so, he made reference to a number of authoritative legal sources, including the Royal Proclamation of 1763 and one of the two imperial statutes I discuss earlier.[59]

Although "the honour of the Crown" has not been subjected to close judicial analysis until quite recently, it was a well-established political concept in Fournier's day, and he invoked it.[60] He advised that the Act was

> objectionable, as tending to deal with lands which are assumed to be the absolute property of the province, an assumption which completely ignores, as applicable to the Indians of British Columbia, the honour and good faith with which the Crown has, in all other cases, since its sovereignty of the territories in North America, dealt with their various Indian tribes.[61]

After making reference to section 109 of the British North America Act, Fournier wrote the following:

> *That which has been ordinarily spoken of as the "Indian title" must, of necessity, consist of some species of interest in the lands of British Columbia.* If it is conceded that they have not a freehold in the soil, but that they have an usufruct, a right of occupation or possession of the same for their own use, *then it would seem that these lands of British Columbia are subject, if not to a "trust existing in respect thereof," at least "to an interest other than that of the province alone."*[62]

The Dominion government accepted his advice and disallowed the Crown Lands Act. In 1927, Duncan Campbell Scott, the deputy superintendent general of Indian affairs, quoted from Fournier's memorandum when he appeared before a parliamentary committee. "It would hardly be possible," he said, "to draft a stronger document in support of the claim for an aboriginal title than this document."[63] Indeed. And what is most important is that Fournier, as a senior officer of the Crown, clearly saw himself as under a duty to assert "such *legal and equitable* claims as may be found to exist on the part of the Indians."[64]

As I said, there was no "interstitial" case in British Columbia, but one did arise in Canada towards the end of the nineteenth century, with similar results. At the heart of the issue was section 109 of the British North America Act – the provision that Fournier had referred to in his 1875 opinion. This section provided that Crown lands in each province belonged to the Crown in right of that province, "subject to any Trusts existing in respect thereof, and to any Interest other than that of the Province in the same." In the *St. Catherine's Milling* case in 1888, the Judicial Committee of the Privy Council confirmed Fournier's interpretation, that is, that Indian title is such an interest under section 109, adding that the province could not use the land as a source of revenue until "the Crown is disencumbered of the Indian title."[65] A decade later, the same court stated that "an interest other than that of the province in the same" denoted "some right or interest in a third party, *independent of and capable of being vindicated in competition with the beneficial interest of the ... province.*"[66] Then in 1910 – the same year that the Nisg̲a'a and the *Victoria Daily Colonist* were engaged in debating Indian title – the deputy minister of justice for the Dominion, invoking these decisions, advised Prime Minister Laurier that

> It has been held distinctly by the Judicial Committee of the Privy Council with regard to the Indian title in Ontario and Manitoba, that the Indians have an interest other than that of the Province within the meaning of Section 109 of the British North America Act – an interest which may be indicated [sic] in competition with the beneficial interest of the Province. *If this rule applies as we contend in British Columbia, it would seem to follow that those portions of the Province which have not been ceded or surrendered cannot be open for settlement until competent arrangements are made to secure the rights of the Indians.*[67]

The deputy minister, E.L. Newcombe, KC, wrote this in the course of reporting to Laurier that the deal he had worked out with British Columbia's deputy attorney general to have the BC Indian Land Question referred to the Supreme Court of Canada had been rejected at the last minute by British Columbia's premier, Richard McBride. The premier, no doubt concerned by the attention this issue had been getting over the preceding four years, believed that allowing it to go to court "would jeopardize the very large sums of money already invested in this province by English and other investors." It was simply "too serious a matter to be submitted to the determination of any court, however competent from a legal point of view."[68] When formally advised of McBride's decision, Laurier told the premier that he regretted that he would not agree to have the courts settle this "vexed question," that is, whether in British Columbia "there is such a thing as the Indian title, as we have always understood and applied it, and whether it has been extinguished or not. This is a fair issue and it ought to be met squarely."[69] But it was not to be – at least not in 1910.

In sum, then, the imperial law of Aboriginal title in 1846 appears to have been as follows. There was clearly *some* sort of interest that

Indigenous peoples had in their traditional lands that survived the assertion of European sovereignty and that was recognized by colonial law, but the content and status of that interest was unclear. Although no court in British Columbia squarely addressed the issue until the *Calder* case, courts in other jurisdictions had done so in cases involving disputes between settlers or between governments about title to land. In these cases – only some of which have been canvased here – and in other writings, the interest was described as a legal one, but different approaches to its substantive meaning can be discerned. These approaches often overlap and are rarely found in their pure form, but I think there are essentially three.

Option 1: Aboriginal Title as a Mere Tenancy at Will

This is the view closest to that held by the editors of the *Daily Colonist* in 1910. In essence, it is that Aboriginal title may have a basis in natural law or international law, but it is not an enforceable legal right in Canadian courts. Domestically, it is only a moral right to occupy traditional lands, and such occupation is a mere licence that may be terminated at the "whim of the sovereign." As a consequence, the question of whether Aboriginal title is a right of property (enforceable, as lawyers say, against the whole world, including the Crown) or some lesser right (the violation of which may entitle the rights holder to compensation if it is violated, but not the land itself) does not arise. No *legal* right is involved.

A representative statement of this view may be found in an article in the *Canadian Magazine* in 1920. The author was J.A.J. McKenna, whose many contributions to Canadian Indian policy included negotiating the agreement that had led to the establishment of the McKenna-McBride Commission on Indian reserves in British Columbia in 1912. "Aboriginal title," he wrote, "is not a claim enforcible [sic] at law. The natural law of nations out of which it arises has no court for its enforcement."[70] Treaties are therefore merely matters of political expediency. As Joseph Trutch, the lands and works commissioner, had said fifty years earlier, speaking of the transactions that came to be known as the Douglas Treaties, they had been "made for the purpose of securing friendly relations between [the] Indians and the settlement of Victoria, then in its infancy, and certainly not in acknowledgment of any general title of the Indians to the lands they occupy."[71] Fifty years after McKenna put pen to paper, Justice Blackburn of the Supreme Court of the Northern Territory in Australia was of a similar opinion. He could find no real authority, he said, "for the proposition that the mere fact of communal occupancy gives a title enforceable in the sovereign's courts against the sovereign or one claiming under him."[72] I would argue that this view is simply that the title issue is not justiciable, and that to conclude that, as a result, Aboriginal title is not a legal right, is mistaken.[73]

Option 2: Aboriginal Title as a Purely Personal Right

In this approach, unlike the first, Aboriginal title *is* a legally enforceable communal interest, but it amounts to no more than a bundle of rights to hunt, fish, trap, and pick berries on traditional lands. These rights can be surrendered only to the Crown and are not, legally, a right of ownership or property. Sometimes – notably by Fournier in 1875 and in the *St. Catherine's* case, referred to above – they are described as merely "usufructuary," meaning a right to use the land for particular purposes, but not otherwise. After the BC Court of Appeal confirmed the existence of Aboriginal rights in 1993, one commentator who had denied for years that there was such a thing as Aboriginal title in British Columbia finally conceded that it might exist. But in a passage that is a vintage statement of this approach, he argued that it was, "at best," only a "right to engage in ... traditional activities for sustenance and ceremonial purposes."[74]

I think it is of interest that, in the article already referred to, McKenna himself slides from the first approach to the second when he deals with a case he does not name but which is clearly *St. Catherine's*. He does not commit himself to a particular version of the content of what he calls Indian title, but he does acknowledge that it is a "burden" on the title of the Crown. He therefore concludes that, in making treaties, Canada had been "not merely politic ... but, in fact, removed a burden which kept the Crown's title, useful as it was for practical purposes, from being what sovereignty's should be."[75] Got that? On the one hand, he seems to be saying that Indian title is a significant legal obstacle and that failing to extinguish it impairs the Crown's sovereignty. On the other hand, he implies that, as a practical matter, such title does not really stand in the way of settlement and resource extraction. This awkwardness is instructive because it is as good a description of the history of the BC Indian Land Question in McKenna's lifetime (and until quite recently) as can be imagined. The province's position – until obliged by the courts in the 1990s to change it – was Option 1: that Aboriginal title did not have to be extinguished before settlement and resource extraction could take place because there was no such title in British Columbia. Others disagreed, preferring Option 2. Or something stronger.

Option 3: Aboriginal Title as a Form of Communal Ownership

Like the second option, in this approach Aboriginal title is seen as an enforceable legal right. But it is a true property right in land that is much like the fee simple of ordinary landowners in Anglo-American law, that is, it is protected by the law of trespass. This view can be discerned in the *Symonds* case in New Zealand and in the cases in the US Supreme Court between 1810 and 1835. As Herman Merivale, the permanent undersecretary of the Colonial Office, told a committee of the House of Commons in 1857, the Māori of New Zealand were virtual proprietors.[76] Indeed, even the Judicial Committee of the Privy Council acknowledged in 1921 that Aboriginal title to land "may be so complete as to reduce any radical right in the Sovereign to one which only extends to comparatively limited rights of administrative interference."[77] This is the approach to defining Aboriginal title (that is, viewing it as a property right) that was adopted by the Supreme Court of Canada in 1997 when it finally settled the matter in its decision in the *Delgamuukw* case.[78]

In my beginning – with apologies to T.S. Eliot – is my end: *Calder* and the role of the doctrine of sovereign immunity in that case and the century preceding it in British Columbia.

In the first place, *Calder* disposed of the notion that Option 1, above, is the law. The BC government had argued strenuously in *Calder* that Aboriginal title was purely a matter of morality and policy, not law. But six of the seven Supreme Court justices disagreed. Justice Judson also discouraged resort to a concept that is part of Option 2: "[T]he fact is that when the settlers came, the Indians were there, organized in societies and occupying the land as their forefathers had done for centuries. This is what Indian title means. And it does not help one in the solution of this problem to call it a 'personal or usufructuary right.'"[79] *Calder* also sheds light on the problem of enforceability, which figures in all discussions of this issue before the BC Crown Proceeding Act was passed in 1974.[80] If the Supreme Court of Canada can affirm that Aboriginal title is a legal right, notwithstanding that Indigenous people could not sue to enforce it without government permission and had to rely instead on the honour of the

Crown, then traditional common-law theory is that it has been a legal right all along. The difference between then and now is not that Aboriginal title was not a legal right before 1974; it is that until then only the Crown could protect it, either through honourable action, including treaties and legislation, or by referring questions about it to the courts.

Prime Minister John A. Macdonald made this point in Parliament in 1881. He said that he was "strongly of the opinion that if the Government raised the question of the Indian title [in British Columbia], the Courts of this country and the Courts of England, at all events, would maintain the right of the Indians and their title to the occupation of the soil until that right whatever it might amount to was extinguished."[81] In those days, it was "the Government" that had to take the issue to court, either by engineering a test case (as we have seen) or by referring it to the courts. Macdonald was not only prime minister but also an experienced lawyer and the superintendent general of Indian affairs; if he thought that the courts would affirm the existence of Indian title, he could not have regarded legal rights as confined only to those rights that could be vindicated directly in court by the affected parties themselves.[82] In other words, the fact that the entities now known as First Nations required government permission to sue did not affect the legal nature of their interest in the land. As legal historian S.F.C. Milsom has remarked, speaking of the law in Blackstone's day, rights were "not less rights because they might be invaded by the Crown, or because the victim's remedy against the Crown would then be at best by petition" (that is, by obtaining a fiat).[83]

The second point to note is that the doctrine of sovereign immunity haunted the *Calder* case from the outset. At trial in 1969, counsel for British Columbia made three preliminary objections, one of which was that the case could not proceed because no fiat had been granted. Justice Gould ruled that although it was unusual to decide the merits before dealing with a preliminary objection, "the comity of our Courts as an institution would have suffered had these plaintiffs been told judicially that their clearly enunciated claim would get no adjudication because it had been brought in the wrong forum." He then found that the Nisg̲a'a title had been extinguished during the colonial period. He added that one "would have to be self-blinded to the events and attitudes of the day to ignore the fact that this litigation is of great concern, and this judgment a deep distress, to the Indian peoples of British Columbia." The costs of an appeal would "probably be beyond [the] financial resources" of the Nisg̲a'a, he said, but "in the context of the Provincial Treasury, would be insignificant."[84]

A year later, when *Calder* reached the BC Court of Appeal, that court noted British Columbia's "formidable" preliminary objections but also chose to rule on the merits, holding in effect that there was never any Aboriginal title to extinguish, but if there were, the trial judge's conclusion was correct.[85]

The Supreme Court of Canada decision in 1973 was the only one to explicitly relegate the merits to obiter. The justices could have simply ruled on the fiat and left it at that – although at trial Justice Gould had made an impressive case against the wisdom of doing so. Or they could have done what both of the lower courts did and rule against the Nisg̱a'a on the merits without deciding the procedural point. Instead, they managed to avoid a binding decision on the merits (which could have gone against the Nisg̱a'a on extinguishment) and, at the same time, say things about Aboriginal title that moved the whole debate forward and into the political realm.

This had two main effects. The first has been stated already: notwithstanding that the ratio decidendi of *Calder* dealt only with sovereign immunity, the fact that six justices agreed that Aboriginal title was a legal right and three held the Nisg̱a'a still had title caused the federal government to reverse course. Ottawa instituted a comprehensive land claims policy for First Nations who had never made a treaty with the Crown (as well as a specific claims policy for First Nations who alleged a treaty breach or unlawful dealings with reserve land). Until then, the policy of the BC government since the 1860s had been to refuse to negotiate or even discuss Aboriginal title, and in 1969 Ottawa had issued a White Paper that, in essence, adopted a similar policy.[86] Until the *Calder* case. Frank Calder made this point as well as anyone at a conference in 2003 marking the thirtieth anniversary of the Supreme Court of Canada's decision. Asked how he felt about the three-to-three ruling on extinguishment, he replied that it was "a major victory." He explained:

> You see, we didn't establish the Indian reservations. Those guys that we faced in court, they did it ... To confine people inside that boundary, you have to be on top of them. You're both in the gutter. Right? If somebody's holding down that First Nation inside that reservation, somebody's got to be on his back and that guy on his back is controlling the law books. So the three-to-three decision meant that he had to get off my back and we'd turn around and face each other and talk. That was the birth of the negotiations, which in my book is the major number one victory of the *Calder* case.[87]

The second effect was more subtle but is nonetheless important and lies at the heart of the present essay. Although the Court split evenly on whether Nisga'a title had been extinguished before 1871, six of the seven justices agreed that Aboriginal title was a legal right, even if a fiat or some other government action was, at that time, necessary to enforce it in British Columbia.

Later cases filled in more of the details. *Guerin* confirmed and made explicit what was implicit in *Calder*, that is, that Aboriginal title existed at common law and did not depend on the Royal Proclamation of 1763 or require other statutory recognition.[88] *Delgamuukw* made it clear that the content of Aboriginal title is best described by Option 3, above.[89] And the *Tsilhqot'in* case removed some doubts about the meaning of *Delgamuukw* and, for the first time, declared that, quite apart from any treaty, a First Nation had Aboriginal title to a defined territory.[90]

But the modern history of the BC Indian Land Question began with *Calder*, a ruling that is quite consistent with the judicial and non-judicial pronouncements canvassed earlier in this essay. Aboriginal title is a legal right at common law, and this is no new principle. It may not be, as the editors of the *Victoria Daily Colonist* in 1910 were wont to say, as old as history itself – but it is old enough.

Notes

1 "The Treaty of Washington," in United States, *Treaties, Conventions, International Acts, Protocols and Agreements between the United States and Other Powers, 1776–1909* (Washington, DC: Government Printing Office, 1910), vol. I. Spain's claims on the coast had been disposed of in the 1790s. Russia's ended with the sale of Alaska to the United States in 1867.

2 *Delgamuukw v British Columbia*, [1997] 3 SCR 1010, in which the Supreme Court ruled that, to establish Aboriginal title to land, plaintiffs must show that their ancestors had enjoyed exclusive (or shared exclusive) use and occupation of that land in 1846.

3 *Victoria Daily Colonist*, June 23, 1910.

4 It is untrue mainly because it confuses sovereignty over territory with ownership of land within that territory. An Australian judge made a similar error when he opined that it was unquestionable that, when the first governor received his commission from George III, all lands in Australia "were already in law the property of the King of England." Sir Kenneth Roberts-Wray has described this statement as "startling and, indeed, incredible." See *Commonwealth and Colonial Law* (New York: F.A. Praeger, 1966), 631, commenting on *Williams v Attorney-General* (NSW) (1913), 16 CLR 404, 409.

5 "In White Man's Way Indians Fight Case," *Victoria Daily Colonist*, June 19, 1910. The assertion that the Royal Proclamation was in effect a statute is a reference to the judgment of Mansfield, CJKB, in *Campbell v Hall* (1774), Lofft 655, 98 ER 1045.

6 *Calder v British Columbia* (1973), 34 DLR (3d) 145 (SCC).

7 The ratio decidendi of a judicial decision is generally regarded as the narrowest rule or proposition in the case that determines the result based on the facts. It is the part of the case that creates binding law. The rest is obiter dicta, extra words that may be quite thoughtful but do not make binding law. Of course, nothing in law is as simple as this, and the concept of the ratio decidendi is in fact an elastic one: see, for example, William Twining and David Miers, *How to Do Things with Rules* (London: Weidenfeld and Nicolson, 1976), 176–81.

8 Douglas Sanders, "The Nishga Case," *BC Studies* 19 (Autumn 1973): 18. As with the names of many First Nations, the spelling of what is now rendered as "Nisg̱a'a" has changed over the years.

9 *Calder et al v AGBC* (1970), 13 DLR (3d) 64 (BCCA). The assertion with respect to the apprehension of other First Nations is based on Sanders (ibid., 14) and on my conversations with the late Frank Calder.

10 At the time, the question whether a fiat was required when only a declaration was sought was less settled, even controversial, outside Canada: see Peter W. Hogg and Patrick J. Monahan, *Liability of the Crown*, 3rd ed. (Toronto: Carswell, 2000), 27n.

11 The rule originated in the feudal principle that a lord may not be sued in his own court. However, the maxim that "the King may do no wrong" was not so much a justification for immunity as an explanation of why fiats – the term is from the endorsement on the petition, *fiat justicia* (let right be done) – should be issued in cases with merit. The standard work is Walter Clode, *The Law and Practice of Petition of Right, etc.* (London: William Cowes and Sons, 1887). See also Arthur S. Bourinot, *Annotation: Petition of Right,* [1928] 2 DLR 625–56 and Sir John Baker, "Magna Carta: The Emergence of the Myth," in *Challenges to Authority and the Recognition of Rights: From Magna Carta to Modernity,* ed. Catharine MacMillan and Charlotte Smith (Cambridge: Cambridge University Press 2018), 19–36 at 25.

12 RSBC 1996, c 89, enacted as the Crown Proceeding Act on August 1, 1974.

13 For details of this history, see, for example, Hamar Foster, "We Are Not O'Meara's Children: Law, Lawyers, and the First Campaign for Aboriginal Title in British Columbia, 1908–1928," in *Let Right Be Done: Aboriginal Title, the Calder Case, and the Future of Indigenous Rights,* ed. Hamar Foster, Heather Raven, and Jeremy Webber (Vancouver: UBC Press, 2007), 61–84.

14 *Calder* (note 9, above) (per Davey, CJBC, para. 10).

15 *R v Sparrow,* 1986 Can-LII 172 (BCCA), 20 and 23. For an assessment of the BC Court of Appeal's record in this area of the law, see Douglas C. Harris, "A Court Between: Aboriginal and Treaty Rights in the British Columbia Court of Appeal," *BC Studies* 162 (Summer 2009): 137–64.

16 The issue did come up before Chief Justice Begbie in 1886 in an application for an injunction. But not only was there no fiat, in that case, the attorney general was denying that the concept of Aboriginal title had any relevance. Begbie therefore held that he could not consider the issue and, somewhat testily, moved on. See *A.G. and I.B. Nash v John Tait,* October 27–28, 1886, BC Archives (BCA), GR-1727, British Columbia Bench Books, 1864–1964, M.B. Begbie, vol. 13, June 1885 to May 1887, 446–52, discussed in Hamar Foster, "Another Good Thing: *Ross River Dena Council v Canada* in the Yukon Court of Appeal, or: Indigenous Title, 'Presentism' in Law and History, and a Judge Begbie Puzzle Re-visited," *UBC Law Review* 50, 2 (2017): 293–319. (I would also like to note an error on page 311 of this article, where the text states that Begbie recommended clemency in eighteen of thirty-eight cases. It should have stated "recommended clemency or remained neutral" in these eighteen cases. I do not know how this error occurred in the editing process, but I accept full responsibility.)

17 At common law, this came to be determined by whether the colony was acquired by conquest (usually followed by a treaty of cession) or settlement of "empty land." But the equation of land occupied by tribal peoples with *terra nullius* was always problematic, and the meaning of the latter term requires analysis. An excellent account is Andrew Fitzmaurice, "The Genealogy of Terra Nullius," *Australian Historical Studies* 129 (2007): 1–15.

18 In fact, although the conflict clearly was a war to the Tŝilhqot'in, Governor Frederick Seymour's early use of the term was probably colloquial, induced by stress caused by the speed and efficiency with which the Tŝilhqot'in had killed or ejected white people from their territory. Although clearly panicked by the news from Bute Inlet, he would not have doubted that Her Majesty was sovereign throughout the colony.

19 I have examined the issue of Indigenous law in British Columbia in the nineteenth century in "One Good Thing: Law, Elevator Etiquette and Litigating Aboriginal Rights in Canada," *The Advocates' Quarterly* 37, 1 (May 2010): 66–86, republished as "One Good Thing: Law and Elevator Etiquette in the Indian Territories," in *Roots of Entanglement: Essays in the History of Native-Newcomer Relations*, ed. Myra Rutherdale, Kerry Abel, and P. Whitney Lackenbauer (Toronto: University of Toronto Press, 2018), 289–312. See also the essay by Kevin Neary and the treaty translations in this volume.

20 RSC 1985, Appendix II, no. 1 (1763). The Royal Proclamation forbade travel into the Indian Territories west of the British colonies without royal licence and required all unceded land, whether in a colony or otherwise, to be respected and sold only to the Crown in a public ceremony.

21 The settlers at Red River were in Rupert's Land and not, technically, in the Indian Territories.

22 Upper and Lower Canada had been merged in 1841 to become the united Province of Canada. Upper Canada was then referred to as Canada West and Lower Canada as Canada East. This union lasted until 1867, when the old division was restored and Canada West became Ontario and Canada East became Quebec.

23 This is essentially what happened on Vancouver Island. On the Mainland, however, an English Law Ordinance was proclaimed at the outset, probably because there had been uncertainty on the Island, and the Colonial Office did not want to risk this on the Mainland because thousands of American gold miners were pouring into the colony: see Hamar Foster, "Law Enforcement in Nineteenth-Century British Columbia: A Brief and Comparative Overview," *BC Studies* 63 (Autumn 1984): 11–14, and "Shooting the Elephant: Historians and the Problem of Frontier Lawlessness," in *The Political Context of Law*, ed. Richard Eales and David Sullivan (London: Hambledon Press, 1987), 139–40.

24 Quebec had been obtained by conquest and treaty, so the law of the inhabitants continued until altered by the Crown – which might, or might not, choose to permit the establishment of a representative assembly. Once the promise of an assembly was made, however, only the imperial Parliament could break it: see *Campbell v Hall* (1774) (note 5, above), the Quebec Act of 1774, and Martin Wight, *The Development of the Legislative Council, 1606–1945* (London: Faber & Faber, 1947), 36–38.

25 See, for example, Desmond Brown, "Unpredictable and Uncertain: Criminal Law in the Canadian Northwest before 1888," *Alberta Law Review* 17, 3 (1979): 497–512. I have tried to summarize some of the issues in "Law and Necessity in Western Rupert's Land and Beyond, 1670–1870," in *Laws and Societies in the Canadian Prairie West, 1670–1870*, ed. Louis A. Knafla and Jonathan Swainger (Vancouver: UBC Press, 2005), 57–91.

26 Joseph Bouchette, *The British Dominions in North America* (London: Longman, Rees, Orme, Brown, Green and Longman, 1832), 1:29. Bouchette was the surveyor general of Lower Canada and testified about the boundaries of Upper Canada in some of the fur trade–era cases.

27 *An Act for extending the Jurisdiction of Courts of Justice in the Provinces of Upper and Lower Canada, to the Trial and punishment of Crimes, and Offences within certain parts of North America adjoining to the said Provinces,* 43 Geo III, c 138 (U.K.), and *An Act for Regulating the Fur Trade, and establishing a Criminal and Civil Jurisdiction within certain parts of North America,* 1 & 2 Geo IV, c 66 (U.K.). These statutes are examined in Hamar Foster, "Long Distance Justice: The Criminal Jurisdiction of Canadian Courts West of the Canadas, 1763–1859," *American Journal of Legal History* 34 (1990): 1–48, and "Forgotten Arguments: Aboriginal Title and Sovereignty in Canada Jurisdiction Act Cases," *Manitoba Law Journal* 21, 3 (1992): 343–89.

28 The 1821 statute provided that civil cases involving land sent to Canada had to be tried according to English rather than Canadian law, but because there were no settlers in the Indian Territories and any land owned by fur traders was in Canada, this provision meant little.

29 The licence provided that the HBC had a monopoly over the Indian trade east of the Rockies, but because of the problem in Oregon with the United States, this monopoly could not extend to the Indian Territories west of the Rockies. There, the licence simply excluded all British subjects other than HBC employees from conducting trade.

30 By "unchallenged" I mean by other British trading concerns. West of the Rockies, the HBC still had to deal with the Russians and the Americans and generally did so quite effectively.

31 *An Act to Provide for the Administration of Justice in Vancouver's Island,* 12 & 13 Vict, 1849, c 48 (UK).

32 In early land law, land was "purchased" with service, and the services were classified as to type. Thus, those whose service was military were said to "hold" their land in or by "knight service." There were many different tenures, or forms of land holding, and this terminology outlived the economic reality of land for service by several centuries. When the military tenures were abolished by statute in 1660, only one other major tenure was preserved: the basic agricultural service known as free and common socage. Even today, if you own fee simple land in British Columbia, you technically (and rather meaninglessly) hold it in free and common socage directly of Her Majesty the Queen as one of her tenants in chief.

33 The Letters Patent are reproduced as the "Charter of Grant to Vancouver's Island to the Hudson's Bay Company," in James E. Hendrickson, ed.," *Journals of the Colonial Legislatures of the Colonies of Vancouver Island and British Columbia, 1851–1871,* 4 vols. (Victoria: Provincial Archives of British Columbia, 1980), 1:374–78.

34 New Caledonia was what is now northern BC (from the vicinity of Kamloops or thereabouts north); the Columbia Department embraced the whole region, from Oregon to Russian Alaska. Permanent undersecretary James Stephens wrote the quoted words. See Paul Knaplund, "James Stephen on Granting Vancouver Island to the Hudson's Bay Company," *British Columbia Historical Quarterly* 9 (1945): 259, 269. Vancouver Island is often incorrectly described as a Crown colony, but until the HBC's title to the soil was repurchased by the Crown it was really a hybrid.

35 *The Times,* August 31, 1848. The *Morning Chronicle,* on August 22, 1848, described the HBC – whose initials were alleged to stand for "Here before Christ" – as "a sort of corporate Nimrod." To the *Morning Herald,* it was "the Worshipful Corporation of

Peltmongers" (February 9, 1849). The *Dublin World* went further, wondering why, given the available land in Britain's other colonies, anyone would "wander to the remoteness of Vancouver? In Heaven's name, what sane man would go there, and for what would he go?"

36 On Wakefield and the effect of his views on settlement in Vancouver Island, see Richard Mackie, "The Colonization of Vancouver Island, 1849–1858," *BC Studies* 96 (Winter 1992–93): 3.

37 House of Commons, *Report from the Select Committee on the Hudson's Bay Company; Together with the Proceedings of the Committee, Minutes of Evidence, Appendix and Index* (July 31, 1857), iv.

38 The negotiations took some time, however, and the conveyance was not completed until 1867: Appendix to RSBC, 1871, 56.

39 See Foster, "Long Distance Justice" and Forgotten Arguments." I examine two of the post-1821 cases in more depth in "Sins against the Great Spirit: The Law, the Hudson's Bay Company and the Mackenzie's River Murders, 1835–1839," *Criminal Justice History: An International Annual* 10 (1989): 23, and "Killing Mr. John: Law and Jurisdiction at Fort Stikine, 1842–1846," in *Law for the Elephant, Law for the Beaver: Essays in the Legal History of the North American West,* ed. John McLaren, Hamar Foster, and Chett Orloff (Regina/Pasadena: Canadian Plains Research Center/Ninth Judicial Circuit Historical Society, 1992), 147.

40 In 1815, the HBC had attempted to have Northwester Duncan Cameron prosecuted in England for a number of crimes pursuant to a Tudor statute – 33 Henry VIII (1541), c 23 – and when told this could not be done unless the charge was murder or treason, it tried to send him back to Canada for trial under the Canada Jurisdiction Act. However, although the Habeas Corpus Act of 1679 permitted the arrest of a prisoner for a capital offence committed in one of His Majesty's Dominions or "foreign plantations" abroad, the Colonial Office advised that the Indian Territories were Indian, not British. There was, in short, nothing in either statute that authorized the arrest in England of a man alleged to have committed a crime "out of His Majesty's Dominions" for the purpose of sending him abroad for trial: see Foster, "Long Distance Justice," 25–26.

41 Reproduced in Alexander Morris, *The Treaties with the Indians of Manitoba and the North-West Territories Including the Negotiations on Which They Were Based* (Toronto: Belfords, Clarke and Co., 1880; reprint, Fifth House, 1991), 298–300.

42 William Dummer Powell to Sir Peregrine Maitland, May 1, 1819, quoted in the dissenting judgment of Strong, J., of the Supreme Court of Canada in *St. Catherine's Milling and Lumber Co v The Queen* (1887), 13 SCR 577, 613–14. Justice Strong concluded that if "the soil was in the aborigines" in 1819, "it must have so remained down to the date of the North West Angle Treaty No. 3 made in 1873," that is, the treaty at issue in the *St. Catherine's* case.

43 *Connolly v Woolrich* (1867), 11 LCJ 197, appeal dismissed at (1869), 1 RLOS 253. The US case relied on was *Worcester v Georgia,* discussed in the text accompanying note 54. *Connolly* was cited with approval by the BC Court of Appeal in *Casimel v Insurance Corp of BC,* [1994] 2 CNLR 22.

44 See notes 31 and 33, above.

45 CO 305/1, 635–47 (March 1849), cited in various sources.

46 On Douglas and his land policy, see the essays in this volume by Graham Brazier, Keith Thor Carlson, John Sutton Lutz, and Sarah Pike.

47 Douglas to the Duke of Newcastle, Secretary of State for the Colonies, March 15, 1861, in British Columbia, *Papers Connected to the Indian Land Question, 1850–1875* (Victoria:

R. Wolfenden, 1875), 19. Compare with what the first European to set foot on Vancouver Island had to say. When Captain Cook landed at Nootka Sound in 1778, he remarked that he had "nowhere met with Indians who had such high notions of everything the Country produced being their exclusive property." Quoted in Gilbert Malcolm Sproat, *The Nootka: Scenes and Studies of Savage Life,* ed. Charles Lillard (Victoria: Sono Nis, 1987), 59. This book was originally published in 1868 as *Scenes and Studies of Savage Life,* and Sproat, who was to become a reserve commissioner in 1876, agreed with Cook's assessment.

48 *Johnson v M'Intosh,* 21 US (8 Wheat) 543 (1823).

49 *R (ex rel McIntosh) v Symonds* (1847), [1840–1932] NZPC Cases 387.

50 David V. Williams, "*The Queen v Symonds* Reconsidered," *Victoria University of Wellington Law Review* 19 (1989): 389.

51 Ibid., 388.

52 *Johnson v M'Intosh,* emphasis added.

53 *R (ex rel McIntosh) v Symonds,* emphasis added.

54 *Worcester v Georgia,* 31 US (6 Pet) 515 (1832).

55 *Mitchell v US,* 34 US (9 Pet) 711 (1835).

56 An exception is *Cherokee Nation v Georgia,* 30 US (5 Pet) 1 (1831), where the Cherokee sued directly, justifying this by arguing that the Supreme Court had jurisdiction over disputes between US states and foreign states. The court ruled, however, that the Cherokee were not a foreign state but a "domestic dependent nation," and jurisdiction was therefore declined.

57 See note 20, above. The proclamation provided that Indigenous land, whether in the Indian Territories or in a colony, had to be acquired by consensual surrender to the Crown in a public setting.

58 What Maine actually said in his *On Early Law and Custom* (London: J. Murray, 1890), 389, is that "[s]o great is the ascendancy of the Law of Actions in the infancy of the Courts of Justice, that substantive law has at first the look of being gradually secreted in the interstices of procedure."

59 See the text accompanying notes 27–28. It is noteworthy that Fournier assumed that the Royal Proclamation of 1763 applied to British Columbia. This seems to have been the consensus among the few lawyers who considered the question – until the BC government's contrary argument in the *Calder* case in the 1960s.

60 See, for example, *Haida Nation v British Columbia (Minister of Forests),* [2004] 3 SCR 511.

61 Reproduced in Appendix B, *Special Committees of the Senate and House of Commons meeting in joint session to inquire into the claims of the Allied Indian Tribes of British Columbia, as set forth in their petition submitted to Parliament in June 1926: Proceedings, report and the Evidence* (Ottawa: King's Printer, 1927), 43. Of course, it was not true that all those who represented the Crown in other parts of North America observed these principles.

62 Ibid., emphasis added.

63 Ibid., 8. Unfortunately, when Ottawa and British Columbia agreed to set up the Joint Indian Reserve Commission later that year, Ottawa approved a new version of BC's Crown Lands Act that was really no different in substance from the 1874 version. However, Fournier's successor as minister of justice, Edward Blake, continued to have serious doubts about the law's constitutionality.

64 Ibid., 40, emphasis added.

65 *St. Catherine's Milling Co v R* (1888), 14 AC 46, 59: "The fact that the power of legislating for Indians and [their lands] has been entrusted to ... Parliament is not in the least degree inconsistent with the right of the province to a beneficial interest in these lands,

available to them as a source of revenue whenever the estate of the Crown is disencumbered of the Indian title," emphasis added. The Dominion government had made a treaty (Treaty 3) allegedly extinguishing the Aboriginal title to a vast swath of land, and the Province of Ontario was disputing the right of the Dominion to issue timber licences with respect to the disencumbered land. It was, thus, a dispute between two settler governments as to which one received the benefit of the surrender of the Aboriginal title. For a more critical look at this case, see Kent McNeil, *Flawed Precedent: The St. Catherine's Case and Aboriginal Title* (Vancouver: UBC Press 2019).

66 *Reference re British North America Act, 1867,* ss 109, 111 (Can), [1896] JCJ No 4, para 13, emphasis added.

67 Newcombe to Prime Minister Laurier, June 16, 1910, Library and Archives Canada (LAC), MG26-G, vol. 634, reel C-892, 172168–172176, emphasis added. The premier had objected to three of the ten questions posed because they raised the issue of unextinguished Aboriginal title.

68 Draft letter from McBride to Laurier, November 19, 1910 (not sent), BCA, GR-441, box 149.

69 Laurier to McBride, December 8, 1910, LAC, MG26-G, vol. 654, reel C897, 177668. Laurier intended to bring a test case and in fact had the Indian Act amended to facilitate this, but he lost the 1911 election. The new Borden administration was not interested in pursuing this initiative: see Hamar Foster, "A Romance of the Lost: The Role of Tom MacInnes in the History of the British Columbia Indian Land Question," in *Essays in the History of Canadian Law,* vol. 8, *In Honour of R.C.B. Risk,* ed. G. Blaine Baker and Jim Phillips (Toronto: University of Toronto Press for the Osgoode Society, 1999), 195–96.

70 J.A.J. McKenna, "Indian Title in British Columbia," *Canadian Magazine* 54, 6 (1920): 474.

71 Memorandum from Trutch contained as an enclosure in Governor Musgrave to Earl Granville, January 29, 1870, in British Columbia, *Papers Connected to the Indian Land Question.* The enclosure is in Appendix B to the "Report of the Government of British Columbia on the Subject of Land Reserves," and the quoted passage is at page 11. This report begins after page 170 of the *Papers* and has its own pagination. Compare with the governor of the New Zealand Company, who wondered in 1843 if the Treaty of Waitangi "could be treated by lawyers as anything but a praiseworthy device for amusing and pacifying savages for the moment." Quoted in Peter Adams, *Fatal Necessity: British Intervention in New Zealand, 1830–1847* (Auckland/Oxford: Auckland University Press/Oxford University Press, 1977), 184.

72 *Milirrpum v Nabalco Pty Ltd,* [1971] 17 FLR 141 at 217. In reaching this conclusion, Blackburn, J, relied in part on the BC Court of Appeal's decision in *Calder* (above, note 9).

73 But I will not argue this at length here. See, instead, Foster, "Another Good Thing" (above, note 16) and "The Royal Proclamation of 1763 in British Columbia: An Indigenous Magna Carta's Chequered Canadian Career," in *Challenges to Authority and the Recognition of Rights: From Magna Carta to Modernity,* 269–95.

74 Melvin H. Smith, *Our Home or Native Land? What Governments' Aboriginal Policy Is Doing to Canada* (Victoria: Crown Western, 1995), 136. The BC Court of Appeal decision referred to is its decision in the *Delgamuukw* case. The report is at (1993), 104 DLR (4th) 470.

75 McKenna, "Indian Title," 472, 474.

76 Merivale's remarks are included in a dispatch from New Zealand Governor Gore Brown to Lord Lytton, October 14, 1858: see "Further Papers Relative to Native Affairs,"

Appendices to the Journals of the House of Representatives, 1860 (Turnbull Library, Wellington, NZ), 1.

77 *Amodu Tijani v Secretary, Southern Nigeria*, [1921] 2 AC 399, 410. By "radical right of the Sovereign," Viscount Haldane meant the underlying title and sovereignty of the British Crown in the colony.

78 See note 2, above.

79 *Calder* (see note 6, above), 156. For an excellent analysis of this aspect of *Calder*, see Michael Asch, "Calder and the Representation of Indigenous Society in Canadian Jurisprudence," in Foster, Raven, and Webber, *Let Right Be Done*, 101–10.

80 See text accompanying note 12.

81 *House of Commons Debates*, 4th Parl, 3rd Sess, vol. 2 (March 11, 1881), 1348.

82 Ibid. He went on to add that, if it were found that the BC government was "acting unjustly with the Indians – which I do not, by any means, expect – or depriving them of their reasonable rights, we might ... be obliged to assert the rights of the Indians to a recognition of their titles to their lands."

83 S.F.C. Milsom, "The Nature of Blackstone's Achievement," in *Studies in the History of the Common Law* (London: Hambledon Press, 1985), 199.

84 *Calder et al v AGBC* (1969), 8 DLR (3d) 59, paras 50 and 52.

85 *Calder et al v AGBC* (1970), see note 9, above. The quoted adjective is in the judgment of Maclean, JA.

86 British Columbia, of course, resisted the implications of *Calder* for another fifteen years or so, not joining the Nisga'a Treaty negotiations until the 1990s: see text accompanying notes 14–15. The White Paper was a policy document of the Trudeau government rejecting, *inter alia*, the notion of further treaties.

87 "Frank Calder and Thomas Berger: A Conversation," in Foster, Raven, and Webber, *Let Right Be Done*, 45.

88 *Guerin v The Queen*, [1984] 2 SCR 335.

89 See note 2, above.

90 *Tsilhqot'in Nation v British Columbia*, [2014] 2 SCR 257.

Part 2

Treaty Texts

4

The Earliest First Nations Accounts of the Formation of the Vancouver Island (or Douglas) Treaties of 1850–54

Neil Vallance

On October 16, 2010, the Douglas Treaties made a brief appearance in the media. The *Victoria Times Colonist* reported that members of the Tsartlip First Nation had blocked a public road running through their reserve in Saanich, a suburb of Victoria. According to Chief Ivan Morris, this was done because "the federal government has failed to live up to the terms of the Douglas treaty signed in 1852."[1] The incident soon dropped out of the news, but First Nations continue to bring unresolved treaty issues to the attention of the public in various ways, including demonstrations and court actions. These events are likely to intensify until non-First Nations people living within treaty territory, on Vancouver Island and across Canada, acknowledge First Nations understandings of the terms of such treaties.

How could an interested reader of the *Times Colonist* article learn more about what happened in 1852? The obvious answer is a quick Google search, which brings up a Wikipedia entry stating that "[t]he Douglas Treaties, also known as the Vancouver Island Treaties or the Fort Victoria Treaties, were a series of treaties signed between certain indigenous groups on Vancouver Island and the Colony of Vancouver Island."[2] The entry goes on to say that "[f]or four years [from 1850 to 1854] the governor, James Douglas, made a series of fourteen land purchases from aboriginal peoples," and "[t]hese fourteen land purchases became the fourteen Treaties that make up the Douglas Treaties." That seems straightforward enough, but what did the First Nations get in exchange? Another Google search brings up a federal government site titled "Treaty Texts – Douglas Treaties,"[3] which confirms that Douglas paid sums recorded in pounds, shillings, and pence by way of the equivalent in Hudson's Bay Company (HBC) blankets, together with promises concerning reserves, hunting, and fishing.

End of story one might think, but there is a problem. In 2006, the Supreme Court of Canada, in *R v Morris and Olsen,* discussed the 1852 Saanich Treaty and noted that "the treaty was concluded orally" and only "subsequently reduced to writing."[4] That raises the question of whether the written document indeed reflects the terms of the oral agreement. Two sources have argued forcefully that it does not. In 1984, Judge Lambert of the BC Court of Appeal, in *R v Bartleman,* reported that, "I have examined, at the provincial archives, the foolscap notebook inscribed 'Register of Land Purchases from Indians,' where the written components of the ... Fort Victoria treaties were recorded," and concluded that "I do not think that the text of the land grant ... should be regarded as anything more than some evidence of what was generally agreed to."[5] In 2008, Lambert's position was echoed by legal historian Douglas Harris, who proposed that "the treaties are best understood as oral agreements" and that the written text "should be considered as evidence of the terms of those agreements, not as the agreements themselves," because the written text "provides little or highly qualified evidence, at best, of how the Native participants understood the agreements."[6] These are very serious allegations that deserve explanation.

The first set of Vancouver Island Treaty meetings took place between April 29 and May 1, 1850, and Chief Factor James Douglas reported to his superiors at Hudson's Bay House in London on May 16.[7] In the last paragraph of the letter, Douglas makes a startling disclosure: "I attached the signature of the native Chiefs and others who subscribed[8] the deed of purchase to a blank sheet,[9] on which will be copied the contract or Deed of conveyance, as soon as we receive a proper form,[10] which I beg may be sent out by return of Post." This "mail-order" template, titled "Form of Agreement for Purchase of Land from Natives of Vancouver's Island," duly arrived some months later. Douglas then filled in the blanks with the name of the relevant "Tribe" or "family," a description of boundaries, and the price paid. The final step in this process was Douglas and his clerks copying the completed texts of the agreements onto the spaces left for that purpose at the top of each sheet of paper, the bottom of which had already been "subscribed" with the "signature of the native Chiefs and others."

The completed forms were then inserted or copied into the "Register of Land Purchases from Indians" and stored in the Lands and Works Office at Fort Victoria.[11] Were copies given to the First Nations participants? There is nothing in the historical record to indicate that this was done.

It is unlikely that the First Nations parties to the Vancouver Island Treaties became aware of the existence, let alone the contents, of the completed forms for decades. (For the balance of the essay, I'll call them the Douglas Forms to avoid confusion with the oral versions, henceforth called the Vancouver Island Treaties.) However, it is important to bear in mind that for most of the time, and for most people (including some First Nations), the Douglas Forms have been treated as if they *were* the treaties, on the assumption that they accurately reduce to writing the terms of the oral agreements made at the treaty meetings.[12]

Even though the written texts are tainted, surely the terms of the oral agreements can be ascertained by reference to contemporaneous records. Again, there is a problem. In 2002, eminent historical geographer Cole Harris stated that "the purchase agreements were oral understandings, the terms of which have been lost."[13] This is a bleak but not unreasonable conclusion when the circumstances surrounding the formation of the treaties are set out. The only contemporaneous report was this laconic entry in the HBC's Fort Victoria Journal for April 29, 1850, made by clerk Roderick Finlayson: "In the evening the proprietors of the tract of country lying between the headland and point McGregor were paid for their land. They ... got 3 [blankets] ... each at which they appeared well satisfied."[14] Eight more treaties were concluded over the next two days, but none of these meetings were described in the fort journal. None of the words spoken by the First Nations representatives or James Douglas were recorded. No minutes or other memorandums of the terms of the agreements were produced at the time, other than lists of the names of First Nations representatives (with crosses beside each name), followed by the names and signatures of two HBC employees.

What documentation *does* reside in the archival record in addition to Finlayson's journal entry and Douglas's two-and-a-half-page letter to HBC headquarters?[15] In 1888, Joseph McKay, who was witness to seven of the nine 1850 treaties, wrote a two-page account, which represents the third and final first-hand account by a European.[16] In his letter, McKay also mentioned the presence of a translator, Thomas, also an HBC employee.[17]

Other than First Nations representatives and HBC employees, who was present? It is impossible to tell from extant records. Richard Blanshard, the first governor of the colony, was not in attendance. Only one independent colonist, Walter Colquhoun Grant, had arrived on the Island, but there is no record of his presence at the meetings. The only clerics in Victoria at the time were the Reverend R.J. Staines,[18] and an Oblate father,

Timothy Lempfrit,[19] but, again, there is no record of their attendance. British and American naval vessels and merchant ships often stopped at Victoria, but there are no ships' log entries or letters by officers or passengers that mention the meetings. The nearest newspaper was in the Oregon Territory, so no journalists were present. One might have expected that such colourful events would be memorialized by a painting or sketch, but there is nothing. The same scenario held true for the remaining five treaties, negotiated between 1851 and 1854. All of the above raises the question of whether a deliberate silencing of other voices took place. On balance, it seems likely that the absence was a result of happenstance rather than malice forethought.

Douglas Harris has suggested that, "given the thin documentary and oral history surrounding the treaties, the written texts assume particular importance."[20] While true, research on the four corners of the document, supplemented only by colonial accounts, has become a largely sterile exercise, generating a stunted literature. Starting in the 1970s, the treaties have received some mention but only as an interesting though unimportant episode in colonial treaty making. In most cases, three pages are devoted to the formation of the treaties, presenting the standard colonial account over and over. Ideally, the information gap should be filled by resort to First Nations accounts of treaty formation.

This brings forward one last problem. While there are five first-person First Nations accounts, only one is clearly first-hand, and all were reduced to writing long after the events described. Without exception, the accounts were translated, and all but one was told to journalists, who published their stories in newspaper articles. Consequently, they are usually rejected by historians as primary sources, thereby reducing or eliminating their perceived usefulness as accounts of what they purport to describe. This is understandable given the unorthodox nature of such accounts and the challenges of extracting useful information from them. However, responsibility for the shortcomings of the accounts does not lie with the authors. They were endeavouring, with remarkable courage and persistence, to voice their understandings in an indifferent and often hostile environment. At the time they spoke, the intended audience was unable to listen, and their message was ignored. Their voices should not be ignored again merely because they fail to meet today's historiographical and legal standards. As well, their accounts represent almost the only window we have into First Nations understanding of what transpired. For these reasons, every effort must be made to identify any insights they are capable of providing. In recent years, the scholarly literature has started to refer to the First Nations accounts, but only as a supplement to the usual recitation of events derived from the colonial record. At this juncture, it is standard practice in the literature on the Douglas Treaties to proceed straight to an account of the treaty meetings based on Douglas's letters to HBC headquarters in London. Not this time. In the case of each meeting, First Nations accounts are presented first, a practice that results in the emergence of a very different picture of the treaties. This picture, in turn, facilitates a reconsideration of the treaties.

The four First Nations spokespeople were attempting to explain their understanding of the treaties to non-First Nations audiences, but at the time they spoke, their words and their message were ignored. The accounts are few, and they are not without serious problems, but to no greater degree than the colonial versions. The five earliest accounts were reduced to writing between 1913 and 1934. Two are by Chief David Latass, who describes the 1850 Esquimalt/Songhees Treaties and the 1852 North Saanich Treaty.[21] The other three describe the Nanaimo Treaty of 1854 from the viewpoint of Snuneymuxw Elders. There are no extant First Nations accounts of the other Vancouver Island Treaty meetings. It should be kept in mind that, unlike contemporaneous accounts, these accounts reflect the understanding of the narrators at the time their stories were told, not at the date of the original meetings.

The Latass accounts are embedded in a long (and rambling) newspaper article published in 1934, and a degree of editorial discretion has been exercised in the choice of extracts reproduced here.[22] The article has not been reproduced in its entirety in any publication. The earliest of the Snuneymuxw accounts is by Dick Whoakum, who gave his version of the Nanaimo Treaty in 1913, in sworn testimony before the Royal Commission on Indian Affairs in British Columbia (commonly referred to as the McKenna-McBride Commission). A typescript of the translation of his statement to, and cross-examination by, the commissioners is available online.[23] The second Nanaimo account, published in a Vancouver newspaper in 1922, was given by Bobby *Yacklum.* The third and most recent Nanaimo account, provided by Quen-Es-Then (also known as Joe Wyse), also appeared in a newspaper article, originally published in 1933 and recently republished in a compilation of the journalist's work.[24]

On the other hand, the five First Nations accounts presented here were provided by people well placed to have a good understanding of what transpired at the treaty meetings: Whoakum was a signatory, Yacklam and

Wyse were the sons of Snuneymuxw signatory Chiefs, Latass (or his father) participated in the Songhees/Esquimalt meetings, and he (or his maternal uncles) participated in the Saanich meetings. To be clear, no attempt is made to speak *for* the authors of the first-person accounts. The only goal is to reveal the message First Nations spokespeople were trying to communicate so long ago. Recent academic literature has started to include short snippets of these First Nations accounts, but the references are largely uncritical.[25] No court decision involving the Vancouver Island Treaties has had occasion to reference these First Nations accounts. The detailed presentation and critical analysis here are intended to remedy this problem.

The Fort Victoria Treaties (1850)

In 1934, Chief David Latass of the Tsartlip First Nation in Saanich gave an interview to Frank Pagett, a reporter for the *Victoria Daily Times*.[26] The article opens with these prescient words: "Tribal groups of Saanich have claims against the Hudson's Bay Company, the Imperial Government, the Dominion of Canada and the British Columbia Government, for a capital sum to make good an agreed rental of Saanich now unpaid for eighty years, according to Chief David Latass, famous orator of the Brentwood division of the Saanich Tribe."[27] According to the article, Latass was "born a member of the Songhees tribe" but at age seven went to Brentwood to live, "joining aunts who had become wives of members of the Saanich tribe." An explanation of his relocation is contained in a letter in support of Latass's claim to receive a share of the proceeds of the sale of the old Songhees Reserve in 1911:

> David Ledtast [sic] born a Songees and both parents lived on the Songhees Reserve in the community house. This man when about fifteen years old and after his mother and his father had died was taken by his aunt who was a Saanich Indian to live at Saanich ... He is now chief of the Saanich tribe and he has been for many years.[28]

He spent the balance of his life with the Tsartlip First Nation at Brentwood in Saanich.

According to the reporter, Latass, who claimed to be 105 years old, was "still mentally keen." In the article, Latass addresses the issue of incredulity concerning his age: "White people doubt my age can be 105 years. They see my bright eyes, they saw me move quickly until a few years ago, they heard me speak in council and address the tribes when long past ninety years old, and they said it was impossible for me to have known James Douglas. But I was a grown man when the big pow-wow was held [in 1850] in Beacon Hill."[29] The results of an extensive search for confirmation or contradiction of Latass's age claim have been wildly disparate, making it impossible to come to any definite conclusion one way or the other.[30] If he indeed exaggerated his age, why did he do so? The question is important because it affects the credibility of everything else he said in the interview. A possible insight is provided by historian Chris Friday, who comments on how important eyewitness status was to Native Americans claiming to have been present at the Stevens Treaty meetings in the Puget Sound area in 1854 and 1855: "For those individuals, having been there was a basis of legitimacy and authority … Such exact knowledge of the treaties and an ability to mobilize it became markers of leadership."[31] It is ironic that a possible attempt by Latass to bolster the legitimacy and authority of his account has had the opposite effect.

Given the uncertainty of his eyewitness status, the frailties of human memory, and the imperfections of translation, the information supplied by David Latass may not be accurate as to the dates and details of the events described. However, for the purposes of this essay, it is his *interpretation* of the events that is important. His unique contribution to the search for the oral terms of the Vancouver Island Treaties is a lifetime spent listening and talking to people knowledgeable about the treaties, absorbing information from many sources along the way, and expressing his views as they evolved over the years. In other words, rather than being an eyewitness, he is the equivalent of the modern "expert witness," the first student of the Vancouver Island Treaties. The views expressed in his 1934 interview were fifty years ahead of their time and would not find expression again until 1989, in an important article by legal historian Hamar Foster on the Saanich Treaty.[32] A review of the editorials and letters to the editor for the two weeks following Latass's provocative article revealed no references, indicating that his account did not prompt outrage, only indifference.

The following excerpt from the transcript of evidence given by Saanich Elder Gabriel Bartleman in 1987 in court proceedings brought by the Tsawout First Nation to prevent the construction of a marina on Saanich Inlet reveals much about the high esteem in which David Latass was held by the Saanich people. Bartleman was seventy-three years old when he was examined by Louise Mandell, counsel for the Tsawout:

Q: Who was the leader of the Saanich people during the time when you were growing up?
A: A gentleman by the name of Chief David Latesse ...
Q: Was David Latesse an elected leader or was he a leader by his birthright or hereditary line?
A: He was a leader by his birthright and became a leader through the merits that he had behind him.
Q: What did you understand that the merits were which the people recognized in him?
A: At that time, Chief David Latesse apparently got to understand some of what is called the treaty, and he tried to inform the people that he looked after the best he could at that time.
Q: Now you mention that Chief David Latesse had knowledge concerning the treaty ...
A: He didn't use the word "treaty," they called it James Douglas' word.
Q: And did Chief David speak about what happened to have that treaty concluded?
A: The understanding that he gave the people at home was that their way of life was never ever going to be disturbed, that they would always be able to take their food and travel as they did before, that nothing would ever be taken away from them.[33]

As a side note, all the First Nations accounts were related by elderly men. Memories implanted at a young age and recalled in extreme old age may have become confused. Apparently, Bartleman is the only person to address this issue with respect to the treaty First Nations in this region. During his court testimony, he justified his clear memory of a meeting in 1924 or 1925, which took place when he was nine or ten years old, explaining that

> whenever my father was called to sit in at a meeting I went along with him, and [that is] how I happened to hear whatever was discussed. I was told to be quiet and sit down and listen. Many of our older people were very disciplining people, and we were told that when there was something especially good to listen to that we should do so. And I think that that's why I have a good memory of some of the discussions that took place on the Saanich Reserve. Usually that was about Douglas' word.[34]

According to Pagett, Latass was "looked after by a well-educated wife, half his age, who aided in interpreting the ancient's vigorous statements."[35] But "the principal interpreter of Chief David's reminiscences was his grandnephew, Baptiste Paull," described as "a boxer and wrestler, whose prowess has won fame throughout the Pacific Coast."[36] What follows are extracts from the interview relevant to the Fort Victoria Treaties:

> I do well remember hearing that Douglas called a meeting of the four sub-chiefs of the Songhees, heads of the groups living at Clover Point, at Cadboro Bay, at Cordova Bay and at Mud Bay [on the same side of the harbour as the fort]. I remember the sense of wealth shared by the Mud Bay group when, after they had agreed to abandon Mud Bay and remove to the old Songhees reserve on the inner harbour, Douglas gave the sub-chief a bale of fifty blankets for distribution among the families of the group. He also gave the other groups presents for waiving their rights of assembly at Mud Bay ...
>
> In the years around 1850 the Indians considered that there was lots of land and had no thought of or fear of extensive settlement by white men. The whites were welcomed, they provided a fine market for the large amount of fur which the tribesmen annually collected. The trade goods the whites gave in return for the furs were highly regarded. The whites at that time also had no idea of asking the Indians to give up their land. Areas proposed to be used by whites were limited and the gifts of blankets and trade goods were considered as annual dues as I shall show. I was twenty-one when Governor Douglas gave a big party to the Indians of southern Vancouver Island. The entertainment took place at Beacon Hill on May 24, 1850,[37] and was to celebrate the birthday of Queen Victoria. For weeks in advance the party was the talk of all encampments within eighty miles of Victoria. Invitations were sent to the Songhees, Saanich, Cowitchen, and other tribes and the gathering included men, women and children.[38] The natives were seated in big circles, the chiefs forming the innermost line, the lesser braves being further to the rear, according to their relative importance or youth. The women and children hung around the outskirts of the circles of men, grouping themselves in eager clusters.[39] Hudson's Bay men distributed hard biscuits smeared with molasses and also other foodstuffs. After all had eaten Governor Douglas addressed the crowd. He was dressed in a coat of blue with gold shoulder pieces and trimmings. He preceded his speech with a salute to the Great White Queen,[40] given with upraised hand. He stressed the desire of the white man to be friends with the tribes. He assured the chiefs that trade in furs with peaceful use of enough land to grow food were the only reasons for

> establishment of the settlement. His statement was welcomed by the peace-loving tribes, whose view of white settlement, had it been voiced at all, would have been that there was lots of land and no harm could come from letting the whites have the use of some of it. It must be remembered that the Indians were great bargainers and they would not have had any idea of letting the whites use their land from year to year unless some equivalent trade or gifts be made each year.

The above passage set out the terms by which First Nations would cede specific tracts of land (including the relocation of a village in the instance recounted) to allow expansion of the HBC establishment outside the palisade. There is another account, a non-First Nations account, of a negotiated relocation, and it is markedly different. In his memoirs, HBC clerk Roderick Finlayson recounts that "I wanted them ['the Indians'] to remove to the other side of the harbor which they at first declined to do, saying the land was theirs, and after a great deal of angry parleying on both sides, it was agreed that if I allowed our men to assist them to remove they would go, to which I consented."[41] Finlayson did not provide a date for this event, but from the context it would appear that it was some time in 1845. The obvious differences in the second account are the date, Finlayson as HBC negotiator, and the lack of compensation for the relocation. One obvious explanation is that the accounts do not describe the same event. If they do describe the same event, memory has played tricks on one or both of the storytellers. However, for present purposes, the differences do not matter so much as the similarities.

In the article, Latass gives an account of a second meeting, held on May 24, 1850. However, the Fort Victoria Journal entry for that date does not mention this "party" and makes no mention of First Nations at all. The journal entry for May 23 does note that "a large number of the natives are at present assembled here for the purpose of collecting camus." Therefore, it is possible that the event took place as described by Latass, even if it did not merit a mention by the ever-laconic Finlayson in his journal. While the first meeting resolved immediate issues, the second was much more open-ended. It seems to have been a public celebration and confirmation of the existing terms of their coexistence on the land. Although not mentioned by Latass, First Nations attendees likely responded to Douglas's pronouncements with speeches of their own. It seems likely that successive annual celebrations of the Queen's birthday over the early 1850s would have reaffirmed the agreement of the parties to maintain the status quo of sharing the land and its resources.

Neither event as recounted by Latass coincides in time with the accounts of Finlayson, Douglas, and McKay, which describe a series of meetings held between April 29 and May 1, 1850, at Fort Victoria. It is difficult to tell if the omission was deliberate or accidental. Latass may have been unaware of them, chosen to ignore them, or believed they never occurred.

The Saanich Treaties, 1852[42]

Over an eleven-year period, Chief David Latass made at least four attempts to communicate his views on the Saanich Treaties to non-First Nations audiences. His first known attempt was made in 1923, when he wrote to Duncan Campbell Scott, deputy superintendent of Indian affairs. While the letter has not survived, Scott made reference to it in the course of a meeting with representatives of the Allied Tribes of British Columbia, held in Victoria in August of that year: "Now, there is an Indian living here today that was alive when Mackay [sic] was negotiating with the Indians, and he states emphatically that no such an understanding was reached between the Saanich Indians as stated in the Treaty; that no such thing ever occurred – that is the Chief, David Lalask [sic]."[43] On this first occasion, his message, as summarized by Scott, seems to be a simple denial of the existence of a treaty. Latass's views were ignored.

In the 1989 *Saanichton Marina* case, Louise Mandell, counsel for the Tsawout First Nation, led testimony[44] from Gabriel Bartleman as to his recollection of a meeting of the Saanich people in 1924 or 1925, called because Tommy Paul had been prevented from selling fish by a federal fisheries officer. According to Bartleman, such episodes took place "about four times a year." Mandell then asked, "[D]o you recall whether ... after Tommy Paul raised ... the problem, whether there was any action which the chiefs recommended from that meeting to do about the problem he raised?" Bartleman answered, "I believe after the meeting Tommy Paul and Chief David went up to Nanaimo to the Fisheries Office ... When they came back they called another meeting, and it was told to them that they could no longer sell fish from ... the Saanich Arm ... [and that] James Douglas's promises weren't any good." That was the end of the second attempt.

In his testimony, Bartleman posed the following scenario: "[M]aybe you could just picture for yourselves that where then could the native people go to ... They had some trust in the Department of Indian Affairs" and apparently went to visit "a gentleman by the name of Ditchburn" in Victoria, who "was "Commissioner of Indian Affairs." It is likely that the purpose of the visit was to deliver two statements dated April 4, 1932,[45] the first of which was by David Latass, and witnessed by a Stó:lō Elder and activist Simon Pierre. The statement began as follows: "I Chief David Latasse, Tsartlip Reserve, Saanich tribe of Indians ... do solemnly deny any knowledge of the so called Saanich treaty, as shown on Exhibit No. 6, filed by PR. Kelly, Chairman of the Allied Indian Tribes of British Columbia, as set forth in their petition, submitted to parliament in June 1926." He averred that the "only knowledge we know is in regards to a dispute between the whites and Indians at the time of James Douglas – that there was a settlement of that dispute (been [sic] regards to timber matter) ... It was not to sell land or surrender any Territory rights." It is apparent that Latass had modified his position somewhat, acknowledging an agreement with Douglas, but only as a means to resolve a specific problem. It is not known why Latass and the other Chiefs decided to protest in 1932 an event that took place in 1926.

His statement was accompanied by one from "the Chiefs and Councillors of the Saanich Tribes," affirming the truth of Latass's statement, based on what had been told to them by "some of our men" who "were present at the time." The statement concludes as follows: "Mr. McKay, interpretering [sic] for James Douglas, saying these blankets is not to buy your lands, but to shake hands [of] the Indian in good Harmoney and good tumtums (heart). When I get enough of your timber I shall leave the place." Thus, the Chiefs went further than Latass, claiming that Douglas had given them his assurance that he did not intend "to buy your lands." Both statements contain many errors in spelling and grammar, indicating that they were composed without outside assistance or influence. In any event, this third attempt was also ignored by the Department of Indian Affairs. To be disappointed once again may have convinced Latass that complaining to officialdom was a dead end and that he had better make his final plea to the public.

Latass made an attempt to reach a much wider audience in his 1934 interview with Pagett. It is clear that the combined efforts of Paget, Latass's wife, and his grandnephew enabled Latass to convey his views clearly and in much greater detail. On the other hand, parts of his argument may have been skewed in the process of translation and editing. Latass began his account of the Saanich agreements with a much more elaborate and colourful rendering of the "timber" dispute:

> For some time after the whites commenced building their settlement they ferried their supplies ashore. Then they desired to build a dock where ships could be tied up close to shore. Explorers found suitable timbers could be obtained at Cordova Bay, and a gang of whites, Frenchmen and Kanakas were sent there to cut piles. The first thing they did was set a fire which nearly got out of hand, making such a smoke as to attract attention of the Indians for forty miles around. Chief Hotutstun of Salt Spring [Island] sent messengers to Chief Whutsaymullet, of the Saanich tribes telling him that the white men were destroying his heritage and would frighten away fur and game animals.
>
> They met and jointly manned two big canoes and came down the coast to see what damage was being done, and to demand pay from Douglas. Hotutstun was interested by the prospect of sharing in any gifts made to Whutsaymullet but also, indirectly, as the Chief Paramount of all the Indians of Saanich.
>
> As the canoes rounded the point and paddled into Cordova Bay they were seen by camp cooks of the logging party, who became panic stricken. Rushing into the woods they yelled the alarm of Indians on the warpath. Every Frenchman and Kanaka dropped his tools and took to his heels, fleeing th[r]ough the woods to Victoria. As they ran they spread the cry that the Indians were on the warpath.
>
> Douglas hastened to meet the two chieftains and found that the party, with scarcely a weapon other than a few fish spears, were camping in harmony with the white members of the logging detachment. All that was asked was pay for trees cut and damage wrought, which Douglas promptly agreed was right and proper. He ordered two bales of blankets brought from the fort and gave each chief one of them. There was no suggestion that the compensation was for anything other than the timber. No suggestion of title to any land was involved in that matter.[46]

According to Latass, the purpose of the meeting was to resolve a dispute. In other words, it was a peace treaty, which was retrospective, in that it resolved a threat to the peace, but also prospective, as it served notice to Douglas that future logging operations would require prior approval by the appropriate Saanich authorities. Latass then went on to provide, for the first time, an account of a second meeting, which he considered to be the actual treaty negotiation:

> When Douglas met with Chief Hotutstun in 1852, and discussed with him and his sub-chiefs the allotment of lands to the Hudson's Bay Company, it was arranged that lands not needed by the natives might be occupied by the whites. The Indians were to have reserved to their use some choice camping sites, were to have hunting rights everywhere and fishing privileges in all waters, with certain water areas exclusively reserved to the use of the tribes.
>
> In return for the use of meadowlands and open prairie tracts of Saanich, the white people would pay to the tribal chieftains a fee in blankets and goods. That was understood by us all to be payable each year. It was so explained to us by Joseph MacKay, the interpreter for Governor Douglas. The governor himself solemnly assured us that all asked to be ratified would entirely be to the satisfaction of the Indians. He stated that the only object of the writing was to secure the Hudson's Bay Company peaceful and continued use of land tracts suitable for cultivation. This was accompanied by a gift of a few blankets. We all understood that similar gifts would be made each year, what is now called rent.
>
> I was unmarried and therefore considered too young to take part in those proceedings as a tribal representative, but I was present, in attendance upon my uncles, who were among the tribal elders. At that time I thought as did the Indians that the proceedings were just a pow-wow for the purposes of receiving a few trade goods. I say truly that I have no knowledge of payment of money as mentioned in papers supposed to have been signed by Chiefs Hotutstun and Whutsaymullet[47] and their sub-chiefs. I know of no act of signing such papers and believe that no such signatures were in fact made by those tribesmen.[48]

Just as Latass described two meetings at Fort Victoria, each with a different purpose, he chose to relate two meetings in Saanich, also dealing with immediate and long-term concerns, respectively. Latass is clear in his assertion that neither of the meetings included a cession of land as described in the Douglas Forms. The first meeting was called by the Saanich to ensure that Douglas acknowledged his obligation to pay compensation for the felling of timber on their land. According to Latass's account of the second meeting, the Saanich agreed that "lands not needed by the natives might be occupied by the whites," specifically "meadowlands and open prairie tracts … suitable for cultivation."[49] Latass neatly turned the usual assumption on its head by asserting that land would be shared with the whites on terms set by the Saanich First Nation. Similarly, in his clever paraphrase of the "promises" in the second half of the Douglas Forms, Latass expanded their scope, making them unrestricted. His choice of words also indicates an acquaintance, acquired at some point in his long life, of the wording of the Douglas Forms.

Latass claimed that the agreements were to be renewed annually, and he used the analogy of an annual rent, something easily understood by newspaper readers in the 1930s but not necessarily an accurate reflection of the understanding of the parties in 1852. The picture that emerges from the Latass description is a patchwork of habitation and resource sites, some to be shared by the Saanich people and European settlers, and some to be occupied exclusively by one group or the other.

Many First Nations accounts of treaty meetings across Canada contain a denial of the surrender of their lands but do not go on to describe how the resultant sharing of the land was going to work. Latass's account is almost unique in its portrayal of how an agreement to share the land would operate. Finally, his accounts indicate that he was aware of the Douglas Forms but was determined to raise his voice in opposition to the false message he believed they conveyed. In a remarkable validation of Latass's interpretation, in 1989 legal historian Hamar Foster independently came to the same conclusion, namely, that the Saanich "believed that they were agreeing to peaceful relations, to share the right to harvest certain resources, and to allow a limited number of colonists to occupy some of the lands they were not themselves occupying."[50]

The above discussion raises a much broader issue: the reliability of oral history and oral traditions. The topic is huge, but the discussion that follows is brief. The phrase *oral history* is used in many contexts and has many definitions, all too often resulting in confusion and misunderstanding. In the First Nations context, the label is commonly used to designate stories of the past told by today's Elders. These stories serve a multitude of purposes, including expressions of Indigenous law concerning land. Another aspect or category is the testimony of modern Elders in court concerning the terms of historical treaties. The courts in Canada have been extremely reluctant to give any weight to such testimony. For all of the above reasons, this essay avoids the term as much as possible. That said, all of the Indigenous accounts presented here can be regarded as examples of oral history reduced to writing. As a practical measure, designed to avoid these accounts being lumped with the oral history of present-day Elders, I adopt a narrow subcategory: the earliest first- and second-hand accounts reduced to writing after the treaty meetings. Given that these oral histories were recounted by a wide variety of people to a wide range of audiences over a considerable span of time, one could reasonably expect a significant disparity in content. Thus, they are all the more remarkable for the consistency of their descriptions of treaty negotiations concerning land.

Definitions of *oral tradition* are also multiple and contested and for present purposes another narrow subcategory has been created, namely, third-hand and subsequent stories of treaty meetings, passed down from generation to generation to the present day. Much more could be said on the subject of oral histories and traditions, but for present purposes the working definitions set out above will suffice. In 2000, Harriet Van Wart of the Tsawout First Nation searched for oral accounts of the Vancouver Island Treaties and found "only one source that relied primarily on the oral history to interpret the meaning of a Douglas treaty. This was the documentation of Saanich oral history."[51] At this point, it is important to state that there is no intent to deny the existence of additional oral traditions, only that they have not as yet made their way into the public domain. That leaves only the Saanich, who have built a multigeneration oral tradition, largely stemming from Latass and three versions of which have been reduced to writing and are described below.

In his evidence before the court in the *Saanichton Marina* case, Gabriel Bartleman recalled what Latass had said at the 1924 meeting concerning a meeting with Douglas. Bartleman began with an account of the dispute over timber, followed by a statement that "it was a time later when Douglas called the people in to what they thought was a peace offering." At this meeting, "There was some blankets and I believe some metal it was called – the money was called metal then, and to make a cross on a piece of paper, on a blank piece of paper, native people thought that that was the sign of the cross." Counsel asked if Latass told this story at "public gatherings," and Bartleman answered, "Many times." Finally, counsel asked if Bartleman had heard the story from any other Elders, and he answered, "Yes, Mr. Elliot [sic], Dave Elliot."[52]

The best-known version of the oral tradition is contained in a booklet published in 1983 titled *Saltwater People, as Told by Dave Elliott Sr.: A Resource Book for the Saanich Native Studies Program,* edited by Janet Poth.[53] Poth notes that the "words in this book are all Dave's. Over twenty hours of oral history on audio-tape have been transcribed then edited for the written word."[54] Elliott was "born May 17, 1910 on the Tsartlip Indian reserve in Saanich" and died on August 5, 1985.[55] He was five years older than Gabriel Bartleman. In his account of the Saanich Treaty meeting, Elliott relates the tree-cutting episode but adds a second cause of friction with the HBC:

> There was another incident besides that, that already made things not exactly in a state of peace. An Indian boy crossing Douglas' property had been shot and killed. Douglas' property was in the area of Mount Douglas. He had a farm there, and this boy was crossing through. For what reason they shot the boy, I don't know.
>
> We weren't in a state of war, but almost. After these loggers left Cadboro[56] Bay and went back to Victoria, our people just turned around and came home. That's the way things stood when they got the message, or invitation to come into Victoria. Douglas invited all the head people into Victoria.
>
> When they got there, all these piles of blankets plus other goods were on the ground. They told them these bundles of blankets were for them plus about $200 but it was in pounds and shillings.
>
> They saw these bundles of blankets and goods and they were asked to put X's on this paper. They asked each head man to put an X on the paper. Our people didn't know what the X's were for. Actually they didn't call them X's they called them crosses. So they talked back and forth from one to the other and wondered why they were being asked to put these crosses on these papers. One after another, they were asked to put crosses on the paper and they didn't know what the paper said.
>
> What I imagined from looking at the document[57] was that they must have gone to each man and asked them their name and then they transcribed it in a very poor fashion and then asked them to make an X.
>
> One man spoke up after they discussed it,[58] and said, "I think James Douglas wants to keep the peace." They were after all almost in a state of war, a boy had been shot. Also we stopped them from cutting timber and sent them back to Victoria and told them to cut no more timber. "I think these are peace offerings. I think Douglas means to keep the peace. I think these are the signs of the cross." He made the sign of the cross. The missionaries must have already been around by then, because they knew about the "sign of the cross"! "This means Douglas is sincere."
>
> They thought it was just a sign of sincerity and honesty. This was the sign of their God. It was the highest order of honesty. It wasn't much later they

> found out actually they were signing their land away by putting those crosses out there. They didn't know what it said on that paper.
>
> I think if you take a look at the document yourself,[59] you will find out, you can judge for yourself. Look at the X's yourself and you'll see they're all alike, probably written by the same hand. They actually didn't know those were their names and many of those names are not even accurate.[60] They are not even known to Saanich People. Our people were hardly able to talk English at that time and who could understand our language?[61]

This account is basically consistent with the Latass version of the timber dispute, with the addition of the shooting incident and the interpretation of the *x*'s as crosses. However, in Elliott's retelling, the treaty meeting was held at the behest of Douglas, with the purpose of paying compensation for the two incidents and re-establishing peaceful relations. Elliott does not mention any agreement to share the land. The powerful imagery of placing the "crosses" is contradicted by Elliott's own observation that all the *x*'s were "probably made by the same hand." He did not attempt to resolve the inconsistency. Elliott's final comments also indicate that HBC officials may not have been overly scrupulous about verifying the status of the signatories as members of the Saanich First Nation.

In 2004, Janice Knighton wrote a master's thesis titled "The Oral History of the 1852 Saanich Treaty" in which she reprised the accounts given by Gabriel Bartleman and David Elliott and introduced a third version based on an interview with John Elliott.[62] His parents were David Elliott and Beatrice Bartleman, and his mother's grand-uncle was Chief David Latass. John Elliott introduced a new twist as to the location of the Saanich Treaty meeting with Douglas and his officials, who "took them [the Saanich people] up to that mountain up there, the one … they call … Mount Douglas today. It's one of the highest mountains in that area. We call it P'kols, and [Douglas] pointed outward where our people could roam freely and not be bothered." According to John Elliott, "that was what I was told by Manny Cooper, he's an elder cousin of mine."[63]

The Nanaimo Treaty, 1854

The Nanaimo Treaty is unique because the "signature" sheets are not accompanied by a Douglas Form. In tangible form, it consists of only a six-page list in ink of 159 names under the heading "Sarlequin Tribe."[64] The Douglas Form has either been lost or, more likely, was never completed. To the right of each name is "his X mark." Pinned to the top of the list is a slip of paper with the following words (written in an unknown hand) in pencil: "Similar conveyance of country extending from Commercial Inlet 12 miles up the Nanaimo River made by the Sarlequin Tribe signed Squoniston and others."[65] The treaty was witnessed by three HBC officers and "James Douglas, Governor Vancouver Island." It is the only Douglas Form signed by Douglas.

The earliest First Nations account of the Vancouver Island Treaties arose out of testimony before the Royal Commission on Indian Affairs for BC, established in 1912 under an agreement entered into by federal representative J.A.J. McKenna and BC premier Richard McBride "to settle all differences between the Governments of the Dominion and the Province respecting Indian lands and Indian Affairs generally in the Province of British Columbia."[66] The mandate sounds broad, but later provisions in the agreement make it clear that the remit of the commission was limited to increasing or decreasing the size of reserves.[67] Revisiting the Vancouver Island Treaties was definitely not on the commission's agenda. The commission was made up of two federal commissioners, two provincial commissioners, and a fifth commissioner, to be chosen by the other four. The commission held hearings around the province, and transcripts were made of the testimony of witnesses, generally First Nations representatives and Indian agents.

The first testimony at the Nanaimo meeting was given by the Snuneymuxw Chief, Louis A. Good, who spoke English fluently and did not need a translator. The second speaker was band member Dick Whoakum, who stated he was eighty-three years old and would have been twenty-four years old when the treaty was signed. His name is included among the 159 names listed on the *Douglas Form*; accordingly, his is the only First Nations account by a signatory to a Vancouver Island Treaty. Whoakum could not speak English, so two interpreters were sworn in. One was Chief Good and the other was Simon Pierre, from the Katzie First Nation on the lower Fraser River. The Snuneymuxw and the Katzie spoke closely related dialects of the Halkomelem language.[68] Pierre's skill as a translator is confirmed by the fact that he was chosen to accompany three prominent Salish Chiefs to London in 1906 and translated their speeches to King Edward VII.[69] Thus, both translators possessed the skill to accurately translate from English to Halkomelem and vice versa. In sworn testimony before the

Royal Commission in 1913, Whoakum recalled his meeting with James Douglas:

> I want to tell you people that I was amongst the first people who found coal in Nanaimo ...[70]
>
> Two months later,[71] Sir James Douglas himself came over to see where the coal was. Sir James Douglas said "I will buy this coal" but he said "I will not buy anything but the coal." "All the wood and the land is yours." "The land where the coal is, is yours, and the land up the River[72] is yours" ...
>
> The Indians that used to live here, their main home was at Departure Bay, at other times they lived on the Island,[73] and on Nanaimo River ... I told Sir James Douglas that these three places were our land. Sir James Douglas said "I don't take any land away from you at all. All these three places where you live at different times are yours." The promise that Sir James Douglas made with us, is being broken. We are being pushed off our land.[74] They are now stopping the Indians from cutting the wood and from taking the fish.[75]

Whoakum is clear that Douglas asked only for permission to take the coal, not their land. Douglas's promise that "[a]ll these three places where you live at different times are yours" is a rare colonial acknowledgment that *village sites* include all seasonally occupied sites, not just winter villages. Finally, Whoakum is also clear that in pushing the Snuneymuxw off their land, and "stopping the Indians from cutting the wood and from taking the fish," white settlers had broken "[t]he promise that Sir James Douglas made with us." In other words, according to Whoakum, Douglas had promised that the Snuneymuxw could keep their land and continue to harvest the resources of the land and water without interference. After listening to Whoakum's statement, Commissioner McKenna engaged in the following exchange:

Q: What do your people want today?
A: What we want is to get the land back or to get some settlement.
Q: You say that you and some other Indians brought down furs to Victoria, and also coal. Before that time, were there no white men here?
A: No there were no white men before that.
Q: Then afterwards Sir James Douglas came out?
A: Yes.
Q: And you made treaty with Sir James?
A: Yes. He said "the land is yours."

Q: And then he paid your people some money?
A: There was no money paid.[76]
Q: The Chiefs agreed that the rest of the land was open to Sir James Douglas, and the other people to come in?
A: There was no white man here.[77]
Q: But they agreed to allow Sir James Douglas and the others to come in?
A: By and by the white men came over and made their home here.[78]

McKenna's questions are blunt, and Whoakum's responses are equally direct and terse, but they disclose a keen awareness of the answers McKenna was trying (without success) to elicit. The statement by Whoakum that "[w]hat we want is to get the land back or to get some settlement" anticipates and encapsulates the present-day claims of treaty First Nations. It bears noting that the use of the word *treaty* by McKenna is an exceedingly rare pre-1964 official acknowledgment of the status of the agreement.

The opening statement and subsequent exchange are important because they directly address the issue of the terms of the treaty, with the First Nations version being provided by an eyewitness under oath. Whoakum acknowledged the fact of a treaty, presumably to arrange for the sale of coal, but steadfastly denied that it was intended to authorize the indiscriminate occupation of their land by whites. He was the only First Nations speaker at any of the commission's meetings on the Island to raise the issue of the Vancouver Island Treaties. It should be noted that the official reports of the commission do not contain any reference to the testimony heard by the commissioners. Unfortunately, Whoakum's name does not appear anywhere else in the archival record, so it is not possible to assess his veracity other than as revealed in his statements to the McKenna-McBride Commission. Sadly, when asked by Commissioner McKenna "Do you have any family?," Whoakum answered, "No sir, I have no family."

Recently, I became aware of the existence of a second-hand account of the Nanaimo Treaty by the son of one of the signatories, published in the *Vancouver Sun* in 1922, as one of a series of articles on BC First Nations.[79] The author of the article styled himself "Chief Buffalo Child Long Lance," but this was a *nom de plume.*[80] It appears that Long Lance was an unreliable source of information about his own past, but there is no indication that he tampered with the story solicited from his informant, Bobby *Yaklam.* How Long Lance learned of Yacklam and who chose the topic of the article are unknown. In any event, Long Lance interviewed Bobby Yaklam, who related the story, as told by his father, Chief Zok-leston:

> The company's [HBC] exploring ship was first attracted to the site of Nanaimo by the rich seams of coal observed along its shoreline. Going ashore, the captain was met by Chief Zok-leston[81] and a party of Nanaimos ... The captain informed the chief that they desired to be friends of his people, and asked him to accept a little present of blankets, shirts and tobacco, as a token of good-will. Chief Zok-leston accepted this offering as a gift and went back to his people with the good news. He gathered them together and distributed these articles among the various heads of families, commanding them to be friendly towards the whites. When the Company began to remove coal from its [the tribe's] land it did not look unkindly upon this, as the Indians had often built fires from it, but had been driven away from them by the disagreeable odor. But, when a few years later the Indians were ordered to clear out of the town and move to their present habitation on the outskirts of Nanaimo, they enquired the reason for this sudden turn of events, and were told that the land which they were occupying belonged to the H.B. Company; that it had been bought from Chief Zok-leston for a number of specified articles, which turned out to be the above blankets, shirts and tobacco.[82]

This account suggests that the Snuneymuxw people were led to believe that the HBC simply sought and obtained their consent to the removal of coal from their land, in return for a "present" of trade goods. While the Yacklum story is brief, it is consistent with Whoakum's claim that the Snuneymux were not made aware that the arrangement rendered their continued presence on the land entirely at the discretion of the company and the Crown.

In 1931 a part-time journalist, Beryl Cryer, was hired by the editor of the *Victoria Daily Colonist* to "submit accounts of native histories and mythologies for the newspaper's popular *Sunday Magazine,*" and over the next three years she contributed more than "sixty articles based on narratives by distinguished native elders."[83] Chris Arnett, as editor of a collection of her stories, conducted a thorough examination of the reliability of her accounts and concluded that "she strived for accuracy and authenticity in the collection of her data."[84]

In 1933, Cryer met several times with Snuneymuxw Elder Quen-Es-Then (Joe Wyse) and his wife, Tstass-Aya (Jennie), at their home on the Nanaimo

Indian Reserve. She recorded a number of stories. On one occasion, the couple decided to tell the story of a meeting between the Snuneymuxw people and James Douglas. Cryer described the Wyses as "a tall, thin, old couple, both speaking good English" and noted that Joe, "in spite of his great age, is remarkably alert."[85] The death certificate of Joseph Wyse lists his date of birth as May 24, 1852, which means he would have been only two and a half years old at the time of the 1854 treaty meeting. After interviewing the couple, Cryer published the story in the *Victoria Daily Colonist.*[86] The interview began with Jennie stating that "My man, he can talk English, but I talk it better, so he will tell me, and I will tell you!" Through Jennie, Joe said "he thanks you, kind white lady, for coming to hear his stories. Always he has wanted to tell what he knows to the white people, but nobody has time to listen."[87] As with Latass's 1934 interview, Wyse's motivation appears to have been having a last chance to tell an important story before he died. The following account, according to Arnett,[88] records the Nanaimo Treaty meeting between the Snuneymuxw First Nation and James Douglas:

> Well, one day a Hudson's Bay man came to see my [Quen-Es-Then's] father. "We want to talk to you and your people about this coal," he said. "We will have a meeting. You and all your people, and you must get another chief and his people, and on a certain day we will all talk this thing over."
>
> So my father, Chief Sugnuston,[89] called all his people, and he told another chief, whose name was Chief Schuna'h'un, to call his tribe, and together they went to the meeting. Now, you know where the big wharf is now where the steamers come? Well, down there is a rock in the water. In those old days it was part of the land, and at that place was a very big house.[90] To that house there went all the Hudson's Bay men, and the two chiefs with their people.
>
> Here, Quen-Es-Then interrupted, "I was at that meeting," he said. "I can remember all the people in that house, and lots outside, but I was only a small boy standing beside my father."
>
> Then the Hudson's Bay men talked to the Indians. "This coal that is here," they said, "is no good to you, and we would like it; but we want to be friends, so, if you will let us come and take as much of this black rock as we want, we will be good to you." They told my father, "The good Queen, our great white Queen over the water will look after your people for all time, and they will be given much money, so that they will never be poor." Then they gave each chief a bale of Hudson's Bay blankets and a lot of shirts and tobacco, just like rope! "These are presents for you and your people, to show we are

> your good friends," they said. The chiefs took the things, and they cut the blankets, which were double ones, in half, to make more, and gave one to every chief man, then the shirts, and to those who were left they gave pieces of the rope tobacco; so that every man in the tribes had a present.
>
> Now you know, said Tstass-Aya, we think there was some mistake made at that meeting, or, maybe, the people could not understand properly what was said; but later, when our people asked for some of the money for their coal, the Hudson's Bay men said to them, "Oh, we paid you when we gave you those good blankets!" But those two chiefs knew that the man had said, "The Queen will give you money."[91]

The detailed description of the circumstances and locale of the meeting make it very likely that it was the meeting of December 23, 1854. The reference to the Queen is a potentially significant indication that the Snuneymuxw by 1854 had gained an appreciation of the Crown as an entity separate from the HBC. There was no mention of a sale of land, just of coal, on the basis that "much money" would be paid for it over time. In other words, the treaty may have ceded mineral rights in exchange for royalties, but nothing more. The account is also consistent with Latass's claim that the distribution of blankets at treaty meetings was not to be considered a one-time event.

Treaty Categories: Old and New

The five First Nations accounts presented here each have significant weaknesses, but in combination they provide a strong denial of the cession or surrender of land in favour of the HBC or the Crown. If the Vancouver Island Treaties are not cession treaties, what are they? What characterization(s) would better suit them? To answer that question, we need to review the standard categories and promote a new one. The three standard categories used to pigeon-hole historical treaties between First Nations and the Crown are "trade," "peace and goodwill," and "cession." Typically, the trade treaties are presented in the literature as the predecessors of peace and goodwill agreements, which were popular in the eighteenth century in the Maritimes and what is now Ontario. Neither category includes a surrender of land by First Nations in favour of representatives of the Crown. The third category emerged in what is now modern-day Ontario when First Nations entered into agreements to surrender parts of their territory to representatives of the Crown, to clear the way for occupation and development of the land by settlers. Starting with the Huron and Superior (also known as the "Robinson") Treaties of 1850 a new era commenced in which the governments of the day favoured cessions of the entire territory of a First Nation, the allocation of small plots of land, and limited rights to hunt and fish over the ceded land. This kind of arrangement was continued via the eleven Numbered Treaties across the Prairies and into northern Canada between 1871 and 1923, as mineral development and settler pressure moved westward and northward.

Where do the Vancouver Island Treaties fit in the history of treaty making across Canada? In short, they don't. In the literature, they are considered outliers, not part of the mainstream development of treaties from east to west to north. They are therefore accorded little attention and dismissed as small and unimportant. In which category *do* they belong? Some would argue that they are mere trade agreements made by Douglas on behalf of the Hudson's Bay Company. Some have argued that they are mere expressions of peace and goodwill. Most scholars, and the courts, accepted them as cession treaties by which local First Nations gave up their land to Douglas, who was acting as agent of the British Crown. Do these three categories adequately describe the major characteristics of all the historical agreements across Canada over the last three hundred years? According to recent scholarship, they do not. What is missing?

All three treaty categories as presented in the literature over-represent colonial interests, demonstrating an urgent need for new categories, for categories that are more inclusive of First Nations interests and understandings. There are many potential candidates, but only one is discussed here. The category "sharing treaty" is already well established in the academic literature, but it has not, as yet, been accepted by the courts in Canada.

A sharing treaty is based on First Nations understandings of treaties as agreements to share their land with newcomers, namely, the settler population of Canada. For example, Aimee Craft produced a book in 2013 dealing with the first of the Numbered Treaties titled *Breathing Life into the Stone Fort Treaty: An Anishinabe Understanding of Treaty One.* The treaty covered southern Manitoba. Craft is a lawyer and Anishinaabe community member, and much of the book is devoted to the Indigenous law that informed First Nations negotiations. She frequently used quotes from newspaper reports of the negotiations, such as this excerpt from Chief Ayee-ta-pe-pe-tung's address to the treaty commissioners: "I understand you are going to buy this land from me. Well God made me out of this very clay that is besmeared on my body. This is what you say you are going to buy from me."[92] She also quotes from recent interviews with Elders, such as Victor Courchene:

> One old man, much older than me, said his grandfather told him about the Treaty and how it was supposed to work. He said it is like a plate and the resources were on that plate. The white man was invited to come and eat from that plate together with the Anishinabe. This is how he understood the Treaty. They never gave up anything.[93]

Craft concluded that "while both the Anishinabe and Crown negotiators viewed the treaty as being related to land," the Crown contemplated "a total and complete surrender and acquisition of land," while the Anishinaabe "did not view Treaty as a sale of land, but as an agreement to share in its bounty." In sum, "This is what the elders refer to as a 'sharing treaty.'"[94]

University of Victoria philosopher James Tully addressed the topic of "Indigenous peoples" in 2008 and had this to say about the early historical treaties between the Crown and First Nations:

> Canada is founded on an act of sharing that is almost unimaginable in its generosity. The Aboriginal peoples shared their food, hunting and agricultural techniques, practical knowledge, trade routes and geographic knowledge with the needy newcomers. Without this, the first immigrants would have been unable to survive ... the Aboriginal peoples formalized the relation of sharing in the early treaties in the following form: they agreed to share this land with the newcomers on the agreement that the newcomers would neither attempt to govern them nor use their land without their consent. The treaties involved other exchanges as well, such as trade, military, educational and medical benefits, and political and legal interrelations, but the sharing of land and trade on this understanding were at the heart of the relationship.[95]

University of Victoria anthropologist Michael Asch, in a recent book on the Numbered Treaties, highlights the two major approaches adopted by the parties to the historical treaties, starting with that of the Crown: "[F]or each of the numbered treaties, governments in Canada (and others) insist that Indigenous peoples consented to transfer all authority to the Crown, thereby leaving Settlers free to do as they please with their lands."[96]

He contrasts this with the understanding of the treaty First Nations: "They speak with one voice in asserting that what the Crown asked for was permission to share the land, not to transfer the authority to govern it."[97] The two viewpoints are radically different, which raises the possibility that there was no common understanding and thus no treaties. Asch responds to that argument as follows: "it is my view that, despite cultural differences, there is every chance that these parties could have achieved a degree of shared understanding at the time of negotiations to conclude an agreement based on mutual consent."[98] Of course, that in turn raises the likelihood that one version is more accurate than the other, and based on his research Asch concluded that "the 'sharing' interpretation more closely reflects what transpired than does the written version."[99]

Do these views have application to the Vancouver Island Treaties? The answer is yes, they are best described as sharing treaties. The pieces of the puzzle contributed by each First Nations account add up to a convincing argument that the Vancouver Island Treaties included the following terms: compensation for land already occupied and resources previously harvested by non-First Nations residents; continuation of the terms of their existing joint occupation and enjoyment of land and resources; and agreement to negotiate expansion of non-First Nations establishments and activities, provided they did not interfere with the existing way of life of the First Nations. In sum, First Nations negotiated with James Douglas an agreement to share, not surrender, their land and its resources.

Notes

1 Katie DeRosa, "Tsartlip Blockade Severs Traffic Artery," *Victoria Times Colonist*, October 17, 2010, 1.

2 "Douglas Treaties," *Wikipedia*, https://en.wikipedia.org/wiki/Douglas_Treaties.

3 Aboriginal Affairs and Northern Development, "Treaty Tests – Douglas Treaties," accessed August 14, 2015, https://www.aadnc-aandc.gc.ca/eng/1100100029052/1100100029053.

4 *R v Morris and Olsen*, 2006 SCC 59, [2006] 2 SCR 915, para 24.

5 *R v Bartleman*, [1984] 55 BCLR 78 (BCCA), para 41.

6 Douglas C. Harris, *Landing Native Fisheries: Indian Reserves and Fishing Rights in British Columbia, 1849–1925* (Vancouver: UBC Press, 2008), 24.

7 The British government had delegated treaty-making power on Vancouver Island to the HBC, which in turn appointed Douglas as its agent for the purpose of negotiating the agreements.

8 The words *signature* and *subscribed* refer to a column of *x*'s on a sheet of paper, with a transliterated name beside each *x*.

9 The "deed of purchase" for the "Sangees" land was ultimately embodied in six separate documents, the "Clallum" in two documents, and the "Soke" in one document, for a total of nine "Fort Victoria Treaties."

10 It is unclear why Douglas requested a "proper form." He may have believed Barclay to be in possession of, or able to acquire, such a form, or he may have felt it more prudent to request a template that Barclay would find acceptable as to "form."

11 Adele Perry, "The Colonial Archive on Trial: Possession, Dispossession, and History in *Delgamuukw v. British Columbia,*" in *Archive Stories: Facts, Fictions, and the Writing of History,* ed. Antoinette Burton (Durham, NC: Duke University Press, 2005), 328–29.

12 Facsimile copies of all fourteen of the Douglas Forms are available on the BC Archives website, https://royalbcmuseum.bc.ca/bc-archives/what-we-have/indigenous-material/vancouver-island-treaty-translations.

13 R. Cole Harris, *Making Native Space: Colonialism, Resistance, and Reserves in British Columbia* (Vancouver: UBC Press, 2002), 25.

14 Fort Victoria Journal, 1846–50, April 29, 1850, Hudson's Bay Company Archives (HBCA), B.226/a/1, reel 1M149 (available online at http://www.fortvictoriajournal.ca/).

15 Hartwell Bowsfield, ed., *Fort Victoria Letters, 1846–1851* (Winnipeg: Hudson's Bay Record Society, 1979), 94.

16 Joseph McKay to Dr. James S. Helmcken, December 3, 1888, BC Archives (BCA), Joseph William McKay Fonds, PR-0560, MS-1917, file 27.

17 Also known as "Tomo Ouamtomy" and "Tomo Antoine." His qualifications as a translator are discussed in Chapter 3 of Neil Vallance, "Sharing the Land: The Formation of the Vancouver Island (or 'Douglas') Treaties of 1850–1854 in Historical, Legal and Comparative Context" (PhD diss., University of Victoria, 2016).

18 Staines, a Church of England minister, arrived at Fort Victoria in March 1849 and started a school for the children of HBC officers. See Madge Wolfenden, "Staines, Robert John," *Dictionary of Canadian Biography,* vol. 8, Université Laval/University of Toronto, 2003–, http://www.biographi.ca/en/bio/staines_robert_john_8E.html.

19 Lempfrit arrived at Fort Victoria in June 1849 on the same ship that carried Douglas and his family to their new home. He immediately set up a school for the children of the company's Métis employees. See Edith E. Down "The History of Catholic Education in British Columbia, 1847–1900," *Study Sessions* 50 (1983): 569–90.

20 Douglas C. Harris, "The *Boldt* Decision in Canada: Aboriginal Treaty Rights to Fish on the Pacific," in *The Power of Promises: Rethinking Indian Treaties in the Pacific Northwest,* ed. Alexandra Harmon (Seattle: University of Washington Press, 2008), 140.

21 There are four variants of his surname: Latass, Latasse, Latess, and Latesse. I have opted to use the first.

22 Frank Pagett, "105 Years in Victoria and Saanich! Chief David Recalls White Man's Coming; 80 Years Rent Unpaid," *Victoria Daily Times,* July 14, 1934.

23 Transcripts of testimony before the McKenna-McBride Commission are available on the BC Union of Indian Chiefs website, "UBCIC Library and Archives," http://www.ubcic.bc.ca/library.

24 Beryl Mildred Cryer and Chris Arnett, *Two Houses Half-Buried in the Sand: Oral Traditions of the Hul'q'umi'num' Coast Salish of Kuper Island and Vancouver Island* (Vancouver: Talonbooks, 2007).

25 Harris, *Making Native Space;* Grant R. Keddie, *Songhees Pictorial: A History of the Songhees People as Seen by Outsiders, 1790–1912* (Victoria: Royal BC Museum, 2003); and John Sutton Lutz, *Makúk: A New History of Aboriginal-White Relations* (Vancouver: UBC Press, 2008).

26 A Google search of "Pagett" yielded only one additional reference to his work, an article on the history of the Victoria Public Library, also published in 1934. Frank Pagett, "Victoria Is Proud of Senior Public Library," *Victoria Times,* July 21, 1934.

27 Ibid.

28 The letter was from a Victoria law firm Hanington and Jackson to the provincial minister of lands. Hanington and Jackson to W.R. Ross, Provincial Minister of Lands, 1911, Library and Archives Canada (LAC), RG 10, Department of Indian Affairs, vol. 3690, file 13,886-4. The discrepancy in the two accounts as to Latass's age when he moved to Saanich does little to support the accuracy of his claim to be 106 years old.

29 Pagett, "105 Years."

30 Provincial archaeologist Grant Keddie, in an article written in 1992 on the ceremonies surrounding a visit to Victoria of the governor general in 1927, quotes from an (unidentified) newspaper story that notes the participation of "Chief David, of the Saanich Tribe, who is approaching ninety years of age": Grant Keddie, "Installation of a Songhees Chief," *Discovery* 20, 1 (Winter 1992): 2. Ethnographer Diamond Jenness notes in his unpublished manuscript "Indians of Vancouver Island" that he used David Latass as an informant and that he "died in 1937 [sic] at the age of over 90": Diamond Jenness, "Indians of Vancouver Island," unpublished manuscript, ca. 1930s, BCA. A search of census records yielded one entry, in the 1921 Canadian Census (available online). David is listed as being sixty-five years old, which, if accurate, would mean that he was born in 1859. He is listed as unable to read or write, but his wife, Genevieve, is listed as literate, so she presumably supplied the information to the census taker. On the other hand, his death certificate at BC Archives, also based on information supplied by Genevieve, states that "David Joseph Latess" died at Brentwood in September 1936, at the age of 110 years, which indicates to me that she is not a reliable source on his age.

31 Chris Friday, "Performing Treaties: The Culture and Politics of Treaty Remembrance and Celebration," in *The Power of Promises: Rethinking Indian Treaties in the Pacific Northwest,* ed. Alexandra Harmon (Seattle: University of Washington, 2008), 157–85.

32 Hamar Foster, "The Saanichton Bay Marina Case: Imperial Law, Colonial History and Competing Theories of Aboriginal Title," *UBC Law Review* 23, 3 (1989): 632.

33 *Saanichton Marina Ltd v Louis Claxton et al,* transcript of proceedings at trial on September 2, 1987, 27–29. Copy in possession of Hamar Foster.

34 Ibid., 28.

35 Pagett, "105 Years," 1. Her name was Genevieve Latess, according to David's death certificate. Death register of David Latesse, BCA, GR-2951, vol. 020, 1936-09-020220, reel B13363.

36 Paull has an entry on Wrestlingdata.com showing a birth date of 1895 and a date of death of 1966. He enjoyed a wrestling career as "Chief Thunderbird" from 1930 to 1955. "Chief Thunderbird," Wrestlingdata.com, http://wrestlingdata.com/index.php?befehl=bios&wrestler=2651&bild=1&details=7&liga=297&jahr=1935

37 The Fort Victoria Journal entry for this date does not mention any public gathering; HBCA, Fort Victoria Journal, 1846–50, B.226/a/1, reel 1M149.

38 The weeks surrounding the Queen's birthday coincided with the height of the camas harvesting season, which drew visitors from Saanich and the Cowichan Valley. See Fort Victoria Journal entries for May 1850.

39 This description gives a unique visual image of the arrangement of First Nations when meeting with Douglas.

40 The reference to the "Great White Queen" is interesting as it is the only indication in the archival record that Douglas invoked the name of the Queen at a treaty meeting.

41 BC Heritage, "Biography of Roderick Finlayson, 1818–1892," "Hudson's Bay Company at Fort Victoria: Fort Life," accessed August 14, 2015, http://bcheritage.ca/fortvictoria/fortlife/rod.html.
42 While there are two Saanich Treaties, most of the literature and historical documents do not differentiate between them, so references to the Saanich agreements can be assumed to apply to both of them, unless otherwise specified.
43 Reproduced in BC Union of Indian Chiefs website, "UBCIC Library and Archives," accessed August 15, 2015, http://www.ubcic.bc.ca/library.
44 Foster, "The Saanichton Bay Marina Case."
45 "Statement by Chief David Latasse," April 4, 1932, BCA, RG 10, vol. 2:303, file 974/1–9.
46 Pagett, "105 Years," 1.
47 *Hotutstun* and *Whutsymullet* were the first names listed on the written versions of the North Saanich and South Saanich treaties, respectively.
48 Pagett, "105 Years," 1.
49 Ibid.
50 Foster, "The Saanichton Bay Marina Case," 632.
51 Harriet Van Wart, "A Bibliography and Discussion of Douglas Treaty Materials: Phase One of Research on the Tsawout First Nation's Douglas Treaty" (master's thesis, University of Victoria, 2001), 40.
52 *Saanichton* (see note 33, above), 28.
53 Dave Elliott, *Saltwater People, as Told by Dave Elliott Sr.: A Resource Book for the Saanich Native Studies Program,* ed. Janet Poth (Saanichton, BC: School District 63, 1990).
54 Ibid., 3.
55 Ibid., 5.
56 Both the Latass and the subsequent Bartleman accounts place the incident at Mount Douglas, which overlooks Cordova Bay, indicating that Elliott was likely in error on this minor point.
57 Here, Elliott departs from the oral history account and makes inferences based on his personal inspection of the document.
58 Elliott clearly reverts to the oral history at this point.
59 Once again, Elliott departs from the oral history to make inferences based on his inspection of the treaty document. He in fact contradicts the oral history, inferring that the *x*'s were not made by the First Nations representatives.
60 It is difficult to ascertain the accuracy of the transliterations of names on the written treaty forms.
61 Elliott, *Saltwater People,* 69–73.
62 Janice Knighton, "The Oral History of the Saanich Douglas Treaties: A Treaty for Peace" (master's thesis, University of Victoria, 2004). Available online at http://web.uvic.ca/igov/index.php/igov-598-community-governance-project.
63 Ibid., 23.
64 See facsimile reproduced on the BC Archives website.
65 The above description is based on a personal inspection, in 2005, of the original treaty document at BC Archives at the invitation of the Chief and Council of the Snuneymuxw First Nation. I have not located any information that would explain the discrepancy in descriptions of the territory conveyed, between the pencilled notation at the top of the treaty document and the description in Douglas's letter. The latter covers a much larger area than the former. According to Wilson Duff, at the top of the first five Fort Victoria documents, "Douglas wrote in pencil a memorandum or

prologue describing the territory of the group concerned. This was likely done in the presence of the Indians and served as the basis for the description to be written later into the body of the text." See Wilson Duff, "The Fort Victoria Treaties," *BC Studies* 3 (Fall 1969): 11.

66 The agreement is reproduced in Robert E. Cail, *Land, Man, and the Law: The Disposal of Crown Lands in British Columbia, 1871–1913* (Vancouver: UBC Press, 1974), 304.

67 Ibid.

68 Wayne Suttles, "Central Coast Salish," in *Handbook of North American Indians,* vol. 7, *The Northwest Coast,* ed. Wayne Suttles (Washington, DC: Smithsonian Institution, 1990), 455.

69 Keith Thor Carlson, *The Power of Place, the Problem of Time: Aboriginal Identity and Historical Consciousness in the Cauldron of Colonialism* (Toronto: University of Toronto Press, 2010), 265–69.

70 In 1852, the presence of coal seams at Nanaimo Harbour was made known to the HBC by members of the Snuneymuxw First Nation. See "Report of Canoe Trip by James Douglas to Colonial Office, August 27, 1852," HBCA, PRO CO 305/3, folios 134–39d. The balance of Whoakum's description of the coal discovery is omitted.

71 Whoakum may have conflated two meetings with Douglas, the first in 1852 when Douglas first visited Nanaimo, and the second in 1854.

72 This is the Nanaimo River.

73 The "island" is Gabriola Island, which is close to Nanaimo. See Homer Barnett, *The Coast Salish of British Columbia* (Eugene: University of Oregon, 1955), 22.

74 According to Joseph McKay, in his 1888 letter, the purpose of the treaty was compensation, because the "Nanaimos had to surrender their principal village sites to make room for the mining operations carried on there." Joseph McKay to Dr. James S. Helmcken, December 3, 1888, BCA, Joseph William McKay Fonds, PR-0560, MS-1917, file 27.

75 Transcripts of his testimony before the McKenna-McBride Commission are available on the BC Union of Indian Chiefs website. BC Union of Indian Chiefs, "UBCIC Library and Archives," accessed August 15, 2015, http://www.ubcic.bc.ca/library.

76 Technically, Whoakum is correct: blankets, not money, were distributed. Alternatively, Whoakum may have meant that the blankets were not a payment but a gift.

77 Presumably, Whoakum understood McKenna's reference to "the other people" to mean settlers.

78 Again, Whoakum is careful to point out that "the others" arrived later and simply "made their home here."

79 My thanks to Donald B. Smith of the University of Calgary for bringing this to my attention.

80 Donald B. Smith, "From Sylvester Long to Chief Buffalo Child Long Lance," in *Being and Becoming Indian: Biographical Studies of North American Frontiers,* ed. James A. Clifton (Chicago: Dorsey Press, 1989), 183–203.

81 By examining the list of names making up the Nanaimo Douglas Form, I found a transliteration of the name of a Chief that appears to be a close match to "Zok-leston."

82 Chief Buffalo Child Long Lance, "Greatest Real Estate Deal Recorded," *Vancouver Sunday Sun,* June 4, 1922.

83 Cryer and Arnett, *Two Houses Half-Buried in the Sand,* 17.

84 Ibid., 23.

85 Ibid., 186.

86 Beryl Cryer, "Ki'et'sa'kun of Nanaimo: Telling How Governor Douglas Renamed Him 'Coal Tyee,'" *Victoria Daily Colonist,* March 5, 1933; reproduced in Cryer and Arnett, *Two Houses Half-Buried in the Sand,* 186–92.

87 Ibid., 187–88.

88 Ibid., 186.

89 *Sugnuston* is a variant spelling of *Squoniston.* Chief Squoniston is identified as the chief signatory of the Nanaimo Treaty in British Columbia, *Papers Connected to the Indian Land Question, 1850–1875* (Victoria: R. Wolfenden, 1875), 11: "and signed Squoniston and others."

90 The relocation of the Snuneymuxw from this village on the harbour to the present "town" reserve took place in 1862. See Booth Good, "Mission to the 'Nanaimo Tribe', Vancouver's Island," *The Mission Field,* 8 (1863): 116–18.

91 Ibid., 191–92.

92 Aimee Craft, *Breathing Life into the Stone Fort Treaty: An Anishinabe Understanding of Treaty One* (Vancouver: UBC Press, 2013), 112.

93 Ibid., 110.

94 Ibid., 61.

95 James Tully, *Public Philosophy in a New Key,* vol. 1, *Democracy and Civic Freedom* (Cambridge: Cambridge University Press, 2008), 245.

96 Michael Asch, *On Being Here to Stay: Treaties and Aboriginal Rights in Canada* (Toronto: University of Toronto Press, 2013), 76.

97 Ibid., 77.

98 Ibid., 78.

99 Ibid., 80.

5

SENĆOŦEN and Lekwungen Texts of the Vancouver Island Treaties

Neil Vallance, STOLȻEȽ John Elliott, Sr., and Elmer George

Little is known about the translations back and forth that surely occurred at the Vancouver Island Treaty meetings.[1] There is only one mention of an interpreter in the historical record, and it was made in a letter by Joseph McKay, who signed as witness to nine of the fourteen written versions of the treaties. He wrote in 1886, over thirty years after the events described:

> Mr. Douglas was very cautious in all his proceedings. The day before the meeting with the Indians, he sent for me and handed me the document above referred to telling me to study it carefully and to commit as much of it to memory as possible in order that I might check the interpreter Thomas should he fail to explain properly to the Indians the substance of Mr. Douglas's address to them.

As is argued by Graham Brazier in this volume, it is no longer clear what document McKay was referring to. To further complicate matters, McKay did not specify whether Thomas spoke in the Chinook Jargon, Lekwungen, SENĆOŦEN, or all three. The problems of communicating the terms of a treaty through the medium of the Chinook Jargon, which has a vocabulary of less than one thousand words, would have been enormous. However, there is sufficient documentation of the abilities of Thomas and McKay as linguists to conclude that Thomas likely addressed the First Nations in their own languages, rather than in Chinook.

In March 1852, James Douglas, governor of Vancouver Island, had recommended McKay for an increase in salary, noting that he "is employed as Indian trader, as he speaks the language fluently, and possesses an uncommon degree of tact and address, in managing Indians."[2] At the time, Thomas Ouamtany (also known as "Tomo Antoine" and "Tomo Omtamy"), who joined the Hudson's Bay Company (HBC) around 1843, was stationed at Fort Victoria as an interpreter, a position he held until 1854.[3] Ouamtany had a considerable reputation as a linguist, as described by Robert Brown, who hired him in 1864 as a translator on an exploring expedition up the east coast of Vancouver Island: "He was at one [time] high in favour with Governor Douglas whose constant factotum he was on every expedition. He served for some time in the H B Company in several capacities, as guide, hunter, and interpreter in all of which capacities he stands unrivalled."[4] Brown commented that "few [Indians] understood any Chinook or English while Tomo spoke English without an accent."[5]

By 1850, some of the First Nations participants at the treaty meetings would have picked up a few words of English in their trade and paid labour relations with HBC employees. However, it is highly unlikely that any had a sufficient grasp of the English language and common law to understand Douglas's speech. Therefore, the words spoken by Thomas are crucial. He faced a difficult task. On the one hand, he had to satisfy McKay that he had adequately translated Douglas's speech. On the other, he had to phrase Douglas's proposal in such a way as to not alienate the First Nations parties. Not addressed in McKay's letter is the issue of whether the First Nations agreed to Douglas's proposal without demur or whether Thomas had to work hard, mediating the respective demands of the parties until some form of consensus was achieved.

Therefore, the key question is how Thomas translated Douglas's words to the assembled First Nations. Did he go to the lengths necessary for the First Nations to comprehend that, in the words of McKay, "the British Government did not admit that nomad tribes had any property in lands which they had not improved nor occupied for permanently industrial or useful purposes, and over which they had not established any form of government nor system of land tenure"?[6] Or did he use words consistent with Chief David Latass's 1934 account of what Douglas said at the treaty meetings: "He assured the chiefs that trade in furs with peaceful use of enough land to grow food were the only reasons for establishment of the settlement"?[7] The simple answer is that his words have not been recorded and thus cannot be known.

At the time of the Vancouver Island Treaty meetings, there was no written form of the languages of the First Nations parties. Does this mean that the English-language version is authoritative by default? Do the later First Nations accounts, and recent Salish-language versions, thereby possess less authority? The Canadian literature and case law on the bilingual aspect of the historical treaties is quite undeveloped, but the principles of international law can provide guidance and useful analogies, particularly the classic treatise *The Law of Treaties*, by Lord McNair.[8] McNair states the general rule on bilingual treaties as follows: "The parties are free to choose the language or languages in which a treaty is expressed. It is customary and desirable that the treaty itself should indicate which text or texts are to be regarded as authentic."[9] However, he went on to confirm that in a bilingual treaty, "In the absence of provision to the contrary neither text is superior to the other."[10]

By analogy, each Canadian historical treaty is bilingual, that is, each exists simultaneously in two languages, with neither version being superior to the other. However, a close reading of the literature and case law indicates that until recently there was an unspoken assumption that the English-language treaty documents were the "gold" standard by which later accounts translated from a First Nations language were to be assessed. According to the logic of international treaty law, this assumption is unwarranted. For example, it is generally accepted that the 1850 Fort Victoria Treaties were at first concluded orally and only later reduced to writing, with the result that the oral versions existed simultaneously in English and Coast Salish prior to written versions in either language. From this it can be inferred that the two oral versions (Coast Salish and English) are equally authentic; neither is superior to the other. The same reasoning applies to the written versions, namely, that the superiority or greater authenticity of the English-language version over First Nations accounts in translation should not be assumed. In other words, the fact that the First Nations versions have been preserved only through recollections in English translation long after the event does not mean that the English-language document should be automatically accorded greater authority, no matter how tempting and convenient it may be to privilege the English-language versions, thereby avoiding the hard work of ascertaining the content of treaty accounts, which have their origins in the Coast Salish languages.

Encouragingly, this hard work began with the presentation of Salish-language versions of the Fort Victoria Treaties at the 2017 conference, "First Nations, Land, and James Douglas." These translations came after the conference organizers approached two Salish-speaking Elders to produce translations of the treaties in their own languages. In hindsight, the instructions were overly terse, as they did not address the complexities of what "translation" might entail, given the unique history of these treaties. The Elders could provide a literal translation of the English-language versions produced by James Douglas and the Hudson's Bay Company, or they could re-create the likely wording of the oral agreements reached during treaty meetings with Douglas, followed by an English-language translation.

Songhees Elder Dr. Elmer George chose the first approach, producing a literal translation of the words of the written version of the Chekonein Treaty of 1850. Unfortunately, Dr. George could not attend the conference; therefore, he did not have an opportunity to discuss the challenges he faced in finding Songhees words and phrases that would approximate the meaning of those in the HBC-Douglas document. Saanich Elder STOLȻEŁ John Elliott, Sr., adopted the second approach, choosing to draw on oral traditions passed down by his Saanich ancestors – David Latass, David Elliott, Sr., and Gabe Bartleman. He then translated his SENĆOŦEN-language version into English.

At the conference, the Songhees and SENĆOŦEN versions of the treaties were formally presented to the Royal BC Museum. The conference attendees fell silent when John Elliott, Sr., read his SENĆOŦEN-language interpretation of the Saanich Treaty. It was an emotional and historic moment, marking the first time that a First Nation–language version of any of the Vancouver Island Treaties has been heard. He then read his English-language translation of the SENĆOŦEN text, which bore little resemblance to the HBC-Douglas document. The Songhees and SENĆOŦEN versions created by Elmer George and John Elliott, Sr., have now taken their place in the museum's collection, alongside the English-language versions, both physically and symbolically. Elliott's re-creation of the oral text of the Saanich Treaty is as follows:

NIŁ ȻE SKÁLS ET̲ ŁNIN̲EŁ WILN̲EW
TŦE WSÁNEĆ

U. WSÁNEĆ ŁTE. U.DOT ŁTE ÁŁE E ŁÁ,E TIÁ TEN̲EW.NIŁ ȻE TŦE ÁLEN̲ENEȻ ŁTE TIÁ. U, SN̲ÁTW ȻE TIÁ TEN̲EW ĆSE LÁ,E ET̲ ŦIŦEŁ SIÁM TIÁ TEN̲EW TŦE ÁLEN̲ENEȻ ŁTE. HIIIŦ JE ȻE ĆÁŁE ET̲ ŁNIN̲EŁ, WILN̲EW ÁŁE E TIÁ TEN̲EW. LÁ,TEN̲ ȻO, U, MEQ TEN̲EW ŁTE ET̲ XÁLS ŦIŦEŁ SIÁM. I, T̲ÁU LÁ,TEN̲ MEQ TŦE SKÁLS I TŦE Ś*ENÁN̲S I, TŦE S,OX,HELI ET̲ ŁNIN̲EŁ WILN̲EW ET̲ XÁLS.NIŁ ȻE TŦE ST̲I, ET̲ XÁLS HIŦ LE SĆELÁ,NEN̲ Ȼs QENT ŁTE TŦE TEN̲EW I, TŦE ÁLEN̲ENEȻ ŁTE E TŦE SȻÁ,s SKALS I, S,OXHELI ȻO ON̲ESTEN̲ E TŦE ĆELÁN̲EN LE ŁTE. SKÁLS E TŦE TEN̲EW, I TŦE SȻÁĆEL, I. TŦE MEQ SELSELI TELETOŦELN̲EW, SKELKELÁLN̲EW, TŦE SĆÁÁNEW, SJESENEN̲EȻ ŁTE, MEQ U, TŦE K̲EPILEN̲ ŁTE. NIŁ ȻE TŦÁ,E Ȼs ST̲I, E TŦE XAXE ET̲

ŁNIṈEŁ ȻS QENT TŦE ÁLEṈENEȻ ŁTE TIÁ. ĆSE, LÁ,E E TIÁ TEṈEW EṮ ŁNIṈEŁ WSÁ,NEĆ WILṈEW E TŦE SȻÁ,s S,TUO,s. LO,E ȻO XELTEṈ EṮ TŦE TEṈEW ŁTE E TŦE O,MET SṈÁNET EṮ XÁLS Ȼs ÁŁE I, ŚETEṈ LE E ŁÁ,E HIŦ LE ȻENTOL TŦE ĆELÁṈEṈ LE ŁTE.

HIŦ LE SĆELÁNEṈ, NIŁ WEXES ŁḴÁLJ TIÁ. AŁE ŁTE SȾÁȾE E TŦE ŦIŦEŁ SṈÁNET PKOLS E TŦE SḴÁPEŁ E ŁÁ,E. ḰOḰEL ŁTE EṮ James Douglas S,HIWEḰ E TŦE ḴÍYES TÁ,ĆEL WELENI,TEM. I, NIŁ TIÁ ÁNEȻ ḰELNEUEL SE ŁTE TŦE XEUES S,TUOs ÍY, NEUEL SE ŁTE OL ÁŁE E TIÁ TEṈEW. ÍY, ŚḰÁLEȻEN. TŦE WELENI,TEM I, TŦE WILṈEW WSÁNEĆ. MEDOST SE, ŁTE E TŦE MEQ SȻÁ, ŁTE TEṈEW WILṈEW.

U, TOLNEW EṮ ŁNIṈEŁ WILṈEW TUE HIŦ SE ŁTE ĆOȻES TŦE TEṈEW I, TŦE Á,LEṈENEȻ ŁTE EMNI,EṈ I *OLE TEW U, *ENÁṈ Ȼs HIŦ LE ĆELÁṈEN.ÁŁE E ŁÁ,E E TIÁ TŦE Á,LEṈENEȻ ŁTE.NIŁ ȻO LÁTEṈ EṮ XA LS. ȻE OṈESTEṈ TŦE SḴÁLS I, TŦE Ś*ENÁṈS Ȼs LÁ,TEN.MEQ EXIN YÁ, OLEXET TŦE SDÁLṈEW I, SJESENEṈEȻ I, IST E TŦE SȻÁ, ŁTE ŚWISTs WILṈEW.ȻENEW ŁTE E TŦE ÁLI SṈÁTW ĆSE LA,E E TŦE ḴÍYES TÁĆEL SĆALEĆE ŁTE.NIL ȻE TŦÁ,E PITNESs Á,TOL EŁ TŦE Ś*ENÁṈS ŚTENIST SE ŁTE E TŦE ŦE,ITḴEN Ś*ENÁṈs. XELTEṈ ŁTE ȻO TŦE SMEDOSTEṈ SXEL LÁ,E E TŦE PIPE. HIŦ SE ŁTE ŚTEṈIST ȻENTOL E TŦE ÍY, ŚḰÁLEȻEN, Á,TOL ÁŁE TIÁ TEṈEW.

His translation of the text into English is as follows:

We are the Saanich People. We are the original people of this land. This is our homeland. This land, our homeland, is a gift from the High Honoured Most Respected One, Creator. Creator made all of this our homelands. And, in making all of this our homeland and the creation, made our laws and beliefs and our Sacred Teachings of Life. Creator wants us to remember these Sacred Teachings of Life. Creator marked our homelands with Monumental Stones for us to remember his presence on these lands with our ancestors of the past.

Many years ago, in the moon of the Frogs, there was a gathering on the top of PKOLS. There was a meeting with James Douglas, the leader of the newly arrived White People. We were talking about a new beginning, on our land together with the White People. A new good beginning together with the White People and the W̱SÁNEĆ People. And, there, we would point out the extent of our Saanich homelands. The lands that our people used for all time for hunting and setting our reef nets. Where we harvested food and medicines and fished. The places that Creator (XÁLS) had made our laws,

Sacred Teachings of Life, and our ways. We were given some gifts to acknowledge that we met and to make a new beginning. Because there was a threat of attack made by the W̱SÁNEĆ on the new Fort in Victoria. There were crosses marked on paper to signify a sacredness to the meeting. And, how the newly arrived people recognized our responsibilities to the land. And, that with the new beginning that we would live on these lands with respectful relationship with one another. The W̱SÁNEĆ and the White People.

This was to make a new beginning because there was a threat on the Fort Victoria by the W̱SÁNEĆ.

The translation by Dr. Elmer George of the text of the HBC-Douglas version of the Songhees/Chekonein treaty is as follows:

čeʼqʼnein nəčʼelŋxʷ- kʷʼatsʼayč iʔ xpeʔ kʷəliq̌a

xčit meqʷ sweqa łniŋeł ta hewas iʔ ta ʔełʼtalʼŋəxʷ eƛ̓čeʼqʼnein. ełəʔ xelʼet ta sneʼs iʔ xelʼet ta xəlʼelās atīa pipa ʔaāʼpn iqʷʔ łixʷ sqʷaʼčel pəxsīsəŋ ʔaāʼpn nečʼəwəč teʔses nečʼəwəč iʔ ta łqʼečəsłšēʔ aneł iʔ aŋest meq̌ʷ woʔ yaθ aŋest ta James Douglas ta siʔems ta Hudsonʼs Bay Company laʼa sqxʷamiš ƛ̓čes ta xʷənitem siʔem iʔ kansel meq̌ʷ ta taŋexʷ sčečeł eƛ̓ kʷʼatsʼayč iʔ pq̓als čicelqaŋ esčʼeyenʼ ata čilcowitč iʔ xʷsapʼsəm ŋənŋənəʔs. ta qʷaƛ̓gʷa wəʼew eƛ̓kʷʼatsʼayč ta xčitʼłta ata sxʷiʼemʼs sgweʼłta sqʷaʼaqʷʼanaqʷal iʔ ta taŋexʷ ʔeʔiʔ əl sqʷeʔłta čaʼaʼwes ta ŋənʼŋenʼna iʔ ta čiʼcelqəŋ səʔ. iʔ ta taŋexʷ xʷcʷitčtəs xə̄lʼet ata pipa. xčitʼs ta taŋexʷ txʷə̄ sqweʼs ta xʷənitem woʔ yaθ xčitʼs łniŋeł xʷəŋ iʔ əmʼnieŋ ata ewʼs čaʼaʼwes taŋexʷ iʔ sčeēʼnəxwłta woʔ yaθ gʷənʼexʷ łta ta sq̓əʼw ata nečtela ta łniŋeł xelʼet ta sneʼs łta iʔ xelʼet ta sxəlʼelā łta laʼa Fort mətūliyə ʔaāʼpn iqʷ łixʷ sqʷeʼčel eƛ̓pəxsīsŋ ʔaāʼpn nečʼəwʼəč teʔses nečʼəwʼəč iʔ łqʼečəsłše?

čayłəm sqʷes xelʼela iʔ tsaʼqwas iqʷ teʔqʷəxʷ

xwilʼŋexʷ

ta laʼa laʔ xə̄leteŋ

Alfred Robson Benson, M.R.C.S.L.

Joseph William McKay

While the two First Nation–language versions of the treaty texts represent the beginning of a new chapter in the life of the Vancouver Island Treaties, it will remain for future First Nations and settler scholars to build on the results achieved by the conference and this volume. Only when First Nations understandings of the Vancouver Island Treaties have received attention and critical scrutiny equal to that already accorded to the colonial accounts will it be possible to accomplish a fair and enduring reconciliation of their differences.

Notes

1 The following description is based on Neil Vallance, "Sharing the Land: The Formation of the Vancouver Island (or 'Douglas') Treaties of 1850–1854 in Historical, Legal and Comparative Context" (PhD diss., University of Victoria, 2016).

2 Hudson's Bay Company Archives, B.226/b/6, folios 39–42.

3 Bruce McIntyre Watson, *Lives Lived West of the Divide: A Biographical Dictionary of Fur Traders Working West of the Rockies, 1793–1858* (Kelowna: University of British Columbia Centre for Social, Spatial, and Economic Justice, 2010).

4 Robert Brown, *Robert Brown and the Vancouver Island Exploring Expedition,* ed. John Hayman (Vancouver: UBC Press, 1989), 26, 49.

5 Ibid.

6 BC Archives, Joseph William McKay Fonds, PR-0560, MS-1917, file 27, Letter from Joseph McKay to Dr. James S. Helmcken, December 3, 1888.

7 Frank Pagett, "105 Years in Victoria and Saanich! Chief David Recalls White Man's Coming; 80 Years Rent Unpaid," *Victoria Daily Times* (Victoria, BC), July 14, 1934, 1.

8 Lord Arnold Duncan McNair, *The Law of Treaties* (Oxford: Clarendon, 1961).

9 Ibid., 30.

10 Ibid., 432.

6

Huu-ay-aht t'ayii ḥawił *ƛiishin's Land Transaction with William Banfield*

Emchayiik, Robert Dennis, Sr., and Kevin Neary

Remarks by Emchayiik, Robert Dennis, Sr., "First Nations, Land, and James Douglas," February 26, 2017

WHAT I WANTED TO TALK about today was to share with the audience that treaties and agreements between two different jurisdictions is nothing new to First Nations people, and in particular not new to the Huu-ay-aht First Nation. My objective today is to share some examples of where we had agreements with neighbouring First Nations, and today we have a modern-day treaty with British Columbia and Canada.

Another main purpose is to say to people that we are not standing still. We are in a modern world. What do we have to do to move ahead in this modern world, recognizing that we have a history? I say let's make our history part of our future in moving forward. One of the things I want to share is that our Chief ƛiishin, our head Chief, has said, "I would like to have all of my hahouthlee back within twenty-five years." He has said that we have to do it in a certain way, though. We can't do it as in the past, where we could go to war and we gain our land back. So, we are using the modern ways of reaching our goals. These can be achieved in different ways.

In our approach, when we use the word *hahouthlee,* it means "domain" – everything within the territory. So ƛiishin always says that "my hahouthlee is exclusive jurisdiction plus shared jurisdiction. And one day, I am going to get 100 percent of my land back. I am going to get 100 percent control of the natural resources in my territory, or one day I am going to have shared comanagement with other jurisdictions." But his overall objective is that "one day I am going to have 100 percent of my land back. I'm going to have 100 percent of my territory back. I'm going to have 100 percent of my hahouthlee, and my people will be back on the land."

We wanted to share that today, and that can be shared by saying here is the modern context of doing things. We know the historical context. We are taking that history of our nation and now applying that history to the modern and contemporary situation. I am really pleased to be able to state today that the Huu-ay-aht First Nation have either full jurisdiction or shared jurisdiction in 100 percent of our territory, right now, as I speak. We have sole management now in 37 percent of our territory, so we are making gradual steps to get where we want.

We have taken a different approach than most First Nations. Some First Nations have chosen to go to court and fight for Aboriginal title. I say, Guess what? Those First Nations that are fighting for Aboriginal title, and they get the court victory – they still have to negotiate. So, twenty or thirty years of going to court might be considered as wasted, just to prove that you have the title. That is not to be critical. It's that we had to decide: Do we want to spend twenty or thirty years going to court and then, after that, we still have to negotiate?

We have completed our negotiations. My negotiations on behalf of ƛiishin shows that, within a time period, we have a really, really good chance of being 100 percent owners again. That's what I wanted to share today.

There are different ways of doing it. I'm not saying our way is right. I am just sharing. I am saying this is the way we have chosen to do it. The reality, I want to say, is we have neighbours who outnumber us by ninety-five to one, or something like that. Our neighbours are here to stay. So, what do we have to do to coexist with our neighbours who outnumber us by a substantial amount? We have to find a mechanism that allows us to be meaningful residents of our homeland. That's where we are getting to, where the Huu-ay-aht First Nation is happy.

One of the good things about a modern treaty is that you negotiate to the best of what you can live with. And that is only the beginning, that is Step 1. Treaty, that is Step 1. And then, after that, you look to see, What can I do next? For example, right now, we just finished getting approval from our citizens that we can log 200,000 cubic metres from our Treaty Lands. We are going to explore having an LNG facility on our lands. That's self-governing. Whereas before, someone would say, "I want to build a facility on your land, and this is what we are going to do." Now we are saying, "Well, let us consider it, and we'll let you know if we want you to build a facility on our lands." In other words, it's our decision.

Huu-ay-aht Traditional Governance

The series of Douglas Treaties completed with various First Nations on Vancouver Island between 1850 and 1854 are well known, documented, and analyzed. Another Indigenous land transaction from the same era, completed between Huu-ay-aht *t'ayii ḥawił* (Head Chief) ƛiishin and government agent William Banfield in July 1859 has not been as well reported.

Investigation of the circumstances around this 1859 transaction can further inform and add depth to discussions about this era in our shared history. The agreement is interesting, not simply as an historical record but also for its underlying context, which reveals significant distinctions between colonial law and Nuu-chah-nulth customary law, especially concerning ownership rights. These distinctions created friction at the time, but they are also particularly significant given that they foreshadow today's issues of Indigenous title and rights.

This essay first examines Huu-ay-aht customary law and traditions and then examines the events of 1859 in their context. It has been reviewed and approved by the Huu-ay-aht leadership.

Huu-ay-aht Histories

The Huu-ay-aht are one of the Nuu-chah-nulth First Nations, whose respective territories extend along the west coast of Vancouver Island and connected waters from Cape Cook in the north to Sheringham Point in the south. Huu-ay-aht Territory includes the lands and waters in and surrounding the southeastern portion of Barkley Sound, including Bamfield Inlet, the Deer Group Islands, Numukamis Bay, Pachena Bay, and adjacent areas (see Figure 6.1).

As referenced by Emchayiik, Robert Dennis, Sr., the Huu-ay-aht First Nation has concluded a modern-day treaty and is a signatory to the Maa-nulth First Nations Final Agreement that came into effect on April 1, 2011. Huu-ay-aht history, though, stretches back to the start of time. Embedded in their histories are cultural teachings and core philosophies that are central to the Huu-ay-aht today. The summary of Huu-ay-aht history and traditional governance that follows will hopefully provide background for better understanding both the Huu-ay-aht's modern treaty and the historic agreement signed by their t'ayii ḥawił in 1859, described later.

Huu-ay-aht oral accounts have been, and continue to be, the traditional method for passing Huu-ay-aht language, culture, traditions, and

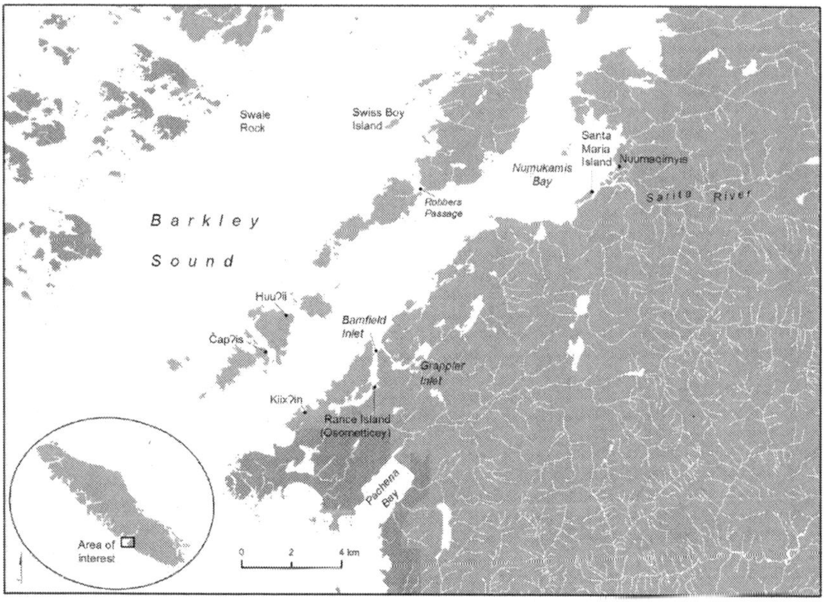

FIGURE 6.1 Regional map with Huu-ay-aht and other place names. | Map by Hillcrest Geographics.

worldview from one generation to the next. Songs, public events, and art are also important means of maintaining and renewing Huu-ay-aht history and culture. Oral histories detail how generations of Huu-ay-aht ancestors occupied and harvested from the land, rivers, lakes, and ocean in their territory and how they fought to obtain and preserve sovereignty over these lands and waters. This knowledge is intimate and detailed, and it is based on thousands of years of experience and observation. Huu-ay-aht Chief Louie Nookmiis provided an important series of Huu-ay-aht histories in 1964 that were tape-recorded by Eugene Arima. This Huu-ay-aht history cycle has been transcribed and published in both Nuu-chah-nulth and in English translation, and it continues to be an invaluable text for understanding the Huu-ay-aht.[1]

Huu-ay-aht chief councillor and historian Emchayiik, Robert Dennis, Sr., observed the following in a written introduction to the histories by Chief Louie:

> From the Huu-ay-aht perspective, these narratives are extremely important. They provide us with unforgettable insights into our history. They tell us who we are, where we came from, the price our ancestors paid to hold on

to our territory, and details of historic and heroic events. Chief Louie Nookmiis died in a hospital in Nanaimo in October of 1964. He is buried in the Huu-ay-aht cemetery at *numuqamyis* village.[2]

One foundational history for the Huu-ay-aht, provided by Chief Louie, describes events during a time when the Huu-ay-aht Territory was overrun by enemies. Huu-ay-aht survivors of this attack retreated to refuges in the Sarita River Valley to recover their strength over decades. They then fought with other Barkley Sound nations to regain their territories (Figure 6.2). Hostilities came to an end when a woman Chief from Ucluelet came to Huu-ay-aht and agreed on a treaty with Chief Louie's grandfather, establishing peaceful relations that continue up to today. These histories are important to Huu-ay-aht today as they work through treaty implementation and other means to recover control of the territory that was unjustly taken from them by a colonial power.

Another account of Huu-ay-aht history, recently published, describes the mysterious time before the Great Flood, a time when the supernatural, animal, and human realms blended into one. This account illustrates how

FIGURE 6.2 Trevor Little's illustration of the fifty Huu-ay-aht warriors who recaptured their territory. | Courtesy of Huu-ay-aht First Nation.

Huu-ay-aht origin stories of First Ancestors combine art, ceremony, history, and cultural teachings (see Figure 6.3):

> The world was a much different place at what we call yaqʷiimit, "the Beginning of Time." The first lady, Ḥuminʔiki (pronounced "Ho-min-iki"), was said to have been from the moon. She came to our lands on her 13th year and upon her arrival, transformed into a woman. She remains connected to the moon through her transformation, and her womanly life-giving cycles are what mark our calendar every 28 days. Every 28 days a new moon starts (we have 13 moons per year), just as a woman has her menses cycles. When she stepped down to this world she was happy to give this world the breath of life, for she is the life giver and a powerful woman.
>
> Načquʔa (pronounced "Nach-ko-ah") looked out from his point and saw the lady descend to Kiixʔin[3] from his perch on the stars. The urge to follow her and build a new home in Kiixʔin was greater than his desire to stay at his home in the stars. Saddened by leaving his family, at 14 years old he transformed into man and now wears the lump of sadness in his throat. This lump is worn by all men when they transform. He is the life taker (the opposite of women, who are life givers) and in order to provide life to his family, he must kill. He is a whaler and is also powerful …
>
> At the main entrance of the Royal British Columbia Museum in Victoria, the original welcoming figures from the National Historic Site of Kiixʔin welcome millions of people each year. Replicas of these figures also stand at the Vancouver Airport. These two figures, Načquʔa and Ḥuminʔiki, were originally raised in Kiixʔin to honour a marriage between the Huu-ay-aht and Makah Nations. These figures represent the time when Načquʔa (the first man) and Ḥuminʔiki (the first woman) came down from the stars in Huu-ay-aht territory.
>
> These carvings of the first ancestors were erected … at Kiixʔin. Načquʔa stands with his arms outstretched as he watches for the Huu-ay-aht, encouraging for them to come home. This gesture is symbolic: he has been welcoming home his people since the beginning of time and will continue to do so for eternity. He stands ready to pull in their canoes and invite them for a community whale feast and potlatch. (A potlatch was a forum for making decisions, certifying events, and announcing new laws to the public.) As well, one sees there is a lump carved on his throat (his Adam's apple) symbolizing the lump of sadness from his transformation into a man. Ḥuminʔiki is holding a baby rattle that symbolizes the lifespan of a person. Symbolically contained within this rattle are all the teachings and traditions of the Huu-ay-aht First Nation.[4]

FIGURE 6.3 Welcome figure carvings of Načquʔa (left) and Ḥuminʔiki (right) at Kiixʔin village, 1903. | Photo by C. Bradbury. Courtesy of the Royal BC Museum and Archives, PN 4659.

Overview of Traditional Huu-ay-aht Governance

As is the case for other Nuu-chah-nulth nations, traditional Huu-ay-aht governance and society was based on rank and its associated rights, privileges, and responsibilities.

The Hereditary Chiefs, known as *ḥa'wiih,* are members of the noble class and own economic and ceremonial privileges. Traditionally, the ḥa'wiih were the only ones who could control rights to access land or territory (*hahouthlee*). They also owned a wide array of other rights, such as village sites, places to land canoes, and places to build houses. Huu-ay-aht traditions dictate that the ḥa'wiih hold the responsibility for the stewardship of the land, rivers, lakes, and ocean and all the resources and living creatures within them.

Within each tribe, there was traditionally one t'ayii ḥa'wił, or Head Chief, who was recognized as the leader of all members of that tribe and who held ultimate responsibility and authority for the nation. The rights, privileges, and responsibilities of the t'ayii ḥa'wił extended into both the economic and ceremonial realms and included rights over resource

FIGURE 6.4 Huu-ay-aht Treasures Repatriation signing, November 2016. *Front row, left to right:* Jack Lohman, CEO Royal BC Museum; Yaalthuu-a, Jeff Cook; t'ayii ḥa'wił ƛiishin Derek Peters (standing); ʔemptiss, Darlene Nookemus. *Back Row, left to right:* Angela Wesley; Hu'miniki, Irene Peters; and Emchayiik, Chief Councillor Robert Dennis, Sr. | Photograph by Heather Thomson.

management.[5] The current t'ayii ḥa'wił of the Huu-ay-aht is ƛiishin, Derek Peters (Figure 6.4), who can trace his title and name back through many generations of ḥa'wiih. Chief ƛiishin can recall details of events and advice received from his grandmothers, Elders, and other ḥa'wiih who guided his training throughout his youth to prepare him for his inherited responsibility.

The relative positions and rank of the ḥa'wiih was, and continues to be, proclaimed and recognized in the arrangement of the "seats" occupied by each ḥa'wił at feasts and Potlatches. Each of the chieftainships and "seats" carry with them an array of hereditary rights, privileges, and responsibilities.

Hahouthlee are chiefly territories, and each hahouthlee is the domain of a Huu-ay-aht chiefly family, which anthropologists called "local groups," headed by a ḥa'wił. The boundaries of the hahouthlee generally follow specific landmarks such as hills, mountains, headlands, beaches, and bays. The Huu-ay-aht hahouthlee includes the ocean "as far as the wind blows" and extend back to the mountain peaks that form the central spine of Vancouver Island.

Each chiefly family is composed of a number of lineages, or "houses." The names of chiefly families are typically taken from the place of origin of the highest-ranking lineage in the group. For example, the name *Huu-ay-aht,* or *huuʔiiʔaht,* translates as "people of huuʔii," referring to a village site on Diana Island. Each chiefly family traces its history back to the creation of First Ancestors in their hahouthlee.

Topati are rights held by chiefly families that verify and proclaim the wealth, privileges, and prerogatives of the ḥa'wiih that have been handed down from ancestors. The topati can include many things, such as hunting, fishing, and trapping rights; drift rights; the use of certain names or the right to use and possess certain carvings, masks and ornaments; the staging of certain ceremonial games and dances; and certain songs.

People who had no senior rights or privileges were *musčim* (community members, citizens). Just as the ḥa'wiih were ranked, so too were the musčim. The ḥa'wiih relied on good relations with their musčim to support them in their enterprises. The ḥa'wiih were traditionally governed by a council known as the *ḥa'wiłpatak ḥa'wiih* (Governing of Our Chiefs).[6] Some of the musčim held formal advisory positions, which were usually also hereditary in nature.[7] Such positions included:

- t'ayiiʔas: Highest Hereditary Female Chief
- čiqhsii: Speaker
- qʷayaċiik: Head Wolf, Law Enforcer
- t'iquwił: Adviser to Chief.

Some designated roles and responsibilities of the musčim specialist advisers related specifically to resource management. As Toquaht Elder Archie Thompson explains:

> There were important people with important portfolios like shore rights and fisheries. They had names for the people that look after the rivers and fish. Like a biologist, they decided when to stop fishing and let some of the fish go by. Others looked after the forests; it was not only the *ḥa'wiih* who made the rules. The advisers did as well.[8]

Some of these specialist roles included:

- *witwaak:* warriors responsible for the nation's security
- *ʔuʔuutahci:* whalers who caught whales for the community
- *hitinkisnak:* "beach keepers" responsible for maintaining the ocean beaches and shorelines and for welcoming guests from other nations
- *cacaluk:* "guardians" who cared for the watersheds and monitored the salmon runs to allow the first wave of fish upstream to spawn; these guardians were also responsible for opening and closing specific runs.

Huu-ay-aht cultural training and ceremonies and the responsibilities of the ḥa'wiih and Huu-ay-aht citizens are guided by core principles that include:

- *Hisukʔis cawaak:* everything is one
- *ʔiisaak:* respect with caring
- *ʔuuʔaaluk:* taking care of.

As stated, within Nuu-chah-nulth traditions, the ḥa'wiih, and only the ḥa'wiih, own the rights to make decisions about access to and use of territory and resources. Today, in keeping with their motto of "Ancient Spirit, Modern Mind," the Huu-ay-aht are governed by an Executive Council that operates in conjunction with an advisory Ha'wiih Council.

Nuu-chah-nulth Ownership and Newcomers

The ownership rights of the ḥa'wiih to their hahouthlee were apparent to the non-Indigenous people who began visiting Nuu-chah-nulth Territory in the late 1700s. Captain Cook, on his well-known third expedition with the vessels *Resolution* and *Discovery,* arrived in Nootka Sound on March 29, 1778, and remained there for twenty-seven days. On April 22, 1778, Cook himself led a party ashore and proceeded into Mowachaht Territory "to the Village at the west point of the Sound," after which he recorded the following:

> Here I must observe that I have no where met with Indians who had such high notions of every thing the Country produced being their exclusive property as these; the very wood and water we took on board they at first wanted us to pay for, and we had certainly done, had I been upon the spot

> when the demands were made; but as I never happened to be there the workmen took but little notice of their importunities and at last they ceased applying. But made a Merit on necessity and frequently afterwards told us they had given us Wood and Water out of friendship.[9]

What Cook failed to grasp was that the demands for payment were assertions of ownership. When the Nuu-chah-nulth perceived that the foreigners did not act in appropriate acknowledgment of their rights, they asserted ownership in another way.

Nuu-chah-nulth customary law included *honi,* or "drift rights," meaning that any goods that floated or landed in a hahouthlee belonged to the ḥa'wił who held rights for that territory.[10] This concept extended to foreign vessels that entered the hahouthlee. Lieutenant King, a member of Cook's expedition, observed that some of the Indigenous groups in Nootka Sound were prevented from trading with the British by the group of people in whose territory Cook's ship had anchored. King wrote: "This violent proceeding we had observ'd often before, & we saw plainly that the [different] Parties in the sound were not Cordial friends, & it seemed clear that those who first came to us, claimd us as their exclusive property." Later, after Vancouver Island became a Crown colony, the Huu-ay-aht learned that their concepts of ownership rights differed from those of the colonial power, as will be described.

The Swiss Boy *Incident*

In early February 1859, a floundering American ship, the *Swiss Boy,* overloaded with a cargo of lumber, ran aground in Barkley Sound to avoid sinking. The *British Colonist* in Victoria initially reported the incident as follows, with exaggerations and commentary that reflect the colonial attitudes of the time:

> The brig Swiss Boy, Capt. Weldon, bound from Port Orchard to San Francisco, with a cargo of lumber, put into Natinat Sound[11] to stop a leak, on February 1st. The Indians boarded her in great numbers, drove the Captain from the wheel and the crew to the forecastle. They then cut away the masts, rigging, and sails, and carried ashore everything. Some three hundred boarded her and completed the work of destruction in two hours. Capt. Weldon attributes the preservation of their lives to a Macaw chief. Prompt measures should be taken by the government to chastise these pirates. And

> if one of H.M. ships would visit their camps and inflict summary punishment on them, they would be taught a profitable lesson.[12]

Governor Douglas, on the same day as the publication of the above report, requested that a vessel from the British naval base in Esquimalt be dispatched to "institute enquiries into the circumstances of the case, and if it shall appear advisable to adopt such measures with the Indians as will make them sensible of the wrong they have committed, and as shall induce them to forbear from similar actions in any subsequent case of a like nature."[13] Captain Prevost, in command of the *Satellite,* a two-hundred-foot screw corvette with twenty-one guns, was ordered to investigate the *Swiss Boy* incident. Douglas's instructions to Prevost directed him to conduct a "searching enquiry into the whole circumstances of the case," and "if upon investigation any of the natives can be identified who were aggressors in the matter, to bring them to Victoria for trial."[14]

After visiting Barkley Sound and talking with members of the Huu-ay-aht, Captain Prevost's investigation revealed a much different story from that reported in the newspaper. The *Swiss Boy* had been seriously overloaded and sinking when it limped into Barkley Sound and anchored, likely near what is now called Swiss Boy Island (Figure 6.1).[15] As previously described, according to Nuu-chah-nulth customary law, any drift goods that floated into or ashore in a particular hahouthlee became the property of the ḥa'wił and his relations who owned the rights to the lands and waters in question.[16] The Huu-ay-aht Chief ƛiishin and his people claimed the *Swiss Boy* as honi, their salvage right, and seized the vessel, towing it farther into their territory and near a village at the west entrance to what is now called Robbers Passage (Figure 6.1). The Huu-ay-aht took the *Swiss Boy*'s crew off the vessel then proceeded to remove what few goods of value they could find. "When a vessel arrives in their country in distress, they think it right to plunder her, considering her their property," reported Prevost.[17] The Huu-ay-aht were disappointed to find that there was little of value to remove from the *Swiss Boy*. *Swiss Boy* crew members were then fed and given canoes by the Huu-ay-aht to make their way to Victoria.

After his investigation, Prevost regained the few goods taken from the *Swiss Boy* by the Huu-ay-aht. Upon returning to Victoria, he prepared a report on his investigations, which ended as follows:

> I would beg to be allowed to bring before His Excellency the Governor's notice the necessity of appointing some responsible person as Indian Agent

> on the West Coast of Vancouver's Island. During my fortnights sojourn with the Indians I have had the opportunity of seeing much of their character, and as far as I can form an opinion in such time, believe them to be well disposed, quiet, inoffensive and easily led by any one capable of gaining their confidence. If this be true how much evil may be prevented by the presence of one who would watch over their interest for good.[18]

The *Swiss Boy* incident resulted in the British exercising their presumed authority in Huu-ay-aht Territory. Prevost provided reasonings to the Huu-ay-aht, but they were emphasized and backstopped by the *Satellite*'s cannons.

The journal of Henry Piers, a surgeon on the *Satellite* during the *Swiss Boy* investigation, conveys recognition of Huu-ay-aht custom coupled with colonial arrogance and prejudice:

> These poor people, whom we consider our Subjects but hitherto have not visited ~~them~~ [sic] to make them acquainted with their relationship to us, appear to have acted only in a manner that might be expected of them. The vessel came in distress, water-logged and entirely at their mercy. The "Lord of the Manor," George, seized & plundered her and let the crew go. In many parts of the world the crew would not have escaped with their lives or freedom. However, the practice is doubtless wrong & must be changed and it is the immediate duty of the Government, without treating the poor ignorant people harshly, to introduce, with the change in this & other respects, the light of Christianity and civilization.[19]

William Eddy Banfield, Government Agent, and Land Agreements

Douglas immediately followed up on Prevost's written recommendation and promptly appointed a trader, William Eddy Banfield, in April 1859 as "Agent on the part of the Government ... to assume a General Supervision of the Indians located on the South West Coast of the Island, and you will be required to reside in the neighbourhood of Barclay Sound." The appointment letter to Banfield stated that he was the best candidate:

> [Your] long experience in this locality and your intimate knowledge of Indian character and habits, will enable you in a great measure to judge of the manner in which your services can be most usefully employed in affording assistance to the Government – to civilized persons who may happen to visit the unsettled districts near to you and to the Indians themselves.[20]

Banfield had become a trader on Vancouver Island's southwest coast after his discharge as a carpenter in the Royal Navy. At his appointment as government agent, Banfield was already acquainted with the Huu-ay-aht and Chief ƛiishin. Banfield had previously reported on the "Ohiat" (Huu-ay-aht) in an article published in the *Daily Victoria Gazette* in 1858:

> The Ohiat Indians are a large tribe, about four hundred and fifty or five hundred strong. They inhabit the eastern side of Netinett [Barkley] Sound ... The Indian villages are numerous from the very point. They are traceable for twelve or fourteen miles up the Sound, but in winter they assemble in one encampment, showing a full mile frontage. One chief controls the whole, his name is Cleshin.[21]

Following his instructions that he reside in Barkley Sound, Banfield set himself up to trade in Bamfield Inlet. He soon found himself directly engaged with Huu-ay-aht traditional law. He was forced by Huu-ay-aht leaders to purchase the rights to reside at and establish a trading station on their property on Rance Island in Bamfield Inlet and later in Grappler Inlet. To document the arrangement, Banfield drew up a letter of agreement with the Huu-ay-aht ḥa'wiih, which read as follows (see also Figure 6.5):

> **Ohiat Barclay Sound July 6th 1859**
>
> Know all men by these present that I William Eddy Banfield Government Agent for the Western Shore of Vancouver Island have this day ... Bought of Cleeshin the Chief of Ohiat and Howeesem the next in rank of the same tribe that Island known among the tribe by the name of Osometticey, all and every part of it for the sum and consideration of two blankets and two shirts its water privileges and timber to be mine forever my heirs and assigns for the aforesaid sum of two blankets and two shirts which these chiefs have acknowledged by affixing the marks and seals here under on which this is the title deed each of aforesaid chiefs holding a copy.
>
> Cleeshins mark and seal
> Howeesems mark and seal
> Witness Howeesems son.[22]

The land transaction was formalized by the addition of crosses made from strips of red cedar bark and affixed with linen and sealing wax. Traditionally, red cedar bark is considered to have inherent sacred qualities and here signifies the ḥa'wiih's "stamp of approval" for the agreement.

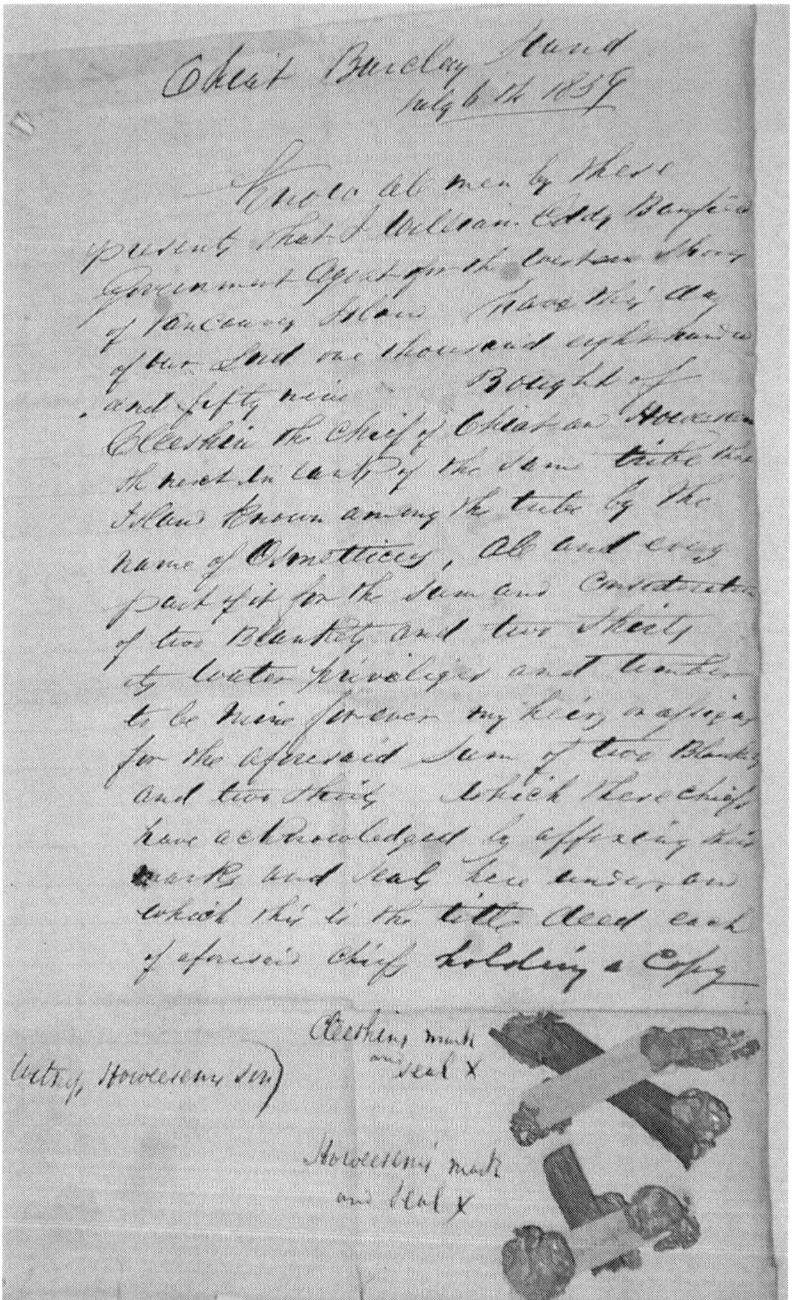

Ohiat Barclay Sound
July 6th 1859

Know all men by these presents that I William Eddy Banfield Government Agent for the western shore of Vancouver Island have this day of our Lord one thousand eight hundred and fifty nine Bought of Cleeshin the Chief of Ohiat and Howeesen the next in rank of the same tribe the Island known among the tribe by the name of Ossmottiecy, All and every part of it for the sum and consideration of two Blankets and two Shirts [illegible] water privileges and timber to be mine forever my heirs & assigns for the aforesaid sum of two Blankets and two Shirts which these chiefs have acknowledged by affixing their marks and seals here under, on which this is the title deed each of aforesaid Chiefs holding a Copy

Witness Howeesens Son

Cleeshins mark and seal X

Howeesens mark and seal X

FIGURE 6.5 Land agreement between Chief ƛiishin and William Banfield, 1859, Royal BC Museum and Archives. | Photograph by Kevin Neary.

Later, in an 1860 report to Governor James Douglas, Banfield described this written land transaction and another that he had later signed with Huu-ay-aht ḥa'wiih:

> I mentioned to his Excellency Sir when at Victoria that I had made a purchase of my place at Ohiat from the Chief. I was almost compelled to do so on my first coming among them they were particularly anxious that I should purchase the ground on which I lived saying that the Americans at Cape Flatery had all bought their ground from the Indians. I pleaded poverty which was very evident to them my stores being very limited but as I gradualy [sic] increased I was [still] pressed to buy the place I lived on at first I did not like – but to save myself the daily annoyance of the creatures – I at length bought it for two blankets and two shirts sir and to impress on them formality I drew out a little deed and explained it to them giving them a duplicate I had no civilized witness none being in the neighborhood.
>
> I removed from that place to another which after becoming acquainted with the localities I prefered [sic] and made [?] myself this time to buy it being a sort of private property of the Chief's the bargain was closed for six blankets some beans molasses &c I again drew out a little deed this time witnessed by three white men – my object at this time was solely to prevent myself from native annoyance sir and as an example of honest dealing that they might perceive that white men would not occupy their valueless ground without purchase they put no value in land as they never cultivate.[23]

A copy of the second "deed" prepared by Banfield, referenced in the above report, does not appear to have survived. The American treaty referred to by Banfield is the 1855 Treaty with the Makah, through which the Makah Reservation was established and the remainder of Makah Territory was ceded to the US government for the sum of $25,000. The Huu-ay-aht, intermarried with the Makah, were well aware of this treaty and used it as a negotiating point in establishing their ownership rights with Banfield.

Based on Nuu-chah-nulth customary law, it is unlikely that the Huu-ay-aht ḥa'wiih viewed the agreement with Banfield as a "purchase" of land in return for two blankets and two shirts, in one instance, and for six blankets, beans, molasses, and other items, in the second. It is more likely that they regarded the blankets and shirts as payments from Banfield in acknowledgment of their hahouthlee rights and allowed him temporary occupation at Rance Island and later at Grappler Inlet.[24] Nuu-chah-nulth customary law specifies that only ḥa'wiih can hold, assign, or otherwise arrange rights of occupation and use of territory.

The Huu-ay-aht ḥa'wiih's agreements with Banfield are significant as Indigenous land transactions conducted during the tenure of Governor Douglas, but they are later and separate from the Douglas Treaties. For the Huu-ay-aht, the surviving agreement is of great significance as a historic document and as an important reminder of their assertion of rights of hahouthlee, traditional law, and government. It must also be noted that Rance Island, the subject of the land transaction in 1859, was reacquired by the Huu-ay-aht Government in 2016 as one of several properties purchased in Bamfield.

On October 24, 1862, the *British Colonist* published a report that Banfield had drowned in Barkley Sound.[25] This incident was widely covered in the Victoria press, with initial reports stating that Banfield had drowned accidentally. Later, letters published in the newspapers accused

FIGURE 6.6 Delegations of Huu-ay-aht and Uchucklesaht people meet with Dr. I.W. Powell, superintendent of Indian affairs for British Columbia in 1874 in Barkley Sound. This photograph, by Richard Maynard, likely portrays the Huu-ay-aht party, led by t'ayii ḥa'wił "Adzik" who succeeded the Chief ƛiishin who signed the agreement with Banfield as Huu-ay-aht Chief. | Courtesy of the Royal BC Museum and Archives, G-05844.

FIGURE 6.7 HMS *Devastation* at Penelakut Island. | Watercolour painting by R. Britten. Courtesy of the Royal BC Museum and Archives, PDP05445.

Huu-ay-aht people of murdering Banfield. The accusations were based on hearsay evidence.[26] Nearly two years after Banfield's death, in September 1864, and in apparent response to repeated accusations in the newspapers, the British gunboat *Devastation* (see Figure 6.7) was dispatched to apprehend the Huu-ay-aht accused of the murder.

There are two surviving written accounts of what occurred when the *Devastation* arrived in Huu-ay-aht Territory, and both reflect the colonial and overtly racist attitudes of the authors.[27] The following is an interpretation of events drawn from these documents.

On arrival in Barkley Sound in September 1864, the *Devastation* first investigated the Huu-ay-aht villages of Kiixʔin and Čapʔis. Finding these villages empty, the warship anchored in Bamfield Inlet, near the Chief's village. That night, Commander Pike went to the house of Chief ƛiishin with an armed party but found that the Chief, having heard of the *Devastation*'s mission, had departed, presumably to avoid capture. Pike took action, seizing Chief ƛiishin's canoes and taking the Chief's daughter as hostage. Pike noted that he found the Huu-ay-aht "fully prepared for resistance, some three hundred men being under arms at Numukamis village, and that they had received information that the object of our visit was to arrest the murderers of Mr. Bamfield [sic]."[28]

The next day, Police Superintendent Smith was dispatched from the *Devastation* in a rowing vessel towards Nuumaqimyis village (see Figure 6.8)

FIGURE 6.8 Huu-ay-aht village of Nuumaqimyis (Tabu Beach) featuring traditional style Big Houses, 1901. | Photograph by Samuel Morse. Courtesy of the Washington State Historical Society, 1917.115.381.

with an assistant and two Tla-o-qui-aht interpreters. As they approached the village, Smith and his party were surprised and surrounded by twelve large canoes that emerged from a hiding place behind Santa Maria Island. These canoes contained some sixty or seventy black-faced Huu-ay-aht warriors who were singing war songs and armed with muskets, spears, and other weapons. In a manoeuvre that was apparently planned, Huu-ay-aht warriors seized Smith's assistant, Lewis, and took him ashore as a hostage, as security, and in retribution for the British having taken Chief ƛiishin's daughter and his canoes.

Commander Pike ordered the *Devastation* to take position directly offshore Nuumaqimyis and threatened the village with wholesale destruction from the ship's cannons. Under such threat, and with a hostage as security against immediate action, the Huu-ay-aht entered negotiations with the British.

During the discussions that ensued, Pike learned that the Huu-ay-aht had been previously warned that if a gunboat did visit their territory, it would fire on them immediately. Pike advised the Huu-ay-aht that he was determined to punish all crimes, regardless of who committed them. Further talks revealed that the Huu-ay-aht had many complaints of rough treatment from visiting white traders to relate, and they requested specifically through Pike that Governor Douglas take measures to stop such behaviour. In the end, three Huu-ay-aht men, "Katmish, Hoth-lu-Seta and

Satch-kool," were seized by the British and taken to Victoria for trial, being accused of Banfield's murder.[29] Chief ƛiishin, who was accused of masterminding Banfield's demise, avoided being taken by the British.

Somewhat ironically, at virtually the same time that Pike and the *Devastation* were threatening to bombard Nuumaqimyis, Huu-ay-aht people some seven kilometres up the Sarita River were providing food, shelter, and canoes to a starving and lost party of members from the government-sponsored Vancouver Island Exploring Expedition, led by Peter Leech.[30]

Later events proved that the threats posed by Pike and the *Devastation* to the Huu-ay-aht and Nuumaqimyis were very real. After the gunboat's visit to Barkley Sound, the vessel proceeded to Clayoquot Sound, where Pike and the *Devastation* played key roles in the bombardment and destruction of seven Ahousaht villages. These actions were meant to make a strong impression on the Nuu-chah-nulth tribes along the coast through a display of British military power.[31]

The series of events during the *Devastation*'s investigation of Banfield's drowning reveals that in 1864 Huu-ay-aht warriors were fully prepared to defend their people, their territory, and their t'ayii ḥa'wił, even when faced with a gunboat. It also indicates that the Huu-ay-aht were able to manage affairs successfully through strategies that included decisive action, diplomacy, and negotiations.

Banfield himself had earlier remarked on Huu-ay-aht diplomatic and negotiation skills. As British naval officer Richard Mayne recorded:

> On missions of peace also this [eagle] down is, as I have said, made use of. One day in talking to Mr. Banfield, the Indian agent on the West coast of Vancouver Island, who has resided among the Ohyat tribe several years, we were comparing many of the Indian customs with those of Europe, and he told me that on the occasion of a quarrel between the Ohyat and another tribe, a chief who was one of the best speakers among them, was employed on several days as envoy, going frequently to the enemy's camp to negotiate, and that his diplomacy averted war. During the whole time of the negotiations the peace-maker wore eagles' down all over his head, so that he looked as if he had been powdered, and eagle feathers in his cap, or secured to a band around his head.[32]

On November 4, 1864, the *British Colonist* reported on the trial in Victoria of "Klatsmick," the Huu-ay-aht man ultimately accused of murdering Banfield. After several witnesses, including Chief ƛiishin, had been called to provide testimony, the accused was acquitted.[33] It transpired that the case against "Klatsmick" could not be confirmed by the evidence, and there were also questions about whether "Indian" testimony was admissible in court.[34] In the end, the reported accusations of Huu-ay-aht agency in Banfield's death were found to be without credible foundation.

Ancient Spirit, Modern Mind

The agreement signed by ƛiishin with William Banfield in 1859 marks an important event. The Huu-ay-aht ḥa'wiih negotiated with a colonial government agent to formalize a land transaction that recognized the Huu-ay-aht's territorial rights. The Huu-ay-aht – aware of the Makah Treaty and the Douglas Treaties negotiated with First Nations around Victoria, Nanaimo, and Fort Rupert – made sure their Chief's hahouthlee rights were recognized by the first government agent in their territory as Banfield established his trading posts.

The land transaction document itself, with its cedar, linen, and wax seals, eventually became part of the records maintained by BC Archives. The significance of the agreement itself, though, has earned scarce attention, being generally overshadowed by the earlier Douglas Treaties. For the Huu-ay-aht, the agreement with Banfield is an important and powerful statement of the historic and long-standing authority of their ḥa'wiih over their hahouthlee and significant evidence of the enduring nature of Huu-ay-aht traditional law, culture, title, and rights.

The Huu-ay-aht's long history is filled with many events that demonstrate their great resilience. They have faced and survived many challenges that include wars, depopulation, imposition of foreign authority, alienation of territory and resources, and having children taken to residential schools. Huu-ay-aht resilience has continuously carried them through, and it has carried them to another major transaction that recognizes Huu-ay-aht First Nation territorial rights – the Maa-nulth First Nations Final Agreement, which came into effect on April 1, 2011.

Today, relationships between Huu-ay-aht ḥa'wiih, their hahouthlee, and the musčim are strong and enduring. The Huu-ay-aht ḥa'wiih on the Ha'wiih Council maintain the traditional rights to the hahouthlee in Huu-ay-aht Territory, as expressed in the agreement with Banfield. The ḥa'wiih have formal input into modern governance as a highly respected advisory body, in keeping with the Huu-ay-aht motto of "Ancient Spirit, Modern Mind."

As outlined above by Emchayiik, the Huu-ay-aht continue to view their history and traditions as essential in setting the course for their stated goals of self-governance and regaining jurisdiction over their hahouthlee.

Notes

1 Chief Louie Nookmiis, "Appendix: Huu-ay-aht History of the ƛiišin Family," in E.Y. Arima, Edward Sapir, Tyee Bob, and Canadian Museum of Civilization et al., *Family Origin Histories: The Whaling Indians West: Coast Legends and Stories, Part 11 of the Sapir-Thomas Nootka Texts/Told by Tyee Bob [and Others]; Prepared by Edward Sapir [and Others]; Edited by Eugene Arima [and Others]*, Mercury Series, Ethnology Paper 145 (Gatineau, QC: Canadian Museum of Civilization, 2009), 281–339.

2 Ibid., 283.

3 Kiixʔin is the traditional capital of the Huu-ay-aht (see Figure 6.1). Occupied for over five thousand years, it has been commemorated as a National Historic Site of Canada.

4 Uu-a-thluk/Nuu-chah-nulth Tribal Council Fisheries, *Practice and Principles: Nuu-chah-nulth Traditional Management Series* (Port Alberni, BC: Nuu-chah-nulth Tribal Council, 2012), 5–7.

5 Uu-a-thluk/Nuu-chah-nulth Tribal Council Fisheries, *Roles and Responsibilities: Nuu-Chah-Nulth Traditional Management Series* (Port Alberni, BC: Nuu-chah-nulth Tribal Council, 2012).

6 Nuu-Chah-Nulth Tribal Council, "ḥa'wił patak ḥa'wiih" poster, n.d.

7 Uu-a-thluk, *Roles and Responsibilities.*

8 Quoted in ibid., 4.

9 John C. Beaglehole, ed., *The Journals of Captain James Cook on His Voyages of Discovery* (Cambridge: Haklyut Society/Cambridge University Press, 1967), 306.

10 Philip Drucker, *The Northern and Central Nootkan Tribes* (Washington: Smithsonian Institution, 1951), 254.

11 Now known as Barkley Sound.

12 "Seizure and Dismantling of a Vessel by Indians," *Victoria Gazette,* February 17, 1859.

13 "Correspondence: James Douglas to De Courcy, February 19, 1859," BC Archives (BCA), Vancouver Island Miscellaneous Letterbooks, no. 2, C/AA/10.4/2, microfilm B-2650, 55–56, Victoria, 1859.

14 "Correspondence: Douglas, Governor Vancouver Island to Captain de Courcy, H.M.S Plyades, February 22, 1859, BCA, Vancouver Island Miscellaneous Letterbooks, no. 2, C/AA/10.4/2, microfilm B-2650, 55–57, Victoria, 1859.

15 M.S.S. Peile, G.S. Gooch, M. Hill, and R. Davey, "Report: Peile et al. to Prevost, 28 February 1859," BCA, Colonial Correspondence, GR-1372, file 1218, Victoria, 1859.

16 Drucker, *The Northern and Central Nootkan Tribes,* 254.

17 George [Oweesum], "Deposition: George to Prevost, 26 February 1859," BCA, Colonial Correspondence, GR-1372, file 1218, Victoria, 1859.

18 "Letter of Proceedings: [James] Prevost to De Courcy, 11 March 1859," ibid.

19 Journal of Henry Piers, Surgeon, HMS *Satellite,* February 28, 1859, Wellcome Library, MS 6110.

20 "Correspondence: Colonial Secretary [W.A.G. Young] to Wm Banfield, 27 April 1859," BCA, Vancouver Island Miscellaneous Letterbooks, no. 2, C/AA/10.4/2, microfilm B-2650, 115–18, Victoria, 1859.

21 W.E. Banfield, "Vancouver Island: Its Topography, Characteristics, &c, Number V; Ohiat District," *Daily Victoria Gazette,* August 28, 1858.

22 W.E. Banfield, "Land Purchase, Osometticey Island, Ohiat, Barclay Sound, 6 July 1859," BCA, Hudson's Bay Company, Fort Victoria, Add MSS 772, vol. 2, file 4, Victoria, 1859.

23 "[Report 5]: W.E. Banfield to Colonial Secretary, February 23, 1860," BCA, Colonial Correspondence, GR-1372, file 107/1a, Victoria.

24 Banfield must have had some ability to communicate with the Huu-ay-aht, but it is questionable if he would have been able to properly communicate some of the language used in the land agreement, such as "water privileges and timber to be mine forever my heirs and assigns."

25 "Drowned," *British Colonist,* October 24, 1862.

26 For an example, see B. [nom de plume], "Letter to Editor: The Murder of Mr. Banfield," *British Colonist,* March 4, 1864.

27 J. Pike, "Report to Rear Admiral J. Denman, September 27, 1864," BCA, Colonial Correspondence, F. 1210/8, Victoria; and "Return of HMS Devastation: Murderers of Bamfield Secured – Defiant Attitude of the Natives," *British Colonist,* September 28, 1864.

28 Ibid.

29 Ibid.

30 P. Leech, Report, September 20, 1864, BCA, Robert Brown Collection, Add MSS 794, vol. 3, file 13, Victoria.

31 Barry M. Gough, *Gunboat Frontier: British Maritime Authority and Northwest Coast Indians, 1846–1890* (Vancouver: UBC Press, 1974).

32 Mayne, R.C. (1862). *Four Years in British Columbia and Vancouver Island:* London, John Murray, 270.

33 "The Assizes (Before Chief Justice Cameron): The Bamfield Murder," *British Colonist,* November 4, 1864; and "The Murderer of Banfield," *British Colonist,* December 5, 1864.

34 Gough, *Gunboat Frontier,* 121–22.

Part 3

The Beginning and End of Treaty Making on Vancouver Island

7

Land, First Nations, James Douglas, and the Background to Treaty Making on Vancouver Island

Graham Brazier

"Land. If you understand nothing else about the history of Indians in North America, you need to understand that the question that really matters is the question of land."

– THOMAS KING, *THE INCONVENIENT INDIAN*

MORE THAN A CENTURY ELAPSED between the completion of the fourteen Douglas Treaties and the first detailed examination of what Wilson Duff called "these untidy and almost-unknown little documents."[1] It was 1969 before Duff's groundbreaking work on the first eleven treaties, which were completed between 1850 and 1852 on southern Vancouver Island (referred to as the "Fort Victoria Treaties"), was published in *BC Studies.* His brilliant interweaving of the tools of anthropology and history whet the appetites of a small body of dedicated scholars who emerged over the course of the next few decades. To the eleven treaties examined by Duff, one signed at Nanaimo and two at Fort Rupert were added, and together they became known as the Douglas Treaties. As scholars poured over the "almost-unknown little documents," the Douglas Treaties gradually moved from obscurity to celebrity, where they have come to be regarded as documents central to the study of the history of Indigenous-white relations and continue to offer important signposts for the future of those relationships as well. And yet, as revealing as these investigations have been, many of us, both Indigenous and non-Indigenous alike, feel there is still more to be learned from close examination of these documents and the context of their times. One of the questions that continues to tease scholars is "why, when only 3% of the land of Vancouver Island had been included in the treaties, were there no further agreements after 1854?"[2]

The question is challenging for many reasons, not the least of which is that trying to explain why something didn't happen is an exercise that is neither familiar nor comfortable for most of us. There is no possibility of a "smoking gun" for an event that didn't happen and, therefore, no possibility of a definitive answer. In addition, there is the fact that, on the subject of treaty making, James Douglas, for whom the agreements were named, wrote remarkably little. Hartwell Bowsfield's *Fort Victoria Letters, 1846–1851,* for example, contains four letters written by Douglas in 1849 – the year preceding the first treaties.[3] In total, the letters contain 104 paragraphs. One of those paragraphs is devoted to the issue of land purchases from the Indigenous inhabitants of Vancouver Island and is quoted in full later in this essay, and the other 103 paragraphs address other matters deemed by James Douglas to be equally important. This pattern is evident once again in the following year: Bowsfield reproduces twenty-three letters written by Douglas in 1850. Taken together, there are 239 paragraphs. Six were devoted to the question of land purchases from Indigenous residents of Vancouver Island. Consequently, other factors, such as Douglas's actions, elements of his personal history, and the context of his times must be considered in addition to his words when attempting to explain the reasons for both the beginning and the end of treaty making on Vancouver Island.

Over the course of the last forty or so years, a number of explanations have been advanced to explain the cessation of treaty making on Vancouver Island. It has been argued that it ended because of a financial and jurisdictional impasse between the Colonial Office and the local legislature, with each believing the responsibility for treaty making rested with the other. It has also been suggested that James Douglas came to believe that the benefits of treaty making for Indigenous peoples were minimal and transitory and, consequently, not worth the considerable effort required to negotiate. Another analysis suggests that Douglas abandoned land purchases because he came to believe that they had harmed Indigenous peoples by isolating them and concluded that they would be better served by assimilation with the settler community. It has also been argued that by 1854 Douglas believed he had purchased all the land the colony could defend and all that was required for settlement at that time; consequently, efforts to conclude further treaties were not warranted. Another argues that Douglas initially felt compelled by law to negotiate treaties but may have interpreted a decision of the Supreme Court of Oregon in 1853 as releasing him from that compulsion; he subsequently abandoned the project.[4]

My own investigations suggest that while there may be elements of all these explanations present among the specific reasons for the cessation of treaty making, a more general cause for its demise is discernible in a close examination of the background and context of its origins. My contention is threefold. First, commitment to treaty making was not a fundamental element of the plan to colonize Vancouver Island but rather was adopted by the Colonial Office and the Hudson's Bay Company (HBC) largely as an afterthought. Second, James Douglas's extensive career in the fur trade fostered a worldview that, while sympathetic to the well-being of Indigenous peoples, did not embrace the notion of Aboriginal title. Third, as a consequence, he wasn't capable of fully committing his energies to the purchase of land from the people he referred to as "children of the forest." Nonetheless, as long as the process didn't take up too much of his time, Douglas was initially prepared to go through the motions to foster good relations with the Indigenous populations of Vancouver Island.

I begin with an overview of how the land of North America was viewed by both European individuals and European nation states and divided by the Oregon Treaty of 1846. I then document the founding of Fort Victoria and the gradual expansion of the agricultural practices of the HBC into the territory of the Songhees in the years before the British government considered the formal colonization of Vancouver Island.[5] Next, I track the evolution of the terms of the grant of Vancouver Island to the HBC and note that the land policy, for the purpose of "disposing of the land" to British colonists, was developed without reference to Indigenous populations. I continue by pointing out that it wasn't until after the grant was finalized that the HBC considered that agreements with Indigenous groups might be advisable. I then document the arrival and settlement of the first British colonists on Vancouver Island before concluding with a close examination and analysis of the process of treaty making under the direction of James Douglas.

Dividing up the Land

From the time of the founding of the HBC in 1670, European-born fur traders crossed and recrossed the continent of North America gathering beaver pelts for the lucrative English market and they did so in the belief that the land they traversed was unowned. Their largely unspoken belief was that land ownership was a concept of "the old country" and not one that applied in the wilds of North America, where they were currently employed and where Indigenous peoples appeared to move about freely, unconstrained by fences or other property markers. As time passed and distant governments became interested in developing colonies in North America, the need to secure the right to pass title of the land along to prospective settlers became paramount, and by the terms of the Oregon Treaty of 1846, it was agreed by the United States and Great Britain that, from June 19 on, Vancouver Island would be within British North America and the government of Great Britain would have the legal right to confer title to prospective settlers.[6] Although the Royal Proclamation of 1763 recognized that the Indigenous peoples of British North America had a legal interest in their lands that predated the Oregon Treaty, this interest was not formally acknowledged by the British government when it assumed sovereignty over the lands north of the forty-ninth parallel and all of Vancouver Island.[7] Nevertheless, sovereignty over Vancouver Island, which was home to an estimated thirty thousand Indigenous people whose ancestry spanned millennia, was, upon agreement by two men meeting in Washington, DC, granted to Great Britain, whose presence on the island was marked by a collection of fewer than forty HBC employees, of whom four had been born in Britain.[8] They resided, along with fellow servants of the company born in Lower Canada and the Hawaiian Islands, within the palisades of Fort Victoria, where the language spoken by a majority of its inhabitants was likely French.

As tenuous as its hold on Vancouver Island may have appeared, two and a half years passed while the British government considered how it might best govern a remote territory where it had no formal representation and only a tiny resident population. During those years – from June 1846 to January 1849 – although the status of the land occupied and cultivated by the HBC was somewhat uncertain, life on the distant southern tip of Vancouver Island, though largely unaffected by the treaty, was not static. The HBC trading post at Fort Victoria continued its slow but steady expansion into the territory of the Songhees, where, necessarily, cross-cultural social and economic relationships continued a process of adjustment first set in motion in 1843, with the founding of the fort. Documentary evidence of the growth of the fort's footprint and its impact on the relationships between the Indigenous residents and the men of the company during this time period is fragmentary. It is found primarily in the Fort Victoria Journal, 1846–50 (which, coincidentally, covers the interval between the Oregon Treaty of 1846 and the first of the Douglas Treaties in April and May 1850), the correspondence of HBC officials and the Colonial Office, and the correspondence of visiting ships' personnel as well as in various ships' logs.[9]

By 1846, relations between the Songhees and the men of the Hudson's Bay Company had taken on some measure of stability. Their paths had crossed briefly four years earlier, in the summer of 1842, when James Douglas first set foot on Vancouver Island and, along with a small party of HBC men, examined several potential sites for the construction of a new trading post in the territory of a number of Coast Salish groups, including that of the Songhees. Though reference to the Indigenous peoples of the area is scant in his report of their findings, it is clear that Douglas had at least one encounter with the inhabitants during the week-long expedition, as he adopted Indigenous names for many harbours and other geographical features. He also cited "Native" advice on the productivity of a fishing stream and made note of many small fields where it was clear that potatoes were being cultivated. Throughout the week-long first convergence of "land, First Nations, and James Douglas," it was clear that the eyes of Douglas were on the land first and its inhabitants second. He was interested in how the land might serve the interests of the HBC, how it might accommodate the arrivals and departures of various ships, and how it may be adaptable to the agricultural needs of a major new trading post.

Douglas concluded his report to John McLoughlin at Fort Vancouver on July 12, 1842, by identifying Camosack (today's Victoria Harbour), where

> there is a pleasant and convenient site for the establishment, within 50 yards of the anchorage, on the border of a large tract of clear land, which extends eastward to Point Gonzalo at the south-east extremity of the Island and about 6 miles interiorly, being the most picturesque and decidedly the most valuable part of the Island that we had the good fortune to discover.[10]

Douglas's enthusiasm for his "valuable" discovery was repeated in a letter to a friend in which he described the area as "a perfect Eden" with an abundance of luxuriant vegetation "indicating a rich productive soil." He also declared he had already identified "the site we intend to build upon" before he acknowledged that the "natives" were "numerous and daring having as yet lost no trait of their natural barbarity so that we will have both trouble and anxiety in the first course of training." Only after he had seen the land did he note the presence of its inhabitants, who he saw as possible impediments to the company's intentions. Rather than suggesting a negotiation or an agreement with them, Douglas concluded that "we must trust, as in other cases, to a kind Providence, whose watchful care has preserved us in many other dangers."[11] Subsequently, in March of the following year, Douglas and a larger party of HBC men returned to the site prepared to begin construction of a new trading post on Vancouver Island, where no other non-Indigenous structure yet stood. There is nothing in the historical record to indicate that either consultation or negotiation with the Indigenous population was undertaken before construction got underway. This was consistent with well-established HBC practice in the Columbia District, which effectively denied an Aboriginal title to the land.[12] On March 16, Douglas wrote in his diary: "[S]poke to the Samose [Songhees] to-day and informed them of our intention of building in this place which appeared to please them very much and they immediately offered their services in procuring pickets for the establishment."[13] Douglas made no reference to seeking permission on behalf of the company, and it is noteworthy that no individual Songhees were identified or named by him as having been present when he announced his intention. Subsequent to the announcement, much cooperative activity was noted by the ever-confident Douglas, and the construction of Fort Victoria got underway.

A few months later, in June, Douglas returned to his home at Fort Vancouver, leaving Charles Ross in charge at Fort Victoria. Under Ross's direction, construction of the fort was largely completed by the summer of the following year. Ross noted no further consultation with Indigenous authority before his death in June 1844. Command then passed to twenty-six-year-old clerk Roderick Finlayson, whose priorities were established by John McLoughlin, chief factor at HBC headquarters in Fort Vancouver, a four- or five-day journey away on the Columbia River. On November 9, 1844, McLoughlin wrote to Finlayson: "You will contrive extending your fields as far as the means at your disposal permit as Fort Victoria will soon be expected to furnish a large quantity of grain."[14] McLoughlin's directive was issued without elaboration, and as a consequence, Finlayson was never specifically required to seek the approval of the Songhees before he expanded the land under cultivation for the benefit of the company.

Subsequently, under Finlayson's supervision, the company's footprint on Songhees land grew appreciably between 1844 and 1849. In August 1845, he reported to McLoughlin that "[a]s soon as our harvest is over all our disposable men and engaged Indians will be employed preparing new land for tillage & erecting fences."[15] In the meantime, the fort itself was expanded from its original enclosure of 330 feet by 300 feet in 1844 to 450 feet by 330 feet by 1848, and numerous buildings were added outside its walls. Among them were two dairies, a barn, a pair of storage sheds 100 feet by 40 feet, and a sawmill and flour mill six miles from the fort. But more significantly, fenced land and land under cultivation expanded substantially in this period. In early 1844, "about ten acres [were] broken up & prepared for the plough," and by August 1848 farmland had been extended to 350 acres, two-thirds of which were devoted to growing wheat.[16] Evidence suggests that a large, but unrecorded, number of acres were fenced during this period, and by May 1849, "HBC properties with their official reserves occupied 20 square miles (52 square kilometres), the major part of the area surrounding the fort."[17]

While the expansion was carried out with the assistance of Indigenous labour, there is nothing specific in the journal to indicate that Finlayson consulted with or sought permission from any Chief or other high-ranking Songhees before or during the five-year project. However, during James Douglas's annual visit to the fort in 1848, Finlayson made an entry in the journal on December 7 that raises intriguing questions in this regard. He wrote, without further elaboration. "The two Songes chiefs were each made a present of a capot a blanket and a shirt."[18] By the standard indicated in the fort journal on January 18, 1847, where five blankets were exchanged for six months' worth of labour, this appears to be a generous gift and raises the question: Was this truly a "present" or part of an exchange and the consequence of some unrecorded negotiation or *makúk* between the parties?[19] And could that exchange have involved permission to fence and cultivate Songhees land? On one hand, it seems quite possible that, as a clerk, Finlayson doubted his ability to fully represent the interests of the company in consultations or negotiations with Songhees Chiefs, but the knowledge that Chief Factor James Douglas, who would have no such doubt, was visiting the fort at the time may give credence to the speculation that the "present" was part of an exchange that he negotiated.

Evidently, in the era before colonization was spoken of on Vancouver Island, the company had been able to build and sustain a reasonably stable trading operation and distribution centre without formal engagement with Indigenous authority. By 1849, it had become a significant presence upon the landscape of southern Vancouver Island, dependent for its daily operations on agreements with numerous Indigenous individuals. As long as the company was simply a trading enterprise, exchanges in the form of employment, trade, and intermarriage had all become essential components of the social and economic fabric in and around Fort Victoria, where Songhees, Hawaiians, Skagits, French-speaking "Canadians," Iroquois, Makah, English, and Scots, along with a dozen or so other Indigenous groups, regularly intermingled. The company had become extremely adept in pursuing agreements likely to directly advance its interests, such as employment contracts with Songhees individuals, and avoiding those with less certain outcomes, such as seeking an agreement with the Songhees to expand its cultivated fields and pasture lands. Perhaps, as seems more likely, the company simply didn't recognize the Songhees as titled owners of the land, and it never occurred to management to seek out an agreement to fence more land with each passing year. Although the highest-ranking members of the two communities were certainly acquainted by 1849, exchange and trust between them was not as frequent as it was among lower-ranking individuals, and the walls of the fort no doubt continued to inhibit dialogue between the two. In any case, there is little evidence that either treaties or land purchases were considered necessary during this period when expansion of the non-Indigenous community continued.

Colonization Considered

Meanwhile, back in London, largely unbeknownst to the population of Vancouver Island, discussions to determine how to best protect British interests on the west coast of North America following the signing of the Oregon Treaty in 1846 got underway at the highest levels of the British government. In short order, colonization was deemed to be the answer, and the Colonial Office, headed by the secretary of state for the colonies, Earl Grey, was assigned the task of developing a colonization plan for Vancouver Island to secure British possession and occupation of the territory north of the forty-ninth parallel. In September 1846, Grey was quick to make the recommendation that, eventually, would be acted upon. On September 10, he wrote: "I think it is of importance to strengthen the British hold upon the territory now assigned to us [by the Oregon Treaty] by encouraging the settlement on it of British subjects; and I am also of opinion that such settlement could only be effected under the auspices of the Hudson's Bay Co. which I am therefore disposed to encourage."[20]

A complex and lengthy dance between the Colonial Office and the Hudson's Bay Company ensued over the course of the next two and a half years while the Colonial Office considered, or at least gave the appearance of considering, at least four other partners (none of whom resided on Vancouver Island) for the colonization project. The Colonial Office may have tipped its hand as early as March 1847, when it referred a request from an individual for a licence to cut spars on Crown lands on the northwest coast of North America to the HBC for comment. Without reference to any possible Indigenous interests, George Pelly, governor of the Hudson's Bay Company, responded that he had no objections to the proposal and, in so doing, demonstrated the company's habit of failing to consider any notion of Aboriginal title.[21]

The Hudson's Bay Company was not everybody's first choice as a colonizing agent, however, and in fact it roused spirited opposition among many influential individuals, none of whom, it seems, doubted that full title to Vancouver Island was in the hands of the United Kingdom. Opponents frequently pointed out that the interests of a fur-trading monopoly were inherently at odds with those of a colonizing agent that sought to push back the wilderness rather than protect the habitat of fur-bearing animals. Nevertheless, in the end, for a number of reasons, the HBC was named as the Colonial Office's choice to colonize Vancouver Island. "For political reasons," wrote historian Barry Gough, "the government could not invest even a farthing in colonial development: it had to be self-sustaining in every sense other than naval protection."[22] As previously noted, the HBC had established a substantial physical presence on southern Vancouver Island, where it had developed the only harbour in what became British territory and had shown itself to be a largely self-sustaining entity since 1843. Perhaps most significantly, it had a long history of successful and profitable trading relations with Indigenous populations throughout much of the continent. Consequently, by way of a Charter of Grant dated January 13, 1849, the Colonial Office granted Vancouver Island to the Hudson's Bay Company on the condition that it undertake a colonization scheme. The Charter of Grant reads, in part:

> And whereas it would conduce greatly to the maintenance of peace, justice and good order, and the advancement of colonization and the promotion and encouragement of trade and commerce in, and also to the protection and welfare of the native Indians residing within that portion of Our territories in North America, called Vancouver's Island, if such island were colonized by settlers from the British dominions, and if the property in the land of such island were vested for the purpose of such colonization in the said Governor and Company of Adventurers of England trading into Hudson's

> Bay, but nevertheless, upon condition that the said Governor and Company should form on the said island a settlement or settlements ... for the purpose of colonizing the said island ... [and further that] ... the said Governor and Company shall establish upon the said island a settlement or settlements of resident colonists, emigrants from Our United Kingdom of Great Britain and Ireland, or from other of Our dominions, and shall dispose of the land there as may be necessary for the purposes of colonization; and to the intent that the said Company shall, with a view to the aforesaid purposes, dispose of all lands hereby granted to them at a reasonable price.[23]

The language of the document suggests that either the Colonial Office was unaware of the 1847 ruling of the Supreme Court of New Zealand in *The Queen v Symonds,* which recognized the existence of Aboriginal title in the common law of the British Empire, or they were deniers, as it implies that, in their view, the United Kingdom of Great Britain and Ireland had unencumbered authority over the land of Vancouver Island, regardless of the fact that there were "Native Indians" residing "within that portion of Our territories."[24] Another possibility is that the Colonial Office was eager to close the file on the tiny, distant Colony of Vancouver Island and consequently hesitant to burden the HBC with the responsibility for dealing with Aboriginal title, for fear the profit-oriented company would not accept the terms of the grant. This may also explain why the Colonial Office failed to require the company to conform with the terms of the Royal Proclamation of 1763. Perhaps it was recognized that the company, with its almost two-hundred-year history of decision making based on profit maximization, was bound to be challenged in its role as a colonizing and governing body and may have found the burden of dealing with Aboriginal title too much to bear. In any case, the Colonial Office, acting on behalf of the government, granted the land of Vancouver Island to the HBC to "dispose" of at a "reasonable price" without requiring it to first extinguish Aboriginal title.

It suggested, but didn't make it a condition of the grant, that the "welfare of the native Indians" should be protected. In so doing, it effectively disconnected "native Indians" from the land by inferring that the protection of their welfare was a moral question related to the general treatment of Indigenous peoples by colonizing agents and not one related to the land they had occupied for millennia. The document implies that, in the view of the Colonial Office, the "native Indians" had no more claim to the land than did the deer or the bears of the forest. In short, the company was not required by the Colonial Office to purchase the land before it disposed of it. The Charter of Grant, in fact, imposed no specific obligations on the part of the company in relation to the "Native Indians" of Vancouver Island. Furthermore, upon the release of the carefully worded charter on January 13, 1849, the Colonial Office was pleased to have set in motion a plan for the colonization of Vancouver Island without any cost to the government of the day. Effectively, it had set the fur-trading monopoly on an undertaking for which it had only limited previous experience and then slipped into the background for five years, when it would be required to evaluate the company's progress in the implementation of the colonization scheme.

Disposing of Land

Two weeks after the Colonial Office officially released the Charter of Grant, the HBC, under the title of "Resolutions of the Hudson's Bay Company: Colonization of Vancouver's Island," announced that it was "ready to make grants of land to any emigrants from Great Britain or Ireland" and listed a series of resolutions passed to define more closely how the lands granted to them would be "dispose[d] of" at "a reasonable price."[25] Underlying the readiness of the company and the set of resolutions was the assumption that the HBC now had unrestricted ownership of the land that comprised Vancouver Island and that it was fully within its power to determine the conditions for disposal. Accordingly, it was announced that purchasers would pay one pound per acre; that the minimum lot size would be twenty acres; "that colonists must pay their own way to the island from Britain; that purchasers of 100 acres or more must take out with them five single men, or three married couples, for every hundred acres"; and, consistent with the view that it had unrestricted ownership of all the land, "that all minerals, wherever found, shall belong to the Company."[26] Presumably, this would apply to the forests as well, though it didn't seem necessary to mention it. There were, as well, provisions for the establishment of schools, churchyards, land districts, land for the Anglican Church, and other public purposes. Much was left unsaid in the document that set out the conditions for the disposal of the land of Vancouver Island. "Native Indians," for example, were not mentioned.

As further evidence that, in the minds of HBC authorities in London, "native Indians" had no legitimate claim to the land of Vancouver Island, the company entered into negotiations for the sale of one hundred acres to Captain Walter Colquhoun Grant several months before the Colonial Office publicly announced that, effective January 13, 1849, the land was granted to the company. Though the hundred acres hadn't yet been specifically identified or set aside, the company assumed that any hundred acres Grant might select would be unencumbered. With equal confidence, Captain Grant, who had been appointed by the company to survey what were to become its "holdings" on Vancouver Island, assembled a group of labourers to establish a farm on the hundred acres he had "purchased" and arranged for their passage from London to Fort Victoria. As a result, before 1848 drew to a close, the first tangible steps towards colonizing Vancouver Island had been taken: the *Harpooner* set sail from England with what became known as "Grant's Men" on board.

While Captain Grant lobbied HBC headquarters in London, James Douglas, the highest-ranking officer employed by the company on the west coast, was visiting Fort Victoria, where he pondered a letter from Sir John Henry Pelly, governor of the same company that had just initiated a colonization plan for Vancouver Island. Pelly asked Douglas for his views on colonization. His response, dated December 5, 1848, was that of a man who had spent close to thirty years devoted to maximizing the profits of a fur-trading monopoly; it contains the declaration that colonization "is a subject that I have never given a moment's consideration."[27] From this, it is clear that the colonization plan for Vancouver Island that had been almost two and a half years in the making had been constructed wholly in London without the benefit of any first-hand knowledge of the Island or its inhabitants. Furthermore, whatever James Douglas had to say about the colonization of Vancouver Island could not be transmitted to London in sufficient time to be considered before January 13, 1849, when the Colonial Office made its public announcement of the grant to the HBC.

Nevertheless, in his reply to Pelly, Douglas went on: "I will however hazard a few observations [on colonization] since you wish me to do so." Much like his initial report on Vancouver Island written in 1842, his first observation related directly to the land. He wrote that the Island contained "some good cultivatable land" and that much more "might soon be reclaimed from the forest by an industrious population." Next, he extolled the virtues of some of the fine harbours of the Straits of De Fuca and their suitability for a naval depot. Then he returned to the products of the land and noted the "abundance of wood and coal fuel." "The Colony and the Naval Depot," he wrote, "would be a mutual benefit to each other, the one producing and the other consuming the products of the land."[28] Whose land? Douglas doesn't say. Instead, he presumes. His simple little equation involving the land of southern Vancouver Island overlooks the Indigenous residents of that land and implies there would be no barriers to the implementation of such a scheme. In fact, Douglas's only reference to "Indians" in his remarks on colonization was in the form of a warning (once again reminiscent of his 1842 report) that prospective settlers would need to be prepared to put up with some "petty depredations" at their hands. These remarks suggest that Douglas shared the view of the HBC and the Colonial Office that, as of January 13, 1849, the land of Vancouver Island was owned, unencumbered, by the company.

His words must have been what Pelly wanted to hear. On May 12, 1849, six months after considering the merits of colonization for the first time, James Douglas, on the recommendation of Pelly, was appointed *pro tempore* governor of the Colony of Vancouver Island and directed to implement a colonization plan he had had no part in shaping. The search for a permanent governor not aligned with the HBC, however, went on as Douglas and his family made their way from Fort Vancouver to their new home in the Colony of Vancouver Island.[29] They arrived on June 6, one week after the colony's first settlers. On May 31, the *Harpooner*, with "Grant's Men," eight miners, and a doctor on board, completed its six-month voyage from England when it dropped anchor in Fort Victoria's harbour. Roderick Finlayson noted their arrival in the fort journal, but there was nothing to indicate he was aware that a plan to colonize the island was officially underway or that a new era in the history of Vancouver Island had just been embarked upon.

The bold plan that was the product of a difficult two-and-a-half-year negotiation between the Colonial Office and the HBC, as outlined in the Charter of Grant, permitted the company to determine many aspects of the implementation process or, as Stuart Banner writes, "virtually unconstrained discretion ... in setting land policy."[30] The "Resolutions of the Hudson's Bay Company on the Colonization of Vancouver's Island," referred to above, were intended to set out in some detail just how colonization should be implemented and included requirements for prospective colonists regarding the terms and conditions for the purchase of land. These details were released just two weeks after the Charter of Grant was announced on January 13, 1849, and contained no reference to the Indigenous occupants of the land that was to be "dispose[d] of"; thus, once again, these details confirm the company's underlying assumption that

British settlement could proceed without constraint. Almost simultaneously, a request for information about the colony and its land policies was received by the Colonial Office from William Adams, Her Majesty's chargé d'affaires in Peru, who wrote on behalf of several British subjects considering relocation to Vancouver Island. His letter was passed along to J.H. Pelly of the HBC, who, on March 31, suggested that

> it would save much time and greatly facilitate emigration from Peru if Mr. Adams would undertake to receive payment for grants of land, and give certificates of purchase to intending emigrants, on the production of which the company's Officers at Ft. Victoria would (according to instructions to be sent from England) put the purchasers in possession of the quantity of land mentioned in the certificates.[31]

As in the case of Captain Grant, Pelly was clearly prepared to accept payment for land the HBC presumed it owned though hadn't purchased.

An Afterthought

Coincidently, in the same month, two words that can't be found in any of the voluminous preceding documentation involving the development of the plan to colonize Vancouver Island were uttered in London by a nameless official in the Foreign Office.[32] The phrase *Indian title* was used in a rather puzzling unsigned memo marked "confidential." In the memo, which was addressed to no one in particular, the unidentified author reviewed the process by which Her Majesty's government had granted Vancouver Island to the HBC and closed by describing the role the company was expected to play in the colonization plan. The writer agreed with the decision of the Colonial Office that "[w]ith regard to the Indians it has been thought on the whole the better course to make no stipulations respecting them in the grant." But it then drew a conclusion apparently overlooked in the Colonial Office: "It must however be added that in parting with the land of the island Her Majesty parts only with her own right therein, and that whatever measures she was bound to take in order to extinguish the Indian title are equally obligatory on the company."[33] While the precise meaning of what might be construed as a warning may be open to interpretation, what is notable is that the phrase *Indian title* became part of the official record of the development of the colonization plan for Vancouver Island for the first time two weeks *after* it had been formally announced. If the HBC land policy now included an acknowledgment of the concept of Aboriginal title, it was, in every sense, an afterthought.

Though the memo is not acknowledged or referenced in any subsequent correspondence of either the HBC or the Colonial Office, nor is it known whose desk it may have crossed, its date, March 1849, coincides with some subtle changes in the writings of the upper echelons of HBC management with respect to land policy on Vancouver Island. Perhaps the memo was seen by senior managers in London, and perhaps it sparked reflection on some of the practicalities of the implementation of an ill-defined land policy, which caused them to realize that, throughout the planning process, the company had failed to imagine the possibility of friction with Indigenous residents as it encouraged boatloads of settlers from Britain to build townsites and establish farms on Vancouver Island. In any case, it was April 5, 1849, when Andrew Colvile, London-based deputy governor, made a suggestion as to how the company might "prevent disputes." In a letter to George Simpson, governor in North America, Colvile wrote: "It would be best to make some bargain with the Indians in the first instance to prevent disputes – and if the consideration to them be by annual payment it will give some kind of hold over them as it could be stopped if they become troublesome."[34] For the first time since its occupation of Vancouver Island had begun in 1843, HBC management contemplated the wisdom of entering into agreements that involved some "consideration" for "the Indians."

Evolving Land Policy

George Simpson seemed to take Colvile's recommendation a step further when, rather surprisingly, he recommended that the company purchase "the coal lands" discovered on northern Vancouver Island. On June 30, he wrote to Governor J.H. Pelly and Committee:

> The Indians occupying that part of the coast near which the coal mine is situated are numerous and, when we first commenced dealings with them, were of a very bold & treacherous character; they have, however, since then by our frequent intercourse, become civilized to a certain degree, and it is thought they may be made useful as labourers at the mine. – in order to guard against future difficulty with them arising from extravagant claims for compensation for the coal lands I have suggested to the Board of

> Management ... that they should be purchased from them with a formal agreement, at an annual payment in goods to the amount of £100 Sterling, at the usual Indian tariff price.[35]

A month later, likely before he received Simpson's letter, Pelly expressed similar thoughts in a letter to Douglas. From London, on August 4, he wrote to James Douglas at Fort Victoria: "[W]e should hope that by kind treatment and by entering into agreements with the chiefs for the occupation of all lands not actually required by them all hostile feeling on their part may be removed."[36] On the one hand, these suggestions from the upper echelons of HBC management betrayed a puzzling lack of cohesion and coordination uncharacteristic of the monopoly, perhaps indicative of the unfamiliarity of the position they found themselves in. On the other hand, they indicated an awakening of sorts – interest in entering "into agreements with the chiefs" was new. The Charter of Grant, it must be remembered, imposed no specific obligations on the company in regard to the "native Indians" of Vancouver Island, and the fifth resolution of the governor and committee specifically stated "that all minerals, wherever found, shall belong to the Company."[37] Agreements to purchase land or minerals from Indigenous peoples were not requirements, nor had they been deemed necessary by their worldview. Consequently, the agreements contemplated by HBC management can be viewed as either small steps along the path to acknowledgment of Aboriginal title or elements of a strategy of appeasement necessary "to guard against future difficulty" and to foster amiable relations couched as land purchase agreements.

Almost simultaneously, on far-off Vancouver Island, it appears that James Douglas may have been entertaining similar thoughts. On September 3, well before he was aware of the above correspondence, he wrote one of his most often quoted letters to Archibald Barclay (secretary, though not a voting member, of the governor and committee of the HBC, the company's management team) in London:

> Some arrangement should be made as soon as possible with the native Tribes for the purchase of their lands and I would recommend payment being made in the Shape of an annual allowance instead of the whole sum being given at one time; they will thus derive a permanent benifit [sic] from the sale of their lands and the Colony will have a degree of security from their future good behaviour. I would also strongly recommend, equally as a measure of justice, and from a regard to the future peace of the colony, that

> the Indians Fishere's [sic], Village Sitis [sic] and Fields, should be reserved for their benifit and fully secured to them by law.[38]

Taken as written, without a context, Douglas's words seem to indicate that he underwent a dramatic change of opinion in nine months. When he first offered his thoughts on colonization in December 1848, it was only as an afterthought that he made reference to "the native Tribes" of Vancouver Island, leaving the impression that, in his view, their rightful interests in the land were negligible. While Douglas's words quoted above are clear and forthright and taken alone might suggest a high level of commitment to an enlightened land policy, there are elements of context that undermine that impression.

Douglas had been in the colony three months when he wrote to Barclay at HBC headquarters in London on September 3, 1849, with a report intended to cover all the important events since his arrival. He wrote thirty-nine paragraphs – twenty-three came before the one quoted above, where he recommended the purchase of land from "the native Tribes." Before he got around to that recommendation, he devoted paragraph 10 to explaining that Scottish emigrants preferred oatmeal to fish. He devoted seven paragraphs to updating Barclay on the progress of the first colonist to buy land on Vancouver Island – land that the company hadn't felt the need to purchase from "the native Tribes" before selling it to Captain Grant. Grant and his men had been on the land at Sooke for slightly more than two weeks when Douglas wrote paragraph 13 of his letter:

> The little body of Colonists, the first independent settlers on Vancouver Island, have commenced their bold enterprise, under the most favourable auspices: they have no enemies to dread, and no obstacles to encounter, beyond those which the hand of nature has interposed through the force of a teeming sail. Instead of thirsting for their blood, the Natives are not only kind and friendly, but ready and willing to share their labours and assist in all their toils, and they regularly bring in large quantities of the finist [sic] salmon and potatoes, which they part with at a low rate in barter for such articles as suit their fancy or necessities. It has been a work of time and labour, to bring the Indians to that state of friendly intercourse, and I have endeavoured strongly to impress on the minds of Captain Grant and his followers, the incalculable importance, both as regards the future well being of the Colony, and their own individual interests, of cultivating the friendship of these children of the forest. The settlers are certainly wanting

> in experience, but are full of courage and have taken to their work with a degree of ardour and tenacity of purpose, which promise great and permanent results.[39]

Much can be said about the passionate energy and hyperbole of Douglas's words, but use of the phrase *children of the forest* in reference to "the native Tribes" of Sooke is worthy of pause, particularly when it is remembered that ten paragraphs later in the same letter Douglas wrote: "Some arrangement should be made as soon as possible with the native Tribes for the purchase of their lands." In the paternalistic Victorian world view of James Douglas, fur trader, it seems highly unlikely that he would have been able to imagine children, least of all "children of the forest," as rightful landowners. One may well question whether Douglas sincerely believed that an arrangement to buy land from "children of the forest" was anything more than a symbolic and strategic move to ensure "the future well being of the Colony" and, in his view, not a land purchase at all.

This impression is sustained in paragraphs 20 through 23, in which Douglas writes at length about some of the agricultural limitations of the land in the vicinity of the fort and then details the need to map out the HBC lands, the Puget Sound Company lands, and a townsite in Esquimalt with building lots for sale. These remarks, which clearly presumed company ownership of substantial amounts of land, all preceded paragraph 23, where his recommendation to purchase the lands of "the native Tribes" appears, and cast doubt on the sincerity of his commitment to enter into purchase agreements for lands already marked out and utilized by the company.

Nevertheless, it is evident that both James Douglas and the governor, as well as a number of deputy governors of the HBC, were independently coming to believe that if the colonization scheme were to succeed, agreements with "the native Tribes" would be necessary components of a land policy. The nature and composition of the agreements proposed, however, varied considerably among company officials, and, furthermore, it's unlikely that Douglas, who had only recently taken up residence in Fort Victoria, was even aware of the changes being entertained in London as he, too, reflected on a land policy appropriate for Vancouver Island. Governor J.H. Pelly, the highest-ranking HBC official, for example, didn't use the word *purchase* when he suggested that "agreements with the chiefs" be considered – a conclusion consistent with the fur-trading monopoly's long-established practice of managing "indians" in the interests of profit maximization. Similarly, Andrew Colvile used the word *bargain* rather than *purchase* in his recommendation; whereas both George Simpson and James Douglas (by his words of September 3) appeared to favour *land purchases.* None of the proposals, however, invoked laws or legal precedents or legal principles or made reference to Aboriginal title or demonstrated any awareness whatsoever of the "imperial law of Aboriginal title," as described by Hamar Foster elsewhere in this volume, leaving the impression that their recommendations were strategic in nature rather than based on legal obligation. In any case, though no formal announcement of a land policy was ever made, a change in thinking among HBC officials became evident in mid-1849 in the correspondence quoted above. The change was not overt but rather seemed to seep into existence, and for that reason it was not always clear just what HBC land policy was with respect to the "native Tribes" of Vancouver Island.

Agreements with "Native Tribes"

It was in this context, without reference to legal obligation or any further communication from HBC headquarters in London or any other obvious provocation, that James Douglas set out at the end of April 1850 to carry out what he had recommended in his letter of September 3, 1849 – that is, to "purchase the lands of the native Tribes." In the eight-month interval between September 3, 1849, and April 29, 1850, Douglas offered no further written reflections on the subject of Indigenous lands in his correspondence with the HBC. During that time, however, he was visited by Governor Eden Colvile (son of Andrew referred to above), who spent much of the winter of 1849–50 at Fort Victoria in his company. Colvile reported details of his visit in letters to J.H. Pelly at HBC headquarters in London, including discussions he had had with Douglas regarding "the settlement of Vancouver Island, a matter in which he [Douglas] takes great interest, and I agree with him in thinking that it would be advisable that he should be authorised to open a Land office in the island and dispose of lots to British subjects."[40] Notably absent from their conversations about disposing of land to British subjects was any reference to Aboriginal title or, indeed, of reference to Indigenous peoples, with the exception of Douglas's observation that the Cowichan Valley was "thickly inhabited by a very uncivilised & treacherous tribe of Indians."[41]

Douglas's first recorded acknowledgment that he had embarked on a project to acquire land didn't appear until a week after he had completed eight of the nine treaties with the "native Tribes" of southern Vancouver Island. This puzzling delay – along with the fact that the recently arrived governor of the colony, Richard Blanshard, didn't participate in the exercise – suggests that perhaps he regarded his efforts as experimental in nature and may not have wanted attention drawn to them. However, as contemporaneous references to the process of treaty making are sparse, few details of the exercise are known.[42] To begin with, it's not known what set James Douglas off on April 29. We are left to speculate. Perhaps he simply became impatient waiting for a response from London, or his actions might have been triggered by events of the previous month at Fort Victoria, when four ships landed almost one hundred emigrants and labourers from Great Britain and the Sandwich Islands, creating a minor population boom and perhaps a need to appease Indigenous interests.[43] It seems more likely, however, that news of a more recent event may have motivated Douglas to initiate the treaty-making process in the area surrounding Fort Victoria. On April 23 he received a despatch from Fort Rupert in which the clerk in charge, George Blenkinsop, revealed that he had acquiesced to the demands of "the Chiefs" to purchase "the land necessary for garden purposes &c ... so we may now consider ourselves the sole owners of the land, or at least appropriate to our use as much as we may require for gardens, mining purposes, &c."[44] This may have alarmed Douglas who quite likely would have preferred to initiate such a process with local Songhees Chiefs rather than have to respond to their demands for payment. In any case, six days later Douglas "summoned to a conference, the Chiefs and influential men of the Sanges [Songhees] Tribe" and the treaty process was underway. However, no details of the assemblies he apparently presided over are known.

It's not known, for example, if advance notice of his purpose had been circulated among the "native Tribes"; if he had been accompanied on his task by a translator (though it was noted in the journal that an interpreter was at Fort Victoria on April 22, 1850); or if he had a prepared text, and, if so, how it was communicated.[45] In any event, on Monday, April 29, 1850, the first of what would become known as the "Douglas Treaties" (though only the Nanaimo Treaty of 1854 bears his signature) was noted by Roderick Finlayson in the Fort Victoria Journal. Without reference to James Douglas, Finlayson wrote: "In the evening the proprietors of the tract of country lying between the headland and point McGregor were paid for their land. They are ten in number & got 3 blankets 2 1/2 points each at which they appeared well satisfied."[46] Finlayson's journal entry marked the beginning of an extraordinary period of ten days, when Douglas apparently completed agreements with nine "native Tribes." Subsequently, he reported some aspects of the process and its outcomes to HBC headquarters in London in his letter of May 16. Documentation of this period – April 29 to May 10, 1850 – sparse as it is, however, suggests that the task of making the first nine treaties didn't go as smoothly as Douglas would have liked.

Curiously, Roderick Finlayson, keeper of the Fort Victoria Journal and resident of the fort (the site of the signing of the first nine treaties) made reference in the journal to the purchases from "the proprietors" of various tracts of land on four occasions without ever mentioning James Douglas. The first occasion, noted above, was on April 29, for which he and Joseph William McKay were named in the handwritten agreements as well as the published versions as witnesses, then subsequently on May 4, when he wrote: "Some of the Songes were repaid paid for their lands to day & a party of Tequetsins arrived to receive a compensation for their lands about Rocky point."[47] Then on May 9 he noted: "The whole of the Soke tribe arrived to day to receive payment for their lands."[48] And finally, on May 10, he reported that the "Sokes were paid for their lands to day."[49] According to the published versions of the treaties, however, one agreement was signed on April 29, five were signed on April 30, and the remaining three were signed on May 1; the handwritten version of the final treaty with the "Sokes" references both May 1 and May 10.[50]

These discrepancies with respect to the dates referenced by Finlayson and those of the handwritten and published versions are puzzling and not readily explained. At the very least, these incongruities would seem to indicate that, after April 29, when Finlayson was called upon by Douglas to witness the first agreement, communication between the two faltered. Finlayson did not witness any further agreements, and, as his subsequent journal entries are not consistent with the handwritten or published versions of the treaty process, it seems he was not included in the planning and organization of any gatherings after April 29, which seemed to fall to Joseph McKay. The main point of difference, apart from the dates, was that Finlayson's journal entries suggest that payments made to the "native Tribes" for their lands were, at least in the case of the "Tequetsins" and the "Sokes," not made at the time of the agreement but, rather, were delayed by several days. This may well be a detail Douglas thought unimportant and not worthy of passing along to HBC headquarters in his letter of May 16, but it also draws attention to the role of witnesses named in the handwritten and published versions, where all agreements indicate that payment was received on the date of the treaty and where there is no indication that any payments were delayed. Furthermore, though Finlayson officially witnessed the first agreement, where, according to the handwritten and published versions, eleven men signed the document in which payment was said to be "twenty-seven pounds ten shillings sterling," his journal entry for April 29 indicates that payment was made in blankets. He wrote that ten men, not eleven, got "3 blankets 2 1/2 points each" not "twenty-seven pounds ten shillings sterling." Douglas also acknowledged, in his letter of May 16, that payment was made in "a quantity of goods" rather than in pounds sterling. Nevertheless, that was both the first and the last of the treaties witnessed by Finlayson, who, if his memoirs are any indication, gave them little further thought.

"Nothing of Importance"

Perhaps more puzzling, however, is Finlayson's journal entry for the following day. For, according to the handwritten and published versions of the treaties, it was on April 30, "at Fort Victoria," that James Douglas presided over momentous gatherings of 111 "Chiefs and men," representing five Indigenous family groups of the region, and created the majority of what we know today as the Fort Victoria Treaties.[51] Inexplicably, this event seems to have escaped Finlayson's attention, for, according to him, what was noteworthy about Tuesday, April 30, 1850, was this:

> Generally overcast with a fresh breeze from the South West. People employed much the same as yesterday. Were busy to day in the Sale Shop packing up the Ft. Simpson Servants' Orders. Some furs & provisions were traded from Nanaimaults who arrived this morning. A ship was seen in the offing last night, going down the Straits apparently from Nisqually.[52]

It's difficult to imagine how a gathering in numbers roughly equal to the non-Indigenous population of the area could go unnoticed by the official recorder of occurrences. But Finlayson was not alone in overlooking the events of April 30, 1850. They also seem to have eluded the governor of the colony. Blanshard wrote that between April 8 and June 15, 1850, "nothing of importance has since occurred in the colony."[53] In addition, neither the Reverend Staines nor Father Lempfrit, both known for recording their observations regarding affairs of Fort Victoria, made any reference to the great gathering of "Chiefs and others" in any of their subsequent correspondence. (Dr. Helmcken was not present – he left Fort Victoria on April 25, bound for Fort Rupert.) It's challenging to draw any conclusions, other than puzzlement, or, indeed, to offer any speculation about such apparent incongruities, the largest being that the governor of the colony was unaware that documents of great historical significance were being created under his nose.[54]

Nor were these the last of the anomalies associated with the treaty-making process. In describing his approach two weeks later, Douglas wrote: "I attached the signature of the native Chiefs and others who subscribed the Deed of purchase to a blank sheet."[55] Even a cursory examination of the handwritten versions of the agreements, however, suggests that Douglas's use of the word *signature* was misleading. Each treaty includes a list of the names of "Chiefs and others" of the relevant families, all written boldly in ink in the same neat hand – believed by Wilson Duff to be that of Douglas.[56] Following each name is an exceptionally uniform *x*, which also appears to have been made by the same hand and suggests that Douglas, rather than attaching "signatures" to the blank sheet, attached a list of names and put an *x* beside each one himself. Furthermore, the remarkable uniformity of the handwritten names suggests that they may have been prepared in advance of the meeting with the "Chiefs and others" rather than in their presence "in the field."

Following his description of attaching the signatures to the blank sheet, Douglas goes on to request that Barclay send out "the contract or Deed of conveyance," which he describes as "the proper form ... by return post."[57] Consequently, there can be little assurance that the words spoken to the gatherings of Chiefs were the same as those that later appeared on "the proper form," which wasn't received at Fort Victoria until November. Furthermore, Douglas's description of the document "signed" by "the native Chiefs and others" as a "blank sheet" indicates that he overlooked reporting a subsequent step taken where, according to Duff's convincing handwriting analysis, Douglas entered an opening paragraph in pencil that identified the boundaries of the land of each specific tribe for each of the nine agreements. Duff concluded that Douglas wrote above the "signatures" of the agreement with the "Teechamitsa": "Know all men, we, the Chiefs and People of the Teechamitsa Tribe, who have signed our names and made our marks to this deed on the twenty-ninth day of April, one thousand eight hundred and fifty, do consent to surrender." He stopped there and left space for the wording he expected to receive from

HBC headquarters in London to be inserted. His assertion that "the Chiefs and People of the Teechamitsa Tribe" signed their names and made their marks to the deed is at odds with Duff's handwriting analysis, which concluded that the names and likely the *x*'s were all in the hand of James Douglas, making it challenging, if not impossible, to assess the extent of participation of the "Chiefs and others" in the whole process.

Taken together, these factors betray an awkwardness and an absence of formality and precision in the whole exercise of treaty making; they undermine any conclusion that the "treaties" were, in Douglas's worldview, anything more than strategic agreements intended to secure the goodwill of local Indigenous groups; they may explain Wilson Duff's conclusion that the resulting documents were "untidy"; and they may account for Douglas's choice of words in his May 7 letter to J.M. Yale at Fort Langley, in which he wrote that he found the process "a rather troublesome business."[58] In the same letter, Douglas claimed to be following orders from England as he had been "engaged in buying out the Indian right to the lands in this neighbourhood and to the westward." Curiously, though no prior orders from England have been uncovered, instructions on how he was to make treaties arrived the following day, May 8.[59] Almost six months earlier, on December 17, 1849, Archibald Barclay, HBC secretary, had written, apparently without knowledge of Douglas's recommendations of September 3, 1849:

> With respect to the rights of the natives you will have to confer with the Chiefs of the tribes on that subject, and in your negociations [sic] with them you are to consider the natives as the rightful possessors of such lands only as they are occupied by cultivation, or had houses built on at the time when the Island came under the undivided sovereignty of Great Britain in 1846. All other land is to be regarded as waste, and applicable to the purposes of colonization ...
>
> In other colonies the scale of compensation adopted has not been uniform, as there are circumstances peculiar to each which prevented them all from being placed on the same footing, but the average rate may be stated at £1 per head of the tribe for the interest of the Chiefs, paid on signing the Treaty ...
>
> The natives will be confirmed in the possession of their lands as long as they occupy and cultivate them themselves, but will not be allowed to sell or dispose of them to any private person, the right to the entire soil having been granted to the company by the Crown. The right of fishing and hunt-

> ing will be continued to them, and when their lands are registered, and they conform to the same conditions with which other settlers are required to comply, they will enjoy the same rights and privileges.[60]

Though it seems surprising that such a major change in company policy should be passed on to Douglas by someone other than the highest-ranking company official – Governor J.H. Pelly – Barclay's letter seemed to mark a significant shift in HBC land policy for Vancouver Island, though, once again, any reference to a specific legal obligation is missing. At the time he wrote, on December 17, 1849, the company's operations on Vancouver Island had been under the direction of the Charter of Grant for almost a year. The charter hadn't required the company to either acknowledge "native Title" or to purchase the land before "disposing" of it for the purposes of colonization, although, as pointed out above, there had been indications that perhaps a change in thinking was taking place at the highest levels of HBC management, where agreements or bargains with "Indians" were being considered. Barclay's letter, perhaps as a result of a directive from the Colonial Office, took this process a step further and had the effect of superseding the charter, as he recommended that Chiefs be paid on the signing of a treaty. Douglas considered the letter for a week before responding on May 16:

> I have the honor to acknowledge your communication of the 17th of December 1849, stating in a more detailed form the views of the governor and Committee respecting the colonization of this island, the rights of the Natives, and their instructions as to the extent to which these rights are to be respected. [Without disclosing that he had received Barclay's letter on May 8, a week after he had initiated nine treaties on southern Vancouver Island, Douglas continued.] On the receipt of that letter I, summoned to a conference, the Chiefs and influential men of the Sanges Tribe, which inhabits and claims the District of Victoria, from Gordon Head on Arro Strait, to Point Albert on the Strait of De Fuca as their own particular heritage. After considerable discussion, it was arranged, that the whole of their lands, forming as before stated the District of Victoria, should be sold to the company, with the exception of the Village sites and enclosed fields, for a certain remuneration, to be paid at once to each member of the Tribe.[61]

Douglas's declaration that "[o]n the receipt of that letter, I summoned to a conference, the Chiefs and influential men of the Sanges Tribe" is puzzling, as it is not supported by the evidence. That he didn't receive Barclay's instructions until he had already completed nine agreements may explain, in part, why he didn't follow Barclay's narrow directive that, as the company had been granted the rights "to the entire soil" by the Crown, it was only necessary to purchase the land occupied by the "Natives of Vancouver's Island." Nevertheless, his motivation remains puzzling. He seems to have regarded Barclay's letter as an opportunity to maintain that the process for the purchase of "Native lands" had been ordered from England and not one he had initiated himself. Perhaps he was eager to put some distance between himself and the process, which had become, and continued to be, awkward and "troublesome."

Nevertheless, six months later, "the proper form" requested by Douglas arrived from London. The "Form of Agreement for purchases of Land from Natives of Vancouver's Island" and the wording dictated by Barclay, based on treaties signed in New Zealand, arrived on November 16 as enclosures to Barclay's letter, in which he offered his assurance that "the Governor and Committee very much approve of the measures you have taken in respect of the lands claimed by the Natives."[62] In his response to Barclay, Douglas acknowledged receipt of the letter but failed to make any reference to the enclosures. He offered nothing further on how or when the "Form of Agreement" would be employed or when the copying of the prescribed text into the spaces left between the opening paragraph and the lists of names of Indigenous men from nine family groups would be undertaken. Rather than expressing his gratitude for receiving the forms he had requested and offering his assurance that they would enable him to complete the treaty process expeditiously, Douglas chose to remind Barclay, in a rather tortuous manner, that the treaty-making process had been difficult. He wrote that while he had been "surrounded ... on all sides by disaffection and unexampled difficulties, it is consolatory to find that the Governor and Committee generally approve of our measures and proceedings, though at times it was a choice of evils."[63]

Six months after the "signing" of the treaties, Douglas offered no evidence to indicate where they were stored or who had custody of them or when and under whose direction the completion of the treaties was to be undertaken. Furthermore, though it is not known when the text received from London was entered on the handwritten versions, it is evident that it was entered in a hand other than that of James Douglas, though the historical record offers nothing further in this regard. In addition, as Neil Vallance has pointed out elsewhere in this volume, there is no indication that Douglas conferred with the original "signatories" regarding the wording before it was inserted.[64] By November 1850, Douglas seems to have put the treaties well behind him and turned his attention to other matters, such as problems associated with coal mining at Fort Rupert and the settlement of retired servants in the vicinity of Fort Victoria. As a consequence, a date for the final steps in the Fort Victoria Treaties process remains unknown.

In summary, it seems clear that Douglas's experience with the nine Fort Victoria Treaties failed to inspire his commitment to, or enthusiasm for, the process; as a result, the majority of the five treaties that followed were entered into in response to specific circumstances rather than as general land purchases for settlement. The South Saanich Treaty, signed at Fort Victoria on February 7, 1851, for example, was initiated to secure the interests of "Vancouver's Island Steam Saw Mill Company," which had been cutting timber within territory belonging to Saanich families, and the spread of settlement into the area was simply a byproduct of the agreement. Likewise, the Fort Rupert and Nanaimo Treaties were initiated for specific purposes – that is, to secure access to profitable coal deposits – and were not related to facilitating settlement.

Conclusion

Though the Fort Victoria Treaties of 1850 followed a detailed and protracted negotiation regarding colonization plans for Vancouver Island that spanned two and a half years, it cannot be said that they were a product of that process. The product was the Charter of Grant, which concluded the discussions between the Colonial Office and the HBC in January 1849 and set out the conditions for the grant of Vancouver Island to the company. Notably absent from those conditions was a requirement that the company purchase land from the Indigenous residents before selling it to prospective settlers from Great Britain. This omission was simply a reflection of the unspoken worldview that "Indians" didn't have rights to the land. It was a long-held, unspoken, deeply entrenched worldview and one that was shared by James Douglas and the HBC servants who had occupied southern Vancouver Island since 1843. It was evidenced by the construction of Fort Victoria and the subsequent annual expansion of the territory under their management, without consultation or agreement with the Indigenous residents. It was also evident in all their assumptions concerning "disposal" of the land to settlers from Great Britain.

The treaties emerged out of what can only be called a series of afterthoughts on the part of the upper echelons of HBC management. It wasn't until after the formal declaration of the Charter of Grant in January 1849 that cracks in the long-held worldview appeared among the London-based managers, who began to consider making "bargains" or entering into agreements with the Indigenous peoples of Vancouver Island as a part of the colonization plan. There was, however, no consensus on the substance of such "bargains" or agreements. Some, including Governor J.H. Pelly and Deputy Governor Andrew Colvile, believed that the function of the agreements was simply to remove "hostile feeling" and "prevent disputes." That is, they were seen to be strategic tools of appeasement, unrelated to rights to the land.[65] Others, notably, Archibald Barclay – whose position in the company hierarchy, described as "secretary," was below that of Pelly and Colvile – saw the agreements as purchases of land occupied by the "native Tribes" of southern Vancouver Island. George Simpson, North American governor, thought it would be wise to purchase land where coal was present to "guard against future difficulty." While this change in attitudes led to acknowledgment that the Indigenous peoples of Vancouver Island were deserving of consideration as colonization was imposed, there was no consensus that the agreements should take the form of land purchases and no clear statement that they were a legal obligation on the part of the company.

James Douglas's personal point of view had also begun to evolve. But the evidence, scarce as it is, suggests that late in 1849, Douglas, whose knowledge of a plan to colonize Vancouver Island was still only months old, was not fully committed to the notion of "Native title" to the land, as he expressed contradictory sentiments in the body of his letter to Barclay dated September 3. Furthermore, he didn't accord the resolution of questions raised by the notion of "Native title" a high priority among his tasks as land agent on Vancouver Island. Eight months passed before he embarked on a low-key campaign with the stated intention of purchasing land from the "native Tribes" of the area surrounding Fort Victoria. From the evidence, Douglas seems to have attached little importance to the exercise, which he executed not only hurriedly and awkwardly but also largely unnoticed and without the knowledge or participation of the governor of the colony. Instead, it seems that after devoting a few days to treaty making, during which he experienced "unexampled difficulties," he was content to put it all behind him.

In 1850, the notion of "Native title" was still new to James Douglas – he is not known to have used the phrase in any of his correspondence. His perspective on Indigenous peoples' rights with respect to the land had formed over the course of thirty years in the fur trade and was not one that could readily be put aside. In 1850, Douglas's image of Indigenous peoples as "children of the forest" lingered. As a consequence, the treaty-making process under his direction failed to ignite his full commitment or to generate any traction or momentum. It would be another eleven years – seven years after the last treaty was concluded at Nanaimo in 1854 – before he more fully accepted the sentiments expressed by Thomas King in the introduction to this essay. In 1861, he wrote:

> As the native Indian population of Vancouver Island have distinct ideas of property in land, and mutually recognize their several exclusive possessory rights in certain districts, they would not fail to regard the occupation of such portions of the Colony by white settlers, unless with the full consent of the proprietary tribes, as national wrongs; and the sense of injury might produce a feeling of irritation against the settlers, and perhaps disaffection to the Government that would endanger the peace of the country.[66]

However, while his eloquent words suggest that by 1861 the fur trader in James Douglas had been fully relegated to the past, they failed to signal a change in his priorities or to trigger a return to the process of treaty making; for reasons explored by other contributors to this volume, no further written treaties were concluded with the Indigenous peoples of Vancouver Island.

Notes

1 Wilson Duff, "The Fort Victoria Treaties," *BC Studies* 3 (Fall 1969): 3. For the purposes of this essay, I have chosen to be consistent with Wilson Duff and refer to the subject documents as "treaties" in full recognition that this term is currently the subject of critical examination among historians. See, for example, the essay by Neil Vallance elsewhere in this volume.

2 See Cole R. Harris, *Making Native Space: Colonialism, Resistance, and Reserves in British Columbia* (Vancouver: UBC Press, 2002), 21.

3 Hartwell Bowsfield, ed., *Fort Victoria Letters, 1846–1851* (Winnipeg: Hudson's Bay Record Society, 1979).

4 See Robin Fisher, *Contact and Conflict* (Vancouver: UBC Press, 1977); Paul Tennant, *Aboriginal Peoples and Politics: The Indian Land Question in British Columbia, 1849–1989* (Vancouver: UBC Press, 1990); Harris, *Making Native Space;* Hamar Foster and Alan

Grove, "'Trespassers on the Soil': *United States v Tom* and a New Perspective on the Short History of Treaty Making in Nineteenth-Century British Columbia," *BC Studies* 138–39 (Summer–Autumn 2003): 51–84; and Stuart Banner, *Possessing the Pacific: Land, Settlers, and Indigenous People from Australia to Alaska* (Cambridge, MA: Harvard University Press, 2007).

5 In the time period examined here, "Songhees" refers collectively to all nine families who lived in what is now Greater Victoria. All shared a common language and so are sometimes referred to as "Lekwungen speaking people" or "Lekwungen" for short. Today's descendants of the nine families comprise two Indian Act designated bands: the Songhees and the Esquimalt.

6 "Oregon Treaty," *Wikipedia,* https://en.wikisource.org/wiki/Oregon_Treaty.

7 For more details on this point, see Hamar Foster, "The Imperial Law of Aboriginal Title at the Time of the Douglas Treaties," elsewhere in this volume.

8 Roderick Finlayson, clerk, was born in Ross-shire, Scotland; Angus McDonald, laborer, was born in Stornoway, Scotland; Norman Martin, carpenter, was born in Stornoway, Scotland; and Charles Ross, Chief Trader, was born in Inverness-shire, Scotland. A majority of the other residents were born in Lower Canada (today's Quebec), and eleven were born in "Woahoo" (Hawaiian Islands).

9 Fort Victoria Journal, 1846–50, April 29, 1850, Hudson's Bay Company Archives (HBCA), B.226/a/1, accessed April 12, 2017, http://www.fortvictoriajournal.ca.

10 James Douglas to John McLoughlin, July 12, 1842, quoted in "The Founding of Fort Victoria," *The Beaver* (March 1943): 83.

11 James Douglas to James Hargrave, February 5, 1843, in G.P.T. Glazebrook, ed., *The Hargrave Correspondence* (Toronto: Champlain Society, 1938), 420–21.

12 There is nothing in the historical record to indicate that negotiations with Indigenous inhabitants preceded the construction of Fort Vancouver (1825), Fort Langley (1827), Fort Simpson (1831), Fort McLoughlin (1833), or Fort Rupert (1849). On the contrary, at the founding of Fort Vancouver on March 19, 1825, Hudson's Bay Company governor George Simpson announced that the object of naming the fort after the "distinguished navigator is to identify our claim to the Soil and Trade with his discovery of the River and Coast on behalf of Great Britain": Frederick Merk, ed., *Fur Trade and Empire: George Simpson's Journal* (Cambridge, MA: Harvard University Press, 1968), 124.

13 Diary of James Douglas, quoted in Derek Pethick, *Victoria: The Fort* (Vancouver: Mitchell Press, 1968), 50.

14 McLoughlin, Fort Vancouver, to Finlayson, Fort Victoria, November 9, 1844, BC Archives (BCA), A/B/40/F49.

15 Roderick Finlayson, Fort Victoria, to McLoughlin, Fort Vancouver, August 29, 1845, BCA, A/B/40/F49.

16 Charles Ross to Donald Ross, January 10, 1844, in "Five Letters of Charles Ross," *British Columbia Historical Quarterly* (April 1943): 111.

17 Michael Layland, *A Perfect Eden: Encounters by Early Explorers of Vancouver Island* (Victoria: Touchwood, 2016), 118.

18 Fort Victoria Journal, December 7, 1848, HBCA, B.226/a/1.

19 For a full examination of the word *makúk,* see John Sutton Lutz, *Makúk: A New History of Aboriginal-White Relations* (Vancouver: UBC Press, 2008), Preface.

20 Quoted in Barry M. Gough, "Crown, Company, and Charter: Founding Vancouver Island Colony – A Chapter in Victorian Empire Making," *BC Studies* 176 (Winter 2012–13): 32.

21 Pelly to Hawes, March 22, 1847, BC Archives GR-0332, Colonial Office Correspondence with the Hudson's Bay Company, transcripts, 1822–80.

22 Gough, "Crown, Company, and Charter," 13.

23 Royal Grant, quoted in James E. Hendrickson, ed., *Journals of the Colonial Legislatures of the Colonies of Vancouver Island and British Columbia, 1851–1871,* 4 vols. (Victoria: BC Archives, 1980), 1:377, Appendix A.

24 Hamar Foster and Alan Grove, "Trespassers on the Soil," *BC Studies* 138–39 (Summer–Autumn 2003): 62.

25 "Resolutions of the Hudson's Bay Company: Colonization of Vancouver's Island," in "Papers Relating to the Colonization of Vancouver Island," in Provincial Archives Department, British Columbia, *Report of the Provincial Archives Department of British Columbia, British Columbia Sessional Papers* (Victoria: King's Printer, 1914), V 73.

26 Richard Mackie, "The Colonization of Vancouver Island, 1849–1858," *BC Studies* 96 (Winter 1992–93): 7.

27 James Douglas, Fort Victoria, to Sir John Henry Pelly, London, December 5, 1848, Bowsfield, *Fort Victoria Letters,* 33.

28 Ibid.

29 A month later, Richard Blanshard accepted the appointment as governor but didn't arrive in the colony until March 1850, when his commission was read publicly and he officially took office. Blanshard's commission as governor was issued by the Colonial Office on July 9, 1849, and none of the forty-one clauses made specific reference to Indigenous peoples or their lands but referred repeatedly to "Our said Island."

30 Stuart Banner, *Possessing the Pacific: Land, Settlers, and Indigenous People from Australia to Alaska* (Cambridge, MA: Harvard University Press, 2007), 204.

31 Pelly to Hawes, Parliamentary Under-Secretary, March 31, 1849, National Archives (UK), 2777, CO 305/2, in *The Colonial Despatches of Vancouver Island and British Columbia, 1846–1871,* ed. James Hendrickson and the Colonial Despatches Project, https://bcgenesis.uvic.ca (hereafter *Colonial Despatches*).

32 See *Colonial Despatches:* "This digital archive contains transcriptions of virtually the complete correspondence between the British colonial authorities and the successive governors of the nascent Vancouver Island and British Columbia colonies, along with a great deal of associated writing, generated within the colonial office, and between public offices, which relates to the colonies. The entire history of Vancouver Island and BC, from 1846 to 1871, is represented here, in the words of those most intimately concerned with the governance and development of the land, its resources, and its population."

33 British Foreign Office to Anonymous, March 1849, CO 305/1, p. 635, *Colonial Despatches,* https://bcgenesis.uvic.ca/getDoc.htm?id=V495PA03.scx.

34 Quoted in Harris, *Making Native Space,* 19.

35 Quoted in Bowsfield, *Fort Victoria Letters,* lv–lvi.

36 Quoted in Harris, *Making Native Space,* 19.

37 "Resolutions of the Hudson's Bay Company," 73.

38 James Douglas, Fort Victoria, to Archibald Barclay, London, September 3, 1849, in Bowsfield, *Fort Victoria Letters,* 43.

39 Ibid., 38–39.

40 Colvile to Pelly, November 22, 1849, in Eden Colvile, *London Correspondence Inward, 1849–52,* ed. E.E. Rich, Publications of the Hudson's Bay Record Society 19 (London: Hudson's Bay Record Society, 1956), 9.

41 Colvile to Pelly, October 15, 1849, in Colvile, *London Correspondence,* 5.

42 Two letters written by Douglas (one on May 7 to J.M. Yale at Fort Langley and one on May 16 to Archibald Barclay, HBC headquarters in London), Finlayson's entries in the

Fort Victoria Journal (for April 29 and the first week in May), and portions of the handwritten agreements themselves provide the only primary documentation of the process of treaty making. The handwritten agreements dated April 29, April 30, May 1, and May 10, 1850, are collected in the "Register of Land Purchases from Indians," BCA, MS-0772. But from the handwriting analysis quoted by Duff in "The Fort Victoria Treaties," it is evident that portions of these documents were completed sometime later, following receipt of the "form" from London on November 16, 1850.

43 The Fort Victoria Journal records that on March 11 the *Driver* arrived from England with the governor; on March 12 the *Mary Dare* arrived from "Ouahu" with eight labourers from the Sandwich Islands; on March 19 the *Cowlitz* delivered seven labourers and two clerks; and on March 24 the *Norman Morrison* arrived from England with approximately eighty "labourers and others."

44 "Fort Rupert Post Journal: 1849–1850," April 15, 1850, Hudson's Bay Company Archives, B.185/a/1, http://pam.minisisinc.com/DIGITALOBJECTS/Access/HBCA%20Microfilm/1M123/B185-A-1.pdf. For a detailed discussion of the agreement, see Daniel Marshall, "Fort Rupert and the Mystery of the Fort Victoria Treaties," *The Orca*, March 30, 2019, https://theorca.ca/resident-pod/fort-rupert-and-the-mystery-of-the-fort-victoria-treaties.

45 Joseph McKay, who witnessed seven of the nine treaties, recalled the process many years later in a letter to Dr. Helmcken. He recalled that Douglas had been guided by a lengthy letter from HBC secretary, Archibald Barclay. McKay wrote: "The day before the meeting with the Indians, he [Douglas] sent for me and handed me the document [the letter from Barclay] above referred to telling me to study it carefully and to commit as much of it to memory as possible in order that I might check the interpreter Thomas should he fail to explain properly to the Indians the substance of Mr. Douglas' address to them." As Douglas didn't receive Barclay's letter of December 1849 (quoted later in this essay) until after the Fort Victoria Treaties were completed, it is evident that the specifics of McKay's memory must apply only to the Saanich Treaties of 1852. See Joseph McKay to Dr. James S. Helmcken, December 3, 1888, BCA, Joseph William McKay Fonds, PR-0560, MS-1917, file 27.

46 Fort Victoria Journal, HBCA, B.226/a/1.

47 Ibid.

48 Ibid.

49 Ibid.

50 Douglas made no references to specific dates in either his letter of May 7 or his letter of May 16.

51 According to the handwritten and published versions of the agreements, 111 Chiefs and men of the area surrounding Fort Victoria gathered at the fort on April 30, 1850 (Kosampson Tribe, 21; Swengwhung Tribe, 30; Chilcowitch Tribe, 12; Whyomilth Tribe, 18; and Che-ko-nein Tribe, 30).

52 Fort Victoria Journal, April 30, 1850, HBCA, B.226/a/1.

53 Blanshard to Earl Grey, June 15, 1850, CO 305/2, *Colonial Despatches.*

54 Evidence that Governor Blanshard was present at Fort Victoria while Douglas was engaged in the treaty-making process between April 29 and May 10 is strong but not conclusive. Blanshard wrote a letter to Earl Grey from Fort Victoria dated April 8, and Douglas, in a letter dated May 15, confirmed his presence on May 11.

55 James Douglas, Fort Victoria, to Archibald Barclay, London, May 16, 1850, in Bowsfield, *Fort Victoria Letters,* 96.

56 Wilson Duff credited Willard E. Ireland for assistance in identifying James Douglas's handwriting in "The Fort Victoria Treaties," 8.

57 James Douglas, Fort Victoria, to Archibald Barclay, London, May 16, 1850, in Bowsfield, *Fort Victoria Letters,* 96.

58 Douglas to J.M. Yale, May 7, 1850, BCA, MS-0105, box 1, file 1.

59 "I have the honor to acknowledge your letters of 17th Decr. 1849 and of the 3rd January and 16th Feby. of this year, which were received here on the 8th of May, the two former by the way of Fort Vancouver, and the last direct from San Francisco." See James Douglas, Fort Victoria, to Archibald Barclay, London, May 15, 1850, in Bowsfield, *Fort Victoria Letters,* 89.

60 Archibald Barclay, London, to James Douglas, Fort Victoria, December 17, 1849, BC Archives, A/C/20/Vi7A, transcript.

61 James Douglas, Fort Victoria, to Archibald Barclay, London, May 16, 1850, in Bowsfield, *Fort Victoria Letters,* 94–95.

62 Barclay to Douglas, August 16, 1850, sent as enclosure to letter of August 23, BCA, A/C/20/Vi7, https://royalbcmuseum.bc.ca/assets/Douglas_Treaties_Correspondence1.pdf.

63 James Douglas, Fort Victoria, to Archibald Barclay, London, November 16, 1850, in Bowsfield, *Fort Victoria Letters,* 130.

64 Neil Vallance, "The Earliest First Nations Accounts of the Formation of the Vancouver Island (or Douglas) Treaties of 1850–54," this volume.

65 This view endured and was still alive in 1888, as evidenced in a letter by prominent physician and politician J.S. Helmcken to Joseph McKay, who wrote in part that the purchase of the land from "the neighbouring Indians ... was unnecessary as the Company held the land by 'grant' from HM." He went on to write, "My feeling is, the blankets &c were given to appease or make friends with Indians, in order that no trouble might arise in case settlers arrived upon the land": J.S. Helmcken to Joseph McKay, November 30, 1888, BCA, Add MSS 1917, file 15.

66 Quoted by Hamar Foster elsewhere in this volume.

8

The Rutters' Impasse and the End of Treaty Making on Vancouver Island

John Sutton Lutz

One of the most puzzling mysteries of British Columbia's colonial period revolves around Governor James Douglas's treatment of Indigenous peoples, particularly the Vancouver Island Treaties he initiated. Fourteen treaties were made on Vancouver Island in rapid succession, from 1850 to 1854, between Douglas, the agent of the Hudson's Bay Company (HBC) acting for the British Crown, and Island First Nations. Why did he make the three small clusters of treaties, ignoring most of the Island? And when a willingness and a precedent had been clearly established, why did treaty making stop? British Columbia would be a much different place today if Douglas had consistently followed his own precedent.

Historian John Weaver states in *The Great Land Rush and the Making of the Modern World:* "There is conjecture about why Douglas stopped."[1] In fact, most of the scholars who have written about the history of Indigenous-settler relations in British Columbia have made an effort to solve this mystery. Many have argued that sometime between the 1854 Nanaimo Treaty and the 1858 Fraser Canyon Gold Rush, James Douglas changed his mind about treaties. Some, like Paul Tennant and Hamar Foster, argue that he realized the treaties had not benefitted Indigenous peoples.[2] Others, like Cole Harris, argue that, with the gold rush, events moved too fast; to negotiate treaties across British Columbia would have been too complicated, too expensive.[3] Leonard Wrinch argues that, with disease and depopulation, Douglas felt Indigenous peoples were going to vanish in any case.[4] George Shankel in his 1945 PhD dissertation argues that procrastination meant that settlement outpaced Douglas's desire for treaties. And Shankel, with Robin Fisher, in his 1977 *Contact and Conflict,* argues that neither Douglas nor his Legislative Assembly were ultimately willing to spend the money. Most recently, Graham Brazier (see his chapter, this volume) has argued that Douglas never fully committed to treaty making and abandoned it as easily as he adopted it.[5]

There are, however, problems with all these explanations. First, James Douglas did not change his mind. This essay shows that Douglas remained a supporter of making treaties on Vancouver Island through to his retirement in 1864, and even his successor, Governor Arthur Kennedy, affirmed the need for treaties in that year. Douglas all but finalized a treaty with the Cowichan in 1862, and he raised the need for treaties in his addresses and budgets submitted to the Vancouver Island Assembly in 1860, 1861, 1862, 1863, and 1864 and to the Colonial Office in 1861. So, if Douglas did not change his mind, three interlocking mysteries remain about the process of treaty making on Vancouver Island:

1 Why did James Douglas make fourteen agreements between 1850 and 1854 with First Nations on the south, middle, and north Island and not with nations in between?
2 Why were no treaties made between 1855 and 1858, when Douglas, as both governor and land agent for the HBC, could have done so unilaterally?
3 Why did he stop treaty making? Why were no treaties made between 1859 and Douglas's retirement in 1864?

Mystery 1: Why a Patchwork of Fourteen Treaties in 1850–54?

The 1846 Oregon Treaty established the border between American and British territory west of the Rocky Mountains at the forty-ninth parallel. Thanks to the HBC, which built Fort Victoria on the southern tip of Vancouver Island below the forty-ninth parallel in 1843, the boundary jogged south so the whole of Vancouver Island went to the British. Almost immediately, the British government opened up negotiations with the HBC to solidify British claims and prevent American filibusters from seizing the territory.[6] The bargain struck was that Vancouver Island would become a colony of Great Britain, effective January 13, 1849, but to save the British taxpayers money, it would be granted to the HBC for the token payment of seven shillings a year.[7]

The HBC was granted all land and minerals on Vancouver Island for ten years on the understanding that (1) it would establish a colony on the Island by selling the land at a reasonable price; (2) it would pay the costs of the colony from the proceeds of these sales, keeping no more than 10 percent for its own profit; (3) at the end of ten years, the British government would repossess unsold land and mines on repayment of the "sums expended by the Company on the island and the value of their establishments"; and (4) "in parting with the land of the island Her Majesty parts only with her own right therein, and that whatever measures she was bound to take in order to extinguish the Indian title are equally obligatory on the Company."[8]

James Douglas, then the HBC's senior official on the Pacific Coast, learned that Vancouver Island had been made a colony and that he was in charge of selling the land to incoming colonists in fall 1849.[9] In September of that year, he wrote to his superiors at the HBC suggesting he purchase title from the "Peoples whose land we occupy," as he once said. As Graham Brazier points out in the previous essay, he started making treaties literally days before he got approval from the HBC in London to do so.[10]

The first six treaties were all small, were made in April and May 1850, and each covered an area of just a few square miles, including much of what is now considered "Greater Victoria": the area from Mount Douglas over to Portage Inlet and what is now Esquimalt and View Royal.[11] This, it turns out, was precisely the extent of the land that Douglas was claiming for the HBC and its subsidiary, the Puget Sound Agricultural Company, for the purposes of farming and stock raising. He wanted secure title.

Because the HBC was claiming all of what is now Victoria and Esquimalt as its own land, settlers had to look elsewhere. When the first settler, Walter Colquhoun Grant, arrived in 1849, Douglas told him he would have to buy land outside of the HBC reserve and recommended Metchosin to the west as good farmland nearby. Grant wanted to have a sawmill, so he chose a spot even farther to the southwest, near the Sooke River, for its water power.[12] Three of Douglas's HBC employees also wanted to buy land, and Douglas also directed them to Metchosin. Therefore, the next three treaties, all signed in May 1850, covered the coastal strip of land west of Victoria from Metchosin to Sooke – land that was in the process of being settled.

As he was making the treaties between Mount Douglas and Sooke, Douglas was asked by representatives of the Cowichan people, who lived to the north of Victoria in what would become known as the Cowichan Valley, to make treaties with them.[13] He wrote: "I declined their proposals in consequence, of our not being prepared to enter into possession; which ought to be done immediately after the purchase or the arrangement may be forgotten, and further compensation claimed by the natives."[14] This is one of the few principles of treaty making that James Douglas ever clearly stated: treaties were only to be signed when an area was immediately needed for settlement. As we will see, he followed this principle until 1858.

Douglas was initially passed over for governor of the colony in favour of Richard Blanshard, who arrived in the colony in March 1850.[15] Despite being present in Victoria when the treaties were made, Governor Blanshard played no part in their creation. Douglas made these agreements as agent for the HBC, which held title to the land. After Blanshard resigned, Douglas became governor in 1851. Douglas continued to make treaties but not in his capacity as governor. All the treaties were made with the authority he had as agent of the HBC, a position he continued to hold along with his governor's commission until late 1858.

The next two treaties were made in 1851 on northern Vancouver Island, skipping over most of the Island. In 1849, coal was discovered at Beaver Cove, and the HBC built its second Vancouver Island post there, calling it Fort Rupert. These coal mines were initially considered very valuable, so the HBC wanted to secure its title for the post and future mines. Several Kwakwa̱ka̱'wakw communities moved their winter villages adjacent to the fort, and two treaties were signed with them.

The next two treaties, made the following year, covered the Saanich Peninsula and abutted the areas around Victoria included in the 1850 treaties. In this case, the principal motivation was that the HBC wanted to establish a sawmill on the peninsula in Cordova Bay.[16] The Saanich Peninsula, adjacent to Victoria, was fine agricultural land, and settlers were already eyeing it as the next site of agricultural settlement.[17]

The coal seam at Fort Rupert did not pan out, and in 1852 the HBC was directed to coal deposits by the Snuneymuxw people in what is now Nanaimo. The HBC built a coal-mining establishment there, and Douglas was instructed that year by HBC governors in London to sign a treaty. Douglas described the negotiations as difficult, and the treaty was not made until 1854. It was his final treaty.

So the answer to the first mystery is that Douglas made treaties only when land was wanted for settlement; initially, this was only on southern Vancouver Island. Over the next four years, he made five more small treaties when he wanted coal at Fort Rupert and Nanaimo and a sawmill site and farmland at Saanich.

Mystery 2: Why Were No Treaties Made between 1855 and 1858?

The answer to the second mystery is simple: there were no new areas proposed for settlement, mines, or sawmills in these years. In the years between the Nanaimo (Saalequun) Treaty and 1858, James Douglas had an unfettered capacity to sign treaties as agent of the HBC, but he opened up no new areas for settlement, so there was, in his view, no reason to sign new treaties. Settlement of the Colony of Vancouver Island was slow and deliberately concentrated by Douglas in Nanaimo and the crescent from Saanich through Victoria to Sooke. Douglas would not sell land to settlers outside these areas, and he even discouraged missionaries from living with First Nations outside the settlement areas.[18]

Then, in March 1858, stories hit San Francisco about gold on the Mainland, and the settler population of Vancouver Island exploded. The miners and the urban infrastructure that grew up to supply the gold rush created a need for agricultural products. Settlers wanted farmland, so in 1859 Douglas opened up agricultural land on the Saanich Peninsula, on Salt Spring Island (a large island just north of Victoria), and in the Cowichan and Chemainus Valleys between Victoria and Nanaimo, for settlement. In 1862, Douglas himself led a party of settlers by ship to Cowichan Bay to settle the Cowichan Valley. In 1864, another large party settled the Comox region farther to the north. So, beginning in 1859, areas were needed and opened for settlement; Douglas had previously established a pattern of making treaties where there was settlement.

Mystery 3: What Explains the End of Treaty Making?

Given the precedents and principles, why were no treaties made between 1859 and Douglas's retirement in 1864? In other words, what explains the end of treaty making?

James Douglas

Did Douglas change his mind? There is an abundance of evidence to show that he did not change his mind and wanted treaties signed through to his retirement. For example, at the beginning of March 1860, James Douglas told the elected House of Assembly it would "have to provide the means for extinguishing native title to Lands in the Districts of Cowitchen, Chemainus and Saltspring Island, which are now thrown open for settlement. The purchase should be effected without delay, as the Indians may otherwise regard the settlers as trespassers and become troublesome."[19]

In 1861, Douglas wrote his superiors in the British government "praying for the aid of Her Majesty's Government in Extinguishing the Indian Title to the public lands in this Colony" in the form of a loan of £3,000 (about $15,000), a lot of money compared to the £107 (about $500) he had settled the Victoria treaties for in 1850. In this case, Douglas said:

> As the native Indian population of Vancouver Island have distinct ideas of property in land, and mutually recognize their several exclusive possessory rights in certain Districts, they would not fail to regard the occupation of such portions of the Colony by white settlers, unless with the full consent of the proprietary Tribes, as national wrongs; and the sense of injury might produce a feeling of irritation against the Settlers, and perhaps disaffection to the Government, that would endanger the peace of the Country.[20]

In March 1862 Douglas told the Assembly that he could not wait and had already "entered into arrangements for the satisfaction of their claims" with the Indigenous inhabitants of the Malahat District between Victoria and Cowichan:

> Agrarian disputes, endangering the public peace and safety, having occurred in Malahat District. I deemed it expedient, in order to remove the immediate cause of contention, to enter into arrangements with the natives for the satisfaction of their claims on the land, upon terms agreeable to them, and advantageous to the Colony. As an essential part of that arrangement, I propose that a portion of land shall be reserved and secured for their exclusive use and benefit – a measure which will remove almost the only cause likely to disturb the harmony existing between the settlers and the natives. Arrangements will, if found necessary, be also made for the settlement of the native claims in Cowichan District.[21]

Apparently, he found it necessary to settle Indigenous tile claims with the Cowichan in August of that year, when he accompanied a wave of settlers to the Cowichan Valley. As recorded by a reporter for the *British Colonist,* who was present, Douglas promised a treaty to the Cowichan people:

> The few natives at present in the district (the major portion of the tribes being absent fishing) agreed without hesitation to the surrender of their lands to the Government, with the exception of their village sites and potato patches, being informed that when the absent members of the tribes had returned to their homes in the autumn, compensation for the lands taken up by settlers would be made at the same rate as that previously established – amounting in the aggregate to the value of a pair of blankets to each Indian – the chiefs of course coming in for the lion's share of the *potlatch.*[22]

"[A]t the same rate as previously established" appears to refer to the treaty payments around Victoria, Nanaimo, and Fort Rupert. The explanation that the payments were in exchange for the surrender of all land except their "village sites and potato patches" is almost the exact language of the 1850 treaties. Legal historian Hamar Foster calls this "a treaty of sorts," because it was described by Douglas in an identical manner to the documented treaties.[23]

Douglas never returned to make the payments to the Malahat or the Cowichan,[24] nor are the agreements he made with these two groups included in the volume where the other treaty agreements are recorded. And although I have not yet found any statements by Douglas on the subject of treaties between his Cowichan promises of 1862 and his 1864 retirement, his surveyor general, Joseph D. Pemberton, and his staff publicly made promises of treaties right up to and beyond Douglas's retirement. As late as 1864, Joseph Pemberton wrote: "Sooner or later the Indian title must be extinguished in Chemainus."[25] Douglas and the colonial officials on Vancouver Island all felt that treaties were needed for settlement to proceed.

The Settlers

You might think that even if the government supported treaties perhaps it was stymied by popular resistance from settlers and the press. On the contrary, there was widespread support from both. Far from opposing treaties, settlers in the newly opened regions of Cowichan and Chemainus put steady pressure on the government to make treaties. Virtually every settler who had bought property in those areas by 1861 signed a petition sent to Governor Douglas in December:

> That the petitioners purchased their lands in the said district under a promise made to several of them, by the Colonial Surveyor at the time he sold these lands, that the Indian title would be extinguished by the Government within a few months of that time …
>
> That the Petitioners believe that if the Indian title be extinguished the Indians will cease to molest civilized settlers in the district.[26]

Four years later, a petition from the Cowichan settlers, published in the *Daily British Colonist* on April 18, 1865, reiterated that the Cowichan people had never been paid for the lands now occupied by whites. It stated that repeated promises of payment for their lands had been made and not honoured and asked that they be settled.[27]

The Press

If there was an opposition party to the government in the period from 1858 to 1864, it was the fourth estate, particularly the anti-Douglas newspaper the *Daily Colonist* (also published as the *Evening Colonist* and the *British Colonist*), founded by Bill Smith, who had assumed the unlikely, and ultimately inaccurate, name Amor de Cosmos (Lover of the Universe). De Cosmos opposed just about anything Douglas did and became known for his particularly racist attitudes towards nonwhites and for his demeaning comments about Indigenous people. Yet even Amor de Cosmos, as editor of the *Daily Colonist,* wrote to chastise Douglas for his failure to extinguish the title of the First Nations inhabiting the Cowichan Valley.[28]

In July 1859, De Cosmos wrote: "Why is Indian title to Cowitchen not extinguished at once? … The country expects it without delay. We want farmers – and the best way to get them is to open the lands of Cowitchen to actual settlers by extinguishing the Indian title."[29] The most significant of his editorial observations reads as follows:

> What therefore is expected is the speedy extinction of this title. We call it the title though lawyers may quibble about an Indian title, and say there is no such thing. But still we hold that they possess an equitable title, disguise it in legal lore as you please, and that it is our policy to respect that title, which may be vested in the government now at a trifling expense compared with its value in the future.[30]

In March 1861, he wrote, "We hold it to be our best policy to pay them [for their land] to avoid even the possibility of a war." All that is needed, he argued, is "a vigorous policy on the part of our government, in order to extinguish Indian title."[31]

The other local papers were also unanimous in their support for settling treaties. The *British Colonist*'s only competitor in 1860, the *Victoria Gazette,* wrote:

> Economy invites the Indian title to be extinguished, custom calls for it … We ask the Executive at once to extinguish the title to land in the Chemainis

> District ... Do it now, for it can be done at a small cost. But let the priests and missionaries once gain the ear of the Indian then farewell to so easy and so inexpensive arrangement.[32]

The *Victoria Daily Chronicle,* which succeeded the *Gazette,* wrote in May 1863: "As to the superiority of Indian title over every other, no person who is not an atheist can logically deny the Almighty for some wise purpose placed the Indians in the regions they now inhabit, generally with an abundance of fruit, game and fish to subsist on, to all of which they have an almighty good title."[33] The editor of the *Victoria Evening Express* complained in May 1863 that until the treaties are made, "Settlers can have no feeling of security."[34] Even the New Westminster–based *British Columbian,* under the direction of the future premier of the province John Robson, advocated for treaties in June 1863.[35] The new editor of *The Colonist* wrote in May 1863:

> We have heard upon very good authority that there prevails among the members of the tribes whose lands have been taken by the Government a great amount of ill feeling towards the dominant race. The cause of this animosity is simply the neglect of the Executive to make the natives compensation for the property we have appropriated belonging to them.
>
> Government have been authorized to expend some $9,000 in satisfaction of Indian claims at Cowichan – so that they only are to blame for any trouble that may arise out of the non payment to the natives of whatever is fair and just under the circumstances.[36]

The popular press was strongly behind the idea of making treaties in Cowichan and other settled areas throughout the first half of the 1860s.

The British Colonial Office

While the charter that granted the Island to the HBC was silent on the issue of title, in its early instructions to the HBC the British government reminded the company that "whatever measures she was bound to take in order to extinguish the Indian title are equally obligatory on the Company."[37] All British colonies were administered through the Colonial Office, led by a member of the cabinet called the colonial secretary. Governors of Britain's colonies reported regularly on all matters of importance to the colonial secretary through his staff at the Colonial Office in

London. When the Colonial Office received reports of treaties being made in the 1850s, it accepted them without comment.

In 1859 the colonial secretary wrote in a letter to Governor James Douglas:

> Her Majesty's Government earnestly wish that when the advancing requirements of Colonization press upon Lands occupied by Members of that race measures of liberality and justice may be adopted for compensating them for the surrender of the territory which they have been taught to regard as their own.[38]

When asked by the colonial Assembly in 1861 to pay for treaties or to make a loan to the colony to purchase the treaties, the answer of the new colonial secretary, Lord Newcastle, was as follows: "I am fully sensible of the great importance of purchasing without loss of time the Native title to the soil of Vancouver Island." He did, however, pass on the views of the Treasury that the funds had to be raised locally.[39] The *Daily Colonist* had predicted this response and saw the referral to London as a delaying tactic: "[W]e might as well ask the London police to quell a fight on the Indian reserve. We are already told 'You must be self supporting.'"[40]

If the Colonial Office was truly in favour of making treaties but would not pay for them, then what about the elected Assembly on Vancouver Island?

The Colonial Legislative Assembly

The practice in British colonies followed the parliamentary practice that taxes should be levied by an elected assembly, so in 1856 the colonial secretary, Henry Labourchère, ordered Douglas to create one.[41] In 1856, Douglas convened the first Assembly, stipulating that voters must be property owners and that candidates must own substantial property. Until 1858, the Assembly was largely composed of HBC employees, but after the gold rush a variety of business people were elected.

If the governor, the British government, the settlers, and the press all wanted treaties, perhaps the Assembly was the obstacle? Not so.

In 1860, Governor Douglas's budget proposed to the Assembly included £2,000 ($9,700) to purchase "Indian title" in the Chemainus District. In the debate in the Assembly, all members expressed support for purchasing title. Members Cole and Waddington agreed that "the Indians have the right to be paid for their lands but the Home Government must do it." Member Tolmie said that the Assembly needed the proceeds of the sale of Crown lands to pay for Aboriginal title. Member Southgate noted that the settlers in Chemainus had been promised that Aboriginal title would be purchased, and member Crease said the government had been guilty of bad faith in not compensating Indigenous peoples.[42] The Assembly agreed that the imperial government, which held the land through the HBC, should pay for it. In 1861, the Assembly asked the British Government to supply the funds:

> That the Indians, well aware of the compensation heretofore given for lands, appropriated for colonization, in the earlier settled districts of Vancouver Island, as well as in the neighbouring territory of Washington, strenuously oppose the occupation by settlers of lands still deemed their own. No attempts of the kind could be persisted in, without endangering the peace of the Country, for these Indians, though otherwise well disposed and friendly, would become hostile if their supposed rights as regards land were systematically violated; and they are still much more numerous and warlike, than the petty remnants of tribes, who in 1855 and 1856, in the western part of the adjacent United States territory of Washington, kept up for nearly a year, a desultory and destructive warfare, which compelled the whole agricultural population of the Country, to desert their homes, and congregate in blockhouses ...
>
> That the House of Assembly respectfully considers, that the extinction of the aboriginal title is obligatory on the Imperial Government.[43]

Great Britain's colonial secretary initially agreed that the title needed to be purchased, so he wrote the Treasury Branch supporting a request for a loan of £3,000 to Vancouver Island, to be paid back when it sold the land purchased from the First Nations to the settlers. Writing to the Treasury Branch, he said:

> Looking to the importance and practical economy of extinguishing a claim which must be a Continual source of danger, and which can scarcely fail to grow in amounts ... the Duke of Newcastle cannot but admit that the Inhabitants of Van Couver Island have strong & peculiar claims for assistance upon this occasion, and his Grace would therefore recommend the Governor's proposal to their Lordships favorable consideration.[44]

As stated above, the Treasury Branch in London took a different view and insisted that this was a purely colonial matter and that the Colony of Vancouver Island would have to finance the purchase itself.[45] Had the Treasury agreed to a small loan to help settle title, there almost certainly would have been treaties made in Cowichan, Chemainus, Salt Spring Island, and elsewhere in the colony.

Rebuffed by the Colonial Office, Douglas reinserted $9,700 into the budget for 1863 to extinguish land title in Chemainus and Cowichan, but the Assembly again struck it from the budget, arguing that this was an issue relating to "the Royal Domain" or Crown land, and, therefore, an imperial matter.[46]

This money was not disbursed in 1863, so it was carried over in the colonial budget to 1864, when Douglas retired, but it was not approved by the Assembly. In 1865, a year after Douglas retired, the speaker of the House of Assembly, John Sebastian Helmcken, told the Assembly: "The Indians at Cowichan had been promised remuneration for their land year after year and the faith of the country should be kept with the Indians as well as any one else." He added that Indian wars in other countries had been caused by land questions and that "the only way to avoid this was to treat the Indians as men of like feelings and passions with ourselves." Fellow Assembly member Dr. William Fraser Tolmie said the "Indians" had certainly been promised payment for their lands and that the sums voted should be expended.[47]

The Assembly agreed that treaties should be made but argued that the extinction of Aboriginal title should fall on the imperial government. Failing that, the issue of payment got caught up in the question of whether the governor or the Assembly should control the revenue from Crown lands, discussed below.

Missionaries

In this period, there were only a few clerics of the Catholic and Anglican Churches operating on Vancouver Island, but they tended to be among the most sympathetic of all settlers to Indigenous peoples. There were rumours circulating among the majority Protestant population that the Catholic priests were behind the Indigenous demand that they be paid for their land. Richard Mayne, a naval officer who visited Salt Spring Island in 1860, wrote in his diary that the colony was going to need a large treaty gathering because, "the Romish Priests put them up to it & prompt them to demand a high price for the land."[48]

Catholic bishop Modeste Demers defended his church from accusations that the missionaries would stir up Indigenous peoples and drive up the cost of treaties:

> The Government buys their lands, to which I have no objection; and whilst on this subject, I may avail myself of the opportunity to assure [you] that the *Indians have not been spoiled by the Roman Catholic Priests,* relative to the sale of their lands. We tell them that finally they shall have to come to terms with the Government, and part with their lands.[49]

Anglican missionary A.C. Garrett carried the complaints of the Cowichan people, who believed they had been promised a treaty but had not been paid for their land, to the colonial surveyor, along with a petition from settlers in the Cowichan Valley asking for a treaty.[50]

First Nations

As we have seen, James Douglas reported when he signed the first nine treaties around Victoria that the Cowichan had, in 1850, asked to sign treaties as well but that Douglas had declined because there was no imminent prospect of settlement.[51] With the sudden pressure of the gold rush, Douglas opened up the Cowichan Valley to settlement in 1859, promising both settlers and the Cowichan people that treaties would be signed.

Mayne, on Salt Spring in 1860, wrote that "[t]he Indians here have given no trouble, only occasionally informing them [settlers] – as Indians everywhere do – the whites had no business there, and that the land belonged to themselves ... They appear anxious to see Mr. Douglas & to be paid for the land."[52]

In 1861, a contributor to *The Colonist* described the Cowichan people's dissatisfaction with Douglas, whom they described as

> a *cultus* man, a *hyas kli-min-a-cut;* or, in other words, he is a no account man, and don't' tell the truth ... Year after year he has promised to buy their land, and as yet, has never done it. We are sorry to hear that Governor Douglas's popularity is on the wane among the oldest families on the island. Soberly, however, the statement of the Cowichans shows that the fault of the non-extinction of Indian titles lies at Governor Douglas's door.[53]

The Colonist recorded, again, in May 1863 the dissatisfaction of the Cowichan tribes on not being compensated.[54] Another visiting naval officer Edward Verney wrote his superior about the situation at Cowichan:

> The only cause of complaint, and it appears to be a just one, is that the Governor has not yet paid the Indians for the land according to his promise; ... they [Indians] plead the non-fulfilment of the Governor's promise, and an affair of this nature might at any time lead to a serious disturbance.[55]

And, in nearby Chemainus, J.T. Pidwell, one of the few settlers in the valley, wrote to Governor Kennedy that, in 1864,

> the Surveyor [Pearse] and "Thomo" were sent as Agents of the Government to lay out, and to point out the land and to inform the Indians that the Governor would compensate them for any lands that might be taken for the settlers so if any potatoe patches or deserted Rancheries were taken possession of, no blame ought to fall on the settlers ... The removal of the Indians to some reserve, or the compensation promised [to them] was never effected.[56]

In April 1865, seventy-nine Cowichan settlers wrote to the governor acknowledging that the Cowichan people's "potato crops are annually destroyed by the cattle and pigs of settlers." The Cowichan settlers told Governor Kennedy that "[n]o compensation has ever been given to those natives for the lands now occupied by the whites," and "[r]epeated promises of a satisfactory arrangement have been made and not performed. They therefore smart under a sense of wrong and have lost their respect for the whites which justice and truth always engender in the savage mind."[57] In 1869, one of the Cowichan leaders, Te-cha-malt, said "the Governor was a liar and had not fulfilled his promise to pay for the land he had taken."[58] At least, we know that the Indigenous peoples in the Cowichan and Chemainus Valleys wanted a treaty to protect their communities and to compensate them for lost land.

Douglas's Successors

When Douglas retired, settlers immediately petitioned his successor, Governor Arthur Kennedy, in April 1865 that "no compensation has ever been given to these natives for the lands now occupied by whites."

Kennedy, in his first address to the Vancouver Island Assembly, committed to signing treaties, including a modest $1,000 for "expenses connected with the Indians" in his budget.[59]

When, in 1866, the Colony of Vancouver Island merged with the mainland Colony of British Columbia and a new governor was appointed, the Cowichan sent a delegation asking to be "[p]aid for the lands taken up by the white men." Colonial Secretary William Young warned the new governor, Frederick Seymour, in a memorandum dated November 19, 1866, that the payment for the Cowichan lands should not be delayed "one day longer than absolutely necessary" because the "faith in the white man had been severely tried."[60]

The Mystery Deepens

If Governor James Douglas, Governor Arthur Kennedy, the Legislative Assembly, the Colonial Office, settlers in Cowichan and Chemainus, newspapers, missionaries, and First Nations all expressed support for treaties, why were there no more treaties on Vancouver Island?

The answer is at once simple and complex. The simple story is that from 1859 on, when settlement spread beyond the areas already covered by treaties, the government of Vancouver Island was paralyzed by two battles: one was between the governor and the Assembly over who had control of the land sale revenue and who could actually spend the money necessary to purchase title, and the other was between the Colony of Vancouver Island and the HBC, which held title to unsold land on Vancouver Island. The combination of these two interlocked disputes killed treaty making even though all parties wanted treaties.

Until 1859, James Douglas could make treaties on his own volition because the HBC had the right to dispose of land in the colony; the HBC controlled the revenue from the sale of land. Even more important, the HBC knew that it would be reimbursed for every pound spent on treaties when the colony reverted to the Crown. The HBC was notified in January 1858 that the Crown was terminating its charter on May 19, 1859, and would be assuming the ownership of unsold land.[61] Close in time was the creation of the Colony of British Columbia in November 1858. James Douglas was offered the joint governorship of Vancouver Island and British Columbia if he severed his connection with the HBC – which he did. After the Crown reclaimed ownership of the colony, Douglas controlled the income from the sale of land, but in his capacity of governor. Land was inherently in the Royal Domain and the governor represented the Crown. All other revenues needed to be raised from taxes and had to be approved by the Assembly.

The termination of the grant of the HBC happened in May, and we see this conflict first in July 1859, when the Reverend Thomas Skinner of the House of Assembly asked if the Assembly had the power "to amend the land system of this colony." Governor Douglas replied

> that the Legislature does not possess that power but if the House of Assembly will grant a civil list which will provide for the expenditures of the Colony, I shall be happy to recommend to the Imperial Government that the management and control of the Crown lands ... and the appropriations of the proceeds of the sales of such lands shall be vested in the Colonial Legislature.[62]

The civil list was the schedule of salaries for the governor, judges, and heads of government departments. In the absence of "granting the civil list" – an unalterable agreement to pay these salaries – an assembly could cut or withhold the governor's salary and thus control the governor. Understandably, the governor here, as in many British colonies around the globe, would not transfer control of the land revenues unless the Assembly approved a permanent civil list.[63] The Assembly wanted control of the land revenue but feared it was not consistent enough to pay all the salaries of the governor, judges, and ministers, so it refused to approve the civil list.[64]

When Douglas included £2,000 in the estimates for 1860 to purchase title at Cowichan, the Assembly agreed that purchase was necessary, but the consensus of the Assembly was that the "Indians have a right to be paid for their lands but ... until the lands are placed in our hands the Home Government must pay these demands."[65]

Douglas told the Colonial Office that so long as he controlled land sales, the Assembly would not approve any taxes, even if the land sales were not sufficient to fund the government: "Mr. Cary introduced a bill providing that the amount voted for the Civil List (£3,200) out of the general revenue, be not paid until the whole of the general revenue and the whole of the land of Vancouver Island and its dependencies be placed under the control of the legislature of the said colony."[66]

When the matter came up again in 1861, the Assembly again agreed that treaties should be made, but because the Crown and not the people

(Assembly) controlled the land, the home government should pay. When Douglas put £2,000 ($9,700) into the estimates for 1862, the Assembly passed a unanimous motion that "the House would view with approval the extinguishment by his Excellency the Governor of the Indian title at Cowichan, from the proceeds of land sales; but inasmuch as they have not yet obtained control of the public lands, the House cannot provide means for this end from the general revenue."[67] The problem for the governor was that the revenue from land sales was only $20,000 that year and dropping, and the civil list alone took $16,000, so there was little left to purchase land.[68]

The Colonial Office attempted to mediate the conflict in June 1863, suggesting that should the Legislature pass a permanent law securing the salaries of the "principal officers of the government," the Legislature would then be given the right to initiate all budget bills and would have the control of Crown revenue.[69] The Legislative Assembly declined the offer, believing that under the current system the British Crown would cover any deficits but that when the Assembly had full control of revenue, any deficits would have to be covered by taxes.[70]

It was a Catch 22 – neither governor nor Assembly could move on land policy. It persisted through Douglas's term, and the situation only got worse when Kennedy arrived, as he had neither the skill nor the experience that Douglas had used to manage the Assembly. The stalemate terminated only when the colony was dissolved and a new constitutional system was established for the merged Colony of British Columbia.

The second basis for paralysis was a battle between the British Crown (as represented both by the Colonial Office in London and the Colony of Vancouver Island) and the HBC over title to the Island. When the colony was created in 1849, the agreement was that at the end of ten years the Crown would compensate the HBC for "money theretofore laid out and expended by them in and upon the said island and premises, and of the value of their establishments, property and effects."[71] In return, the HBC would transfer back unsold land to the Crown.

Three problems arose when the Crown ended the tenure of the HBC. First, the HBC claimed over four thousand acres of the most valuable land as its own without payment based on its occupation of Victoria before the creation of the colony. The claim included the entire townsite of Victoria. The British government and the colonial Assembly balked at this seizure of the most valuable land in the colony. Second, even granting that the HBC was entitled to these lands, it was not offering to transfer land within these reserves, land that was clearly government land, back to the colony. Third, the company wanted compensation for all its costs in settling Vancouver Island and presented an unrealistic bill of £225,699.9.11, which the British government refused to pay.[72]

In this awkward moment, the HBC's governor, Henry Berens, noted that "in the absence of any reconveyance and the termination of the Grant to this Company neither the Company as still possessing the legal Title or the Crown in right of their repurchase will be in a position to make any Grants of Land."[73] Douglas wrote in November 1859:

> [I]n consequence of the refusal of the Hudson's Bay Company to liquidate the current expenses of the Colony, and in the absence of any instructions from Her Majesty's Government upon the subject, I have been forced to apply the monies arising from the sale of Public Land to that purpose, though those funds should properly be paid into the hands of the Hudson's Bay Company until the Charter of Grant is determined as it is evident that until then, no Title to Land would be legal even if sold by the Crown.
>
> No official announcement has been yet made to me of the revocation of the Grant. I have at present therefore no power either to grant a legal Title or to make sales of Public Land and I am in consequence placed in a position of extreme embarrassment.[74]

When Aboriginal title came up in the Assembly in 1860, the subject was punted to the British government because "until the lands are placed in our possession the Home Government certainly should pay all these demands."[75]

The dispute was referred by the HBC and the Colonial Office to the Privy Council,[76] and an interim agreement was worked out in March 1860 in which the company accepted a down payment of £25,000 pending the decision of the Privy Council. In exchange, the company agreed to "grant authority to the Governor to make grants of land," excepting any land claimed by the HBC and still in dispute.[77]

The grant was over – the HBC could no longer sell land, but it still had title until it returned it, and it would not return it to the Crown until the government met its conditions. The HBC no longer had authority to make treaties, and the Assembly would not because it would not accept the HBC's claim that it was entitled to the most valuable lands in the Island by right of occupation before the establishment of the colony. This, together with the civil list question, meant the Assembly would not accept transfer of control of the land.

In 1863, Douglas again submitted $9,700 for treaties "unexpended because of the civil list deadlock and the Assembly responded the same as the last year, refusing to approve the Civil List and the expenditures for treaties in exchange for control of Crown lands."[78] In June 1863, Newcastle offered the Assembly control of Crown lands if they approved a permanent civil list, and the Assembly appointed a committee to study the matter.[79] In its response to the colonial secretary's offer, the Assembly declined, stating that the proposed governor's salary was too high; along with the liability for settling treaties and a new house for the governor, the revenues from Crown land would not cover the expenses.[80] The assembly wanted to avoid incurring liabilities that require levying taxes which they themselves would have to pay.

In fact, lack of money was not the real issue. Actual expenditures for 1862 were $158,000, revenues $124,00. This was the first year the colony ran a deficit. Douglas's salary alone was $14,000 per annum, and the colony borrowed $200,000 to improve the harbour. When Vancouver Island Colony joined British Columbia in 1866, the colonial debt was $294,000. Treaty costs could have been added onto that and hardly noticed.[81]

There was one lingering issue – a dispute over what were legitimate government lands within the area claimed by the HBC – and this was litigated by the colony through 1865. The Assembly created its own commission to investigate what they considered the irregular or illegal transfer of land ownership by the HBC in 1863. The committee issued a voluminous report in 1865, shedding some light but not much clarity on the situation. The Assembly's hope that the HBC could be forced to pay for some of the land it had claimed by prior occupation or, better yet, the value of that same land when it had been sold to purchasers during the gold rush, added to their disinclination to accept control of Crown lands in exchange for assuming the costs of the civil list and other colonial expenses. When the Assembly reported in June 1864, it concluded that the only way that it could accept control of the Crown lands in exchange for the civil list was if the land, which had been granted free to the HBC because of its prior occupation, was transferred back to the colony. In November that year, the Assembly wrote to Governor Kennedy, "This house regrets its inability to take over the Crown Lands and grant a specific civil list until the extent and nature of the said Crown Lands shall be determined and submitted to this House."[82]

When Kennedy was offered the opportunity to purchase all of Discovery Island as a reserve for the Songhees in February 1865, he declined because "pending the final adjustment of the Crown Lands questions I am not armed with sufficient power to do what I think is desirable."[83] When, in December 1865, Amor De Cosmos, then in the Assembly, asked that the Indian reserve in Cowichan be thrown open to settlement, Kennedy replied that "he is without power to take any practical measures … pending the reconveyance of the public lands of the Colony to the Crown or to the local legislature," and the paper reported, "we are afraid [treaties are] not likely to be carried out until the people have full control of Crown Lands."[84] In October that year, Kennedy urged the Assembly to vote a civil list and assume control of Crown lands, pointing out that "the growing difficulties with the Indian population must continue to increase while the extent of their lands is undefined and their just claims unliquidated" as one of the "inconveniences and injuries to the public interest arising from the unsettled state of this question."[85]

The dispute over the company's claim to the Victoria townsite and other land by prior occupation occupied the Assembly, the governor, and the Colonial Office until the latter capitulated and basically accepted the HBC's claim to the free land. The British government did manage to negotiate down the amount it paid to the HBC to compensate for its expenses, paying £32,500 on top of the £25,000 already paid (a total equivalent to $279,000), a fraction of the HBC's original claim of £225,699 ($1,095,000).[86] But all this took until 1867, a year after the colony had ceased to exist.[87]

Sadly, the mystery of the end of treaty making on Vancouver Island has been solved, but not by identifying a nefarious villain or a great hero. Rather, the solution lies in the same sort of dumb misfortune that occurs when two rutting bull moose smash heads and their antlers are locked by the force of the blow; they are both stuck in an awkward dance, neither able to move forward. Two battles – one over who should be responsible for the government salaries of the colony and, therefore, control the land that generated revenue, and a second over how much land and money the British Crown needed to transfer to the HBC to extinguish its title – paralyzed James Douglas and his successors, the Vancouver Island Assembly, the Crown, and the HBC. Even when all parties wanted to continue making treaties after 1859, they were stuck in the rutters' impasse. Antlers locked, there was no way to make treaties, indeed, to move in any direction. Paralyzed but still trying to make treaties on Vancouver Island as he assumed the simultaneous governorship of British Columbia, James Douglas never once raised the idea of treaty making in the six years he oversaw the newer colony.

Notes

1 John Weaver, *The Great Land Rush and the Making of the Modern World, 1650–1900* (Montreal/Kingston: McGill-Queen's University Press, 2003), 173.

2 See Paul Tennant, *Aboriginal Peoples and Politics: The Indian Land Question in British Columbia, 1849–1989* (Vancouver: UBC Press, 1990). Hamar Foster and Allan Grove argue that Douglas might have been influenced by changing jurisprudence in Washington: "'Trespassers on the Soil': *United States v Tom* and a New Perspective on the Short History of Treaty Making in Nineteenth-Century British Columbia," *BC Studies* 138–39 (Summer–Autumn 2003): 58–61.

3 R. Cole Harris, *Making Native Space: Colonialism, Resistance, and Reserves in British Columbia* (Vancouver: UBC Press, 2002), 21, 32–34.

4 Leonard A. Wrinch, "Land Policy of the Colony of Vancouver Island, 1849–1866" (master's thesis, University of British Columbia, 1932), 260.

5 See George Shankel, "The Development of Indian Policy in British Columbia" (PhD diss., University of Washington, 1945), 49. Shankel also notes an instance where the Assembly prevented a treaty because it did not control land revenue. See also Robin Fisher, *Contact and Conflict: Indian-European Relations in British Columbia, 1774–1890* (Vancouver: UBC Press, 1977), 153; in Fisher's *BC Studies* article on Trutch's Indian policy, he argues that it was a dispute between the Vancouver Island Assembly and the Colonial Office, each insisting the other pay, that stopped the process, a conclusion I think is part of the answer. See Robin Fisher, "Joseph Trutch and Indian Land Policy," *BC Studies* 12 (Winter 1971–72): 3–33.

6 J.H. Pelly to Earl Grey, September 7, 1846, National Archives (UK) (hereafter NA), 1074, CO 305/1, in *The Colonial Despatches of Vancouver Island and British Columbia 1846–1871,* ed. James Hendrickson and the Colonial Despatches Project (hereafter *Colonial Despatches*).

7 "Charter of a Grant of Vancouver's Island to the HBC, 1849," in Great Britain, Colonial Office, *Vancouver's Island: Returns to three addresses of the Honourable the House of Commons, dated respectively 16 August 1848, 6 February & 1 March 1849: viz. address, 16 August 1848, for Copies or extracts of a despatch to the … Hudson's Bay Company* (London: HMSO, 1849), 13–16.

8 Foreign Office to Anonymous, March 1849, NA 635, CO 305/1, *Colonial Despatches,* http://bcgenesis.uvic.ca/getDoc.htm?id=V495PA03.scx.

9 J.H. Pelly to James Douglas, August 4, 1849, BC Archives (BCA), A/C/20/Vi7.

10 See Graham Brazier's chapter, this volume, for a full discussion of the timing of his treaty conference.

11 The extent to which there was a common understanding of the treaties and what that might have been is the subject of Neil Vallance's chapter in this volume.

12 James Douglas to Archibald Barclay, September 1, 1850, in Hartwell Bowsfield, ed., *Fort Victoria Letters, 1846–1851* (Winnipeg: Hudson's Bay Record Society, 1979), 115.

13 Douglas to Barclay, May 16, 1850, Hudson's Bay Company Archives (HBCA), A11/72, folios 246–47, in Bowsfield, *Fort Victoria Letters,* 95.

14 Ibid.

15 Richard Blanshard to Earl Grey, February 12, 1851, NA 4441, CO 305/3, p. 6, *Colonial Despatches.*

16 A plan they later abandoned and instead put the sawmill on Rowe Stream in View Royal.

17 The W̱SÁNEĆ people tell a different story about the origin of the treaty. See Dave Elliott, *Saltwater People, as Told by Dave Elliott Sr.: A Resource Book for the Saanich Native Studies Program,* ed. Janet Poth (Saanichton, BC: School District 63, 1990).

18 Douglas to Earl Grey, April 15, 1852, NA 104, CO 305/3, *Colonial Despatches.*

19 James Douglas, Address to the Legislative Assembly, March 1, 1860, in James Hendrickson, ed., *Journals of the Colonial Legislatures of the Colonies of Vancouver Island and British Columbia, 1851–1871,* 4 vols. (Victoria: Provincial Archives of BC, 1980), 2:157.

20 Douglas to Lord Newcastle, March 25, 1861, NA 4779, CO 305/17, p. 126, received 27 May, *Colonial Despatches.*

21 James Douglas, Address to the Legislative Assembly March 19, 1862 in James Hendrickson, ed., *Journals of the Colonial Legislatures of the Colonies of Vancouver Island and British Columbia, 1851–1871,* 4 vols. (Victoria: Provincial Archives of BC, 1980), 2:345.

22 "The Cowichan Expedition," *British Colonist,* August 22, 1862, 3.

23 When Douglas did not return in the fall to honour the promise, the Cowichan complained, but to no avail. The evidence that Douglas was midstream in creating another treaty in Cowichan in 1862 is further substantiated by the joint federal-provincial Indian commissioner, Gilbert Malcolm Sproat, when he was establishing reserves in the Cowichan Valley in 1878. He recorded a Cowichan account of the treaty promise in a memorandum. An 1865 letter from A.C. Garrett, an Anglican minister who worked among the Cowichan, to the surveyor general also vouched for the story. See G.M. Sproat, "Rough Memorandum on Cowichan Reserve," February 1878, Library and Archives Canada (LAC), RG 10, Department of Indian Affairs, vol. 3662, file 9756, pt. 1. These events are described in Foster and Grove, "Trespassers on the Soil," 58–61, and in Hamar Foster, "Letting Go the Bone: The Idea of Indian Title in Nineteenth-Century British Columbia," in *Essays in the History of Canadian Law,* vol. 6, *British Columbia and the Yukon,* ed. Hamar Foster and John McLaren (Toronto: University of Toronto Press for the Osgoode Society for Canadian Legal History, 1995).

24 Assembly member and long-time associate of Douglas, W.F. Tolmie said in 1865 that Douglas withheld payment from the Cowichan because of "their bad conduct in murdering some white men." "House of Assembly Report," *British Colonist,* February 22, 1865, 3.

25 Joseph D. Pemberton, "Memorandum of Report on Letter of Horace Smith Police Superintendent Concerning Indian Reserves at Chemainaus," August 10, 1864, BCA, C/AA/30–7/J3, p. 277; and J.T. Pidwell to Governor Kennedy, August 26, 1864, BCA, GR-1085, F1369.

26 "Petition," BCA, Colonial Correspondence, file 1354, no. 5, microfilm B01354.

27 *Daily British Colonist,* April 18, 1865.

28 He wrote at least six editorials between 1859 and 1862.

29 "Indian Title," *British Colonist,* July 4, 1859.

30 "Editorial," *British Colonist,* August 22, 1860. See also July 4, 1859, and July 8, 1859. De Cosmos was not consistent, however. In 1865, as a member of the Legislative Assembly, he urged the government to shrink the Cowichan reserves.

31 Amor de Cosmos, "Editorial," *Daily British Colonist,* March 8, 1861.

32 "Editorial," *Victoria Gazette,* April 13, 1860.

33 *Victoria Daily Colonist,* May 6, 1863. See also July 3, 1864, and January 10, 1866, and the chapter "Aboriginal Title and the Victoria Press," in Kenton Storey, *Settler Anxiety at the Outpost of Empire* (Vancouver: UBC Press, 2016), 103–28.

34 *Victoria Evening Express,* April 29, 1863.

35 *British Columbian,* June 13, 1863.

36 *British Colonist,* May 12, 1863.
37 Foreign Office, "Vancouver's Island" Confidential Memo, 1849, CO 305:1, 635, *Colonial Despatches.*
38 Earl Carnarvon to James Douglas, 11 April 1859, CO 410:1, 195.
39 Newcastle to Douglas, October 19, 1861, LAC, RG 7, G8C/2, p. 573; NA 334, CO 410/1, *Colonial Despatches.*
40 *British Colonist,* March 8, 1861.
41 Henry Labouchère to Douglas, August 23, 1856, LAC, RG 7, G8C/1, p. 485, received October 21, 1856.
42 *British Colonist,* June 30, 1860.
43 "House of Assembly, Thursday June 28, 1860," *British Colonist,* June 30, 1860; and "J.S. Helmcken, Speaker of the House of Assembly, Feb 6th 1861," enclosed in Douglas to Newcastle, March 25, 1861, NA 4779, CO 305/17, p. 126, received May 27, *Colonial Despatches.* See also Tolmie, in "Assembly," *Daily Colonist,* January 29, 1861. Not everyone in the Assembly agreed to buying title. Mr. Foster claimed that he was in favour of compensating Indians for moving, not for title: "Assembly," *Daily Colonist,* March 22, 1860.
44 T.F. Elliot, Undersecretary to George Hamilton, Treasury, June 22, 1861, included with Douglas to Newcastle, March 25, 1861, NA 4779, CO 305/17, p. 126, *Colonial Despatches.*
45 Newcastle to Douglas, October 19, 1861, LAC, RG 7, G8C/2, p. 573.
46 "Abstract of the Sums Required to Defray the Expenses of the Colonial Government of Vancouver Island ... for the Year 1863," in James Hendrickson, ed., *Journals of the House of Assembly, Vancouver Island, 1856–1863* (Victoria: BC Archives, 1980), 447. See also Peter Fourie Palmer, "A Fiscal History of British Columbia in the Colonial Period" (PhD diss., Stanford University, 1932), 190.
47 "House of Assembly Report," *British Colonist,* February 22 1865, p. 3.
48 Richard Charles Mayne, April 5, 1860, "Journal of Admiral Richard Charles Mayne, Feb 17 1857–Dec 31 1860," ed. Winnifred Macintosh, n.d., British Columbia Archives, E/B/M45a, p. 181.
49 *British Colonist,* July 25, 1862.
50 A.C. Garrett to the Surveyor General, March 10, 1865, BCA, C/AA/30.7 1K; and *British Colonist,* April 18, 1865.
51 Douglas to Barclay, May 16, 1850, HBCA, A.11/72, folios 246–47, reprinted in Bowsfield, *Fort Victoria Letters,* 95.
52 Mayne, "Journal of Admiral Richard Charles Mayne," April 5, 1860, 181.
53 *The Colonist,* March 20, 1861.
54 *British Colonist,* May 12, 1863.
55 Edward Verney to Commodore Spencer, May 10, 1862 [sic – should be 1863] in Allan Pritchard, ed., *Vancouver Island Letters of Edmund Hope Verney* (Vancouver: UBC Press, 1996), 211.
56 J.T. Pidwell to Governor Kennedy, August 26, 1864, BCA, GR-1085, F1369.
57 *British Colonist,* April 18, 1865.
58 J. Morely to Joseph Trutch, April 27, 1869, in British Columbia, *Papers Connected to the Indian Land Question 1850–1875, British Columbia Legislative Assembly, 1876,* 59.
59 March 3, 1865, in Hendrickson, *Journals of the House of Assembly,* 3:280.
60 W.A.G. Young to Frederick Seymour, November 19, 1866, BCA, B1375, 144, F1939.
61 Newcastle to Douglas, July 12, 1859, LAC, RG 7, G8C/2, *Colonial Despatches.*
62 Skinner in the "Assembly" and Douglas to the Assembly, *The Colonist,* July 15, 1859. The dispute is the subject of two chapters in Wrinch, "Land Policy of the Colony of Vancouver Island."

63 For description of a similar struggle and information on the history of the "civil list" see D.C. Harvey, "The Civil List and Responsible Government in Nova Scotia," *Canadian Historical Review*, 28, 4 (December 1947): 365–82.
64 "House of Assembly, July 10th, 1860," *Daily Colonist,* July 12, 1860.
65 *Daily Colonist,* June 30, 1860, and July 5, 1860.
66 "House of Assembly, July 10th, 1860," *Daily Colonist,* July 12, 1860.
67 *Daily Colonist,* April 1, 1862.
68 Palmer, "A Fiscal History," 217.
69 Newcastle to Douglas, June 15, 1863, NA, CO 398/2, *Colonial Despatches.*
70 "Civil List," in "Reply to the Duke of Newcastle Despatch, June 15, 1863," February 8 and 9, 1864, BCA, C/AA/10.5/1, Vancouver Island Governor Correspondence – Inward Communications from the House of Assembly, 1864–66.
71 Charter of Grant of Vancouver's Island to the Hudson's Bay Company, in Hendrickson, *Journals of the Colonial Legislatures,* 1:374– 78.
72 H. Merivale to John Shepherd, January 20, 1858, HBCA, A.8/8, folios 58d–59; and Shepherd to Merivale, January 21, 1858, NA 750, CO 305/9, p. 420, *Colonial Despatches.*
73 H.H. Berens to Newcastle, July 16, 1859, NA 7160, CO 305/13, p. 112, *Colonial Despatches.*
74 Douglas to Newcastle, November 24, 1859, NA 871, CO 305/11, 261, *Colonial Despatches,* http://bcgenesis.uvic.ca/getDoc.htm?id=V59058.scx.
75 Cooper, in "Assembly," *Daily Colonist,* June 28, 1860.
76 The Privy Council was a group of advisors to the Crown including politicians, senior clergy, and members of the royal family.
77 Berens to Newcastle, June 15, 1860, NA 6239, CO 305/9, p. 152, *Colonial Despatches,* http://bcgenesis.uvic.ca/getDoc.htm?id=B605MI03.scx; and Berens to Newcastle, March 2, 1860, NA 2290, CO 305/15, p. 408, *Colonial Despatches.*
78 *Daily Colonist,* February 7, 1863.
79 Newcastle to Douglas, June 15, 1864, NA, CO 398/2, p. 139, *Colonial Despatches,* https://bcgenesis.uvic.ca/getDoc.htm?id=B637026A.scx.
80 *Daily Colonist,* February 4, 1864, 4.
81 Palmer, "A Fiscal History," 229, 290.
82 "Resolutions Reported from the Committee of the Whole 21 Novr. 1864 Confirmed by the House 22 Novr. 1864," BCA, C/AA/10.5/1, Vancouver Island Governor Correspondence – Inward Communications from the House of Assembly, 1864–66.
83 Governor Kennedy to Jay and Co., February 11, 1865, BCA, Colonial Correspondence, file 838.
84 Kennedy to Assembly, December 18, 1865, in Hendrickson, *Journals of the House of Assembly,* 3:394; and *British Colonist,* April 18, 1865.
85 Kennedy to the Assembly of Vancouver Island, October 31, 1864, in Hendrickson, *Journals of the House of Assembly,* 3:212–13.
86 Newcastle to Douglas, October 1, 1864, LAC, RG 7, G8C/3, p. 144 (CO 410/1, p. 389).
87 Roundell Palmer and R.P. Collier to Edward Cardwell, July 26, 1865, NA 7205, CO 305/27, p. 95, *Colonial Despatches,* http://bcgenesis.uvic.ca/getDoc.htm?id=V655LW02.scx. The reconveyance is recorded in Thomas W.C. Murdoch to Thomas F. Elliot, April 18, 1867, NA 7205, CO 305/27, p. 95, *Colonial Despatches.*

Part 4

After the Treaties

9

The Colony of British Columbia's Unsurveyed Land System

Sarah Pike

Once sworn in as governor of the new Colony of British Columbia on November 19, 1858, James Douglas had to follow many directions from England. His overarching duty was to make laws "for the peace, order, and good government of Our subjects and others residing in Our said Colony and its Dependencies."[1] His most detailed mandate was his "Instructions," a list of thirty-four things he was to do or not to do in exercising his broad powers.[2]

Among other things, Douglas was required to "take especial care that Almighty God be devoutly and truly served throughout your Government," to give "most serious attention to the consideration and appliance of all proper methods for the erecting and maintaining schools," and to send to the Colonial Office, from time to time, "an account of the wants and defects of Our said Colony."[3] The list of things Douglas was not to do was longer, more specific, and related mostly to the types of laws he was not allowed to create.

Yet, in all Douglas's formal imperial directions, not one mentioned what he was to do with respect to Indigenous peoples who lived in the area over which Britain had cast its colonial net. "This question," according to a letter Douglas received from his overseer, the secretary of state for the colonies, "is of so local a character that it must be solved by your knowledge and experience, and I commit it to you in the full persuasion that you will pay every regard to the interests of the Natives which an enlightened humanity can suggest."[4]

Nowhere was Douglas's knowledge and experience more necessary than in dealing with the question of land. In the mid-nineteenth century, the question of colonial land – in particular, how to distribute land in the colonies to British emigrants – gripped British politicians and bureaucrats.[5] Yet distributing land to settlers presupposed that the land was not already occupied. If not of specific concern in Britain, Indigenous occupation of land concerned colonial governors in general, and Governor Douglas in particular. Historian Robin Fisher describes it bluntly: "The basic conflict between settlers and the indigenous people of North America, as on other settlement frontiers, was over land."[6]

This essay examines what may be called "British Columbia's unsurveyed land system," a set of rules Douglas devised to balance the colony's needs with the Colonial Office's directions and to meet settlers' insistent demands for land while preserving – or, at least, intending to preserve – Indigenous interests in land.[7] The unsurveyed land system's focal point was the right of pre-emption, a practice adopted from the United States that allowed British subjects to acquire unsurveyed land without paying for it prior to occupying it.[8] Yet through the unsurveyed land system as well, Douglas sought to preserve for Indigenous peoples the lands they had occupied before the settlers came by exempting an "Indian reserve or settlement" from lands available for pre-emption.

One of the best explanations of the elements of the BC unsurveyed land system is Robert Cail's masterwork, *Land, Man, and the Law: The Disposal of Crown Lands in British Columbia, 1871–1913*.[9] Yet Cail addresses "colonial land settlement policy" ten chapters away from "Imperial colonial Indian policy."[10] In this essay, I suggest that the BC unsurveyed land system is best understood by conceiving it *as a system* – that is, by understanding how Douglas intended all of the interests in land, Indigenous and settler, to relate. One can better apprehend the system by understanding its larger context: how Douglas's "knowledge and experience," on which his instructions in part rested, contributed to his development of the system; how the land alienation rules in the adjacent American territories affected Douglas's decisions; and, most broadly, what role the system played in a colony that Britain envisaged as "but one step in the career of steady progress, by which Her Majesty's dominions in North America may ultimately be peopled by an unbroken chain, from the Atlantic to the Pacific, by a loyal and industrious population of subjects of the British Crown."[11]

A contextual understanding of the BC unsurveyed land system also sheds light on one of the outstanding "major puzzles" concerning BC Indigenous land issues: why Douglas did not take steps to extinguish Aboriginal title in the Colony of British Columbia.[12] Although many answers have been suggested, this essay suggests another: Douglas intended the unsurveyed land system to create an orderly means for providing settlers with access to land while also protecting Indigenous interests and deferring – but not necessarily rejecting – treaties and the extinguishment of Aboriginal title. Douglas did what needed to be done to allocate interests in land and, importantly, to address and attempt to eliminate conflicts over land, while waiting for the issue of who would pay for the extinguishment of Aboriginal title and how they would pay for it to be worked out.

Douglas in the Oregon Territory and the Colony of Vancouver Island

When James Douglas became the governor of the new Colony of British Columbia at fifty-five years of age, he had had considerable experience in two other jurisdictions. Douglas lived in the Oregon Territory from 1830 to 1849, from his mid-twenties to his mid-forties.[13] He spent the next ten years as chief factor of the Hudson's Bay Company (HBC) fort at Victoria and, from 1851, as the governor of the Colony of Vancouver Island. By the time he became governor of the Colony of British Columbia at the end of 1858, Douglas had had nearly thirty years' experience trying to navigate the tensions between the new immigrants, their governments, and Indigenous peoples, especially in regard to the occupation of land. That experience informed what he attempted to do with his system for unsurveyed land in British Columbia.

Oregon Territory

The pre-emption right that formed the centrepiece of Douglas's system was borrowed from the United States. *Pre-emption,* according to one definition, means simply "the purchase by one person or party before an opportunity is offered to others; the right of making such a purchase in certain circumstances."[14] At least as far back as 1799, the US Congress had authorized individuals, when their original transactions turned out to have been legally faulty, to purchase land in priority to others through a "right of pre-emption."[15] In 1841, a federal Act allowed settlers a right of pre-emption over public lands, except lands to which the Indian title had not been extinguished.[16] Under this Act, settlers had a right to occupy and cultivate up to 160 acres and pay for it when the land was surveyed, in preference to others, provided they had occupied and improved the land. Occupation and cultivation came first; payment came second. Douglas would incorporate these basic principles into his British Columbia unsurveyed land system some thirty years later.

However, the 1841 Act did not apply to the Oregon Territory until 1854.[17] To understand the situation in the Oregon Territory once settlers began to arrive around 1840, one must look to the legislation put in place by the Oregon Provisional Government.

Until 1846, Great Britain and the United States jointly occupied the Oregon Territory pursuant to an 1818 treaty.[18] Britain's occupation was reflected mostly by the Hudson Bay Company's presence, centred at its main site at Fort Vancouver (today's Vancouver, Washington) on the north shore of the Columbia River, James Douglas's home for twenty years. By 1843, the new American settlers had established the Provisional Government of Oregon and passed several laws aimed at enabling settlers to acquire land. The Law of Land Claims gave settlers pre-emption rights to *free* grants of land and, unlike Congress's pre-emption legislation, did not exclude lands over which the Indian title had not yet been extinguished.[19]

A year and a half after passing the first set of laws, the Provisional Government passed another Act, appearing on its face to protect Indigenous rights although in reality aiming to preserve only a small percentage of Indigenous lands. The Act in relation to Indians was premised on the assertions that "the Indians inhabiting this country are rapidly diminishing, being now mere remnants of once powerful tribes, now disorganized, without government, and so situated that no treaty can be regularly made with them," and that "the Indians are not engaged in agriculture, and have no use for, or any right to, any tracts, portions, or parcels of land, not actually occupied or used by them." Based on these assertions, the Act protected Indigenous peoples only "in the free use of such pieces of vacant land as they occupy with their villages or other improvements, and such fisheries as they have heretofore used."[20] The Provisional Government made no effort to establish reserves out of the Indigenous lands protected by the Act.

On June 15, 1846, Britain and the United States agreed on what is commonly known as the Oregon Treaty, giving the United States sovereignty over the Oregon Territory to the south of the forty-ninth parallel (except on Vancouver Island and the adjacent Gulf Islands, where the boundary between the two territories ran farther south) and giving Britain sovereignty over the land to the north.[21] The Provisional Government, however, continued to administer the Oregon Territory for another two years.

In August 1848, the US Congress finally exerted its statutory jurisdiction over the Oregon Territory by passing An Act to Establish the Territorial

Government of Oregon.[22] Among the statutory provisions was one invalidating the previous land laws.[23] The Act also confirmed that only the federal government had the right to make laws about or treaties with Indigenous peoples and that the "Indian" rights "of person or property" that "remain unextinguished by treaty between the United States and such Indians" continued unimpaired.[24] By virtue of this federal legislation, both the earlier settlers and the thousands of new immigrants found themselves in a precarious position with respect to rights built on the Provisional Government's Law of Land Claims.[25] They clamoured for additional federal legislation to resolve their land-title situation.[26]

In June 1850, Congress passed a statute authorizing the negotiation of treaties with Indigenous tribes in Oregon "for the extinguishment of their claims to lands lying west of the Cascade Mountains," a prerequisite to its taking steps with respect to settler rights to land.[27] Congress then passed another Act pertaining to Oregon, titled, in part, An Act ... to make Donations to Settlers of the said Public Lands. This Act authorized "donations" of land – free grants – claimable by the settler at the time the land was surveyed upon proof of the "settlement" and "cultivation" requirements of the Act.[28] The settler was required to have been settled on the land for at least four years, whether the settlement had been "made under the laws of the late provisional government or not."[29] In this manner, Congress validated the settler titles to land already occupied under the Oregon Provisional Government's Law of Land Claims, side-stepping both its 1841 Pre-emption Act as well as its practice not to alienate lands until the Indian title had been extinguished.[30]

In 1853, Congress established out of the Oregon Territory the separate Territory of Washington (the precursor to today's Washington State), extending all laws applicable to Oregon (including the 1850 Donation Land Act) to the new territory.[31] In 1854, Congress made its 1841 Pre-emption Act applicable to both the Oregon and Washington Territories.[32]

Thus, by 1859, when Governor Douglas brought in his preliminary pre-emption provisions in British Columbia, a settler in the adjacent Washington Territory could obtain up to 160 acres of land "to which the Indian title had been at the time of such settlement extinguished," on the condition that he "inhabit and improve the same," build a house, and agree to pay the minimum price of such land ($1.25 per acre) when the land was surveyed.[33] These provisions bear remarkable similarity to Douglas's January 1860 Pre-emption Proclamation – but for the provision concerning the extinguishment of Indian title.

Based on the authorization in the 1850 Indian Treaty Act, US federal officials carried out a "treaty-making spree" in western Oregon in the 1850s.[34] This spree has been described as "not a diplomatic negotiation between equals but an aggressor offering terms to a subordinate people"[35] and the results of the "spree" as "warfare, Aboriginal displacement, and defeat."[36] Most of the land in what is now Oregon and Washington became subject to an Indian treaty between 1853 and 1855.[37] These treaties "retroactively legalized ten years of intensive colonization and land speculations"[38] and resulted in the large-scale removal of Indigenous peoples from parts of Oregon and the creation of reservations far from traditional homelands.[39]

Thus, during his twenty years in Oregon, Douglas saw settlers who acted in a largely self-interested way when it came to land and a local government, of and by the settlers, whose legislative actions focused almost exclusively on securing settlers' rights. He saw the considerable problems that settler occupation of land before the extinguishment of Aboriginal title by treaties caused for all stakeholders, but most especially for Indigenous peoples. They suffered "Indian wars" and conflicts, treaties that came after settler occupation, and their removal away from long-occupied lands. By the end of the 1850s, as Keith Carlson also observes in his chapter in this volume, Douglas may have wished to avoid much of what he had seen in Oregon.[40]

The Colony of Vancouver Island

In the spring of 1849 – after Congress had passed the Oregon Territorial Act but before it had passed the 1850 Acts relating to Indian treaties or to land donations in Oregon – James Douglas moved north to become the Hudson's Bay Company's chief factor at Fort Victoria.[41] Throughout his time there, he displayed his knowledge of Oregon land laws in his discussions with HBC officials in urging them to make land acquisition both easier and cheaper in the new colony.[42]

Britain's primary motivation for establishing a colony on Vancouver Island in early 1849 had been to create a British settler colony to check northward American designs.[43] As Graham Brazier explores in more detail in his chapter in this volume, the Charter of Grant of Vancouver Island to the Hudson's Bay Company obligated the HBC to "establish upon the said island a settlement or settlements of resident colonists, emigrants from Our United Kingdom of Great Britain and Ireland, or from other

Our dominions, and … dispose of the land there as may be necessary for the purposes of colonization."[44] As the HBC's appointed agent in the colony responsible for the disposal of land from 1849 until his retirement from that position in 1858, and as governor from October 1851 until 1864, Douglas would have been all too familiar with the pressures to attract British settlers.[45]

To meet the HBC's obligations to sell land and attract settlers, Douglas made his first concession to an intending settler in January 1851, giving him a qualified right of pre-emption "on condition of his residing upon it, and bringing the land into cultivation, and paying the regular price of one Pound Sterling an acre when the lot is surveyed and Titles issued."[46] Settlers ultimately would clamour not only for the delayed payment aspect of the US pre-emption right but also for a land price comparable to the US price. While Douglas acquiesced to the first demand for this intending settler, he was unable for many more years to make this provision or a lower purchase price part of either colony's land scheme.[47]

Although settlers made sporadic requests over the next eight years to be able to acquire land by pre-emption – that is, with no initial payment, a requirement of occupation and cultivation, and a cheap ultimate price – they voiced their first concerted demands in Victoria in spring 1859.[48] On June 22, Albert Waddington – an Englishman who had published a book containing a demand for pre-emption rights – organized a "land reform" meeting.[49] Attendees voiced concerns about the high price of agricultural land and the probability that intending settlers would "leave our shore for the American side."[50] They formed a committee to draw up a petition to the Vancouver Island governor and Assembly calling for a land-price reduction to $1.25 per acre and the implementation of a pre-emption system – precisely the terms available in the Washington and Oregon Territories.[51]

A few days later, a larger land-reform meeting produced a similar petition calling on the governor and council to "open" the Crown lands of the colony "at once to actual settlers" on terms comparable to those available in the US territories.[52] This Land Reform Committee presented its petition to the governor, who, according to the *British Colonist,* advised that while he was "personally opposed to the present system" – that allowed only the sale of land at the much higher rate of one pound per acre – and "would even advocate a free gift of a quarter section to each early settler," he had no power to alter the system on Vancouver Island.[53]

Throughout July, settlers increased their pressure on Douglas to amend the rules, and he was clearly sympathetic. He described one set of petitioners as “a large and respectable body of immigrants chiefly from the province of Upper Canada” who had made “out a truly distressing case”: they had spent so much money getting to the colony that they had no money left with which to purchase lands and were “rendered incapable of settling, unless they at once obtained leave to settle on the public land.” Although he did not agree to make significant changes to the land regulations without being authorized by the Colonial Office, he was “anxious ... to relieve their distress, and to retain a fine active body of working men in the Colony,” so he allowed them to delay making their first payment instalment upon claiming land.[54]

It is clear that by this date Douglas supported relaxing the stringent land alienation rules the Colonial Office had imposed upon the Colony of Vancouver Island. Concession by concession, Douglas inched closer and closer to the American rules for alienating land to settlers. In just a matter of weeks, he would implement an American-style pre-emption right almost exactly, beginning in the mainland colony.[55] Yet, at the same time, Douglas knew what the American rules had meant for Indigenous peoples, at least as they had been applied in Oregon, and he applied some of the lessons from Oregon's experience in developing the BC unsurveyed land system.

The BC Unsurveyed Land System

The BC unsurveyed land system incorporated provisions for recognizing both settler land rights, through pre-emption, and Indigenous land rights, through Indian reserves and settlements. To fully comprehend the system, as well as its role in James Douglas's broader thinking about Indigenous peoples and land in the Colony of British Columbia, it is important to examine both aspects of the system.

Settler Rights to Land: "Lands May Be Lawfully Acquired by Pre-Emption"

In October 1859, just a few months after the settler Land Reform Committees coalesced in Victoria, Douglas, as governor of the adjacent Colony of British Columbia (which, at the time, encompassed only the mainland and not Vancouver Island), put in place the first elements of his system through instructions to five magistrates in unsurveyed areas. The cornerstone of the system was permission for British subjects to acquire unsurveyed agricultural lands "by pre-emption." Douglas formalized the authorization a few months later in what is known as the Pre-emption Proclamation under which British subjects could claim, occupy, "improve," and then receive a Crown grant in fee simple for land, without an obligation to pay for the land until the government surveyed it. The operative recital and provision in the Pre-emption Proclamation were as follows:

> Whereas, it is expedient, pending the operation of the survey of agricultural lands in British Columbia, to provide means whereby unsurveyed agricultural lands may be lawfully acquired by pre-emption in British Columbia by British subjects ...
>
> British subjects and aliens who shall take the oath of allegiance to Her Majesty and her successors, may acquire unoccupied and unreserved, and unsurveyed Crown land in British Columbia (not being the site of an existent or proposed town, or auriferous land available for mining purposes, or an Indian Reserve or settlement,) in fee simple, under the following conditions.[56]

Under Douglas's system, the settler and the Indigenous interests each began in relatively undefined states: pre-emption claims were based on land marked off by the settler and registered with a district magistrate; Indian settlements lacked a definition although provided one basis for establishing an Indian reserve. Both types of occupation could transform into more defined interests under the settler legal system: pre-emption claims could become Crown grants in fee simple; Indian settlements could be designated as Indian reserves.

But one of the critical weaknesses of Douglas's system was that the Pre-emption Proclamation codified the path by which a settler could acquire a legal interest in land but not by which an Indigenous group could. As a result, almost from the outset there was confusion about and conflict over what an "Indian settlement" was, whose responsibility it was to identify such a settlement, and the precise steps to be taken to create an Indian reserve from an Indian settlement.[57] Since the proclamation entwined settler land rights with Indigenous land rights by setting up an inherent conflict between them – land that was an Indian settlement or reserve was not supposed to be pre-empted – the lack of codification of the Indigenous side of the system contributed, no doubt, to the disregard of the Indigenous land interests. In 2018, the Supreme Court of Canada, in *Williams Lake Indian Band v Canada*, addressed this very issue: the conflict between settler pre-emption land rights and Indigenous "Indian settlement" rights in the Colony of British Columbia.[58] While the Supreme Court of Canada's decision addresses some of the underlying problems, the malfunctioning of the BC unsurveyed land system certainly deserves further attention, and I suggest some of the reasons for its lack of success later in this essay. However, here I focus on analyzing how Douglas *intended* the system to operate. To understand this, one must go back to the British Colonial Office's original plan for land alienation in the new colony, a plan that did not include allowing settlers to acquire land by a right of pre-emption.

On July 31, 1858, having nearly completed shepherding through the British Parliament the new Act to Provide for the Government of British Columbia, the secretary of state for the colonies, Edward Bulwer-Lytton, wrote to Douglas to emphasize that "whilst the Imperial Parliament will cheerfully lend its assistance in the early establishment of this new Colony, it will expect that the Colony shall be self supporting as soon as possible." The sale of lands, according to Lytton, would be the best way for the colony to raise money.[59] In his reply, Douglas agreed with Lytton that "the disposal of public lands" would provide "a prolific source of revenue; besides having the effect of opening the country for permanent settlement."[60]

A few days later, in August, Lytton again reminded Douglas that the colony would need to pay its own way from its inception.[61] In a separate letter of the same date, Lytton gave Douglas five "provisional rules" to guide him "on the subject of the disposal of Land in British Columbia," "a subject of such great importance to the future welfare of this new Colony."[62] Key among them were a direction to sell agricultural land at the highest price possible while still being guided by the US price and a direction to sell only surveyed land or land "ready for immediate survey."[63]

In October, on a trip to review the Fraser River Gold Rush, but not yet having received the official documentation appointing him as governor and granting him authority to sell land, Douglas could respond only to the "most urgent appeals" for land by giving intending settlers leases with "a pre-emption right" to purchase the land once he had sufficient authority to sell it.[64]

By the time Douglas proclaimed the Colony of British Columbia at Fort Langley on November 19, 1858, two things were clear: the Colony of British Columbia was to be self-supporting, and it was to become so largely from the proceeds of land sales.[65] Douglas aimed his first administrative actions at these two goals.

On December 2, Douglas issued a proclamation "to enable the Governor of British Columbia to convey Crown Lands sold within the said Colony."[66] The proclamation provided that "it shall be lawful for the Governor … by an instrument … to grant to any person or persons any lands belonging to the Crown in the said Colony, and every such instrument shall be valid … for all the estate and interest expressed to be conveyed by such instrument in the lands therein described."[67]

To generate revenue for the colony through the sale of "public lands," Douglas issued a proclamation on February 14, 1859, setting out "the method to be pursued with respect to the alienation and possession of agricultural lands and of lands proposed for the sites of towns in British Columbia." Among other things, the proclamation declared that "[a]ll the lands in British Columbia, and all the mines and minerals therein belong to the Crown in fee," and it set the price of land at ten shillings per acre, payable one-half in cash at the time of the sale and the other half at the end of two years from such sale.[68] These provisions were significant relaxations over the rules that applied in the Colony of Vancouver Island.

Even though Douglas had set a relatively low price for land in British Columbia in an attempt to compete with the US territories, settlers in both colonies continued to demand a US-style pre-emption right.[69] The same day that the *British Colonist* published the Land Reform Committee's petition from Victoria residents – July 4, 1859, six months after Douglas had first authorized the sale of land in British Columbia – Douglas reported to Lytton on various matters associated with settling the new colony. Foremost among them were questions of how best to settle the land and who best to settle on it. For the first time, Douglas raised the possibility that, because of the inability to survey lands quickly enough for sale and the need for agricultural settlers, he might have to establish "some temporary system of occupation, which would enable settlers to hold and improve certain specified tracts of land under a preemption right until the surveys are completed."[70]

When the Colonial Office received Douglas's letter, it was taken aback but willing to consider his proposal. Herman Merivale, the Colonial Office permanent undersecretary who had extensive London experience with British emigration to the colonies, considered that Douglas's proposal "raises a question of very great importance to the future welfare of the colony. The admission of squatters to preemption rights (American fashion) is an evil if it can be avoided, but difficult or impossible to avoid under such circumstances."[71] The Duke of Newcastle, the new secretary of state for the colonies, felt "we *must* resort to the American fashion. The very neighbourhood to US territory renders it next to impossible to maintain the present system."[72]

The Colonial Office sent Douglas's letter to the Emigration Commission, a three-man board established in 1840 to facilitate emigration from Britain to the various colonies that frequently advised the Colonial Office with respect to colonial legislation and settler acquisition of land in the British colonies.[73] Thomas Murdoch, the chairman of the commission, responded to the Colonial Office that, in no uncertain terms, "no countenance should be given to Govr Douglas's proposal to sanction the occupation with preemptive rights of unsurveyed land."[74] Among his reasons for opposing Douglas's proposal were the "confusion and uncertainty of title," "rival claims to the same land," and the difficulty of fitting irregularly shaped claims into a subsequent survey.[75]

Murdoch's refusal to support Douglas's plan led to much discussion back in the Colonial Office. Most of the officials, however (including, importantly, Merivale and Newcastle), sympathized with the argument that "the vicinity of the Americans makes it almost impossible to maintain the system of disposing of land in the Colonies which is so easily indoctrinated at Whitehall."[76] In the end, Newcastle postponed making a decision on Douglas's proposal. He preferred a plan presented to him days earlier by Captain Andrew Clarke, the former surveyor general of the Australian colony of Victoria, the most distinctive aspect of which was using a public auction as the primary vehicle to alienate Crown lands.[77] Before making a decision, Newcastle wanted further information from Clarke.[78]

In August and September, Colonel R.C. Moody, the chief commissioner of lands and works in the Colony of British Columbia, also pressed Douglas to allow settler occupation of land by pre-emption right. He proposed that the system be implemented for two to three years only and allow for the occupation of unsurveyed land on condition of clearing and cultivation, the construction of a dwelling, occupation of the land, and payment upon survey, terms that Douglas would largely incorporate into his 1860 Pre-emption Proclamation.[79] Yet even before he put his proclamation in place, Douglas implemented a pre-emption right through provisional instructions to magistrates in October 1859.

On October 1, not yet having received any reply from the Colonial Office to his July 4 letter suggesting he might have to offer a right of pre-emption, Douglas issued a lengthy circular to the five "Gold Commissioners and Magistrates" in the new colony, all resident in the unsurveyed areas affected by the gold rush. This circular is the foundational document for Douglas's unsurveyed land system, introducing pre-emption into the BC land alienation scheme for the first time. It contains Douglas's most complete explanation of how he envisaged settler and Indigenous interests in land to relate under the unsurveyed land system. Following an introductory provision, the circular continues:

2. […] I find that not so few British Subjects who are desirous of settling in the country cannot accomplish their object in consequence of not being able to get land either by purchase or by preemption, as the public land is not yet surveyed, and the surveys cannot be completed for some time to come.
3. As delays of that nature have the effect of compelling useful settlers whom we are desirous of encouraging, to leave the country, and will be in many other ways injurious, and greatly retard its settlement, I have decided on introducing a Preemption Law, for the purpose of enabling such persons to settle at once on any unoccupied Crown land, which may suit their purposes on condition of occupation and immediate improvement.
4. You will therefore permit all such persons, being British subjects, or registering their intention of becoming British subjects, to occupy and improve sections of Country Land, not exceeding *160 acres* in extent, on the conditions moreover, that they will not be required to make any payment till the land is surveyed, and then payment will be required at a price not exceeding ten shillings per statute acre.
5. I beg you however to bear in mind that the proposed Law will not apply to Town or suburban land or to rural land immediately beyond the suburban Lots contiguous to Towns, all of which will be reserved for Government purposes and for the purpose of raising an immediate revenue to meet the want of the Country.
6. You will also cause to be reserved the Sites of all Indian villages, and the land they have been accustomed to cultivate, to the extent of several hundred acres round each village, for their special use and benefit.
7. I will hereafter address you more in detail in respect to the proposed pre-emption Laws, and now send you these hints for your direction,

> and that no time may be lost in carrying out the plan, and in permitting British Subjects to occupy Sections of Land as soon as they arrive in the country.[80]

Douglas sent a copy to Moody on October 7.[81] In reference to the intersection of the pre-emption authorization and the Indian reserve instructions, he told Moody (although this is not a precise restatement of the circular), "You will also observe from the Circular … that … the sites of all Indian Villages and the Land which they have been accustomed to cultivate, to the extent of several hundred acres round each village, have been reserved and are not to be subjected to the operation of the proposed pre-emption Law."[82]

Douglas next sent Newcastle a letter on October 18, advising of his recently completed "official tour" of British Columbia and his observation that the colony was "yet destitute of one highly important element, it has no farming class."[83] In order to attract this class of settlers, and in response to lagging land sales and settler pressure, Douglas explained the instructions he had given the magistrates, which were "in fact the basis of a pre-emption law founded on occupation and improvement."[84] When it received this news, the Colonial Office did not object. Merivale felt that even though Newcastle "has already before him the question of admitting the tenure of land before survey & that of preemptive rights," the governor "has now practically solved" the problem, "for it will not be easy, if desirable, to recede from what he has done."[85] Newcastle agreed:

> I consider this a very satisfactory despatch as regards the *future* of this Colony. I have already expressed my preference of Captn Clarke's Victoria plan to the *preemptive* scheme, but the latter is a great improvement in such a Colony as B. Columbia upon the *slow* process of Survey & Sale and I have no doubt it will give an impetus to Agricultural speculation – without which the Colony will never thrive.[86]

A few months later, Newcastle concluded that, despite the opposition of the emigration commissioners, "the price of land in Vancouvers Island and in B. Columbia must be reduced to 5s per acre and that occupation before surveys are completed must *in some form* be sanctioned."[87] However, he still preferred Captain Clarke's plan to a right of pre-emption, so he instructed that Clarke's letter and report be sent to Governor Douglas for his consideration and comment, before he made any official decision approving the pre-emption system Douglas had put in place.[88]

In January 1860, still without having heard from the Colonial Office about his proposed or actual implementation of a pre-emption right, Douglas formalized his circular to the magistrates in the Pre-emption Proclamation.[89] He sent Newcastle a copy of the proclamation with a letter describing how the system would work:

4. I now forward herewith, a Proclamation giving to my previous instructions the force of Law, and also providing for the purchase, with the same limitation of the ultimate price, of larger tracts of unsurveyed country land ...
6. The District Stipendiary Magistrates will record the applications for land, and immediately report the same to the Commissioner of Lands and Works, and to the Colonial Secretary; so that it will not cause any further drain on the funds of the Colony.
7. The object of the measure is solely to encourage and induce the settlement of the Country; occupation is therefore made the test of Title, and no prëemption Title can be perfected without a compliance with that imperative condition.
8. The Act distinctly reserves, for the benefit of the Crown, all Town Sites, auriferous land, Indian Settlements, and public rights whatsoever; the Emigrant will therefore on the one hand enjoy a perfect freedom of choice with respect to unappropriated land, as well as the advantage which is perhaps of more real importance to him, of being allowed to choose for himself, and enter at once into the possession of land, without expense or delay; while the rights of the Crown are, on the other hand, fully protected, as the land will not be alienated, nor Title granted, until after payment is received.[90]

Upon receiving this letter, Newcastle declined to approve or disapprove the Proclamation until he had received Douglas's report on Clarke's scheme for the disposal of Crown lands.[91]

It was not until the end of August that Douglas finally submitted his comments on Captain Clarke's scheme to Newcastle, along with seventy-five pages of comment from Judge Matthew Baillie Begbie, the chief justice of British Columbia.[92] Although Begbie disagreed with some of the details of Douglas's Pre-emption Proclamation, he thought the "laws regarding both the land and the gold mines in this colony are tolerably correct."[93] Douglas praised Clarke's proposal lightly and declared it "not widely different" from British Columbia's scheme, but he felt that Clarke's proposed initial payment requirement would "be disastrous to the Colony," tending to "retard settlement" and "check the sale of public land."[94] Once again, Douglas resorted to comparisons with the US territories to defend his system, concluding that unless the BC system gave comparable rights to the American, "[e]migrants will be forced into the neighbouring Territories of the United States, where they may freely select from millions of acres, equal to any land in British Columbia, at the low price of one dollar and a quarter per acre, payable only after survey."[95] In concluding, Douglas did "not recommend any change in our present laws until the 'Pre-emption Act' of 4th January 1860 has been fairly tested."[96]

The emigration commissioners subsequently advised the Colonial Office that in light of Douglas's and Begbie's "clear and decided opinions," the "peculiarity of the circumstances of British Columbia," and Newcastle's sanction of "the principle of preemptive occupation before survey," they felt that Douglas's proclamation could be supported.[97] Finally, in December 1860, over a year after Douglas had implemented the pre-emption right in British Columbia, Newcastle conveyed Douglas "Her Majesty's sanction" of the Pre-emption Proclamation.[98]

Douglas would amend the Pre-emption Proclamation several times before his retirement, but the basic elements remained, and the right of pre-emption would endure under BC land law for over a century. When the province finally eliminated pre-emption "as a mode of land disposition" in 1970, the deputy minister of lands described it as "the vehicle by which thousands of rural settlers established roots throughout the Province."[99]

Through the proclamation, Douglas met settlers' demands and, in so doing, also addressed the colony's desire for agricultural settlers. The Colonial Office was not enthusiastic about the pre-emption system – the sale of land was the well-trodden path by which a colony arrived at self-sufficiency – but Douglas's arguments about the colony's unique situation convinced the Colonial Office that a right of pre-emption was worth trying. By establishing the pre-emption right, Douglas had satisfied the needs of three of the four main stakeholders in the new colony's land system.

Indigenous Rights to Land: "Not being ... an Indian Reserve or Settlement"

The Pre-emption Proclamation allowed a British subject to acquire lands that were not, among other things, "an Indian reserve or settlement." As Keith Carlson discusses in greater detail in this volume, Douglas put in place an Indian reserve creation system before he put in place the pre-emption system, so it is relatively easy to understand what he meant by "Indian reserve." It is less obvious what he meant by "Indian settlement," but understanding which lands he proposed become Indian reserves can shed some light.

As Carlson explains, during the first few months of 1859, while Douglas still contemplated that settlers could acquire land in the Colony only by purchase, he began to solidify his ideas about "Indian reserves." By mid-March, he wrote to the Colonial Office describing his plan:

> Anticipatory reserves of land for the benefit and support of the Indian races will be made for that purpose in all the districts of British Columbia inhabited by native tribes. Those reserves should in all cases include their cultivated fields and village sites, for which from habit and association they invariably conceive a strong attachment, and prize more, for that reason, than for the extent or value of the land.[100]

When his letter reached the Colonial Office, the officials were generally receptive, although the Colonial Office reminded Douglas of "the importance of exercising due care in laying out and defining the several reserves so as to avoid checking at a future day the progress of the White Colonists."[101] Later in 1859, in the circular to the magistrates and in accordance with his plan, Douglas instructed the magistrates to "cause to be reserved the Sites of all Indian villages, and the land they have been accustomed to cultivate, to the extent of several hundred acres round each village, for their special use and benefit."[102]

A year later, in September 1860, Douglas toured British Columbia, as Carlson explores in greater detail. He met with "the native Indian tribes, who assembled in great numbers" at Cayoosh (Lillooet) and Lytton and

> explained to them that the magistrates had instructions to stake out, and reserve for their use and benefit, all their occupied village sites and cultivated fields and as much land in the vicinity of each as they could till, or was required for their support; and that they might freely exercise and enjoy the rights of fishing the lakes and rivers, and of hunting over all unoccupied Crown lands in the colony.[103]

Douglas adjusted his Indian reserve policy many times throughout his term as governor, but he never strayed far from his initial principles. If anything, Douglas's instructions became more expansive as to the amount of land he wished to set aside as Indian reserves.[104] In his last explanation of his mainland policy, Douglas wrote:

> The principle followed in all cases was to leave the extent and selection of the land entirely optional with the Indians who were immediately interested in the Reserve; the surveying Officers having instructions to meet their wishes in every particular, and to include in each Reserve, the permanent Village sites, the fishing stations, and Burial Grounds, cultivated land, and all the favorite resorts of the Tribes, & in short to include every piece of ground to which they had acquired an equitable title through continuous occupation, tillage or other investment of their labour.[105]

Turning to the other Indigenous reference in the Pre-emption Proclamation, Douglas does not appear to have ever provided further details about what he considered to be an "Indian settlement," but some insight can be gleaned from the kinds of lands he wished reserved. The 1859 circular to magistrates instructed them to reserve "Indian villages, and the land they have been accustomed to cultivate, to the extent of several hundred acres round each village." It thus seems likely that these lands comprised, in Douglas's mind, an "Indian settlement." Arguably, an "Indian settlement" may have extended, as well, to what he described in 1874 it had been his policy to reserve: "the permanent Village sites, the fishing stations, and Burial grounds, cultivated land, and all the favorite resorts of the Tribes, & in short to include every piece of ground to which they had acquired an equitable title through continuous occupation, tillage or other investment of their labour."[106]

But while Douglas appears never to have further defined "Indian settlement," an 1864 decision on Vancouver Island provides a contemporaneous official perspective on the phrase. In a long-running dispute between a pre-empting settler and Indigenous people claiming an "Indian settlement" on the pre-empted land, a three-man commission (consisting of the surveyor general, the colony's treasurer, and another colonial official) had to determine what constituted an "Indian settlement" under the Vancouver Island pre-emption legislation (equivalent to the BC proclamation on this point). Somewhat surprisingly, the commission appears to have looked at the matter largely from an Indigenous perspective:

> We understand an Indian Settlement to be not a permanent standing Village but such a Village or Home as Indians are accustomed to have and it

> appears to be an understood custom with the Indians of this District as with many others to leave their Homes or Villages for months together taking their Houses with them.
>
> It is asserted ... that the portion of Land in question has always been an Indian Settlement in the Indian sense of the word, a place which the Indians looked on as their Home which they from time to time inhabited[.] Houses actually stood on the spot when the Land was taken up.
>
> This fact of an Indian settlement existing on the spot is one which we think can only be decided satisfactorily by the evidence of reliable Indians of the tribe or White men who have known the spot for some years and more particularly by a careful examination of the spot itself which to the eye of one experienced in Indian matters will, we are told, bear indisputable evidence of continued occupation and residence if such there ever were for any lengthened piece of time even before 1859.[107]

While a definition of an "Indian settlement" like this one given in 1864 – after Douglas's retirement – was never codified, I suspect Douglas would have agreed with it, as he seems to have been intent on preserving for Indigenous peoples the lands they had occupied prior to the settlers' arrival. His BC unsurveyed land system was based on the principle that these lands – Indian settlements and Indian reserves – were not available to settlers to pre-empt.

It is now apparent that, when implemented, the land system had enormous shortcomings. More study is needed as to why these shortcomings arose, but some immediate answers present themselves.

First, the system set up a direct conflict between settlers and Indigenous peoples with respect to land ownership and occupation: any piece of land possessed by a settler could not also be possessed by Indigenous people. The almost complete codification of the pre-emption right, juxtaposed with virtually no official description of what constituted Indigenous occupation, no doubt contributed in significant measure to the frequent crystallization of settler rights under the system at the expense of Indigenous rights.[108]

Second, the system was based on a similar one in the United States. Thus, even if a pre-empting settler was not familiar with the American system, he would have felt quite at home with its broad strokes: private land ownership, interests granted by the government, and an agricultural improvement requirement in return for either a delay in payment or a reduction in price. On the other hand, the Indigenous peoples of British

Columbia had never encountered such a system, based broadly on British legal principles.

Finally, as Paul Tennant points out, Douglas's policies and proclamations were one thing, but the magistrates and other colonial officials also played an important role.[109] At best, Douglas's instructions left room for mistakes and misinterpretations. At worst, officials' attitudes and motivations were not always as benevolent towards Indigenous interests as Douglas's may have been. Racism and elements of "stadial theory" – based on ideas that "purported to chart and to explain the transmutation of human societies from crudeness to mannered refinement through distinct stages"[110] – contributed to the malfunctioning of the BC unsurveyed land system. Nearly twenty years after Douglas created the system, the Indian reserve commissioner, Gilbert M. Sproat, lamented the "deep race prejudice" that had permeated the colonial and provincial provincial governments with respect to Indigenous land matters since Douglas's retirement and wished that the Colony of British Columbia had focused on creating Indian reserves from the lands Indigenous peoples wanted, used, and occupied.[111] Following that approach, he said, he had "solved several apparently insoluble problems this year, by discovering, that what the Indians really wanted was not so much good ploughland, as some old 'places of fun' up in the mountains or some place of fishing-resort where, at certain seasons, they assemble to fish, dig roots and race their horses."[112]

A deeper understanding of the BC unsurveyed land system no doubt will help in understanding its failures. But it can also suggest another answer to the question of why Douglas never attempted to extinguish Aboriginal title in British Columbia, particularly when considered in the context of the steps Douglas and the House of Assembly were taking to extinguish Aboriginal title in the Colony of Vancouver Island in the early 1860s.

The Colony of Vancouver Island's Efforts to Extinguish Aboriginal Title

The story of the Colony of Vancouver Island's steps to extinguish Aboriginal title has been told several times, and John Sutton Lutz re-examines the circumstances in this volume. However, the story bears repeating, particularly in the context of analyzing Douglas's intentions behind the BC unsurveyed land system.[113]

On March 1, 1860, Governor Douglas delivered a speech at the opening of the Colony of Vancouver Island's second Legislative Assembly.[114] Towards the end of his speech, he told the Assembly:

> The House of Assembly will have to provide means for extinguishing, by purchase, the native Title to the Lands in the districts of Cowitchan, Chemainis, and Salt Spring Island, which are now thrown open for settlement. The purchase should be effected without delay, as the Indians may otherwise regard the settlers as trespassers and become troublesome.[115]

The Assembly, elected from Victoria's small settler society, disagreed that they had ever "acknowledged" the "Indian titles," although they did "acknowledge that a compensation is due to them for changing their position."[116] However, within a few months, they drafted a petition requesting the Imperial Government to undertake "the extinction of the aboriginal title" on Vancouver Island:

> We, Her Majesty's Faithful and loyal subjects, the Members of the House of Assembly of Vancouver Island in Parliament assembled, would earnestly request the attention of your Grace to the following considerations:
>
> 1. That many Colonists have purchased land, at the rate of one pound sterling per acre, in districts to which the Indian title has not yet been extinguished.
> 2. That, in consequence of the non-extinction of this title, these persons, though most desirous to occupy and improve, have been unable to take possession of their lands – purchased, in most cases, nearly three years ago; and of this, they loudly and justly complain.
> 3. That the Indians, well aware of the compensation heretofore given for lands, appropriated for colonization, in the earlier settled districts of Vancouver Island, as well as in the neighbouring territory of Washington, strenuously oppose the occupation by settlers of lands still deemed their own. No attempts of the kind could be persisted in, without endangering the peace of the Country, for these Indians, though otherwise well disposed and friendly, would become hostile if their supposed rights as regards land were systematically violated; and they are still much more numerous and warlike, than the petty remnants of tribes, who in 1855 and 1856, in the western part of the adjacent United States territory of Washington, kept up for nearly a year, a desultory and destructive warfare,

which compelled the whole agricultural population of the Country, to desert their homes, and congregate in blockhouses.

4. That, within the last three years, this Island has been visited by many intending settlers, from various parts of the world. Comparatively few of these have remained, the others having, as we believe, been, in a great measure, deterred from buying land as they could not rely on having peaceable possession; seeing that the Indian Title was still unextinguished to several of the most eligible agricultural districts of the Island.
5. That the House of Assembly respectfully considers, that the extinction of the aboriginal title is obligatory on the Imperial Government.
6. That the House of Assembly, bearing in mind, that from the dawn of modern colonization until the present day, wars with aborigines, have mainly arisen from disputes about land, which by timely and moderate concession on the part of the more powerful and enlightened of the disputants concerned, might have been peaceably and economically adjusted, now earnestly pray that Her Majesty's Government would direct such steps to be taken, as may seem best, for the speedy settlement of the matter at issue, and the removal of a most serious obstacle to the well being of this Colony.[117]

Governor Douglas forwarded the petition to the secretary of state for the colonies, adding his own words of urgency to the plea to extinguish the Aboriginal title to the public lands in the colony.[118] For Douglas, the urgency lay in Indigenous views about their ownership of lands:

> As the native Indian population of Vancouver Island have distinct ideas of property in land, and mutually recognize their several exclusive possessory rights in certain Districts, they would not fail to regard the occupation of such portions of the Colony by white settlers, unless with the full consent of the proprietary Tribes, as national wrongs; and the sense of injury might produce a feeling of irritation against the Settlers, and perhaps disaffection to the Government, that would endanger the peace of the Country.[119]

Douglas explained that his practice up until 1859 had been "to purchase the Native rights in the land, in every case, prior to the settlement of any District," a practice that, because of the termination of the Hudson's Bay Company's charter over Vancouver Island and the lack of colonial funds, he had not been able to continue. To that date, he had "bought from the Indians" all the settled districts, with the exception of Cowichan,

Chemainus, and Barkley Sound. Douglas estimated that the cost to buy these three districts would amount to about £3 per Indigenous family or about £3,000. He concluded: "It would be improper to conceal from Your Grace the importance of carrying that vital measure into effect without delay."[120] From Douglas's perspective, the only real question was the source of the funds, and he suggested that the imperial government extend the colony a loan, to be repaid from the public land sale proceeds.[121]

On receiving Douglas's letter and the Assembly's petition, the Colonial Office consulted the Emigration Commission on the documents. The commission agreed with Douglas and the Assembly that the only real question was the source of the necessary funds to extinguish Aboriginal title, as "there can be no question" of "the importance & practical economy of at once extinguishing a claim which must be a continual source of danger, and which can scarcely fail to grow in amount as time goes on."[122] From the commission's perspective, extinguishing the claim was "due" to the settlers "who have paid for Land of which, so long as this claim exists, they cannot take possession without risk to the peace of the Settlement."[123]

The emigration commissioners suggested that the Colonial Office ask the Lords Commissioners of the Treasury, who held the British purse strings, for a loan. Back at the Colonial Office once more, an officer suggested that the colony itself should be required "to find this £3000 for extinguishing the native Titles to Land" since "[w]e have scarcely a colony which might not allege the same Reason as an excuse for an appeal to the English Exchequer. And a young Colony cannot too soon be taught to look to itself alone for the accomplishment of an object of primary importance to its welfare."[124] Newcastle, the secretary of state for the colonies, seemed to agree but thought it would not hurt to ask the Treasury for a loan. He noted, however, "I fear we shall get a refusal."[125]

In the covering letter to the Treasury, the Colonial Office recommended the governor's proposal of a loan of "about £3000 to be eventually repaid out of the Colonial land fund." In doing so, it pleaded the settlers' case: "Looking to the importance and practical economy of extinguishing a claim which must be a continual source of danger, and which can scarcely fail to grow in amounts ... the inhabitants of Vancouver Island have strong & peculiar claims for assistance upon this occasion."[126]

As Newcastle had predicted, the Treasury refused to fund the loan. In fact, Treasury officials doubted they were being asked for a loan at all because of the Vancouver Island Assembly's assertion that buying the Aboriginal title was the imperial government's responsibility.[127] The Treasury was "hardly prepared to give authority for the purchase, at the expense of this Country, for the sum of £3000, of the Native title in certain tracts of land in Vancouver's Island."[128] The Treasury suggested that Douglas should continue the practice he had described in his letter of purchasing Indigenous rights only when the colony needed the land for settlement.[129]

There was now a growing consensus within the Colonial Office that the colony should be told to borrow the money itself. One senior official put it this way: "Of course the duty of buying up the Indian Title rests with those who receive the profits of Land when sold."[130] However, the Colonial Office consulted with the emigration commissioners once again before responding to Douglas. This time, the commissioners expressed the obvious conclusion:

> As the matter therefore stands the Colony cannot provide the required sum, and the Home Government declines to make a grant of it. The result will be that the opportunity will be lost of extinguishing the Native Title on very moderate terms, and that faith cannot be kept with the persons to whom the Government sold the land 3 years ago without endangering the peace of the Country.[131]

The only alternative left, according to the emigration commissioners, was for the governor to raise a loan on the best terms he could.[132]

With the matter back in their hands once more, the Colonial Office officials discussed the response to give Douglas. There was general consensus: "1st That the land ought to be purchased, and 2nd That it ought not to be done by English money or by English credit."[133] Newcastle's final comment was that "[i]t is miserable work to see the Colony objecting to pay so small a sum for an object at once essential to their interests and purely Colonial in its character."[134] Newcastle sent his reply to Douglas, declining any financial assistance, on October 19, 1861.

Back on Vancouver Island and having yet heard nothing back from England, the Assembly agreed on October 8, 1861, to make "a renewed application" to "the Home Government for the extinction of the Indian title in districts partially, or soon to be occupied, such as Barclay's Sound – Kawitchin [Cowichan] and Komax [Comox]."[135] However, there is no evidence that the Assembly or the governor ever sent a new petition to England before the Assembly's session concluded in early February 1862.[136] Despite this, there is an intriguing letter on December 5, 1861, from

Joseph D. Pemberton, then the colony's surveyor general and prior to that in charge of lands in the colony for the HBC. Pemberton was responding to a statement Douglas had been told Pemberton made in 1858 "in regard to extinguishing the Indian title at Cowichan."[137] Pemberton explained:

> That although I have no recollection of any conversation upon the subject with any of the gentlemen who have signed the Petition – I believe that if in 1858 any purchaser of those lands asked me whether within a reasonable time the Indian title would be extinguished as had been previously the practice I should have expressed a strong opinion in the affirmative.

The Assembly opened its next session on March 19, 1862. The following day, two years after Douglas had first advised the Assembly that it would need to take steps to extinguish Aboriginal title and one year after Douglas had conveyed its petition along with his request for a loan to extinguish Aboriginal title, Douglas sent the Assembly Newcastle's letter refusing the requested loan. Newcastle had written:

> I am fully sensible of the great importance of purchasing without loss of time the Native title to the soil of Vancouver Island: but the acquisition of the title is a purely Colonial Interest and the Legislature must not entertain any expectation that the British Taxpayer will be burthened to supply the funds or British Credit pledged for the purpose. I would earnestly recommend therefore to the House of Assembly that they should enable you to procure the requisite means; but if they should not think proper to do so, Her Majesty's Government cannot undertake to supply the money requisite for an object which, whilst it is essential to the interests of the people of Vancouver Island, is at the same time purely Colonial in its character, and trifling in the charge that it would entail.[138]

Yet this was not the end of the story with respect to the extinguishment of Aboriginal title on Vancouver Island. Just a few weeks later, the Assembly committed two-thirds of the amount requested from England – £2,000 – towards the "Road to Cowichan & extinction of Indian Title."[139] The following year, in 1863, the house voted for $25,705 "for the Civil List and Indian Titles under the same proviso as last year."[140] The year after that, the Assembly still contemplated payments to extinguish Aboriginal title. On February 9, 1864, the House advised Douglas, now the outgoing governor, that since the colony had lowered the price of land, thereby reducing the colony's revenue, and purchasers were still few, "that the Revenue from this source will, in future years, be less whilst a considerable sum will be requisite for the extinction of the Indian Title to and the surveying of Crown Lands."[141]

On February 22, the Assembly considered the "unexpended" amount of $9,700 for "Indian Claims" – that is, to purchase the Aboriginal title. On being asked whether the $9,700 included "the Comox lands also," the colonial secretary replied that he "believed it did; calculations had been made of the number of Indians, and the amount required to buy them off." In the end, the Assembly voted again for the $9,700, recording in its statements, "Indian Claims – Payment for Lands at Chemanis, Cowichan, &c., unexpended in 1863."[142]

On April 29, the Legislative Council considered a resolution on the perennial matter of the amount of revenue the colony could expect from the sale of public lands. The council considered that no net income could be expected for a number of reasons, including "[b]ecause the amount of money necessary to be paid to Indians to extinguish the Indian title to portions of the land will absorb a considerable sum of the proceeds of sales thereof."[143] The council passed this resolution on May 2, 1864, shortly after Douglas's successors, in both colonies, took office.[144] On November 1, 1864, the new governor of the Colony of Vancouver Island considered that "[t]he growing difficulties with the Indian population must continue to increase while the extent of their lands is undefined and their just claims unliquidated."[145]

Notwithstanding these many statements about the importance of purchasing Indian title to facilitate settlement during the 1860–64 period, there is no evidence that any of the monies put aside were ever paid out to extinguish the Aboriginal title.[146]

Why Were There No Efforts to Extinguish Aboriginal Title through Treaties in British Columbia?

In the context of all these efforts to obtain funds to extinguish Aboriginal title in the Colony of Vancouver Island, let us return to the Colony of British Columbia and consider the comparable situation there. In 1990, Paul Tennant enunciated the "major puzzle" about Douglas as the governor of the Colony of British Columbia: "Why did he fail to arrange further treaties [beyond those he negotiated in the Colony of Vancouver

Island] to extinguish aboriginal title in British Columbia?"[147] Since then, scholars have suggested a multitude of answers, including that the colony lacked the funds,[148] that Douglas found negotiating treaties too difficult and thought that they did not adequately protect Indigenous interests in any event,[149] that Douglas only negotiated treaties when it made sense to do so or when he was required to do so,[150] and that Douglas followed a recent American legal precedent that suggested that treaties for the extinguishment of Aboriginal title were unnecessary.[151] Graham Brazier and John Sutton Lutz, in their chapters in this volume, each offer their own interesting answers to Tennant's question, albeit in the context of the Colony of Vancouver Island, to which slightly different considerations apply. Each successive scholar generally agrees with the preceding interpretations but suggests a fuller and more complete explanation. I am no different.

I agree with Cole Harris and with Hamar Foster and Alan Grove that the "lack of funds" argument cuts both ways: the mainland colony was in dire financial straits, and extinguishment would have been extremely costly, but, when necessary, Douglas did find significant amounts to invest in settler-attracting infrastructure.[152] I am unconvinced by Foster and Grove's hypothesis about the impact of a particular decision in the Oregon Territory, but I agree that Douglas clearly was influenced by his time in Oregon, particularly the manner in which settlers might acquire land.[153]

In general, I am more convinced by Tennant's emphasis on the importance of Douglas's provision for Indigenous pre-emption and by Harris's focus on Douglas's pragmatism. Tennant points to the Indigenous pre-emption provision as an underrecognized indicator of Douglas's thinking, and I agree. Douglas supported and envisaged eventual Indigenous assimilation into the new colonial society and economy.[154] Indigenous pre-emption would hasten this assimilation. As Tennant puts it:

> Pre-emption would be a process drawing out those Indians most amenable to assimilation and to co-operation with Whites … Douglas ignored treaty-making on the Mainland not because of lack of funds but because his system anticipated assimilated Indians who, having abandoned traditional communities for their homesteads, would maintain neither Indian identity nor Indian land claims.[155]

Yet, Tennant goes too far, I think, when he claims that "Douglas came in practice to deny Indian title and so to deny the relevance of the aboriginal past." This argument is not sustainable in light of the Vancouver Island colony's apparently sincere pursuit of funds to extinguish Aboriginal title well after the 1859–60 period, when Douglas was constructing his BC unsurveyed land system.

In my view, Harris provides the best general explanation for Douglas's failure to continue with treaties:

> He stopped, I think, because of the costs and the logistical problems involved, and because there was no pressure from the Colonial Office to make such purchases. I doubt he had ever been deeply committed to the principle of Native title, but ... had thought it wise to clear the land of possible Native claims as long as it was not prohibitively costly or troublesome to do so. On the mainland, land purchases would be costly and troublesome, and no one insisted that he buy land. At the same time, he sought to provide for Native people through an inevitable period of transition from savagery to civilization. As always for Douglas, I think, the challenge was practical rather than theoretical. When he became governor of British Columbia he faced, among all the other demands, the task of somehow achieving a relatively generous resolution of the Native land question with little cost or administrative effort.[156]

However, I would quibble – and perhaps Harris would agree – that Douglas did not "stop" pursuing treaties so much as *suspend* pursuing them on the mainland, pending the decision about how to pay for treaties and the extinguishment of Aboriginal title on Vancouver Island. More problematically, Harris's explanation does not address the other crucial piece of Douglas's land policy: the system for enabling settlers to acquire land. The consideration of this aspect of BC's unsurveyed land system, I think, can contribute to answering the question, Why no treaties in the mainland colony?

To adopt Tennant's wording, Douglas "failed" to arrange treaties in the mainland colony because his immediate goal was not to extinguish Aboriginal title but, rather, to meet urgent settler and Indigenous needs and demands for land in a manner that minimized conflict between them. Douglas thought the BC unsurveyed land system could achieve this goal more quickly, cheaply, and effectively than attempting to negotiate the immediate extinguishment of Aboriginal title. The beauty of Douglas's system, at least from the perspective of a busy governor (of two colonies!) pressed from all sides in countless ways – not the least of which was figuring out how to manage who got what when it came to land – was that it allowed for the future possibility of negotiating to extinguish Aboriginal title. By the time the major pieces of his BC unsurveyed land system were in place in January 1860, he had not yet announced to the Assembly in the Colony of Vancouver Island that it would "have to provide means for extinguishing by purchase, the native Title to the Lands" in settled districts on Vancouver Island. He still had years ahead of attempting to find the funds to extinguish the Aboriginal title in the Island colony. The new mainland colony's unsurveyed land system allowed it to wait for the outcome of the older and more sophisticated colony's steps to extinguish Aboriginal title in the districts settled by the new immigrants.

Minimizing "Agrarian Disturbance"

A close reading of Douglas's statements about land in the Colony of British Columbia – in particular, his use of the word *agrarian* – reveals that Douglas's overriding objective was to minimize conflict over land between Indigenous peoples and incoming settlers. *Agrarian*, to our modern ears, means "agricultural," and this was also one of its definitions in the mid-nineteenth century.[157] However, each time that Douglas used the word in the context of Indigenous land issues, "agricultural" does not seem to fit. Instead, the more general definition of *agrarian* – "concerned with landed property and the rights and issues associated with it, as its allocation, ownership, distribution, enclosure, etc." – is a better fit and also provides fresh insight into what Douglas intended with his unsurveyed land system.[158]

In 1856, Douglas opened the first Vancouver Island House of Assembly by vowing "to conciliate the good will of the native Indian Tribes, by treating them with justice and forebearance [sic], and by rigidly protecting their civil and agrarian rights."[159] In February 1859, Douglas wrote to the Assembly in reply to its desire to remove Indigenous peoples from "that piece of land inside Victoria Harbour known as the Indian Reservation." Douglas refused, declaring instead:

> When the Settlement at Victoria was formed certain reservations were made in favour of the native Indian tribes.
>
> They were to be protected in their original right of fishing on the Coasts and in the Bays of the Colony, and of hunting over all unoccupied Crown Lands; and they were also to be secured in the enjoyment of their village sites and cultivated fields.

> These rights they have since enjoyed in full and the Reserves of land covering their Village sites and cultivated fields have all been distinctly marked on the maps and surveys of the Colony, and the faith of Government is pledged, that their occupation shall not be disturbed.
>
> For that reason the Government will not cause them to be removed, because it is bound by the faith of a solemn engagement to protect them in the enjoyment of those *Agrarian rights.*[160]

In both of these instances, Douglas uses *agrarian rights* to describe land interests generally, not simply agriculture.

Finally, in 1862, Douglas told the Assembly that he had come to an "arrangement" with the Malahat people and had created a reserve for them because of "agrarian disputes, endangering the public peace and safety."[161] This was a reference to disputes over land, which were in part a result of settler desire for agricultural land, but Douglas was not referring to agricultural disputes in particular.

With respect to the mainland Colony of British Columbia, in 1858, Secretary of State Lytton gave Douglas, as the governor of the new Colony of British Columbia, vague instructions with respect to Indigenous peoples (as discussed above), making no mention of anything related to agriculture.[162] Yet, in his reply, Douglas wrote that he would "not fail to give the fullest scope to your humane considerations for the improvement of the native Indian Tribes and shall take care that all their civil and agrarian rights be protected."[163] In 1864, when addressing the new British Columbia Legislative Council, Douglas advised that "the Native Indian Tribes are quiet and well-disposed," and "the plan of forming Reserves of Land embracing the Village Sites, cultivated fields, and favorite places of resort of the several tribes, and thus securing them against the encroachment of Settlers, and for ever removing the fertile cause of agrarian disturbance, has been productive of the happiest effects on the minds of the Natives."[164] Finally, a decade later, Douglas told the new federal superintendent of Indian affairs in British Columbia that his Indian reserve plan had had "the object of securing to each community their natural or acquired rights; of removing all cause for complaint on the ground of unjust deprivation of the land indispensable for their convenience or support, & to provide against the occurrence of Agrarian disputes with the white settlers."[165] In each instance, Douglas used *agrarian* to refer generally to land-related disputes or rights or interests, not agriculture. From this perspective, it becomes clearer that Douglas considered his BC unsurveyed land system to have "for ever remov[ed] the fertile cause of [*land-related*] disturbance" between Indigenous peoples and settlers.

Through the BC unsurveyed land system, the lands Douglas aimed at securing for Indigenous peoples in British Columbia – "Indian settlements" and "Indian reserves" – were comparable to or perhaps more than the lands secured to Indigenous peoples on Vancouver Island under the fourteen agreements he had entered into between 1850 and 1854, known as the Douglas or Vancouver Island Treaties and analyzed in detail throughout this book. The system allowed Douglas to allocate lands that would have been secured to Indigenous peoples under comparable agreements while permitting settler occupation and awaiting the outcome of the Colony of Vancouver Island's pursuit of funds to extinguish Aboriginal title. In this way, the unsurveyed land system was intended to reserve important Indigenous lands, pending a decision as to when, how, and even whether treaties would be negotiated. In other words, just as in Oregon, settler occupation in the Colony of British Columbia preceded the extinguishment of Aboriginal title. However, unlike in Oregon, Douglas may have felt that he had nonetheless preserved Indigenous-occupied lands.

Thus, instead of seeing Douglas's BC unsurveyed land system as an *alternative* to the extinguishment of title through treaties, it is possible to see it as deferring that extinguishment while maintaining it as a possibility. The advantage of Douglas's system – in the confusing, chaotic, and provisional circumstances of a colonial governor in a distant-from-England, mid-nineteenth-century colony – was that it did not require him either to confirm or reject Aboriginal title. He could meet the needs of settlers and Indigenous peoples without, he thought, substantially compromising the interests of either. Extinguishment and treaties could wait. He would address settler demands and preserve Indigenous interests by means other than treaties.

As it turned out, Douglas's BC unsurveyed land system malfunctioned almost from its inception, leading to disputes to this day between Indigenous peoples, the Crown, and settlers over land in this province.[166] So much for "for ever removing the fertile cause of agrarian disturbance."

Further, as is now well known, Douglas's "failure" to pursue treaty negotiations with Indigenous peoples has haunted the province ever since. Although British Columbia and Canada finally began a formal treaty process with Indigenous peoples in 1992, the process has been slow, expensive, and complicated, factors that may have resonated with Governor Douglas.[167] The Supreme Court of Canada's decision in *Tsilhqot'in Nation v British Columbia,* the first judicial finding of Aboriginal title, has added another layer of complexity to an already monumentally complex situation.[168] While we may never understand fully why Governor James Douglas did not pursue treaty making in the Colony of British Columbia, we now understand, all too well, the results of his failure to do so.

One approach British Columbia and First Nations have taken to work around the cumbersome aspects of the BC treaty process is to enter into either interim measures agreements that provide First Nations with economic benefits and a role in decision making arising from timber-harvesting activities taking place in their traditional territories[169] or incremental treaty agreements that transfer lands pending eventual treaty settlement.[170] Canada's Department of Fisheries and Oceans has entered into similar provisional agreements with First Nations concerning fishery resources.[171] Neither the provincial nor the federal arrangements rest on agreements about or the extinguishment of Aboriginal title.

Clearly, the tensions Douglas faced – between expediency and certainty, between settler and Indigenous occupation – are with us still. And even today, when, like Douglas, we face the choice between provisional solutions and final fixes, the provisional solutions sometimes still prove the more attractive choice – or at least the more achievable.

Acknowledgments

The views I express and the positions I take in this chapter are solely mine. They are not to be attributed to my former employer, the Government of Canada (or to any department thereof). I thank Professor Douglas Harris of Peter A. Allard School of Law at UBC for his helpful comments on drafts of this chapter.

Notes

1 Her Majesty the Queen, "Letters Patent under the Great Seal appointing James Douglas, Esquire, to be Governor and Commander-in-Chief in and over the Colony of British Columbia and its Dependencies," September 2, 1858, in James Douglas; Edward George Earle Lytton-Bulwer; British Columbia, Governor; and Great Britain, Colonial Office, *Papers Relative to the Affairs of British Columbia: Part I ...* (London: G.E. Eyre/W. Spottiswoode, 1859), 3 (hereafter *Papers Relative I*).

2 Her Majesty the Queen, "Instructions to Our trusty and well-beloved James Douglas, Esquire, Our Governor and Commander-in-Chief in and over Our Colony of British Columbia and of its Dependencies," September 2, 1858, in *Papers Relative I,* 5.

3 Ibid., ss 28–30.

4 Edward Bulwer-Lytton to Douglas, July 31, 1858, National Archives (UK) (NA), Records of the Colonial Office (hereafter CO), 410/1, in *The Colonial Despatches of Victoria Island and British Columbia, 1846–1871,* ed. James Hendrickson and the Colonial Despatches Project, https://bcgenesis.uvic.ca (hereafter *Colonial Despatches*).

5 Jeremy Mouat, "Situating Vancouver Island in the British World, 1846–49," *BC Studies* 145 (Spring 2005): 7.

6 Robin Fisher, "Indian Warfare and Two Frontiers: A Comparison of British Columbia and Washington Territory during the Early Years of Settlement," *Pacific Historical Review* 50, 1 (1981): 41.

7 Paul Tennant also refers to Douglas's "system," picking up on Douglas's own reference in his letter to Lytton of March 14, 1859: see Paul Tennant, *Aboriginal Peoples and Politics: The Indian Land Question in British Columbia, 1849–1989* (Vancouver: UBC Press, 1990), chap. 3. Yet Douglas, in his 1859 letter, refers primarily to his plan to create Indian reserves, and Tennant's reference carries the same connotation.

8 Though Indigenous people were allowed to pre-empt freely for a time, and after 1866 with the permission of the governor (per *Pre-emption Ordinance, 1866,* s. 1), this practice was rare enough that I will not address it further in this essay. For further discussion of the Indigenous exercise of the right of pre-emption, see R. Cole Harris, *Making Native Space: Colonialism, Resistance, and Reserves in British Columbia* (Vancouver: UBC Press, 2002), 35–36; Tennant, *Aboriginal Peoples and Politics,* 34–36; and Dorothy I.D. Kennedy, Dennis Madill, and Indian and Northern Affairs Canada, *A Reference Guide to the Establishment of Indian Reserves in British Columbia, 1849–1911* (Ottawa: Indian and Northern Affairs Canada, Claims Research and Assessment Directorate, 1995).

9 Robert E. Cail, *Land, Man, and the Law: The Disposal of Crown Lands in British Columbia, 1871–1913* (Vancouver: UBC Press, 1974).

10 Ibid., chaps. 1 and 11.

11 "The Queen's Speech, given by the Lords Commissioners on August 2, 1858, on the close of the session of Parliament in which (and on the day on which) the Act to provide for the government of British Columbia was passed," in F. Sidney Ensor, *The Queen's Speeches in Parliament: From Her Accession to the Present Time* (London: W.H. Allen, 1882), 146.

12 Paul Tennant uses the phrase *major puzzle* in *Aboriginal Peoples and Politics,* 26: "There remains about James Douglas a major puzzle. Why did he fail to arrange further treaties to extinguish aboriginal title in British Columbia?" "Extinguishing the Indian title" or "purchasing the land" appear to be common phrases that colonial actors used to discuss this kind of transaction. Douglas himself, in perhaps the first written indication of an intention to purchase the Aboriginal title in the Colony of Vancouver Island, recommended to HBC secretary Archibald Barclay, on September 3, 1849, the "purchase of their lands": James Douglas to Archibald Barclay, September 3, 1849, in Harwell Bowsfield, ed., *Fort Victoria Letters, 1846–1851* (Winnipeg: Hudson's Bay Record Society, 1979), 43. While the historical actors appear to have used the terms "Indian title," "native title," and "Aboriginal title" interchangeably, "Indian title" was the most often used. I have attempted to use the modern term "Aboriginal title" in this chapter, except when discussing the historical documents in their context, when I tried to use the term the historical actors used.

13 John Adams, *Old Square-Toes and His Lady: The Life of James and Amelia Douglas* (Victoria: Horsdal and Schubart, 2001), 32, 74. *Oxford English Dictionary,* 3rd ed., s.v. "pre-emption," accessed June 21, 2017, https://www.oed.com.

14 *Oxford English Dictionary,* 3rd ed., s.v. "pre-emption," accessed June 21, 2017, https://www.oed.com.

15 *An Act to Authorize the Sale of Certain Lands between the Great and Little Miami Rivers in the Territory of the United States Northwest of the Ohio; and for Giving a Pre-Emption to Certain Purchasers and Settlers, Statutes at Large of the United States of America, 1789–1873,* 1 Stat 728 (March 2, 1799), https://www.loc.gov/law/help/statutes-at-large/5th-congress/c5.pdf.

16 *An Act to Appropriate the Proceeds of the Sales of the Public Lands, and to Grant Pre-Emption Rights, Statutes at Large of the United States of America, 1789–1873,* 5 Stat 453 (September 4, 1841), https://www.loc.gov/law/help/statutes-at-large/27th-congress/session-1/c27s1ch16.pdf.

17 *An Act to Amend the Act Approved September Twenty-Seven, Eighteen Hundred and Fifty, to Create the Office of Surveyor-General of the Public Lands in Oregon, Etc., Statutes at Large of the United States of America, 1789–1873,* 10 Stat 305 (July 17, 1854), s 3, https://www.loc.gov/law/help/statutes-at-large/33rd-congress/session-1/c33s1ch84.pdf.

18 *Convention with Great Britain, US-UK,* October 20, 1818.

19 "Law of Land Claims, July 5, 1843," in La Fayette Grover, *The Oregon Archives: Including the Journals, Governors' Messages and Public Papers of Oregon* (Salem, MA: Asahel Bush, 1853), 35.

20 *An Act in relation to Indians,* December 23, 1844, *Laws of a General and Local Nature Passed by the Legislative Committee and Legislative Assembly, at Their Various Successive Sessions from the Year 1843, down to and Inclusive of the Session of the Territorial Legislature, Held in the Year 1849* (Salem: Asahel Bush, 1853), 70–71. In Hamar Foster and Alan Grove, "'Trespassers on the Soil': *United States v. Tom* and a New Perspective on the Short History of Treaty Making in Nineteenth-Century British Columbia," *BC Studies* 138–39 (Summer–Autumn 2003): 71n83, the authors point out the similarities between this wording and that in the agreements Douglas made on Vancouver Island, known today as the Douglas or Vancouver Island Treaties, as well as the probable influences of Emer de Vattel, a nineteenth-century jurist.

21 *Treaty of limits, westward of the Rocky Mountains, between the United States of America and the British government,* June 15, 1846, Library of Congress, portfolio 232, folder 40, https://www.loc.gov/resource/rbpe.23204000/?st=gallery. According to the treaty, the boundary line between American and British territories actually runs along the forty-ninth parallel from the east to the west only "to the middle of the channel which separates the continent from Vancouver's Island, and thence southerly through the middle of the said channel, and of Fuca's straits to the Pacific Ocean." Thus, the forty-ninth parallel actually runs through Vancouver Island at approximately Ladysmith, leaving all of Vancouver Island and the Gulf Islands south of that point below the forty-ninth parallel.

22 *An Act to Establish the Territorial Government of Oregon, Statutes at Large of the United States of America, 1789–1873,* 9 Stat 323 (August 14, 1848), http://www.loc.gov/law/help/statutes-at-large/30th-congress/session-1/c30s1ch177.pdf.

23 Ibid., s 14.

24 Ibid., s 1.

25 Jerry O'Callaghan, "Disposition of the Public Domain in Oregon" (PhD diss., Stanford University, 1951), 8.

26 Champ C. Vaughan, *A History of the United States General Land Office in Oregon* (Washington, DC: Department of Interior, Bureau of Land Management, 2014), 11, https://www.blm.gov/or/landsrealty/glo200/files/glo-book.pdf.

27 *An Act Authorizing the Negotiation of Treaties with the Indian Tribes in the Territory of Oregon, for the Extinguishment of Their Claims to Lands Lying West of the Cascade Mountains, and for Other Purposes, Statutes at Large of the United States of America, 1789–1873,* 9 Stat 437 (June 5, 1850), http://www.loc.gov/law/help/statutes-at-large/31st-congress/session-1/c31s1ch16.pdf.

28 *An Act to Create the Office of Surveyor-General of the Public Lands in Oregon, and to Provide for the Survey, and to Make Donations to Settlers of the Said Public Lands, Statutes at Large of the United States of America, 1789–1873,* 9 Stat 496 (September 27, 1850), s 7, https://www.loc.gov/law/help/statutes-at-large/31st-congress/session-1/c31s1ch76.pdf.

29 Ibid.

30 William G. Robbins, "The Indian Question in Western Oregon: The Making of a Colonial People," in *Experiences in a Promised Land: Essays in Pacific Northwest History,* ed. G. Thomas Edwards and Carlos A. Schwantes (Seattle: University of Washington Press, 1986), 54–55; and O'Callaghan, "Disposition of the Public Domain in Oregon," 8.

31 *An Act to Establish the Territorial Government of Washington, Statutes at Large of the United States of America, 1789–1873,* 10 Stat 172 (March 2, 1853), https://www.loc.gov/law/help/statutes-at-large/32nd-congress/session-2/c32s2ch90.pdf.

32 *An Act to Amend the Act Approved September Twenty-Seven,* s 3.

33 *An Act to Appropriate the Proceeds,* ss 10, 15.

34 Robbins, "The Indian Question in Western Oregon," 56.

35 Ibid.

36 Foster and Grove, "Trespassers on the Soil," 67. See also Robbins, "The Indian Question in Western Oregon," 61–62.

37 Stephen D. Beckham, "History of Western Oregon since 1846," in *Handbook of North American Indians,* vol. 7, *The Northwest Coast,* ed. Wayne Suttles (Washington, DC: Smithsonian Institution, 1990), 186; and Cesare Marino, "History of Western Washington since 1846," also in Suttles, *Handbook,* vol. 7, *The Northwest Coast,* 170.

38 Gray H. Whaley, *Oregon and the Collapse of Illahee: U.S. Empire and the Transformation of an Indigenous World, 1792–1859* (Chapel Hill: University of North Carolina Press, 2010), 196.

39 Beckham, "History of Western Oregon since 1846," 181–82.

40 In Foster and Grove, "Trespassers on the Soil," 71, the authors make some similar observations about what Douglas "would have known."

41 "Introduction," Margaret Ormsby, in Bowsfield, *Fort Victoria Letters,* xxii.

42 Douglas to Barclay, September 3, 1849, and Douglas to Governor, Deputy Governor and Committee, October 27, 1849, in Bowsfield, *Fort Victoria Letters,* 44 and 58. In Foster and Grove, "Trespassers on the Soil," 69–71, the authors detail Douglas's involvement in Oregon land affairs during his twenty-year residence there.

43 Douglas to Barclay, November 16, 1850, in Bowsfield, *Fort Victoria Letters,* 135.

44 James E. Hendrickson, ed., *Journals of the Colonial Legislatures of the Colonies of Vancouver Island and British Columbia, 1851–1871,* 4 vols. (Victoria: Provincial Archives of British Columbia, 1980), 1:377–78.

45 Ibid., 1:xxix.

46 Douglas to Barclay, January 29, 1851, in Bowsfield, *Fort Victoria Letters,* 147.

47 Richard Mackie details Governor Douglas's distaste for and attempts to circumvent the "Wakefieldian" land system London imposed on the colony but notes that Douglas found it "impossible to dismantle" the £1-per-acre purchase price, which remained in effect until 1860: Richard Mackie, "The Colonization of Vancouver Island, 1849–1858," *BC Studies* 96 (Winter 1992–93): 4, 7–8, 10–13, 15, 17, 30–31, and 34.

48 Phyllis Mikkelsen, "Land Settlement Policy on the Mainland of BC, 1858–1874" (master's thesis, University of British Columbia, 1950), 79–81. See also "Cheap Lands," *Daily British Colonist,* June 13, 1859.
49 Alfred Waddington, *The Fraser Mines Vindicated, or the History of Four Months* (Victoria: P. De Garro, 1858), Foreword, 49.
50 "Land Reform Meeting," *British Colonist,* June 24, 1859.
51 "Land Reform Meeting," *British Colonist,* July 4, 1859.
52 Ibid.
53 "Report of the Land Reform Committee," *British Colonist,* July 8, 1859.
54 Douglas to Lytton, July 20, 1859, CO 305/10, 8944, *Colonial Despatches.*
55 Though Douglas would create a similar pre-emption right on Vancouver Island after he created the mainland system, the two differed slightly. For the purposes of focusing on the BC unsurveyed land system, I restrict my discussion to the pre-emption right Douglas created in the Colony of British Columbia.
56 Proclamation 17, January 4, 1860, enclosed with Douglas to Lord Newcastle, January 14, 1860, CO 60/7, 2316, *Colonial Despatches.* The punctuation is as per the printed version of the proclamation; the second parenthesis was written in by hand.
57 BC Indian reserve commissioner Gilbert M. Sproat, in 1878, discussed the colonial and provincial legislation affecting "Indian settlements" repeatedly. He noted that "[n]obody knows precisely what an 'Indian settlement' is nor what period of occupation of land by Indians gives it that character. Its nature and extent are entirely undefined, but dwellings and ploughed or fenced fields could hardly be excluded from any definition of a 'settlement'": Sproat to Superintendent General of Indian Affairs, "Second Condensed Report by the Joint Commissioner Appointed by the Governments of Canada and British Columbia," December 1, 1877, Ottawa, Library and Archives Canada (LAC), RG 10, Department of Indian Affairs, vol. 3612, file 3756-16. See also Sproat and McKinlay to Provincial Secretary, "Second Condensed Report of the Commissioners Acting for the Province," January 1, 1878, Victoria, BC Archives, (GR-494, p. 489); and Sproat to Superintendent General of Indian Affairs, February 4, 1878, Ottawa, LAC, RG 10, vol. 3657, file 9323.
58 *Williams Lake Indian Band v Canada,* 2018 SCC 4.
59 Lytton to Douglas, July 31, 1858, CO 410/1, *Colonial Despatches.*
60 Douglas to Lytton, October 11, 1858, CO 60/1, 12180, ibid.
61 Lytton to Douglas, August 14, 1858, CO 410/1, ibid.
62 Ibid.
63 Ibid.
64 Douglas to Lytton, October 11, 1858.
65 "Letter from New Fort Langley," *Victoria Gazette,* November 25, 1858.
66 Proclamation, December 2, 1859, in Edward George Earle Lytton-Bulwer; British Columbia, Governor; and Great Britain, Colonial Office, *Further Papers Relative to the Affairs of British Columbia: Part II* (London: G.E. Eyre/W. Spottiswoode, 1859), 41–42 (hereafter *Papers Relative II*).
67 Proclamation, December 2, 1859.
68 Proclamation, February 14, 1859, in *Papers Relative II,* 65–66, ss 1–2.
69 Douglas to Lytton, February 19, 1859, CO 60/4, 3826, *Colonial Despatches.*
70 Douglas to Lytton, July 4, 1859, CO 60/4, 8579, *Colonial Despatches.*
71 Herman Merivale, notes on Douglas to Lytton, July 4, 1859. Merivale, among other things, was the author of "Lectures on Colonization and Colonies" (1841). See, generally, David T. McNab, "Herman Merivale and Colonial Office Indian Policy in the Mid-Nineteenth Century," *Canadian Journal of Native Studies* 1, 2 (1981): 277–302.

72 See notes on Douglas to Lytton, July 4, 1859.

73 Merivale to Land and Emigration Commissioners, September 2, 1859, CO 60/4, 8579, *Colonial Despatches.* House of Commons, "Commission under the Royal Sign Manual Appointing T.F. Elliot and Robert Torrens, Esquires, and the Honourable Edward E. Villiers, Land and Emigration Commissioners," January 10, 1840, Proquest Parliamentary Papers, https://parlipapers.proquest.com/parlipapers.

74 Thomas Murdoch to Merivale, Permanent Under-Secretary, September 23, 1859, CO 60/5, 9516, *Colonial Despatches.*

75 Murdoch to Merivale, September 23, 1859. Most, if not all of these fears, in fact, would be realized in British Columbia.

76 Handwritten notes of Arthur Blackwood to Merivale on Murdoch to Merivale, September 23, 1859. See also handwritten notes of the Duke of Newcastle on the same letter and of Frederick Elliot, the Assistant Undersecretary in the Colonial Office, on draft, Merivale to Emigration Commissioners, February 24, 1860, CO 60/6, 10396, *Colonial Despatches.*

77 See Captain Andrew Clarke's letter and attached draft Order-in-Council: Clarke to Under-Secretary of State, "Monday" 1859, received October 18, 1859, CO 60/6, 10396, *Colonial Despatches.*

78 Notes of the Duke of Newcastle on Murdoch to Merivale, September 23, 1859.

79 Colonel R.C. Moody to Douglas, August 13, 1859; Moody to Douglas, August 14, 1859; Moody to Douglas, August 15, 1859, all at BC Archives (BCA), Colonial Correspondence, GR-1372, Lands and Works Department, July to September 1859, file 917/39; Moody to Douglas, September 14, 1859, ibid., file 917/27; and Moody to Douglas, September 28, 1859, and Moody to Douglas ("Private"), September 28, 1859, ibid., file 917, Proclamation no. 17, January 4, 1860.

80 Douglas to Gold Commissioners and Magistrates of British Columbia, copy of a circular, October 1, 1859, BCA, GR-1372, Douglas, James (Governor) 1859, file 485/8f.

81 Douglas to Moody, October 7, 1859, ibid.

82 Ibid.

83 Douglas to Newcastle, October 18, 1859, CO 60/5, 12499, *Colonial Despatches.* In the trial judgment in *Delgamuukw,* Chief Justice McEachern reviewed the chronology of colonial land ordinances in the Colony of British Columbia, including this letter and the subsequent Pre-emption Proclamation. Chief Justice McEachern noted that "the differing opinions of Douglas and the Colonial Office about selling unsurveyed land was impeding settlement in the mainland colony" but that "Douglas believed that he had tacit permission to proceed with arrangements permitting occupation without survey": *Delgamuukw v British Columbia* (1991) 79 DLR (4th) 185 (BCSC).

84 Douglas to Newcastle, October 18, 1859.

85 Merivale's notes on Douglas to Newcastle, October 18, 1859.

86 Newcastle's notes on ibid.

87 Newcastle's handwritten notes on Douglas to Newcastle, December 17, 1859, CO 305/11, 1545, *Colonial Despatches.*

88 Ibid.

89 Proclamation no. 17, January 4, 1860.

90 Douglas to Newcastle, January 14, 1860. Chief Justice McEachern, in *Delgamuukw v British Columbia* (1991), 79 DLR (4th) 185 (BCSC), concluded that "[t]his Proclamation did not receive easy or early approval in London as had been the case with [two earlier ordinances]. The reasons for this included the fact that the Colonial Office had experienced bad results in other colonies allowing settlers onto unsurveyed land

and it accordingly referred the Governor's proposal to the Land and Immigration Commissions [sic] for study. In addition, a Captain Clark, who had some experience in Australia, had sent a letter to the Colonial Office making suggestions for the disposition of land in British Columbia. Captain Clark assumed that ... "no claims have arisen to the soil of British Columbia excepting isolated claims of the Hudson's Bay Company ... and that no Indian title exists of if any that it has been extinguished, and separate provision made for them.

"The Duke of Newcastle, after receiving the reluctant approval of the Land and Immigration Commissions [sic] allowed the Proclamation to be laid before Parliament, but declined to proceed with it pending a reply from the Governor regarding Captain Clark's proposal."

91 Newcastle to Douglas, May 7, 1860, LAC, RG 7, G8C/9, *Colonial Despatches.*

92 Douglas to Newcastle, August 24, 1860, CO 60/8, 9598, *Colonial Despatches.* In his response, Begbie makes one of the more enigmatic comments about the extinguishment of Aboriginal title in British Columbia. Captain Clarke's proposed first section established the public auction of land. In his notes, Clarke wrote that "I must at the outset remark that the proposed scheme is suggested under the impression that ... no Indian title exists, or if any that it has been extinguished & separate provision made for them": draft Order-in-Council enclosed with Clarke to Under-Secretary of State, "Monday" 1859, received October 18, 1859. Against this notation, Begbie noted, "I may also observe that the Indian title is by no means extinguished. Separate provision must be made for it, and soon: though how this is to be done will require some consideration. – From the friendly intercourse with the natives however, no serious difficulty is to be apprehended": Begbie to Douglas, April 30, 1860, 48, included with Douglas to Newcastle, August 24, 1860. Whether Douglas ever noticed this comment, buried in the middle of Begbie's extensive comments that Douglas forwarded to London, is questionable. Hamar Foster has recently discussed Begbie's notation in "Another Good Thing: *Ross River Dena Council v Canada* in the Yukon Court of Appeal, Or: Indigenous Title, Presentism in Law and History, and a Judge Begbie Puzzle Revisited," *UBC Law Review* 50, 2 (2017): 297–300. Foster concludes that "Begbie was speaking as an advisor to the executive, which he quite properly regarded as being under an obligation to extinguish Aboriginal title before land was opened for settlement" (299).

93 Douglas to Newcastle, August 24, 1860.

94 Ibid.

95 Ibid.

96 Ibid.

97 Murdoch to Rogers, Permanent Under-Secretary, November 20, 1860, CO 60/9, 10940, *Colonial Despatches.*

98 Newcastle to Douglas, December 6, 1860, LAC, RG 7, G8C/9, *Colonial Despatches.*

99 British Columbia Land Service, *Report of the Lands Service for the Year Ended December 31, 1970* (Victoria: Queen's Printer, 1971), 9, https://www.for.gov.bc.ca/hfd/library/annual/DoLFWR_LS_AR1970.pdf.

100 Douglas to Lytton, March 14, 1859, CO 60/4, 4800, *Colonial Despatches.*

101 See handwritten notes on Douglas to Lytton, March 14, 1859; Lord Carnarvon, Parliamentary Under-Secretary, to Douglas, May 20, 1859, LAC, RG 7, G8C/8, *Colonial Despatches.*

102 Douglas to Gold Commissioners and Magistrates of British Columbia, October 1, 1859.

103 Douglas to Newcastle, October 9, 1860, CO 60/8, 11678, *Colonial Despatches.*

104 Harris, *Making Native Space,* 35. See, generally, Douglas to Newcastle, October 9, 1860, 34–44; Cole Harris, "The Native Land Policies of Governor James Douglas," *BC Studies* 174 (Summer 2012): 109–17; Tennant, *Aboriginal Peoples and Politics,* 36–38; and Kennedy et al., *A Reference Guide.*

105 Douglas to Israel Powell, October 14, 1874, LAC, RG 10, vol. 3611, file 3756-1, reel C-10106.

106 Douglas to Powell, October 14, 1874.

107 Wood, Pemberton, and Weston to the Acting Colonial Secretary, October 3, 1864, BCA, GR-1372, Lands and Works Dept. (V.I.), 1864, file 907.

108 Cail, *Land, Man, and the Law,* 175.

109 Tennant, *Aboriginal Peoples and Politics,* 32.

110 Mark Hickford, "'Decidedly the Most Interesting Savages on the Globe': An Approach to the Intellectual History of Maori Property Rights, 1837–53," *History of Political Thought* 27, 1 (2006): 124.

111 Gilbert M. Sproat to Superintendent General of Indian Affairs, November 26, 1878, LAC, RG 10, vol. 3670, file 10,769.

112 Sproat to Superintendent General of Indian Affairs, October 26, 1878, LAC, RG 10, vol. 3612, file 3756-18.

113 See, for example, George Shankel, "The Development of Indian Policy in British Columbia" (PhD diss, University of Washington, 1945), 43–49; James E. Hendrickson, "The Aboriginal Land Policy of Governor James Douglas, 1849–1864" (paper presented to the BC Studies Conference, Simon Fraser University, November 4–6, 1988 [corrections to December 1, 1988]), 14–17; Fisher, *Contact and Conflict,* 151–53; Tennant, *Aboriginal Peoples and Politics,* 21–25; and Harris, *Making Native Space,* 23–24.

114 In addition to the governor, Vancouver Island had an appointed Council (commonly called the Legislative Council) and an elected General Assembly (commonly called the Legislative Assembly or House of Assembly): Hendrickson, *Journals of the Colonial Legislatures,* 1:xxvi–xxxiv.

115 Ibid., 2:155–57.

116 "House of Assembly," *The British Colonist,* March 24, 1860.

117 Hendrickson, *Journals of the Colonial Legislatures,* 2:278. The February 1, 1861, petition is enclosed with Douglas to Newcastle, March 25, 1861, CO 305/17, 4779, *Colonial Despatches.*

118 Douglas to Newcastle, March 25, 1861.

119 Ibid.

120 Ibid.

121 Ibid.

122 Murdoch to Rogers, Permanent Under-Secretary, June 12, 1861, CO 305/18, 5329, *Colonial Despatches*

123 Ibid.

124 See handwritten notes on Murdoch to Rogers, June 12, 1861

125 Murdoch to Rogers, June 12, 1861.

126 Thomas Elliot to G.A. Hamilton, Treasury, June 22, 1861, CO 305/17, 4779, *Colonial Despatches,* filed with Douglas to Newcastle, March 25, 1861, CO 305/17, 4779, *Colonial Despatches.*

127 Frederick Peel to B.F. Rogers, Permanent Under-Secretary, September 25, 1861, CO 305/18, 8612, *Colonial Despatches.*

128 Ibid.

129 Ibid.

130 Handwritten notes of Frederic Rogers on Peel to Rogers, September 25, 1861.
131 Stephen Walcott to Rogers, Permanent Under-Secretary, October 4, 1861, CO 305/18, 8941, *Colonial Despatches.*
132 Ibid.
133 Elliot's notes on Walcott to Rogers, October 4, 1861.
134 Two clerks' and Newcastle's notes on Walcott to Rogers, October 4, 1861.
135 Hendrickson, *Journals of the Colonial Legislatures,* 2:317.
136 Ibid., 2:325, 342.
137 J.D. Pemberton to W. Young, Colonial Secretary, December 5, 1861 (BCA), Colonial Correspondence, GR-1372, Lands and Works Department (V.I.) 1861, file 904.24.
138 Newcastle to Douglas, October 19, 1861, LAC, RG 7, G8C/2, *Colonial Despatches.*
139 Hendrickson, *Journals of the Colonial Legislatures,* 2:353 and 446. Hendrickson, in "The Aboriginal Land Policy of Governor James Douglas," 17, notes that the colony spent nearly £1,000 of this 1862 figure, but he surmises that the money was likely spent on roads, surveys, or presents and not on the extinction of Aboriginal title.
140 Hendrickson, *Journals of the Colonial Legislatures,* 2:419–21. I have been unable to determine to what "under the same proviso as last year" refers. See also p. 449, which itemizes an estimate of $9,700 for "Indian claims at Cowichan."
141 Hendrickson, *Journals of the Colonial Legislatures,* 3:69.
142 "House of Assembly – The Estimates," *Daily British Colonist,* February 23, 1864, reporting on the Assembly's proceedings on February 22, 1864. See journal of the House of Assembly, February 22, 1864, at which "The House went into 'Committee of Supply'": Hendrickson, *Journals of the Colonial Legislatures,* 3:77. See also "Colonial Estimates and Accounts, 1864," ibid., 3:566.
143 Ibid., 1:257.
144 Ibid., 1:258.
145 Ibid., 3:213.
146 Shankel, "The Development of Indian Policy in British Columbia," 47–48.
147 Tennant, *Aboriginal Peoples and Politics,* 26.
148 See, for example, Fisher, *Contact and Conflict,* 152–53.
149 Tennant, *Aboriginal Peoples and Politics,* 36–37.
150 Harris, *Making Native Space,* 30–34.
151 Foster and Grove, "Trespassers on the Soil," 63–74.
152 Harris, *Making Native Space,* 32; and Foster and Grove, "Trespassers on the Soil," 55.
153 Foster and Grove, "Trespassers on the Soil," 65–67.
154 Harris, *Making Native Space,* 33.
155 Tennant, *Aboriginal Peoples and Politics,* 35–36.
156 Harris, *Making Native Space,* 34.
157 *Oxford English Dictionary,* 3rd ed., s.v. "agrarian," https://www.oed.com.
158 Ibid.
159 Quoted in Hendrickson, "The Aboriginal Land Policy of Governor James Douglas," 8.
160 Hendrickson, *Journals of the Colonial Legislatures,* 2:71–72, emphasis added.
161 Ibid., 2:345.
162 Lytton to Douglas, July 31, 1858, CO 410/1, *Colonial Despatches.*
163 Douglas to Bulwer-Lytton, October 11, 1858, CO 60/1, 12180, *Colonial Despatches.*
164 Hendrickson, *Journals of the Colonial Legislatures,* 4:180–81.
165 Douglas to Powell, October 14, 1874.
166 See, for example, the Supreme Court of Canada's important judgment concerning colonial obligations in respect of Indigenous settlements in the Colony of British

Columbia (and federal obligations arising after the Colony of British Columbia joined Confederation in 1871) in *Williams Lake Indian Band v Her Majesty the Queen in Right of Canada as represented by the Minister of Aboriginal Affairs and Northern Development Canada,* 2018 SCC 4.

167 See BC Treaty Commission, "Overview," http://www.bctreaty.ca/about-us.

168 *Tsilhqot'in Nation v British Columbia,* 2014 SCC 44.

169 These are known by different names, but see, for example, the list of similar agreements at Government of British Columbia, "Forest Consultation and Revenue Sharing Agreements," http://www2.gov.bc.ca/gov/content/environment/natural-resource-stewardship/consulting-with-first-nations/first-nations-negotiations/forest-consultation-and-revenue-sharing-agreements.

170 These also are known by different names, but see, for example, the list of similar agreements at Government of British Columbia, "Incremental Treaty Agreements," https://www2.gov.bc.ca/gov/content/environment/natural-resource-stewardship/consulting-with-first-nations/first-nations-negotiations/incremental-treaty-agreements.

171 See, for example, "Canada's Aboriginal Fisheries Strategy," https://www.dfo-mpo.gc.ca/fisheries-peches/aboriginal-autochtones/afs-srapa-eng.html.

10

"The Last Potlatch" and James Douglas's Vision of an Alternative Settler Colonialism

Keith Thor Carlson

On April 27, 1864, William McColl, a retired royal engineer turned contract surveyor, was still working with Fraser Valley Indigenous leaders to identify lands to be included as Indian reserves when an editorial appeared in the *British Columbian* under the headline "The Last 'Potlatch.'" In the article, John Robson directs vitriol at the man who had provided McColl with his instructions – the outgoing governor, James Douglas.[1] Setting himself up as the voice of British Columbia's emergent settler colonial population, Robson works his prose to undermine Douglas's authority by suggesting the governor's well-known empathy and sympathy for Indigenous peoples had caused him to betray the interests of white colonists and, by extension, the future of British Columbia:

> The Last "Potlatch" – It is pretty generally known that shortly before vacating Government House Sir James Douglas held a grand "Potlatch" at which most of the Indians living in the Lower Fraser were present, and amongst whom, as was his Excellency's wont, "biscuit and molasses" were distributed. But it would appear that on this occasion something more was *potlatched,* as several of the Sumas white settlers are down, who aver that seven or eight miles square, including their ranches, were given to the Indians on that day! We hope this affair is susceptible of a satisfactory explanation; but certainly it wears an awkward aspect at the present time. Several thousand dollars have been expended upon the ranches by some of the settlers in the district, and by one fell swoop, to throw so large a tract of settled country into the hands of the Indian would almost seem like seeking to create trouble between the white settlers and natives.[2]

Imbedded in the editorial are not only thinly veiled threats that Douglas's policies, if left unchecked, would provoke white settlers to violence but also what contemporary political analysts would call "dog whistle" call-outs to British Columbia's rising settler colonial political base. In accusing Douglas of "potlatching" to Indians property that settler colonial logic regarded as properly belonging to whites, the newspaper editor (and, it should be noted, future provincial premier) was implying that the old Hudson's Bay Company (HBC) trader had "gone Indian"; he was also implicitly reminding readers of the governor's African ancestry and the Cree and Métis genealogy of his wife, Amelia Connolly.

In the eyes of the disgruntled white settlers of Sumas and those of the editor of the colony's leading newspaper, Douglas had attempted to chart a course antithetical to securing their financial fortunes, and that course was inconsistent with the advancement of British society and civilization. And, of course, as has been well documented, under Douglas's successor, Frederick Seymour, the settler colonial base consolidated control over the formal instruments of government to such a degree that within three years Douglas's personal commitments to Indigenous peoples had been dismissed, his directives to McColl (who died shortly after completing the work) discredited, and the legitimacy of the Indian reserves disavowed. By 1867, Fraser Valley Indian reserves had been reduced by 92 percent (and even larger reductions occurred to Indian reserves in the Interior).

Today, with classic settler colonialism firmly entrenched and its handmaiden, racism, having consistently enabled its goals, it can be difficult to imagine a time when alternatives were genuinely possible. The fragility of white racial identity implicit in Robson's comments, however, hints at a profound insecurity in the minds of colonial settlers in the early 1860s.[3] This is not to suggest that Douglas was any less interested than Robson in attracting immigrants to British Columbia to build the colony's economy or that he resisted the idea of white British immigrants gaining access to, and control over, lands and resources. As Robert Cail, Peter Carstens, Paul Tennant, and Cole Harris have each persuasively argued, Governor James Douglas worked to implement a liberal political and economic order, and he believed in that order's inherent superiority to other economic and political systems – including Indigenous ones. Rather, what caused anxiety among settlers was Douglas's vision of a settler colonialism that was not predicated on assumptions of Indigenous peoples' racial inferiority serving as a structural barrier to their meaningfully engaging with modernity.

Douglas was attempting to create an alternative expression of settler colonialism in British Columbia that was distinct from any other that had been attempted elsewhere in North America, and it was profoundly different from what would ultimately be implemented in British Columbia after his retirement. Understanding the personal and the political factors that enabled and empowered his vision, as well as the forces that thwarted it, puts us in a position to contribute to contemporary conversations aimed at dismantling settler colonialism and building meaningful reconciliation between Indigenous and non-Indigenous residents located on the geography and within the polity referred to as Canada.

To that end, at least two questions emerge. How did Douglas come to conceive of such a drastically alternative vision of settler colonialism, and what convinced him that his ideas would be workable in British Columbia and acceptable to imperial authorities back in London? Finding answers requires an appreciation of the extent to which Douglas interpreted the Colonial Office's approval of his innovative actions to mitigate violence between Indigenous people and miners during the summer of 1858 as signalling its confidence not merely in his ability to protect British sovereignty from American expansionists but also its support for his vision of a colonial society in which Indigenous peoples would hold and exercise distinct Indigenous rights as well as racial equality with white settlers. Helping to contextualize this examination, historian Adele Perry has examined Douglas's biography to shed light on the way race was negotiated on the fringes of the British Empire.[4]

In this essay, I posit that in the eyes of Governor James Douglas (and, indeed, in the eyes of most of the Indigenous population on the Mainland with whom he directly conversed), British Columbia between April 1858 and May 1864 was not yet understood to be a settler colonial society. Rather, it was at most a nascent settler colonial society, one pregnant with settler colonial potential but whose settler colonial fate had yet to be sealed. British Columbia during Douglas's tenure as governor was, in other words, liminal (in a state of transition; a state of *becoming* – but where what it was becoming was still uncertain and filled with possibilities that caused worry among those who took settler colonialism for granted).[5]

For colonists such as Colonel R.C. Moody, Colonial Secretary Arthur Birch, Chief Commissioner of Lands and Works Joseph Trutch, and others of their ilk, there was no question that British Columbia was destined to be a settler colony, and as good settler colonists who stood to profit from that transition, they sought to hasten its arrival. But for Douglas, evidence suggests that while the liminality was apparent (i.e., he recognized that the territory of British Columbia was certainly *becoming* something), the specific form and expression of what was emerging was less clear and less certain. More to the point, he genuinely believed that he possessed both the insight to design the structure and the political power to implement the systems that the new colonial society would assume. And he was confident that the Colonial Office approved, or at least did not disapprove, of his vision.

Thus, what appears increasingly clear is that Douglas's power and authority was representative of not only a peculiar set of circumstances (American miners on the lower Fraser) but a particular time in British imperial history (one that was rapidly passing by the time he was put in charge of British Columbia). Historians of the British Empire have long made the case that the global expansion of British military and economic power allowed all sorts of people who did not fit into English "proper" society to find an avenue for advancement and social recognition in the periphery – from the Scots who dominated Indian administration to the ne'er do wells who made money in Jamaica. But Douglas's story reveals that a more accurate version of this would be to say that it was the long era of empire pursued by commercial mercantile companies that provided this opportunity. These companies – the East India Company, the West Africa Company, the Hudson's Bay Company, and others – relied on whomever they could find to run their enterprises. They were often little concerned with the race and class (and sometimes even character) of the people they inserted into various levels of administrative authority. And, of course, they were well accustomed to engaging with Indigenous peoples, either as allies with whom political agreements were needed or as independent contractors with whom predictable labour policies were required to help ensure corporate profits. Neither of these arrangements mitigated the increased tendency towards regarding Indigenous peoples largely as obstacles who needed to be displaced or assimilated.

This was the context of empire that enabled someone with James Douglas's social and racial background to achieve the particular authority he did in 1858. But by the time Douglas was being ushered into retirement in 1864, such a milieu was rapidly waning. The increasingly racialized idea of a natural order in which white British society sat atop a pyramid of civilization to which those relegated to the lower rungs were expected to aspire was now providing a moral authority to those who sought to undo what Douglas had established. In this way, settlers' views of the inherent correctness and inevitability of a settler colonial order where Indigenous peoples were displaced from their lands and marginalized from decision-making processes that affected Indigenous bodies and lands were given a cloak of moral authority. Douglas, therefore, existed as a liminal figure in a liminal world where non-Indigenous settlers felt comfortable dismissing him as anachronistic and his vision of the future as hopelessly fantastic and contrary to the economic interests of colonial society.

Setting the Scene

The scholarship on colonial-era Indian policy in British Columbia is both deep and robust. Starting in earnest with the works of the anthropologist Wilson Duff in the 1960s, James Douglas's Indian policies on the Mainland have been the subject of careful study and reflection. Both Duff and historian Robin Fisher (who mentored under Duff at UBC) have each explored what they both determined was the distinguishing feature separating Douglas's policies on Vancouver Island from those on the Mainland – that is, the governor's abandonment of treaty making. Without sufficient financial reserves to extinguish Aboriginal title, Duff and Fisher argue, the generally well-meaning Douglas instead opted to create larger reserves, the geographic extent of which Indigenous peoples could identify for themselves. This good will, however, quickly dissolved in the early 1860s, when nefarious representatives of settler development interests took over the reins of power and conveniently argued that Indigenous peoples neither deserved nor required extensive tracts of agricultural land. These interests, led subtly by Arthur Birch, the colonial secretary, and boldly represented by Joseph Trutch, the chief commissioner of lands and works, quickly undermined Douglas's directives by disavowing the actions of those who enacted them.[6]

Conducting research at roughly the same time, Robert Cail was more interested in the social systems and the bureaucratic institutions that gave shape and expression to colonial society and expressions of colonial power than to the personality or private corporate interests of the men who alternatively collaborated and bickered within those systems. In his assessment, the differences between Douglas's policies and those of Joseph Trutch were ones of degree not direction. For Cail, "both Douglas and Trutch ... merely reflected trends in the status quo" – a status quo characterized by nineteenth-century liberalism designed to defend the priorities of settler colonial society. Similarly embracing a structuralist approach to British Columbia's history, Peter Carstens picked up where Cail left off

(Cail died tragically while completing his PhD) to conclude that "the personality of Douglas should not be considered relevant, and we should look to the wider socio-economic implications of colonial rule for insights" if we want to understand the way Indian policy unfolded in British Columbia's colonial era.[7]

In 1990 political scientist Paul Tennant charted an interpretive path that drew from both these historiographical genealogies. He recognized, for example, the power of the socioeconomic forces of liberalism while acknowledging examples of meaningful individual agency within this system. His assessment of the evidence suggested that Douglas had actually abandoned the idea of dealing with Indigenous title long before the 1858 Fraser River Gold Rush propelled him into the governor's chair on the Mainland and that, as governor, Douglas was much more susceptible to the pressures of the colony's emerging economic elite than Duff and Fisher had been willing to concede. Early efforts to create relatively large reserves for Indigenous peoples on the the Mainland were abandoned without much resistance from Douglas, Tennant posited, once it became clear that colonial society wanted all Indigenous lands and would be satisfied with nothing less.[8]

More recently, Cole Harris has shown that "even [Douglas's] mainland policies evolved during his few years as governor" and that how they have been interpreted has been complicated by the fact that Douglas's "statements about them were not always consistent."[9] What is most innovative about Harris's approach is that he situates British Columbia's colonial-era Indian policies within the body of theoretical postcolonial literature to highlight the multiple ways in which power was projected (discursively, administratively, cartographically, militarily, and so on).

As a historical geographer, Harris is principally concerned with assessing the ways in which power was mustered to displace Indigenous peoples from their territories so as to consolidate their actions and influence onto tiny Indigenous spaces (Indian reserves). Harris recognizes the way social, cultural, and economic systems restricted people's ability to act, but he is likewise attuned to the agency people had within those systems, especially figures such as James Douglas who, Harris argues, believed in a universal humanity that rendered race, culture, and ethnicity porous. Douglas's views reflect "liberal humanitarian values" that, unfortunately for Douglas, were a waning philosophical force within London's Colonial Office when he assumed the governorship.[10] James Douglas believed that regardless of (he would likely have phrased it "despite") skin colour or pedigree, all people had the ability within the span of a single lifetime (as opposed to the potential over multiple generations of evolution) to become meaningful participants in colonial society. Harris is careful to point out that Douglas's relatively liberal views did not erase the fact that he carried prejudices common to British traders and settlers; rather, even with these prejudices, Douglas could envisage a future world where assimilated Indigenous peoples participated successfully within colonial society.[11]

Harris's work and the growing body of postcolonial scholarship of which it is a part inform my discussion here. I accept, for example, the premise of Patrick Wolfe and Lorenzo Veracini that settler colonialism is an expression of colonial power distinct from other forms of colonialism (such as the extraction colonialism that occurred under British colonial rule in India or Italian colonial rule in Ethiopia). In settler colonialism, Indigenous peoples were valued less for how their labour could be exploited to enrich colonists back in imperial metropolises than for how their land and resources could enrich an inevitably growing resident population of colonial settlers. These first-generation settlers knew and understood that they were taking land and resources from Indigenous peoples, so they designed and implemented tactics that would alienate Indigenous peoples from their territories and disenfranchise them from politics. "Indians," to early settler colonists, were a problem, an impediment to accessing coveted agricultural lands and mineral and forest resources. Over time, subsequent generations of settlers came to regard themselves not as creating a colonial society but as inheriting a settler colonial one. For them, Indigenous peoples who had already been displaced and marginalized were less a problem than they were people with problems. Consequently, an important insight emerging from settler colonial studies is the recognition that settler colonialism is an ongoing structure of domination that has not ended. Thus, to the extent that contemporary non-Indigenous Canadians (and Americans, and Australians, and New Zealanders, and so on) do not regard Europe or Asia or Africa as homes to which they can return, settler colonialism is intractable.[12]

Settler colonialism was additionally built upon a convenient myth. Historian Brian Dippie has shown that North American Indian policy prior to the early twentieth century was based on the premise that Indigenous peoples were a doomed race destined either to physically disappear or, at a minimum, to culturally and legally assimilate. And politicians and developers did not necessarily need to point to the steadily declining Indigenous demographics throughout the nineteenth century to justify their assumptions. "Proof" of the myth's veracity could be found in the novels, poetry, and art that settler colonial society created to characterize itself.[13]

In British Columbia, where in 1862 a smallpox epidemic devastated Indigenous populations in almost all parts of the colony, except the lower Fraser River where Catholic missionaries had been able to administer vaccinations, settler colonists were emboldened to take a host of actions and inactions that, in turn, served to accelerate Indigenous population decline and political and economic marginalization. Unanticipated Indigenous population rebound since the 1930s has thus disrupted and confounded one of the key logics of settler colonialism and exposed as cruel self-serving hypocrisies the rationales that were used to justify residential schools, Indian reserves, the banning of cultural traditions, the denial of the franchise, and a host of other initiatives. The implications of this today are that the dubious legal and ethical means used to displace Indigenous peoples from their lands cannot be swept away or forgotten in a world where Indigenous peoples continue to survive and find new ways to exist not only as individuals but as collectives with distinct cultures and worldviews intact.

Historical studies that reveal the complexities and nuances of how settler colonialism came to be imposed in different geographies and among different Indigenous groups, therefore, can shed light on the fissures and fracture lines within contemporary settler colonialism. Understanding the structural flaws within the bricks and mortar of settler colonialism can, in turn, contribute to creative ways of thinking about and innovative ways of strategizing the dismantling of it, ideally in ways that need not be stymied by the conundrum that, today, both Indigenous and non-Indigenous peoples have a sense of belonging in the territory known as Canada. It is hoped that this essay contributes in some way to such conversations.

Douglas was familiar with the establishment of settler colonialism in other parts of the Pacific Slope and sensitive to the social consequences that accompanied it. From his time as chief factor at Fort Vancouver on the Columbia River, Douglas carried with him memories of the displacement experienced by Indigenous peoples at the sudden arrival of American homesteaders on the Oregon Trail. Douglas witnessed the aggressive actions of American settlers arriving under the dubious and constitutional legality of the Donation Land Act, which sparked a war between the United States military and Indigenous communities in Puget Sound and the

Columbia Plateau in 1855–56. Additionally, we also know that Douglas was aware of both the threat posed by American miners and the fact that most miners were by definition transient and tended to abandon a region once the gold fields had played out.[14] And fresh in Douglas's mind was the difficulty he had experienced as governor of Vancouver Island in attracting British agricultural settlers to populate the new colony. These factors undoubtedly raised questions in Douglas's mind as to the pace with which mainland British Columbia *might* become a bustling agricultural and industrial society with a large and permanent non-Indigenous population, as well as concerns about what burgeoning settler colonialism might imply for the future of British Columbia as a British space.

Historian Adele Perry has illustrated that Douglas's life story, though distinctive in many details, reveals him to have been a typical man of the fur trade who grew up inculcating sensibilities that were common of biracial families located on the geographic fringe of the British Empire. Her work allows us to be increasingly confident in regarding Douglas's sense of liberal humanism as having been informed at least in part by the fact that his grandmother Rebecca Ritchie was a British Guyana woman of African descent who, through initiative and a skilful navigation of Caribbean colonial economics, went on to own black slaves herself.[15] Likewise, both Perry's and historian Sylvia Van Kirk's analyses of the written records Douglas and his family left to posterity reveal the extent of his love for his wife, Amelia, and his respect for his mother-in-law, Miyo Nipay (a Cree woman raised on the bison hunts of the prairies who, after a strategic marriage, saw her children become prominent figures in the bicultural world of Red River Métis society).[16] We know from Perry's review of documents associated with court proceedings that Douglas shared deeply the pain his wife experienced when her prominent father (and Douglas's early mentor) sought to disavow his country marriage to Miyo Nipay so that he could disinherit his children and then, as a Roman Catholic, (re)marry a (second) wife, who was white.[17] And together, Perry's and historian Jean Barman's examination of Douglas's diary and personal papers reveal the extent to which he agonized over whether his daughters, Cecilia and Martha, would be disqualified from respectable British society because of their father's and mother's ancestry.[18]

It is these disjunctures that make Douglas's efforts to shape Indigenous-settler relations in colonial British Columbia so compelling and revealing. But such personal biographical insights tell only part of the story.

Complimenting and complicating Douglas's position is the exceptional scope of executive authority bestowed on him by the Colonial Office as well as the feedback Douglas received from top Colonial Office officials in the early years of his tenure highlighting their confidence in what they regarded as Douglas's unique ability to steer British Columbia into the future. These matters, I believe, enabled Douglas's sense of his own ability as someone who could create a new and different settler colonialism than existed elsewhere.

This situation gave Douglas a sense that the present and future of British Columbia could be different from the past and present of California, Oregon, and Washington – settler colonial sites where violent wars had recently been waged by settler militias and the American army alike to ensure the displacement and marginalization of Indigenous peoples. For Douglas, from his liminal position, there were opportunities to imagine different British Columbias – alternative settler colonialisms. He rejected the inevitability of a future in which Indigenous peoples would be restricted to merely huddling on tiny Indian reserves. Rather, his vision was for a society where self-governing Indigenous peoples would continue to hunt and fish on unclaimed forests, meadows, streams, lakes, and ocean beyond their reserves and, importantly, where Indigenous peoples would become self-sufficient, prosperous Christian farmers, labourers, property owners, and, eventually, business leaders, people who would participate meaningfully in the colony's political and economic life.[19]

Others have pointed out that Douglas envisaged Indigenous people acquiring fee-simple title to farm lands, but overlooked are his successful efforts to protect certain mining lands for Indigenous people's exclusive use. Insights into this aspect of Douglas's historical consciousness are provided through colonial-era documentary records as well as through Indigenous oral histories – oral histories that have too often been ignored.

Power and Authority in the Summer of 1858

Officials in the Colonial Office in London were well aware that the earlier contestation with Mexico had facilitated the 1848 annexation of Mexican Alta California by the United States (and that the 1849 Gold Rush had then sparked massive American migration to the region). Likewise, fresh in their memory was the unprecedented influx of American farmers into the Oregon Territory in the 1840s, which had resulted in Britain losing rights to more than half of what had previously been jointly claimed territory with the United States. Thus, the arrival along the lower reaches of the Fraser and Thompson Rivers of more than thirty thousand mostly American gold miners from California in the spring and summer of 1858 caused the secretary of state for the colonies, Sir Edward Bulwer-Lytton, not a little anxiety. But if, as historian James Hendrickson has noted, the rush presented the Colonial Office with "both a threat and an opportunity," less well understood is how that perception also created possibilities for James Douglas.[20]

Lytton was not displeased when he learned that James Douglas, from his base in Victoria where he held the dual positions of governor of the Colony of Vancouver Island and chief factor of the Hudson's Bay Company's vast Columbia District on the mainland north of the United States,[21] had started issuing proclamations asserting the Crown's domain over the territory's gold and requiring miners to acquire licences. Although his legal authority to do so was dubious, the quick action reminded Lytton of Douglas's competencies and convinced him of the merits of appointing him governor of the new Colony of British Columbia and of investing in him special authority no longer associated with senior administrators of settler colonies within the British Empire. That is to say, unlike on the neighbouring Colony of Vancouver Island, where his executive authority was constrained by both a legislative and an executive council, in British Columbia Douglas was about to be appointed the colony's sole executive as well as its sole legislator.

One particular initiative by Douglas especially caught Lytton's attention, and his positive reaction to Douglas's recounting of it perhaps did more than anything else to convince Douglas not only that he had Colonial Office support for his Indian policies but also that the British government approved of his taking creative steps to shape the future of the colony in ways that would potentially distinguish it from emerging settler colonial societies elsewhere in western North America. The incident occurred in early June 1858. Writing to Lord Stanley on the fifteenth of that month, Douglas described his actions relating to a dispute that had broken out between white miners and Indigenous people at a site on the Fraser River that the miners had informally christened "Hill's Bar." Arriving on the scene just as violence was erupting, Douglas interceded by refusing the miners exclusive rights to the land and affirming the rights of Indigenous people. He also appointed Indigenous people as government agents and magistrates on terms that provided them agency and a meaningful degree of responsibility and authority as interlocutors with colonial society:

> The quarrel arose out of a series of provocations on both sides, and from the jealousy of the savages who naturally feel annoyed, at the large quantities of gold taken from their country by the white miners ...
>
> I lectured them soundly about their conduct on that occasion, and took the leader in the affray, an Indian, highly connected in their way, and of great influence, resolution and energy of character,[22] into the Government service, and found him exceedingly useful in settling other Indian difficulties ...
>
> I also appointed Indian Magistrates, who are to bring forward when required any man of their several Tribes, who may be charged with offences against the Laws of the country, an arrangement which will prevent much evil ...
>
> I also spoke with great plainness of speech, to the white miners ... I refused to grant them any rights of occupation to the soil and told them distinctly that Her Majesty's Government ignored their very existence in that part of the country which was not open for the purposes of settlement, and they were permitted to remain there merely on sufferance; – that no abuses would be tolerated, and that the Laws would protect the rights of the Indians no less than those of the white man.[23]

Several weeks later, at a different gold bar, Douglas intervened in another skirmish between Indigenous people and miners that had resulted in the deaths of two Americans and was threatening to escalate into a wider affray. On this occasion, as he explained to Lytton, the Indigenous people "made no secret of their dislike of their white visitors." The "Indians," he explained, had

> laid claim to a particular part of the river, which they wished to be reserved for their own purposes ... a request that was immediately granted, the space staked off, and the miners who had taken claims there, were immediately removed and public notice was given that the place was reserved for the Indians, and that no one could be allowed to occupy it without their consent.[24]

Together, these two incidents suggest the potential breadth of Douglas's emerging vision for a colonial society where Indigenous peoples would be meaningful players in both economics and politics. In the first letter,

Douglas waited until the last paragraph to discuss the geopolitical issues of British sovereignty and the land rights of non-British miners – issues that would have been forefront among the concerns of officials in the Colonial Office. In the initial paragraphs, Douglas (who at this time was still without official jurisdiction) highlights two innovative actions that would have been regarded as provocative by any Brit or American familiar with the recent Indian wars in Washington and California. By adopting an influential Indigenous leader into the government's service, Douglas was undeniably seeking to co-opt Indigenous power, but more than that, he was also signalling to Indigenous peoples that, at least to some extent, he respected their existing governance structures and saw them as being not incompatible with colonial governance.

His second action, appointing Indigenous people as magistrates, was even more creative. While there can be little doubt that in doing this Douglas was motivated in large part by a desire to gain influence within Indigenous communities by arming certain individuals with authority derived from the British Crown, his action additionally spoke to Douglas's sense of the competencies of Indigenous peoples at that moment in time, and not merely to their aptitude for acculturation.

In the second letter, Douglas describes his creation of what for all intents and purposes was the first Indian reserve on the Mainland (and what in the broader context of the history of British colonialism on the Pacific Coast was the first Indian reserve not associated with the negotiation of a treaty). The bargain that Douglas struck to resolve the conflict on the shore of the Fraser River illustrates his sense of the legitimacy of Indigenous peoples' interests in land and resources (in this case, gravel bars and gold) beyond their immediate village sites, cultivated fields, and subsistence-associated harvesting and provisioning sites. Indigenous peoples' interests, for Douglas, should not be considered only when their traditional hunting, fishing, and gathering interests were being threatened but also when their interests in a commercial commodity were being compromised. Likewise, Douglas's effort to recognize Indigenous peoples' stake in protecting as-yet untapped gold for themselves, and in adapting Western technology (e.g., sluices and gravel rockers) to allow them to partake in commercial resource extraction, indicated a recognition on his part that Indigenous rights need not be tied to precontact subsistence or cultural activities. Indeed, prior to the gold rush, Douglas had suggested to HBC officials that it would be in both Britain's and Indigenous peoples' interests to leave gold mining in Indigenous hands.

Meanwhile, back in London, news of the American miners' bellicosity was trickling in from a variety of sources. Sensitivity to Mexico's recent inability to stay American expansion in California, and memories of the HBC's impotence in stemming the flow of Yankee pioneers to Oregon, highlighted for London officials just how tenuous was Britain's ability to project power against a large and growing American population. If largely transient American men were the problem, loyal British settler families were, for officials in the Colonial Office, the first and most obvious solution. In a letter dated July 1, 1858, Lytton told Douglas, all "claims and interests must be subordinated to that policy which is to be found in the peopling and opening up of the new country, with the intention of consolidating it as an integral and important part of the British Empire."[25]

Additionally, on July 31, 1858, having become aware of Douglas's innovative actions in creating reserve lands for Indigenous miners and appointing Indigenous people as government agents and magistrates, Lytton penned a dispatch to Douglas encouraging him to follow a humane policy towards "the Natives." Significantly, in the letter, Lytton explains to Douglas that, ultimately, it would be Douglas who would have to determine how best to interpret and apply imperial instructions on the ground:

> I have to enjoin upon you to consider the best and most humane means of dealing with the Native Indians. The feelings of this Country would be strongly opposed to the adoption of any arbitrary or oppressive measures towards them.
>
> *At this distance and with the imperfect means of knowledge I possess, I am reluctant to offer as yet any suggestion as to the prevention of affrays between the Indians and the Immigrants. This question is of so local a character that it must be solved by your knowledge and experience, and I commit it to you in the full persuasion that you will pay every regard to the interests of the Natives which an enlightened humanity can suggest* ... Above all it is the earnest desire of Her Majesty's Government that your early attention should be given to the best means of diffusing the blessings of the Christian Religion and of civilization among the Natives.[26]

If after reading this letter, Douglas retained doubt as to whether officials in London would approve of his actions towards Indigenous peoples, a second letter, dated August 14, 1858, must have allayed any remaining anxieties. In it, Lytton confirms that he approves of Douglas's policies and assures the soon-to-be governor of the British government's support in whatever reasonable measure he devises to protect Indigenous peoples, regulate their relations with non-Indigenous people, and facilitate Indigenous peoples' transition to self-supporting agriculturalists:

> *I highly approve of the steps which you have taken, as reported by yourself, with regard to the Indians.* It is in the execution of this very delicate and important portion of your duties that Her Majesty's Govt. especially rely on your knowledge and experience obtained in your long service under the Hudson's Bay Co. *You may rely on their support in the execution of such reasonable measures as you may devise for the protection of the natives, the regulation of their intercourse with the whites and whenever may be commenced, their civilization.*[27]

Whether Lytton was specifically approving of the underlying strategic elements of Douglas's vision, along lines similar to the way I have interpreted them above, or whether he was signalling his approval of the on-the-spot tactics Douglas used to prevent costly and embarrassing conflicts between Indigenous peoples and Americans for fear that they might lead to American efforts to annex the region will likely never be known. But the possibility that Douglas understood Lytton as endorsing his larger vision of a genuinely alternative form of settler colonialism is likely and well within the realm of possibility. Certainly, at a minimum, Douglas would have felt greatly empowered when he learned from Lytton in the coming weeks not only that he was the British government's choice for governor of the proposed new British mainland colony but also that the Colonial Office's vision for British Columbia, at least for the short term, would be a Crown colony in which Douglas would govern with incredibly far-reaching discretionary powers unencumbered by either a legislative or executive assembly.

It was late July 1858 when the secretary of state for the colonies fully apprised the veteran HBC trader of his plans. Lytton reiterated that he saw the American miners as a political threat, and so the apparatus of representative government would be "temporarily" withheld in British Columbia until "by the growth of a fixed population the materials for those Institutions shall be known to exist."[28] In Parliament, Lytton clarified that "the immediate object" in providing Douglas with his exceptional powers was "to establish temporary law and order amidst a motley inundation of immigrant diggers ... of whom perhaps few if any, have any intention to become resident colonists and British subjects."[29]

From Douglas's perspective, the evidence suggests, a permanent population of loyal British farmers was not the only solution to the threats posed to British imperial interests by American Manifest Destiny. In addition, and in the meantime, Indigenous people themselves could help stem the tide of American expansion. Recent events had revealed that Indigenous people had no love for the Boston men who dug for gold. Their interests, Douglas believed, coincided with those of Britain.

Two letters that arrived from Lytton, each dated August 11, 1858, spoke to the confidence the secretary had in Douglas's judgment. In the first, Lytton states that to accomplish his mandate Douglas must *"take without hesitation such steps as you may deem absolutely necessary."* In the second letter, Lytton reassures Douglas that despite not yet having received a formal Order-in-Council confirming his powers as governor, Douglas should *"continue ... to act as you have hitherto done ... and take without hesitation such steps as you may deem absolutely essential."*[30] Such feedback could only have reinforced in Douglas a sense of his potency as an agent with the potential to create a settler society that reflected his personal sensibilities.

Back in London, Lytton did not want to be criticized for delaying democracy indefinitely, and so the Act to provide for governance in British Columbia contained a clause clarifying that the life of Douglas's executive rule would expire at the end of 1862. But the fact that the Colonial Office as late as 1862 (four years later) saw fit to arrange for a new Order-in-Council that reaffirmed the ongoing "very serious and unusual extent" of the powers invested in Douglas could only have served to reaffirm in Douglas's mind that his ability to govern was as exceptional as the historical circumstances that had thrust him into the governorship in the first place.[31]

Importantly, however, if it was the perceived threat that American miners posed to British sovereignty that provided the context for Douglas being invested with an unusually broad political power, it was in large part the threat the American miners posed to Indigenous people that informed the way Douglas initially conceived of, and then exercised, those powers. More to the point, it was concerns over Indigenous people's safety (albeit no doubt in large part as related to how a failure to protect Indigenous peoples might adversely affect the government's reputation among the British population) that informed the way colonial officers discussed that power with Douglas in official correspondence.

Starting in May 1858, increasingly gruesome reports of violence by miners against Fraser River Indigenous peoples were making their way back to London. By early August, news had reached Britain describing how hundreds of well-armed and organized American miners had embarked on what one of the leaders of the self-declared militias described as a "war of extermination" against Indigenous peoples between Lytton and Yale.[32] The Indigenous peoples themselves, along with some of the less bloodthirsty Americans, were ultimately responsible for bringing peace to the region.[33] But Douglas played a role. As historian Daniel Marshall has shown, Douglas – as the conduit for official communications with the Colonial Office – made sure that Lytton appreciated his contribution to preventing a race war from expanding (if not actually preventing it from happening).[34]

A little over a month later, on September 2, Lytton composed a short letter in which he reminded Douglas that the subject of the "treatment of the Native Indians" was one "which *now demands your prompt and careful consideration.*"[35] Included in his missive was a copy of a letter from Britain's Aborigines Protection Society "invoking the protection of Her Majesty's Government on behalf of these people." In its letter, the society warned the Colonial Office that the predominantly American population participating in the mining probably regarded Indigenous lives in British Columbia "as cheaply as they have, unfortunately, down in California" and, further, that "unless wise and vigorous measures be adopted by the representatives of the British Government in that Colony, the present danger of a collision between the settlers and the natives will soon ripen into a deadly war of races, which could fail to terminate as similar wars have done on the American continent, in the extermination of the red man." The society therefore regarded the need for "Her Majesty's Government to adopt measures to protect the Indians against this class of diggers" as being "too obvious to require any further illustration or argument."

The Aborigines Protection Society's letter explained further that it appreciated that Indigenous peoples were well aware of their rights to the land:

> It is certain that the Indians regard their rights as natives as giving them a greater title to enjoy the riches of the country than can possibly be possessed either by the English Government or by foreign adventures. The recognition of natives rights has latterly been a prominent feature in the aboriginal policy of both England and the United States. Whenever this principle has been honestly acted upon, peace and amity have characterized the relations of the two races, but whenever a contrary policy has been carried out, wars of extermination have taken place; and great suffering and loss, both of life

> and property, have been sustained both by the settler and by the Indian. We would beg, therefore, most respectfully to suggest that the Native title should be recognized in British Columbia, and that some reasonable adjustment of their claims should be made by the British Government ... No nominal protector of aborigines, – no annuity to a petted chief, – no elevation of one chief above another, will answer the purpose. Nothing short of justice in rendering payment for that which it may be necessary for us to acquire, and laws framed and administered in the spirit of justice and equality can really avail.[36]

Lytton, however, was at pains to make Douglas understand that while the British government shared the society's concerns for Indigenous peoples' safety and rights, that did not mean he was recommending that Douglas necessarily follow the society's recommendations as to how best to accomplish this. But nor was he suggesting that Douglas chart a course separate from that outlined by the society. Indeed, ambiguity was lightly sprinkled throughout Lytton's missive. One can only speculate as to how Douglas interpreted the statement "I beg to observe that I must not be understood as adopting the views of the Society as to the means by which this [i.e., the protection of Indigenous people, or the protection of Indigenous rights and interests?] may best be accomplished."[37] What is certain is that facing the prospect of governing British Columbia with neither a local legislative council to challenge his decisions nor a hovering imperial overseer in far-off London dictating policy, Douglas could be forgiven for thinking that Lytton was giving him the freedom to shape a colonial future that included Indigenous peoples.

Likely reinforcing his sense of what might be possible was a line in a second dispatch from Lytton dated that same day, September 2, 1858, that accompanied the formal Order-in-Council legitimating Douglas's political authority on what is now the Mainland. In the letter, Lytton reminds Douglas not only of the unusual circumstances that had led to his being invested with such broad powers but also of the heavy responsibilities that accompanied those powers and, implicitly, in his trust in Douglas's abilities to exercise them:

> These powers are indeed of a very serious and unusual extent ... You are aware that they have only been granted in so unusual a form on account of the very unusual circumstances which have called into being the Colony committed to your charge, and which may for some time continue to

> characterize it. To use them except for the most necessary purposes, would be in truth to abuse them.[38]

Douglas took some time to contemplate the contents of the September 2 letters. It was not until November 5, 1858 (less than two weeks before he took the oath of office as governor), that he composed his reply. By then, the spectre of open warfare that had hovered over the gold fields during the summer months had dissipated. But there can be little doubt that Douglas's thinking about how best to protect Indigenous peoples' interests was informed by what he regarded as his successes during those previous months:

> While you do not wish to be understood as adopting the views of the [Aborigines Protection] Society as the means by which that [protection] may be best accomplished, you express a wish that the subject should have my prompt and careful consideration, *and I shall not fail to give the fullest effect to your instructions on that head,* as soon as the present pressure of business has somewhat abated. I may, however, remark that *the Native Indian Tribes are protected in all their interests to the utmost of our present means.*[39]

To better appreciate what Douglas meant by this, we can look to text he composed as part of a separate dispatch to Lytton a month earlier. In it, Douglas refers back to the comment Lytton had made in his letter of July 31, wherein the secretary emphasizes that it was Her Majesty's government's priority to see Douglas devise means to "diffuse the blessings of the Christian Religion and of civilization among the Natives." Douglas notes that, indeed, he had

> already taken measures as far as possible to prevent collisions between those tribes and the whites, and have impressed on the miners the great fact that the law will protect the Indian equally with the white man, and regard him in all respects as a fellow subject. *That principle being admitted will go far towards the well being of the Indian Tribes.*[40]

For the next month, both Douglas and Lytton were preoccupied with setting up the administrative apparatus of the new colony, particularly finding ways to create revenue streams for government. But that did not mean that for each of these men the issue of Indigenous peoples' place in an emerging settler colony did not remain a priority. On December 10, 1858, Lytton, inspired by George Grey's rationale that relocating a community of nomadic Indigenous people in South Africa into permanent villages would facilitate their transition into civilization, sent an unexpected letter to Douglas inquiring if a similar policy might work in British Columbia. Pointing to what he considered the success of Douglas's Indigenous policies to date, Lytton posited that settling Indigenous peoples "permanently in villages civilization at once begins. Law and Religion would become naturally introduced amongst the red men, and contribute to their own security against the aggressions of immigrants."[41]

The fact that Lytton did not understand that most of the Indigenous peoples along the coastal regions of British Columbia and Vancouver Island already lived in large permanent villages throughout the winter months speaks to how uninformed the Colonial Office was about its far Pacific Coast North American colonies. The lacunae in the secretary's knowledge, however, were not something Douglas saw fit to raise in his reply. Instead, Douglas embraced the opportunity implicit in the South African model to begin conceiving broad structural change as a component of his own Indigenous policy. Additionally, citing efforts by certain settlers to bypass his office to deal directly with Indigenous peoples over land, and with specific reference to events on Vancouver Island and his discussions with the House of Assembly there, on February 9, 1859, Douglas wrote the first of two letters to the secretary of state for the colonies in which he articulated the specific elements of what had become a cohesive and comprehensive "Indian" policy:

3. Attempts having been made by persons residing at this place to secure those lands for their own advantage by direct purchase from the Indians, and it being desirable and necessary to put a stop to such proceedings I instructed the Crown Solicitor to insert a public notice in the Victoria Gazette to the effect that the land in question was the property of the Crown, and for that reason the Indians themselves were incapable of conveying a legal title to the same, and that any person holding such land would be summarily ejected.
4. ... I have informed the House of Assembly [Vancouver Island Colony] of the course I propose to adopt with respect to the disposal and management of the Indian Reserve at Victoria; that is to lease the land, and to apply all the proceeds arising therefrom for the exclusive benefit of the Indians.
5. ... *[I]t will confer a great benefit on the Indian population, will protect them from being despoiled of their property, and will render them self-supporting, instead of being thrown as outcasts and burdens upon the Colony.*[42]

A month later, on March 14, 1859, Douglas provided the second of his two missives outlining the pragmatics of his policy. In it, after cloyingly referring to Lytton's idea of settling Indigenous peoples in villages, he moves on to discuss what for him was the more important element of the vision, namely, a system that would tackle racial inequality and prevent Indigenous peoples from being degraded by settler colonialism.

It is important to recognize that key features in the early paragraphs of this letter are aimed at addressing the specific crisis associated with the Songhees Reserve in Victoria on Vancouver Island; Douglas was, of course, still serving as governor of that colony, where he was legislated to work with a legislative assembly. But as the later paragraphs make clear, Douglas considered his solution to the Songhees situation useful in giving form and expression to a broader policy that would address the growing crisis of conflicting Indigenous-settler land use on the Mainland:

> I have much pleasure in adding, with unhesitating confidence, that I conceive the proposed plan [to move people onto village settlements] to be at once feasible, and also the only plan which promises to result in the moral elevation of the native Indian races, in rescuing them from degradation, and protecting them from oppression and rapid decay. It will, at the same time, have the effect of saving the Colony from the numberless evils which naturally follow in the train of every course of national injustice, and from having the native Indian tribes arrayed in vindictive warfare against the white settlements ...
>
> ... The [Songhees] Indians should be established on that reserve, and the remaining unoccupied land should be let out on leases at an annual rent to the highest bidder, and that the whole proceeds arising from such leases should be applied to the exclusive benefit of the Indians.
>
> *... [A]ny surplus funds remaining over that outlay, it is proposed to devote to the formation and support of schools, and of a clergyman to superintend their moral and religious training ...*
>
> *The support of the Indians will thus, wherever land is valuable, be a matter of easy accomplishment, and in districts where the white population is small, and the land unproductive, the Indians may be left almost wholly to their own resources, and, as a joint means of earning their livelihood, to pursue unmolested their favourite calling of fishermen and hunters.*
>
> *Anticipatory reserves of land for the benefit and support of the Indian races will be made for that purpose in all districts of British Columbia inhabited by*

> *native tribes.* Those reserves should in all cases include their cultivated fields and village sites, for which from habit and association they invariably conceive a strong attachment, and prize more, for that reason, than for the extent or value of the land.
>
> *In forming settlements of natives, I should propose,* both from a principle of justice to the state and out of regard to the well-being of the Indians themselves, *to make such settlements entirely self-supporting, trusting for the means of doing so,* to the voluntary contributions in labour or money of the natives themselves; and secondly, to the proceeds of the sale or lease of a part of the land reserved, which might be so disposed of, and applied towards the liquidation of the preliminary expenses of the settlement …
>
> I would, for example, propose that every family should have a distinct portion of the reserved land assigned for their use, and to be cultivated by their own labour … that they should be taught to regard that land as their inheritance; *that the desire should be encouraged and fostered in their minds of adding to their possessions, and devoting their earnings to the purchase of property apart from the reserve, which would be left entirely at their own disposal and control; that they should in all respects be treated as rational beings, capable of acting and thinking for themselves;* and lastly, that they should be placed under proper moral and religious training, and *left, under the protection of the laws, to provide for their own maintenance and support.*[43]

Acting quickly to communicate and implement his plans for creating Indian reserves, on March 25, 1859, Douglas shared his letter to Lytton with the members of the Vancouver Island Legislative Council. Though the Island Assembly had no legal jurisdiction on the Mainland, these settler representatives typically owned land in both colonies and regarded themselves as the voice of settler interests in both places. Much of the information in Douglas's address therefore pertained to the Colony of British Columbia. To this body he explained *"that he had made anticipatory Reserves in the various districts, including the Cultivated fields & village sites of the Indians"* and that *"he proposed that the Indians shd. Be located on certain parts of those Reserves, & the remainder be leased & the proceeds applied to their temporal and spiritual elevation"*; he recommended that this "system" should eventually become "self-supporting."[44]

Responding to Douglas on April 11, 1859, and clearly indicating the Colonial Office's vision of harmonized policies on the Island and

Mainland, the Earl of Carnarvon (writing in the absence of Lytton as secretary of state for the colonies) indicated his agreement with the plan:

> *Proofs are unhappily still too frequent of the neglect which Indians experience when the white man obtains possession of their country, and their claims to consideration are forgotten at the moment when equity most demands that the hand of the protector should be extended to help them.* In the case of the Indians of Vancouver Island and British Columbia, Her Majesty's Government earnestly wish that when the advancing requirements of colonization press upon lands occupied by members of that race, measures of liberality and justice may be adopted for compensating them for the surrender of the territory which they have been taught to regard as their own. Especially I would enjoin upon you, and all in authority in both colonies, *the importance of establishing schools of an industrial as well as an educational character for the Indians, whereby they may acquire the arts of civilized life which will enable them to support themselves, and not degenerate into the mere recipients of eleemosynary* [i.e., charitable] *relief.* If it is to be hoped that by such and other means which your experience will enable you to devise, the Indians may in these, the most recent of the British settlements, be treated in a manner worthy the beneficent rule of Our Gracious Sovereign.[45]

Thus, we see in Douglas's March 1859 correspondences a more complete articulation of the vision whose seeds had been sown the previous summer in his response to contestation on the gold bars of the Fraser River and then refined in the communications between himself and Lytton. His plan would protect space for Indigenous peoples to live unmolested and self-supporting, but, importantly, these reserves were also to be anticipatory reserves. In setting the boundaries of reserves, Douglas was expressing that government agents needed to ensure that they included sufficient land to accommodate not only Indigenous people's needs based on their current traditional subsistence activities but also sufficient land for individual families to cultivate crops or raise animals in a manner that enabled them to accumulate sufficient financial resources, which they could subsequently use to purchase additional fee-simple land off reserve. Lands within the reserve could, therefore, be genuinely thought of as "anticipatory" in that, until such time as they were being used for cultivation purposes by Indigenous peoples themselves, they could be leased out to non-Indigenous people, with the money being retained by the community for its own use.[46]

This was a vision of a colonial society that was dramatically different from the settler colonial societies Douglas had knowledge of elsewhere in North America. In this model Indigenous people were not segregated away from the white settler society. Nor were they compelled to assimilate and integrate on terms dictated by settler society – that is, on the bottom rung of a racial hierarchy. In the gold fields of the Fraser River Douglas had seen, and acknowledged, Indigenous peoples' interest in, and rights to, the resources of their territory. He was aware that many Indigenous people were eager to engage not simply in subsistence farming but in the commercial marketing of western introduced crops and livestock. But he was sensitive to the fact that many, and perhaps most, Indigenous people were not interested in giving up a traditional lifestyle and becoming farmers or full-time wage labourers – at least not yet. In Douglas's mind, these people needed time, but in taking their time he did not believe that they should be penalized or have future opportunities diminished. The anticipatory reserve system provided communities with land that they could immediately use for farming, or could lease out to non-Indigenous people in anticipation of the time when they themselves might be interested in farming.

Over the coming years, as Robin Fisher and Cole Harris in particular have documented, Douglas found it necessary to tweak certain tactical elements of his overall strategy and policy. In particular, he determined this was essential because Colonel R.C. Moody, in his capacity as commanding officer of the Royal Engineers (whom, to Douglas's chagrin, London dictated were the only people permitted to perform government surveys in the colony)[47] and chief commissioner of lands and works (where he determined the sequencing of surveys throughout the colony), consistently worked to undermine Douglas's authority and vision. Moody's opposition took four forms:

1 Passive aggression (simply not doing what Douglas directed and then later when questioned providing excuses that Douglas clearly regarded as unsatisfactory).[48]
2 Undermining the tactical elements of Douglas's policy by inserting caveats into the governor's directives.[49]
3 Undermining Douglas's strategic capacity by sending covert letters to senior officials in London criticizing Douglas's competencies.[50]
4 Discrediting Douglas's legitimacy as governor within British Columbia and Vancouver Island settler society by creating and contributing to a

> discourse of gossip that highlighted Douglas's racial ambiguity and his lack of cosmopolitan sensibilities.[51]

It was in light of this opposition that Douglas occasionally communicated his Indigenous policy and his visions for the future of Indigenous peoples in British Columbia directly to Indigenous peoples themselves. Certainly, the archival records are replete with documentary evidence of Indigenous people travelling to either New Westminster or to Victoria to lay before the governor their concerns and complaints about people such as Moody and settlers who were moving into their territory from Britain and the United States. Some of the most detailed records we have of Douglas's conversations with Indigenous people come from the governor's own hand.

On October 9, 1860, for example, while travelling throughout the colony, Douglas wrote to the Duke of Newcastle, describing his communication with, and commitments to, the Indigenous peoples he met along the way. Stopping at Cayoosh (present-day Lillooet), he attended the trial of two Indigenous men charged with the murder of two Asian miners. One man was acquitted, the other convicted of manslaughter following an "indecent assault" on the Indigenous man's wife by the Asians. Whether because of the trial or because word had spread of the governor's visit, there were "great numbers" of representatives of multiple Indigenous nations in attendance. It was to these crowds that Douglas explained:

> I made them clearly understand that Her Majesty's Government felt deeply interested in their welfare, and had sent instructions that *they should be treated in all respects as her Majesty's other subjects; and that the local magistrates would attend to their complaints, and guard them from wrong,* provided they abandoned their own barbarous modes of retaliation, and *appealed in all cases to the Laws for relief and protection ...*
>
> I also explained to them that the Magistrates had instructions to stake out, and reserve for their use and benefit, all their occupied village sites and cultivated fields, *and as much land in the vicinity of such as they could fill, or was required for their support; and that they might freely exercise and enjoy the rights of fishing the Lakes and Rivers, and of hunting over all unoccupied Crown Lands in the Colony; and that on their becoming registered Free Miners, they might dig and search for Gold, and hold mining claims on the same terms precisely as other miners: in short, I strove to make them conscious that they were recognized members of the*

> *Commonwealth, and that by good conduct they would acquire a certain status, and become respectable members of society.* – They were delighted with the idea, and expressed their gratitude in the warmest terms, assuring me of their boundless devotion and attachment to Her Majesty's person and the Crown, and their readiness to take up arms at any moment in defence of Her Majesty's dominion and rights.[52]

Continuing on the same journey, Douglas next stopped at Lytton, where, he recorded, "the Indians mustered in great force." His communications with them, he explained to Newcastle, "were to the same effect as to the Native Tribes who assembled at Cayoosh; and their gratitude, loyalty, and devotion, were expressed in terms equally warm and earnest."[53]

The second portion of Douglas's trip is described in a separate letter to Newcastle, dated October 25, 1860. In it, Douglas explains that he travelled from Lytton to Similkameen and then to Rock Creek. Along the way, he

> fell in with detachments [of Indigenous peoples] at different points of the route, where they had assembled to offer a rude but cordial welcome.
>
> I received them with every mark of respect and kindness, entered freely into conversation with the Chiefs, assuring them of the warm regard of Her Majesty's Government, and leading them into the discussion of their own affairs in order to discover if they entertained any real or fanciful grievance which might lead to dissatisfaction, or induce them to make reprisals on the white settlers.
>
> *There was one subject which especially pre-occupied their minds, as I discovered by frequent allusions they make to it, namely the abject condition to which the cognate Native Tribes of* Oregon [contemporary Oregon and Washington States] *have been reduced by the American system of removing whole Tribes from their native homes into distant reserves where they are compelled to stay, and denied the enjoyment of that natural freedom and liberty of action without which existence becomes intolerable. They evidently looked forward with dread to their own future condition, fearing lest the same wretched fate awaited the natives of British Columbia. I succeeded in dis-abusing their minds of those false impressions by fully explaining the views of Her Majesty's Government, and repeating in substance what I have in a former part of this report informed your Grace was said on the subject to the assembled Tribes at Cayoosh and Lytton.* Those communications had the effect of re-assuring their minds and eliciting assurances of their fidelity and attachment.[54]

In Douglas's accounts of his conversations with Indigenous peoples, we are provided not only with his clearest explanations of his Indigenous policies but also descriptions of what he thought Indigenous peoples' future would look like within the colony society he was establishing for British Columbia. His descriptions outline a society in which Indigenous peoples would be recognized as full members of the Commonwealth, not only legally but socially. As the original residents of the territory that had now become a British colony, they retained their rights to continue their traditional hunting and fishing activities over the vast geography that remained unoccupied by settlers. Additionally, as Indigenous peoples, they were entitled to have lands reserved and set aside for their exclusive use. These Indian reserves would include more than simply their villages and existing cultivated fields: they would be large enough to accommodate future anticipated uses – and such uses were not to be restricted to traditional precontact activities. Importantly, they did not need to wait for Moody's Royal Engineers to arrive to conduct formal surveys before their reserves would be identified and demarcated. Magistrates tasked with treating them without prejudice or bias would be the ones who would work with Indigenous peoples to identify their lands. Indigenous peoples were also encouraged to engage fully with the emerging resource-extraction industries – no legal barriers would prevent them from becoming miners. And unlike what had happened to their neighbours to the south (where the Dart and Stevens Treaties had relocated Indigenous peoples onto land reservations away from prime agricultural lands), they would be permitted to continue residing in their Traditional Homelands.[55]

Given the record Douglas left in the archives, it is not at all difficult to understand why the Indigenous people who heard Douglas articulate his vision would later recount that the governor had

> said for which land I have surveyed it belongs to the Indians only, that no white men shall intrude on your land. And for all the outside lands Her Majesty Queen Victoria will take and sell to the white people and that which is taken away from the Indians will be like a fruit tree and from this fruit Her Majesty Queen Victoria will give it to the Indians for their lasting support.[56]

Indeed, Douglas's explanations to the Indigenous peoples of what they could now expect and what they could expect in the future were consistent with his earlier articulations to the Colonial Office. But they additionally contained phrases that provide clearer windows into his conception of race and identity within settler colonialism. He was careful to explain that the way people lived their lives (what we would today call culture) did not affect people's legal status under British law. The only exception to this was intercommunity warfare ("barbarous modes of retaliation"), which, by its very nature, was contrary to the peace and order of society.

While there can be no doubt that Douglas aspired for Indigenous peoples to become Western-educated Christians who owned private property and participated in the colonial economy, he did not make these prerequisites for being entitled to the protection (and associated obligations) of the British law – as did legislation in the United Canada colonies, as reflected in the Gradual Civilization Act of 1857 (which, when amalgamated with the Graduate Enfranchisement Act of 1869, became the Indian Act of 1876, which was applied to all First Nations people across the Canadian Dominion). In other words, as a collective within the settler colony that Douglas was building, all Indigenous people would not only retain some of their Indigenous rights but would acquire the rights of British subjects, no different than the white, British-born, and immigrant residents of the colony.

But, importantly, while race provided no barrier to the full rights of British subjecthood, Douglas anticipated and expected that an individual's behaviour would largely determine social "status" within the colonial order. Here, we see a principled aspirational statement by a man who during his years in the fur trade had come to respect the initiative, hard work, sobriety, and good behaviour of others, regardless of whether they were Scots, English, Canadian, Métis, or Iroquois. Further, "by good conduct," Douglas explained to the Indigenous peoples of British Columbia that "they would acquire certain status and become respectable members of society." *Would* not *could*.

Douglas was not pretending that in the future other people (white people) would not continue to be ascribed status by virtue of having being born into good families, or by virtue of economic wealth, or by virtue of having had access to elite schools. What he was acknowledging was that there were things, such as race, over which one had no control and that did not, in his view, determine character. While one could not change the colour of one's skin or alter the position that one's birth into a particular family ascribed within the social hierarchy, one could, presumably, demonstrate through one's conduct that one was deserving of status and in that way become a respectable and respected member of society. A century before Dr. Martin Luther King Jr., Douglas was envisaging a world in which white privilege would erode as people came to judge others less according to the colour of their skin and more according to the content of their character.

There can be little doubt that to some extent Douglas's aspirations for Indigenous peoples was derived from his own personal experience. Historiographically, however, the bigger riddle is what ultimately came to curb the political potency and social optimism that Douglas felt so keenly during summer and autumn 1858. What was it, in other words, that undermined what he initially regarded as his ability to be an agent capable of creating a different kind of settler colonial society? What is clear is that it was not the motley band of American diggers that Lytton worried would compromise British sovereignty but rather the very men (and their spouses) that Lytton had sent to help Douglas build the colony, men who wielded white privilege as if it were a sword made by their own hand from materials given them by God.

As Adele Perry's research has revealed, Colonel Moody held Douglas in disdain, and so did the colonel's wife, Mary. Her private letters to her mother in England reveal the way racial prejudice and metropolitan snobbery worked to undermine the status of anyone not of the correct birth: "I had a visit from the Gov:r today. I don't get over his formal politeness at all. He certainly is not 'the right man in the right place.' I do wish they wd send us another or make [my husband] Richard Gov:r. I sh:d not object to that!!!"[57] Even more revealing are quotes from the diary of Victoria's Anglican bishop, George Hills. During a trip to London just a few months after Douglas's visit to Cayoosh and other First Nations communities, Hill made a point of visiting the Colonial Office, where he and several other disgruntled settler colonists made it their business to ensure that the officials were aware of what they regarded as Douglas's shortcomings, principally, his naïveté, which Hill ascribed to Douglas's unfamiliarity with metropolitan life: "The Governor is a fine specimen of a loyal Englishman, but never having seen a Dock, or a Railway he could not be up to the day, but of his integrity there could be no doubt." A year earlier, Hills had recorded in his journal that Douglas's "appointments have been of persons subservient to himself & not men of independent feeling and high intelligence." As Perry notes, the Anglican bishop felt this could be attributed "partly to his [Douglas's] never having lived in England or in any civilized community."[58]

Potlatch Reconsidered

When John Robson, the editor of the *British Columbian,* accused James Douglas of having held a "grand 'Potlatch'" and of having "given ... seven or eight miles square ... to the Indians," he was not only articulating the sentiments of British Columbia's aspiring white settler colonial population, he was also reflecting British and American ignorance concerning the Indigenous meaning of *Potlatch* (a Chinook Jargon word meaning "to give"). The nineteenth-century Coast Salish Potlatch was, and remains today, a gift-giving ritual at the centre of a ceremonial system of wealth distribution that historically affirmed compacts of sharing between people with different types of riches. Potlatches took several forms, but the most common was initiated when two families from different tribes arranged a marriage between their children with the goal of securing access to resources (fishing sites, berry patches, *wapatos* (potatoes), shellfish, and so on) that were either unavailable or scarce within their own territory.[59] Quite the contrary of impoverishing one community at the expense of another, Coast Salish potlatching actually enriched by ensuring that wealth resources that were more "available at one place than another, and more in one season than another, and often more in one year than another" became accessible to those whose tribal territories lacked specific resources.[60] By definition, Potlatch ceremonies transformed in-laws in one generation into blood relatives in the next. Ironically, the concept of Potlatch as it was understood by the Coast Salish leaders who heard Governor Douglas articulate his vision of an alternative expression of settler colonialism, and who had secured from Douglas the promise that McColl would demarcate their reserve boundaries in 1864, actually embodies important elements of the spirit and intent behind Douglas's Indigenous policies.

From Douglas's perspective, Indigenous peoples and British settlers were entering into a long term relationship. His vision was to ensure that it was mutually enriching and sustaining. Each side would give, and in return each side would ultimately be assured of receiving more than it had originally conferred. The reciprocation would be ongoing, and, as part of the arrangement, both settler communities and Indigenous communities would give up certain privileges to secure mutual advantages.

Under the system Douglas envisaged, the sacrifices would not necessarily have been symmetrical, nor the advantages equally shared. But for the system to work, incoming settlers would have to abandon the idea that all the land and resources within the colony would be theirs alone, with none left for the Indigenous population; they would need to also give up their belief that being members of the white race set them apart as inherently superior to Indigenous peoples. And, of course, settler colonists would be expected to invest financial resources and import Western technologies into the colony, creating new economic, industrial, agricultural, and commercial opportunities that would, theoretically, benefit Indigenous peoples and settlers alike.

On the other side, under Douglas's vision, Indigenous peoples would be expected to abandon any sense that they would be left alone as the sole occupants of their Ancestral Territories and sole users and managers of their Ancestral Resources. In exchange for sharing access to, and authority over, lands and resources, Indigenous peoples would be investing in their own future and, therefore, could anticipate ongoing benefits. As part of the exchange, Indigenous peoples would be expected to embrace a degree of change within their spiritual, social, political, and economic ways of thinking and acting – but this, in Douglas's vision, was an accommodation that would be conducted at least in part on Indigenous terms and on an Indigenous schedule. Transition was inevitable, but it was not intended to be coercive nor violent.

In this regard, my interpretation of Douglas's vision differs from that of Cole Harris. In Harris's view, Douglas "held that the only long-term solution for Native people in a settler colony was their assimilation … within white settler society."[61] The evidence seems clear to me, however, that Douglas did not envisage for British Columbia a settler colonial society as then currently existed elsewhere in North America. Rather, in his view, the future could be much more hybrid and much less intolerant of, and less assimilative towards, Indigenous peoples and culture. In this alternative settler colonialism, individual First Nations communities could accommodate themselves to, integrate into, and generally help influence and shape British Columbia society, at their own speed (or at least until expanding settler development compelled a response). They would, in other words, retain a meaningful degree of social, political, economic, and cultural agency and autonomy.

Douglas would have been the first to concede that the pressure on Indigenous peoples to become part of the expanding colonial system would have been great and would only increase over time. But nothing indicates that he would have compelled people to change if they were not so inclined themselves, and his decision in January 1864 to protect giant tracts of land for Indigenous peoples right in the centre of British Columbia's most easily accessible and desirable agricultural lands (such as the 9,400-acre Matsqui Reserve in the central Fraser Valley) indicates that he was willing to see this happen despite settler interests to the contrary. Thus, not only would Indigenous peoples be able to continue governing themselves and continue potlatching with and among one another, but they would additionally become participants in the emerging new colonial society and have roles to play in its administration.[62] Importantly, First Nations traditional leaders under Douglas's system would continue to serve as representatives of their communities in interactions with colonial authorities, while First Nations individuals were additionally welcome to move off reserve to "pre-empt land as freely as the white man" and in other ways acquire private property and commodities. Such actions did not imply any reduction in an Indigenous person's Indigenous right to hunt and fish on open and unoccupied lands beyond reserve boundaries.

I am not suggesting that Douglas ever thought explicitly or in detail about how a Potlatch ceremony could serve as a metaphor and a template for the future of Indigenous-settler relations in British Columbia, but I do think it likely that Salish people interpreted aspects of Douglas's policies and actions through the lens of potlatching. Moreover, and perhaps more importantly, Douglas would have been aware that this was how Indigenous peoples would have interpreted and understood his message. Oral histories recorded throughout the last century, and that continue to circulate in Coast Salish communities today, speak to their understanding that Douglas had assured them that their own generosity towards whites would be repaid several fold in the future.

On January 10, 1915, for example, while testifying before the Royal Commission established to look into the issue of reserve lands, Chief Johnny of Chehalis (on the Harrison River) presented the following written petition to the commissioners:

> When the white men came into our country we treated them as friends and brothers as they came along. Sir James Douglas, the first Governor, made a verbally [sic] promise to us Indians on his first surveying the lands. He said for which land I have surveyed as Indian lands it really belongs to the Indians only. That no white man shall intrude in your lands, and for all the outside of your lands, H.M. Queen Victoria will take and call to the white people, and that land will be owned as a lasting fruit trees to the Indians.

Her Majesty will take the said fruits and give it to the Indians as their lasting support ... and that we shall hold just as much privilege as a white man, and that we must treat the white man the best way possible, and that we shall be treated the same way as if we were brothers. Now for this last many years standing we have been expecting to receive those good promises in the name of Queen Victoria.[63]

The following day, Andrew Phillip answered questions and elaborated on Chief Johnny's written statement:

Sir James Douglas's promises – well Douglas knew very well that this territory is an Indian territory, that is the reason he made verbal promise to us ... The BC government say we have no rights to the lands of BC and refuse to recognize our aboriginal title, and hide those good promises of Queen Victoria ... Sir James Douglas knew well that we are the aborigines – for that reason he made a verbally [sic] promise. Said for all the lands I survey as Indian Lands it really belongs to the Indians only. That no white man shall intrude in your lands, therefore we claim that no other has right to claim a share on our reserves but us Indians only.[64]

One day later, the commissioners travelled across the Fraser to Matsqui, where they heard similar things from Chief Charlie:

In the time of Sir James Douglas he made a lasting promise to us Indians, as all the Indians Reserve a lasting support and benefit by the name of Queen Victoria. Also Governor Seymour the second Governor. He also made a lasting promise to us Indians in New Westminster that we will receive or deserving one fourth from all taxes this money for our support and to improve our land. The promises were never kept ... We want to obtain a lasting and secure title to our Indian land.[65]

Two days later, on January 13, 1915, when the commissioners arrived in Chilliwack, they were informed by Chief Harry that

[i]n the early days we used to hold more land than what we are holding today. Yes, this bargain which has been made by the first Chief, and the first Governor Sir James Douglas, and this land in Chilliwack which has been surveyed by Sir James Douglas and surveyed a second time and now it has been surveyed over for the third time and it has left us with very little land

> which now shows on the map. This is why we say to-day that the BC Government has taken our land away from us – that is why our land is too small for us to-day.[66]

The following day, when the commission met at Skowkale, Chief Billy Sepass commented:

> This last fifty years what has become of it [my reserve], or where the changes have been made I cannot get an understanding – The only people that I see is white settlers in this reserve which belongs to me. I haven't got the slightest idea of how this is being changed or transacted. Sir James Douglas was the one that surveyed this property for us. The grievances which I am laying before you is what I have already said. After this reserve was surveyed for me by Sir James Douglas from then I came to learn that there would be compensation made to us Indians for all the land in the Province ...
>
> I made my complaint to Sir James Douglas and I wish these lands to be returned back to me. If I got compensation I would not ask for the return of these lands.[67]

And then, several years later, in 1921, the following statement by Fraser Valley Salish leaders was recorded by the ethnographer and political activist James Teit:

> If this original reserve given to us by Gov. Douglas had not been taken from us there would now be no trouble about lands, for we would have had enough, and perhaps a little for sale ... It is not the Indian's fault that the neighbouring country is now all taken up by whites and that it is now hard to get land for the Indians. This matter of adequate reserves should have been settled many years ago before there was much settlement.[68]

These oral histories describe Indigenous populations that were not afraid of the changes that were coming because they believed that the vision Douglas articulated would adequately (but not perfectly) account for their long-term interests. They believed him when he said that they would become like "brothers" with the British settlers. Significant portions of the land outside of their reserves would be gradually lost, but Indigenous peoples would retain the right to hunt and fish on open and unclaimed lands. And in return for sharing access to their territories, Indigenous peoples would additionally receive financial compensation and meaningful social and economic opportunities. Meanwhile, the lands included within the reserves would be sufficient to grow crops, raise stock, and accumulate capital, thereby facilitating Indigenous peoples' anticipated transition into self-sufficient and commercially successful farmers and ranchers.

The archival records are not sufficiently detailed to permit us to say with certainty the extent to which Douglas's actions and policies towards Indigenous peoples were motivated by his own sense of racial vulnerability, or the degree to which his detractors sense of their own racial fragility might be credited with inspiring them in their efforts to undermine Douglas's plans. As noted, Adele Perry has pointed out that Douglas's life, with its complex racial intersections, was common in the fur trade era, even typical. But having someone with his background and his sensibilities rise to a position of political power during the critical period when settler colonialism was establishing itself was anything but typical. Indeed, it was unprecedented. So, too, was the scope of power invested into Douglas as a governor of a Crown colony by the Colonial Office, in that it lacked even the appearance of any sort of local responsible government – that is, any check on executive prerogative by the settler colonial population.

If London's objective in bestowing such power was primarily to protect vulnerable British sovereignty from the threat of American expansion, the lens through which Douglas interpreted his mandate was in important ways shaped and informed by his sense of his and his wife Amelia's own personal, economic, and professional accomplishments. Importantly, it was also a product of his sincere concern over the vulnerability of Indigenous peoples and his naive faith that the British settlers who would replace the American miners would come to respect Indigenous peoples just as the officers and employees of the HBC and later the Colonial Office had come to do with him and his family. Nothing in the archival records suggests that Douglas ever perceived that senior officials in the Colonial Office may have failed to share his vision and his faith in its achievability.

Importantly, for Douglas, the threat to Indigenous peoples was principally anchored in the personal prejudices and greed of settlers (as opposed to the liberal economic order that he was charged with building). His confidence in the correctness and inevitability of Western Christianity, economics, and society was too solid for him to imagine a future that was not part of that system. He saw liberalism as inevitable, and he saw it largely as good – as progress. But he did not see it as something that would immediately or even quickly eclipse Indigenous systems of government and economics. There would be a period of transition when the two systems would not only exist side by side but, importantly, would inform each other. Thus, unlike both the American miners and the newly transplanted elites of the British colony (men such as Moody), Douglas did not see Indigenous peoples as incompatible with the emerging liberal settler order. And more to the point, he felt the settler order needed to be sensitive to, and responsive to, Indigenous peoples and their interests.

Douglas constructed policies and envisaged a world from within the liminality of what was still a nascent settler colonialism.[69] His vision, now more than 150 years old, was not necessarily what Indigenous peoples or their allies (people such as myself) would endorse today, but it was certainly something that Indigenous peoples then regarded as workable and that in hindsight was greatly preferable to what replaced it following Douglas's retirement. Thus, his vision is worthy of reflection again today, as Canadian society seeks strategies and tactics to dismantle and fundamentally decolonize that particular (and now typical) expression of settler colonialism that ultimately came to replace the one Douglas envisaged.

Notes

1 Robson, as a member of the Colonial Legislative Assembly, would later make a formal motion to reduce the Fraser Valley Indian reserves. He subsequently went on to serve as the ninth premier of the province of British Columbia.

2 Editorial, "The Last 'Potlatch,'" *British Columbian,* April 27, 1864. Immediately following this article was a notice that within the Legislative Assembly, "a communication from the Governor [Seymour] respecting the appointment of Mr. Trutch to the office of Surveyor General was read; also dispatches from the Colonial Office respecting the same subject. Moved by Hon. C. Brew, second by Hon. J. Orr, that this Council disapproves of Mr. Trutch holding a public office of great importance while holding interest in speculations not unconnected with the department superintended by him in the colony. Moved in amendment by Hon. J.A.R. Homar, seconded by Hon. H. Holbrook, That to the above resolution be added the words 'also while he holds large interests, public and private, in Vancouver Island.' The amendment was lost and the original motion carried unanimously. Moved by Hon. J. Orr, seconded by Hon. C. Brew, That it is requisite to purchase from Mr. Trutch the Alexandra Bridge and other interests he holds in the Colony. His Excellency be requested to appoint a party to act as arbitrator to fix the price of the same."

3 For a rich discussion of how settler anxieties shaped attitudes towards Indigenous peoples on Vancouver Island, see Kenton Storey, *Settler Anxiety at the Outposts of Empire: Colonial Relations, Humanitarian Discourse, and the Imperial Press* (Vancouver: UBC Press, 2018).

4 Adele Perry, *Colonial Relations: The Douglas-Connolly Family and the Nineteenth-Century Imperial World* (Cambridge: Cambridge University Press, 2015).

5 My use of *liminality* is informed by Homi Bhabha's writings in *The Location of Culture* (London: Routledge, 2004).

6 Wilson Duff, *Impact of the White Man* (Victoria: Royal BC Museum, 1992); and Robin Fisher, *Contact and Conflict: Indian-European Relations in British Columbia, 1774–1890* (Vancouver: UBC Press, 2014). Duane Thompson picks up the interpretive framework created by Duff and refined by Fisher, a framework that focuses on individuals, personalities, and private interests, but shifts the geographic focus of his analysis from the Coast to the Interior. See Duane Thompson, "Opportunity Lost: A History of Okanagan Reserves in the Colonial Period," *Okanagan Historical Society Report* 42 (1978): 43–52.

7 Peter Carstens, *The Queen's People: A Study of Hegemony, Coercion, and Accommodation among the Okanagan of Canada* (Toronto: University of Toronto Press, 1991), 58–59.

8 Paul Tennant, *Indigenous Peoples and Politics: The Indian Land Question in BC* (Vancouver: UBC Press, 1990).

9 Cole Harris, "The Native Land Policies of Governor James Douglas," *BC Studies* 174 (Summer 2012): 102.

10 Ibid., 104.

11 R. Cole Harris, *Making Native Space: Colonialism, Resistance, and Reserves in British Columbia* (Vancouver: UBC Press, 2002).

12 See Patrick Wolfe, *Settler Colonialism and the Transformation of Anthropology: The Politics and Poetics of an Ethnographic Event* (New York: Cassell, 1998); and Patrick Wolfe, "Settler Colonialism and the Elimination of the Native," *Journal of Genocide Research* 8 (December 2006): 387–409. More recently, Lorenzo Veracini has provided settler colonial studies with a theoretical framework. See Lorenzo Veracini, *Settler Colonialism: A Theoretical Overview* (New York: Palgrave Macmillan, 2010). Adam Baker provides an overview of settler colonialism studies in "Locating Settler Colonialism," *Journal of Colonialism and Colonial History* 13 (Winter 2012): 1–28.

13 Brian Dippie, *The Vanishing American: White Attitudes and U.S. Indian Policy* (Lawrence: University of Kansas Press, 1991).

14 The United States annexed California during the Mexican-American War of 1846–48, and gold was discovered shortly thereafter in January 1848.

15 Perry, *Colonial Relations.*

16 Sylvia Van Kirk, *Many Tender Ties: Women in the Fur Trade Society, 1670–1870* (Winnipeg: Watson and Dwyer, 1980).

17 Adele Perry, "'Is Your Garden in England, Sir?': Nation, Empire, and Home in James Douglas' Archive," *History Workshop Journal* 70 (Fall 2010): 67–85.

18 Amelia Connolly was a member of one of Red River's most elite Métis families. Through her marriage to James Douglas, she eventually became wife of an HBC chief factor and the chatelaine of the first Vancouver Island Colony and then the Colony of British Columbia. She eventually assumed the title "Lady Douglas" when James was appointed to the Order of the Bath in 1864. Yet, by the early 1860s, it was becoming painfully clear to both Amelia and her husband that their Indigenous and African ancestry were becoming liabilities. As Perry has noted, "Connolly had a limited circulation in Victoria's polite society and none in the imperial world beyond it. Indigenous women could be wives and even ladies, but their status was local, untranslatable, and contingent": Adele Perry, "James Douglas, Amelia Connolly, and the Writing of Gender and Women's History," in *Feminist History in Canada: New Essays on Women, Gender, Work,*

and Nation, ed. Nancy Janovicek and Catherine Carstairs (Vancouver: UBC Press, 2013), 23–40.

19 Hamar Foster's scholarship has likewise revealed that Chief Justice Matthew Baillie Begbie shared aspects of Douglas's vision. Begbie spoke of a future in which Indigenous peoples would be "self-supported and self-supporting" and where Indigenous people would be a "race of independent workers."

20 James Hendrickson, "The Constitutional Development of the Colonies of Vancouver Island and British Columbia," in *British Columbia: Historical Readings,* ed. W. Peter Ward and Robert A.J. McDonald (Vancouver: Douglas and McIntyre, 1981), 260.

21 Richard Mackie, *Trading beyond the Mountains: The British Fur Trade on the Pacific Coast, 1793–1843* (Vancouver: UBC Press, 1997).

22 This is likely Chief Liquitim. In Stó:lō oral histories, Liquitim is described as having worked with Governor Douglas and also as having on his own initiative negotiated a series of peace treaties with American miners during the July 1858 Fraser River War.

23 James Douglas to the Rt. Hon. Lord Stanley, Victoria, June 15, 1858, BC Archives (BCA), CO 60/1, 100684, 54–57.

24 Douglas to Edward Bulwer-Lytton, no. 3, October 12, 1858, Colonial Office 60/1, no. 12721, 213, in *The Colonial Despatches of Victoria Island and British Columbia, 1846–1871,* ed. James Hendrickson and the Colonial Despatches Project, https://bcgenesis.uvic.ca (hereafter *Colonial Despatches*).

25 "Dispatch from Lytton to Douglas, no. 1, July 1, 1858," in James Douglas; Edward George Earle Lytton-Bulwer; British Columbia, Governor; and Great Britain, Colonial Office, *Papers Relative to the Affairs of British Columbia: Part I ...* (London: G.E. Eyre/W. Spottiswoode, 1859), 41.

26 Lytton to Douglas, London, July 31, 1858, BCA, CO 410/1, 100684, 147–57, emphasis added.

27 Lytton to Douglas, London, August 14, 1858, BCA, CO 60/1, 100684, 38–49, emphasis added. Moreover, my analysis is not meant to suggest that either the Colonial Office or Douglas felt that Indigenous interests should always be placed above those of settler colonists. In May 1859, Lord Carnarvon explained to Douglas that "whilst making ample provision under the arrangements proposed for the future sustenance and improvement of the native tribes, you will, I am persuaded, bear in mind the importance of exercising due care in laying out and defining the several reserves, so as to avoid checking at a future day the progress of the white colonists." In reply, on August 15, 1859, Douglas informed the Colonial Office that "Her Majesty's Government may rest assured that due care will be taken" and that the Indian reserves being created under his plan would "in no way interfere with the progress of the white Colonists": Douglas to Lytton, Victoria, August 15, 1859, BCA, CO 60/5, 10041, 13. And, indeed, Douglas was not reluctant to compromise Indigenous rights when he felt that they conflicted with the core requirements of the non-Indigenous settler economy. At Hope, for instance, he consented to relocating Indigenous people from a village site to another thousand-acre site of their choosing farther downriver, and at Chilliwack Landing he directed that a township be laid out despite the presence of Indigenous gardens and settlement. In both these cases, the sites were considered necessary to the development of colonial travel infrastructure. See "Carnarvon, in absence of Right Hon. Sir E.B. Lytton, Bart., to Governor Douglas, C.B., London, May 13, 1859, Colonial Office 60:4, no. 4800, 47, *Colonial Despatches,* hhttps://bcgenesis.uvic.ca.

28 Lytton to Douglas, no. 6, July 31, 1858, CO 410/1, 147–57, *Colonial Despatches,* hhttps://bcgenesis.uvic.ca.

29 "Speech of Sir Edward Bulwer Lytton, Government of New Caledonia Bill, 2nd Reading, July 8, 1858," *Hansard's Parliamentary Debates,* 3rd series (London: Cornelius Buck, 1858), 1100–2.
30 Lytton to Douglas, no. 7, August 11, 1858, BCA, CO 410/1, emphasis added.
31 See Hendrickson, "The Constitutional Development," 262.
32 "British Columbia," *Times of London,* 5 August 1858. See also *San Francisco Times,* June 7, 1858.
33 See Daniel Marshall, *Claiming the Land: British Columbia and the Making of a New Eldorado* (Vancouver: Ronsdale Press, 2018). See also Keith Thor Carlson, *The Power of Place, the Problem of Time: Aboriginal Identity and Historical Consciousness in the Cauldron of Colonialism* (Toronto: University of Toronto Press, 2010), chaps. 6 and 9.
34 Marshall, *Claiming the Land.*
35 "Copy of Despatch from the Right Hon. Sir E.B. Lytton, Bart., to Governor Douglas (no. 12)," September 2, 1858, in British Columbia, *Papers Connected to the Indian Land Question* (Victoria: R. Wolfenden, 1875), emphasis added.
36 "Enclosure from Aborigines Protection Society," in "E.B. Lytton to Governor Douglas: F.W Chesson to the Right Honourable Sir Edward Bulwer Lytton, M.P., Her Majesty's Principal Secretary of State for the Colonies, London, September 2, 1858," in British Columbia, *Papers Connected to the Indian Land Question,* 12–14.
37 Lytton to Douglas, no. 12, September 2, 1858, BCA, CO 398/1, 65.
38 Lytton to Douglas, no. 16, September 2, 1858, BCA, CO 398/1, 73–87; and Lytton to Douglas, no. 20, September 2, 1858, BCA, CO 398/1, 93–99.
39 Douglas to Lytton, November 5, 1858, BCA, CO 60/1, 366, emphasis added.
40 Douglas to Lytton, no. 43, October 10, 1858, BCA, CO 60/1, 188–89, emphasis added.
41 "Right Hon, Sir E.B. Lytton, Bart., to Governor Douglas (no. 62.), December 30, 1858," British Columbia, *Papers Connected to the Indian Land Question,* 15.
42 Douglas to the Lytton, February 9, 1859, BCA, CO 398/1, 185–87, emphasis added. Five days later, on February 14, 1859, Douglas issued a proclamation that it was the Executive that held authority "at any time, to reserve such portions of the unoccupied Crown Lands, and for such purposes as the Executive shall deem advisable": "Proclamation by His Excellency James Douglas Victoria, February 14, 1859," in British Columbia, *Appendix to the Revised Statutes of British Columbia 1871 …* (Victoria: R. Wolfenden, 1871), 55.
43 "Governor Douglas to the Right Hon. Sir E.B., Lytton, Bart., Victoria, March 14, 1859," in British Columbia, *Papers Connected to the Indian Land Question,* 16–17, emphasis added.
44 "Journals of the Council, Executive Council, and Legislative Council of Vancouver Island, 1851–1866, Friday, the 25th day of March, 1859," in James Hendrickson, ed., *Journals of the Colonial Legislatures of the Colonies of Vancouver Island and British Columbia, 1851–1871,* 4 vols. (Victoria: Provincial Archives of British Columbia, 1980), 1:24–25, emphasis added.
45 Lord Carnarvon for Lytton, Secretary of State for the Colonies, to Douglas, April 11, 1859, BCA, C/AB/10.2/1, 89–93, emphasis added.
46 What Douglas may have intended by *anticipatory* in this context could have been a land base identified in advance of and in anticipation of settler arrival and localized claims to land. He may have also intended that it was acceptable for these reserves to be marked out informally in "anticipation of formal surveys."
47 See Lytton to Douglas, no. 2 and no. 8, September 2, 1858, as well as October 16, 1858, BCA, CO 398/1, 58–62, 133.
48 For example, Moody side-stepped a commitment made in Douglas's presence to provide Fraser River Indigenous peoples with official white stakes and to allow them to use

them to demarcate the boundaries of their desired reserves in advance of the arrival of formal surveyors: see Father Leon Fouquet, OMI, to Colonel R.C. Moody, December 22, 1862, BCA, GR-1372, file 584/1b, reel B-1346; Moody to Fouquet, December 22, 1862, BCA, Lands and Works Correspondence Outward, vol. 4, 54; and Fouquet to Moody, December 29, 1862, BCA, GR-1372, file 584/I, reel B-1328.

49 For example, on several occasions, Moody inserted the phrase *within reason* into instructions that Douglas had provided, which simply stated that reserve lands were to include all the lands that the "Indians" themselves identified. See "Charles Good (for Colonial Secretary) to Moody, March 5, 1861," British Columbia, *Papers Connected to the Land Question,* 21; Captain R.M. Parsons, R.E., to Moody, April 15, 1861, BCA, C/AB/30.6J/5; and Moody to E.H. Sanders, June 2, 1863, BCA.

50 Margaret Ormsby, "Moody, Richard Clement," *Dictionary of Canadian Biography,* vol. 11, Université Laval/University of Toronto, 2003–, http://www.biographi.ca/fr/bio/douglas_james_10F.html.

51 See Perry, especially Chapter 5 in *Colonial Relations.*

52 Douglas to Newcastle, October 9, 1860, BCA, CO 60/80, B-1427, 196–226, emphasis added.

53 Ibid.

54 Douglas to Newcastle, October 25, 1860, BCA, CO 60/8, no. 26, 232–55, emphasis added; and "Governor Douglas, C.B., to His Grace the Duke of Newcastle, Victoria, October 25, 1860," in James Douglas and Great Britain, Colonial Office, *Further Papers Relative to the Affairs of British Columbia: Part IV* (London: G.E. Eyre/W. Spottiswoode, 1862), 27–28.

55 For an overview of American treaty making (and breaking), see Alexandra Harmon and John Borrows, eds., *The Power of Promises: Rethinking Indian Treaties in the Pacific Northwest* (Seattle: University of Washington Press, 2009).

56 "Evidence from Hearings: Meeting with the Harrison River Band or Tribe of Indians at Chehalis I.R. #4, on Monday, January 10th, 1915," *Royal Commission on Indian Affairs for the Province of British Columbia.* Report available at https://www.ubcic.bc.ca/mckenna_mcbride_royal_commission.

57 Mary Moody to "Mamma," March 21, 1859, BCA, Mary Moody Outward Correspondence, 27, cited in Perry, *Colonial Relations,* 193.

58 George Hills, Journal, December 26, 1861, cited in Perry, *Colonial Relations,* 194.

59 Wayne Suttles, "Variation in Habitat and Culture on the Northwest Coast," *Coast Salish Essays* (Burnaby, BC: Talon Books, 1987), 32.

60 Ibid., 40.

61 See Harris, "The Native Policies of James Douglas," 103.

62 In this regard, Douglas's vision shared certain similarities with ones later articulated in H.B. Hawthorn, C.S. Belshaw, and S.M. Jamieson, *The Indians of British Columbia: A Study of Social Adjustment* (Toronto: University of Toronto Press, 1958), and by Alan Cairns in his book *Citizen Plus: Aboriginal Peoples and the Canadian State* (Vancouver: UBC Press, 2001).

63 "Royal Commission on Indian Affairs for the Province of BC, Meeting with the Harrison River Band."

64 Ibid.

65 "Evidence from Hearings: Meeting with the Matsqui Band or Tribe of Indians on Monday, January 11, 1915," *Royal Commission on Indian Affairs for the Province of British Columbia.* Report available at https://www.ubcic.bc.ca/mckenna_mcbride_royal_commission.

66 "Evidence from Hearings: Meeting with the Chilliwack Band or Tribe of Indians, at Chilliwack, BC, January 13, 1915," ibid.

67 "Evidence from Hearings: Meeting with the Skulkayn Band or Tribe of Indians, at Chilliwack, BC, January 14, 1915," ibid.

68 "Inspector of Indian Agencies – New Westminster Agency – Correspondence, Reports, Re: Bands Including Questions of Reserve Status and Valuations, Economic Situation," Library and Archives Canada, RG 10, Department of Indian Affairs, C-II-4, vol. 11302, emphasis added. Reports refer to royal commission findings and include reports of meetings in 1922 by Andrew Paul.

69 Agnes Horvath, Bjørn Thomassen, and Harald Wydra, "Introduction, Liminality and Culture of Change," *International Political Anthropology* 2, 1, (2009): 3–5.

Reflections

Robert Clifford, Stephen Hume, and Maxine Hayman Matilpi

Robert Clifford, Stephen Hume, and Maxine Hayman Matilpi were three attendees of the conference who, following Coast Salish tradition, were called to witness the events and to remember, recall, and share the messages they heard. These are their reflections.

Rob Clifford

ÍY SȻAĆEȽ. I'm Rob Clifford. I'm W̱SÁNEĆ and a member of the Tsawout First Nation. I carry the name YELḰATŦE, which comes to me from my late grandfather Earl Claxton, Sr. I study law and am working to complete my PhD in law through Osgoode Hall Law School, York University. I live at home at Tsawout while I work and write on the revitalization of Indigenous legal traditions, specifically the W̱SÁNEĆ legal order.

I was honoured to be asked by John Sutton Lutz and my cousin Nick Claxton to witness the work being done at the "First Nations, Land, and James Douglas: Indigenous and Treaty Rights in the Colonies of Vancouver Island and British Columbia, 1849–1864" conference, held at the Songhees Wellness Centre. I was welcomed as a visitor on to Songhees Traditional Territory and to hear the work and thinking that is being done by many people on the Douglas Treaties. I raise my hands and say "HÍSW̱ḰE SIÁM" to all those who attended, presented, spoke, listened, drummed, danced, shared, witnessed, provided a prayer, provided food, and opened their community to us. I also raise my hands and say "HÍSW̱ḰE SIÁM" to all those who held on to our Indigenous teachings, who passed them along to the next generation, who sat, listened, and engaged with those teachings, and to all those who, in their own ways, strive to right wrongs and to forge a better future for us all.

I often find myself reflecting upon W̱SÁNEĆ laws and teachings in both an historical and contemporary context. While damaged through colonial oppression and suppression, W̱SÁNEĆ laws remain alive, valid, and authoritative. For W̱SÁNEĆ, we speak of *ĆELÁṈEN,* our ancestry or birthright. ĆELÁṈEN includes our SENĆOŦEN language, our *S,OXHELI* (sacred teachings of life), and our *SKÁLS* (beliefs/laws) and forms a significant basis of our traditional governance structure. Our W̱SÁNEĆ culture, attitudes towards land, and our SENĆOŦEN language are therefore at the heart of W̱SÁNEĆ law. Much of this is contained in our creation stories, which are often tied to specific places and SENĆOŦEN place names. We have creation stories for the islands, lands, water, animals, plants, and other beings in W̱SÁNEĆ Territory, all of whom we view as our relatives. It is through W̱SÁNEĆ law that we honour and maintain these relationships. And it is through W̱SÁNEĆ law, and the legal orders of other Indigenous communities that are signatories to the Douglas Treaties, that we must understand the intent and application of those Douglas Treaties. So, as I sat and listened to all those involved over the course of February 24 to 26, 2017, I was struck by all those who were engaged. I heard the voices of lawyers, historians, academics, nonacademics, non-Indigenous community members, Indigenous members from various communities, from women, men, young, and old. And I knew these voices were only some of all those who attended. And of those who attended, they were only part of the larger whole who are engaged, in one way or another, in these larger issues. We, of course, need even more people to be engaged in these issues. And we, of course, may not all always agree. But in no way does that detract from all those who already are engaged and committed to building a better future together. How many gifts each of these people bring to their work and engagement.

It was at that moment I was struck by a W̱SÁNEĆ story that has been passed to me. A story I shared with all those who attended.

The bear, too, was a human being before becoming an animal. His name was SPÁEŦ. XÁLS made him to be an animal of the forest. He gave SPÁEŦ a strong body covered with fur, as well as strong teeth and claws to find his food. His warm fur and strong body were a gift to him. SPÁEŦ fished the streams and ate berries.

One day, SPÁEŦ was travelling to the hills in MÁLEX̱EȽ (Mill Bay). He reached SX̱OX̱IYEM (Willis Point) and walked to the shore. He looked across the inlet and sat on the shore thinking to himself that he would like to swim across to the other side. He thought, *If it wasn't so far he could probably make it. If the water wasn't so cold, he could probably make it across without much problem.* So SPÁEŦ sat on the shore thinking of more reasons why he

> shouldn't, and couldn't, swim across the inlet. SPÁEȾ didn't know that the Creator, XÁLS, could hear his thoughts.
>
> XÁLS appeared to SPÁEȾ. He said, "SPÁEȾ, I have given you many gifts. You have a strong body, and a thick fur coat to protect you from the cold. It is only your cowardly manner that prevents you from swimming to the other side. It is wrong to be cowardly and to not use your gifts. You should never hesitate to do something you have to do." XÁLS moved his hand over SPÁEȾ on the shore near SX̱OX̱IYEM and changed him into a huge boulder. Today, you can still see the huge boulder at that place near SX̱OX̱IYEM, which is named SPÁEȾ.

We can never be afraid to use our unique gifts to do what we know has to be done, regardless of how far our swim might appear to be.

Stephen Hume

I'm grateful to the wise men and women of the University of Victoria who organized the 2017 conference on First Nations, James Douglas, and the Indigenous and treaty rights from the beginning of British Columbia's colonial period, which continue to shape relationships on Vancouver Island more than 150 years later. I'm grateful to the Lekwungen Chiefs and Elders who generously hosted the gathering and on whose territory the proceedings took place; to the contributors from both communities who brought big-hearted sagacity; and, last but not least, to the members of the public who came to offer their own insights, to listen, and to discuss. Sometimes those conversations were passionate and visceral; sometimes rarefied, theoretical, and cerebral. None left doubt that they were part of an historic event.

For a lay observer like me to be asked to serve as one of the official witnesses to the transactions taking place according to traditional rules of order is a humbling and instructive honour. To be asked to witness at such an event is a grave responsibility. It requires a particular kind of participation. It imposes a duty not simply to observe but to become an active part of the process. It demands mindfulness; it demands presence. One must pay attention and then share the experience of what happened through the telling of its story.

Many of us caught up in the twenty-first-century technology of instant and ubiquitous communication tend to forget that stories are what we are. We tell ourselves the stories of our lives. We tell others the stories of who we think we are and who we want to be. We fill our children with stories from our own pasts, and they carry those stories into their futures to infuse their own children.

There is a saying in ancient Welsh, the endangered language of another Indigenous people pushed to the margins by powerful, globe-straddling, homogenizing, mainstream cultures. It goes: "A fo ben, bid bont." It means: "He who would be a leader; let him be a bridge."

That story tells of a long-ago chieftain who lay himself down so that his people could cross a dangerous water by walking upon his body. I learned the saying from my wife, who took up the task of learning the difficult language of her ancestors so that she could hear their stories as they were told, a reminder that no language and the stories it contains need ever be lost.

Remembrance of that saying sprang to mind in a broader context during the conference. I realized after listening to many of the presentations – scholarly, traditional, in translation, and not – that I was witnessing the building of bridges. They were bridges of knowledge; bridges of understanding; bridges of awareness; bridges of friendship; bridges of enlightenment; bridges of tolerance; bridges of acceptance; and, ultimately, bridges of reconciliation across the gulfs of past wrongs, both deliberate and inadvertent, and of current misunderstandings, both inadvertent and unconscious but sometimes wilful and deliberate too.

The past is a foreign country, observed the late scholar and historian David Lowenthal, borrowing his title from a line used in another writer's earlier novel – a story – about how we must all reconstruct our knowledge of the past from our understanding of the present and about how, no matter how keenly we observe it, we can't travel there either to experience it or to change what has already happened. We can, however, allow ourselves to become hostages to the past like Jacob Marley, the ghost in Charles Dickens's story, who is doomed to wear for eternity the chains of what he has done. But we don't have to be hostages. We have the power to change the future. In his remarkable book, Professor Lowenthal wrote about how the past – while partly a creation of the present through our reshaping of memory, through the refashioning of the significance of icons, and through the rewriting of history – nevertheless reaches towards the future. The past continues to shape the future precisely through our changing responses in the present to what we persuade ourselves once was. History – which resides in the present, not the past – is a story continually revised to serve present needs. Some aspects are expunged, some celebrated and enhanced; figures once thought illustrious are toppled from their pedestals while those once thought of little account may be rehabilitated and elevated. Residential schools, which once were regarded as beacons of enlightened policy, are now recognized as dark holes of cultural oppression and intolerance. The lustre of Sir John A. Macdonald becomes tarnished; the once-besmirched Louis Riel is burnished anew. Yet if the past has lost some of its power to justify settler privilege in the present, it's also energized political resurgence, cultural renewal, and a powerful sense of rebirth for Indigenous communities of the future.

Elders like John Elliott, Sr., Rupert Wilson, Elmer George, and Margarita James, scholars like Hamar Foster, Nick Claxton, Keith Carlson, John Sutton Lutz, and Adele Perry, leaders like Chief Ron Sam, Chief Councillor Robert Dennis, Sr., and University of Victoria President Jamie Cassels, all limned the fascinating ways in which our perceptions of the past – as characterized through the treaties signed between 1850 and 1854 – differed according to point of view, culture, and language. And yet, despite differing interpretations of what the treaties actually meant to whom, in the larger frame of awareness, treaties remain powerful symbols as well as legal instruments of agreement. They represent acknowledgment of rights. They seek to frame how we will live and deal with one another in a future for which we may hope and strive but ultimately as individuals will never know. Treaties are the figurative commitment to build bridges, however rickety or sturdy they may prove to be. Conferences like the one convened at the Songhees Wellness Centre in the bleak winter months of 2017 serve to lay more planks on the bridge. Let us hope the construction will continue in future conferences, for the alternatives are not pleasant to contemplate.

Bridges, of course, are but one way to cross troubled water. More than half a century ago, as a teenaged student at the University of Victoria, I persuaded my then girlfriend (the same woman who later taught me the Welsh saying), to drive me from Victoria to Port Alberni so that I could talk about the nature of art with George Clutesi. He was then, along with Dan George, one of those at the epicentre of cultural renewal. They were carrying forward a torch handed down from Charles Edenshaw, through Mungo Martin. And they, in turn, would hand that torch on to the Hunt family, to Bill Reid and Ron Hamilton, to Dorothy Grant and Jill Setah, whose work has moved Indigenous design from museums to the haute couture runways of New York. I knew Mr. Clutesi because the Tseshaht writer and artist, the one to whom the now renowned painter Emily Carr willed her brushes, oils, and naked canvases – and my not-long-off-the-boat immigrant father, a reporter for the since defunct *Nanaimo Free Press* – had become close friends. Two unlikely bridge builders or, as Mr. Clutesi put it, fellow paddlers on the same long journey upon which we are all embarked.

Sitting in his kitchen so long ago, he used the analogy of a canoe to reference precisely what, it struck me, the Songhees conference – where people of good will came together to talk about land, rights, colonialism, treaties, and what they signified then and signify today by way of obligation – was intended to address.

Like it or not, Mr. Clutesi said, we are all, settlers and Indigenous people alike, now sharing the same canoe. We may think we know where we have journeyed from in the past, and we may think we know where we are headed to on the uncharted ocean of the future, but one thing is certain: we can either learn to paddle together, or we can capsize the canoe and drown together. People learning to paddle together, leaders becoming bridges for their people – that is what I witnessed.

Maxine Hayman Matilpi

A Solemn Promise: Indigenous Perspectives on the Douglas Treaties

Alright Vancouver Island peeps. Listen up:

If you live on southern Vancouver Island, or in Nanaimo or around Fort Rupert (where my people, the Kwakiutl and Komoyue, call home), and whether you are Indigenous or not, you are bound by a treaty – a solemn promise made between James Douglas, representing the Crown, and one of fourteen First Nations.

These words were repeated throughout the conference "First Nations, Land, and James Douglas: Indigenous and Treaty Rights in the Colonies of Vancouver Island and British Columbia, 1849–1864," which brought together historians and legal scholars as well as Indigenous people who are direct descendants of the signatories to the Vancouver Island Treaties (a.k.a. Douglas Treaties).

Together, we had rich conversations about our profoundly different views of land and resources, as well as what it means to live under these treaties today. Because these are pre-Confederation treaties, they are foundational to Canada's Constitution and protected under section 35, but it's unclear exactly what that means on the ground.

The conference began Friday night with opening words from the keynote speaker, W̱SÁNEĆ Elder STOLȻEȽ John Elliott, Sr., who grounded us with stories. He shared an Indigenous cosmological perspective, and we were reminded of the connectedness to sacred places. This connectedness is illustrated through teachings about nonhuman beings such as the wind beings.

John told us the light, that first light we see in the morning, used to be a human being, and his wife was the Morning Star. He told us about pebbles that grew into mountains and about how, even today, some people will take one of those black stones as a prayer stone and as a reminder of the relationship to islands who are relatives – sisters – who grew from those stones that had been tossed into the ocean.

And he shared a beautiful teaching about cedar. To many people around the world, cedar is considered sacred. In my Kwakwa̱ka̱'wakw community, cedar is known as the Tree of Life, and its image is used on regalia such as button blankets and is integral to our ceremonies. Other people use cedar for medicine or prayers. John told us cedar trees were made from the kindest people and that cedar serves as a reminder of the responsibility we have to be kind to one another.

The next morning, John again reminded us of the sacred trust the Creator gave the W̱SÁNEĆ people to look after the land. "Natural resources are relatives," he said. The wind, the life in the salt water, animals, birds – all are deserving of respect, and, from a W̱SÁNEĆ perspective, we have obligations to look after them.

Through the work of John Elliott and XEMŦOLTW̱, Dr. Nick Claxton, we know the law of this land is based upon the values and beliefs included in these W̱SÁNEĆ perspectives and that laws and beliefs are inseparable. Nick reminded us that Indigenous languages such as SENĆOŦEN are the voice of the land. Songs, prayers, and place names also help us understand that relationship between humans and land.

These understandings of home and connections to the lands and waters, along with the creation stories that tell how the W̱SÁNEĆ people got here, create the context and backdrop to the Douglas Treaties. This cosmology and worldview, and the loving relationship with land, bring responsibilities. And, importantly, these perspectives come from a time long before any treaties were signed. So, from their perspective, the starting place for treaty interpretation is with the concept that land is a sacred gift from the Creator. A sacred gift from the Creator is not something that could ever be surrendered or the subject of a real estate deal.

I was never taught this in law school.

Our ancestors who signed these treaties were reasonable and reasoning people. Through stories like the ones we've been analyzing through the RELAW Project (Revitalizing Indigenous Law for Land, Air and Water), we know the signatories to the treaties cared deeply about – and were connected to – the environment around them. W̱SÁNEĆ (and other Indigenous perspectives) can benefit everyone living in treaty territory by reminding us about what it means to have an ongoing loving relationship and responsibility to the lands and waters around us.

I appreciate what Ojibwe artist and environmentalist Manzinapkinegego'anaabe/Bombgiizhik Isaac Murdoch says about treaties:

> When they signed those treaties, our Nations did not sign up for an Environmental Catastrophe. Let's unite and organize a full-on massive resistance against fossil fuels. We have nothing to lose and everything to gain. ❤ #WaterIsLife #Powertothebabies

Right now, the planet needs what Indigenous perspectives have to offer – and we all need to listen deeply, to treat the land and waters as our beloved relatives, deserving of our respect, care, gratitude, and kindness.

HA'em!

Contributors

Graham Brazier is an independent scholar with an interest in the human history of the islands in the Salish Sea. He lives on Denman Island where he co-edited "Islands of British Columbia 2004: Conference Proceedings" and, in 2010, edited and transcribed "The Fort Victoria Journal: 1846–1850."

Keith Thor Carlson holds the Canada Research Chair in Indigenous and Community-Engaged History at the University of the Fraser Valley. His research is driven by questions that emerge from within Indigenous communities. Individually and with partners, Carlson has authored or edited eight books and over fifty articles, among which are *A Stó:lō-Coast Salish Historical Atlas* (2001); *The Power of Place the Problem of Time: Aboriginal Identity and Historical Consciousness in the Cauldron of Colonialism* (2010); and *Towards a New Ethnohistory: Community-Engaged Scholarship History among the People of the River* (2018).

Robert YELḰÁTŦE Clifford is a doctoral candidate at Osgoode Hall Law School, York University, and an assistant professor at the Peter A. Allard School of Law at the University of British Columbia. He is W̱SÁNEĆ and a member of the Tsawout First Nation.

Peter Cook grew up in the Ottawa River Valley and in 2010 joined the department of history at the University of Victoria. He researches and writes about the history of Indigenous-settler relations in eastern North America before 1850, with a particular focus on alliances and treaty making.

Emchayiik, Chief Councillor Robert Dennis, Sr., has studied Huu-ay-aht history all his life, learning from Elders Chief Louie Nookemus, Willie Sport, Alec Williams, Fanny Williams, Simon Dennis, Arthur Peters, and others. He has served as Huu-ay-aht Chief Councillor for twenty-one years and was Chief Treaty Negotiator for eighteen years. Huu-ay-aht traditional knowledge "turned things around" for his community and formed the basis for the Huu-ay-aht's modern treaty.

John Elliot STOLȻEŁ is an elder of the W̱JOŁEŁP Tsartlip First Nation. In 1999, he co-founded FirstVoices, a ground-breaking online Indigenous language archiving and teaching resource. He paved the way for the ŁÁU, WELṈEW̱ Tribal School to employ full-time SENĆOŦEN immersion teachers. A fluent speaker of *SENĆOŦEN*, he served for many years as a member of the BC First Nations Education Council sub-committee on language and on the board of First Peoples' Cultural Council, Chairman of the Saanich Native Heritage Society, and language and culture teacher at the ŁÁU, WELṈEW̱ Tribal School. He holds an honorary doctorate from the University of Victoria.

Hamar Foster is an emeritus professor of law at the University of Victoria, where over the years he taught criminal law and procedure, trial advocacy, evidence, property law, legal history, and the law respecting Aboriginal title and rights. He has been researching and writing about comparative criminal law, Indigenous law, and legal history since the 1970s.

Elmer Seniemten George is an elder in the Songhees First Nation and one of the last remaining speakers of Lekwungen. He worked as a boom man and in a shake mill in the logging industry and handled backhoe operation, carpentry, plumbing, and electrical work as the Songhees Band's maintenance man for 35 years. He built and designed the Songhees Big House with former Songhees Chief John Albany and others, rebuilt the Indian Shaker Church in Brentwood Bay, and rebuilds racing canoes with his son. He has an honorary doctorate from Royal Roads University.

Stephen Hume came to Douglas Treaty lands and to the ancestral home of the Lekwungen and W̱SÁNEĆ peoples in 1948. Poet, essayist, reporter, and author of ten prize-winning books, Hume's writings have for more than fifty years chronicled First Nations justice issues extending from the polar deserts of the High Arctic to the antelope brush deserts of Southern BC; from the earliest fur trade to contemporary resource disputes and the emerging struggle to find a path to genuine reconciliation.

John Sutton Lutz is a professor in the department of history at the University of Victoria with a research focus on the Pacific Northwest from the 1770s to the 1970s. He is the author of *Makúk: A New History of Native-White Relations* and editor or co-editor of several volumes including *Towards a New Ethnohistory, Community-Engaged Scholarship among People of the River, Myth and Memory: Myth and Memory: Stories of Indigenous-European Contact,* and is founding co-director (with Keith Carlson) of the Ethnohistory Field School with the Stó:lō.

Maxine Hayman Matilpi "Lakwa" is a member of the Kwakiutl Nation (Tsakis) and also has Tlingit, Ma'amtigila, and Scottish/English roots. She serves as Program Lead for RELAW (Revitalizing Indigenous Law for Land, Air and Water) at West Coast Environmental Law and is a happy grandmother living on a northern Gulf Island.

Kevin Neary has been researching and writing on First Nations and history in British Columbia since 1972. After studying anthropology, he worked twenty-four years at the Royal BC Museum as an ethnology collections manager and curator. He has worked as a consultant specializing in applied research as principal of Traditions Consulting Services since 1997. Most clients are First Nations. He has collaborated with Emchayiik, Chief Councillor Robert Dennis, Sr., and the Huu-ay-aht since the 1990s. He co-authored a book on Huu-ay-aht history, *Voices of the Elders.*

Adele Perry is a settler who was born and raised in southern British Columbia. Since 2000 she has taught at the University of Manitoba, where she is distinguished professor of history and women's and gender studies, and a senior fellow at St. John's College. Perry is interested in histories of colonialism in the nineteenth and twentieth-century North American west.

Sarah Pike is a lawyer who practises Aboriginal and constitutional law in British Columbia with her own firm, SPIKE Law. She is also a legal historian whose study focuses on the intersection of land, Indigenous occupation and ownership of land, and settler occupation and law about land and Indigenous peoples. Sarah wrote her chapter in this volume in 2017, while pursuing her LL.M. at the University of British Columbia. In 2018, she completed her thesis, *Gilbert Malcolm Sproat, British Columbia Indian Reserve Commissioner (1876–1880), and the "Humanitarian Civilizing" of Indigenous Peoples.*

Laura Spitz was born in southwestern Ontario within the boundaries of Treaty 2, and she grew up in the lower mainland of British Columbia on traditional Stó:lō territory. Her ancestors – British and Ukrainian – came to Canada at the turn of the 20th century. Today, Spitz is a professor at the University of New Mexico School of Law, where she teaches on land once occupied by Tiwa-speaking Pueblo people. Her research focuses on the consequences and limits of legal subjecthood.

Neil Vallance retired in 2010 from a long career practising property law in Victoria. In 2016 he obtained a PhD from the Faculty of Law at the University of Victoria with a dissertation on the formation of the Vancouver Island (or "Douglas") Treaties of 1850–54. He currently undertakes ethno-historical research on Vancouver Island Treaty claims and occasionally teaches property law at the University of Victoria.

Index

Note: "(i)" after a page number indicates an illustration or map